GABRIEL'S REBELLION

GABRIEL'S REBELLION

The Virginia Slave Conspiracies of 1800 and 1802

DOUGLAS R. EGERTON

The University of North Carolina Press

Chapel Hill & London

The paper in this book meets the guidelines for permanence
and durability of the Committee on Production Guidelines
for Book Longevity of the Council on Library Resources.

Library of Congress Cataloging-in-Publication Data

Egerton, Douglas R.

Gabriel's rebellion : the Virginia slave conspiracies of 1800
and 1802 / Douglas R. Egerton.

p.   cm.

Includes bibliographical references and index.

ISBN 0-8078-2113-6 (alk. paper).—

ISBN 0-8078-4422-5 (pbk. : alk. paper)

1. Slavery—Virginia—Insurrections, etc.   2. Virginia—
History—1775–1865.   3. Prosser, Gabriel, ca. 1775–1800.

I. Title.

F230.E37   1993

975.5′03—dc20   93-18534

CIP

97   96   95   5   4   3

FOR LINDA

CONTENTS

Preface, ix

PART ONE. RICHMOND 1800

1. The Revolutionary Storm, 3

2. An Upright Man, 18

3. The Year 1800, 34

4. The Preparation, 50

5. A Plot Discovered, 69

6. Cemeteries Take What Is Given Them, 80

7. A Companion Picture, 95

PART TWO. HALIFAX 1802

8. Recalled to Life, 119

9. The Footsteps Die Out, 132

10. A Place of Asylum, 147

11. The Power in That Name, 163

Appendix 1. Gabriel's Religion, 179

Appendix 2. The Frenchmen, 182

Appendix 3. Slaves Executed, 186

Notes, 189

Bibliography, 237

Index, 253

PREFACE

The spring of 1800 found Richmond, Virginia, a feverish tribute to partisan politics; the April elections for the General Assembly were crucial for both Federalists and Republicans in the upcoming presidential contest. The accompanying unrest, discord, and rumors of impending disunion inspired a young slave named Gabriel to conceive of what was perhaps the most extensive slave conspiracy in southern history. Most of his contemporaries, white as well as black, believed that his plan stood a good chance of succeeding. Had it done so, it might have changed not only the course of American race relations but also the course of American political history.

It is peculiar, therefore, that Gabriel's conspiracy has been either ignored or misunderstood by historians. Despite a wealth of documentation, the plot and its tragic aftermath have never been treated in full. True, Gabriel typically receives a perfunctory mention in most American history textbooks, although many identify him as Gabriel Prosser, thus giving him the surname of his owner, Thomas Henry Prosser (which no extant contemporary document does). Far too many scholars identify him as a free man, although his tenuous ties to his master make this error somewhat understandable. One writer has even insisted that Gabriel must have been Haitian, although the Virginia census of 1783 clearly places the then-seven-year-old boy on the Prosser plantation nearly a decade before Saint Domingue exploded into revolution. But of all the myths surrounding the events of 1800, surely the most durable is the erroneous idea that Gabriel was a messianic figure, an early national Nat Turner who wore his hair long in imitation of his biblical hero, Samson.

Several fictional treatments have attempted to rescue the slave rebel from the Samson legend, but in the process they have led readers and audiences into yet new myths. Arna Bontemps's vivid 1936 novel, *Black Thunder*, depicted Gabriel as a meek, apolitical bondman driven to revolt only by his master's cruel murder of an elderly slave. Thirty-two years later, Clifford Mason's powerful play *Gabriel: The Story of a Slave Rebellion*, placed the Virginia revolutionary in a generic plantation setting. By day, Mason's Gabriel was a common laborer in "Charlie" Prosser's cotton fields. By night, Mason's hero—in a development oddly reminiscent of the fiction that justifiably offended critics of William Styron's Nat Turner—was a sexual athlete who attended to the needs of the love-starved plantation mistress.

The historical Gabriel who emerges from the voluminous trial records was none of these things. The young husband was no rustic farmhand but a highly skilled blacksmith who hired out his time around the Richmond area. Far from being meek or timid, this born rebel had so little prejudice against violence that he once bit off the left ear of a white neighbor during an angry dispute over a stolen hog. Most of all, the Gabriel who engineered a complex conspiracy with branches in at least three Virginia cities was no apolitical servant but a literate artisan whose breadth of vision was truly international. Far from praying for the religious day of jubilee, the black Jacobin labored to gather together "the most redoubtable democrats in the state" to destroy the economic hegemony of the "merchants," the only whites he ever identified as his enemies.

This book unapologetically tells a story. This currently unfashionable approach need not, of course, eschew analysis. But Gabriel's short life—and the chain of events he precipitated—were dramatic, and it would be a nearly criminal act if the story did not unfold for the reader as it did for those who lived through it. In hopes of giving equal attention to both story and interpretation, the book is presented in two sections. Part 1 seeks to re-create the context of the conspiracy. The first chapters explore the political and economic landscape of Virginia during the two decades following the Revolution. The disorder of war and the climate of insubordination produced by the rebellious patriots, as well as the gentry's growing recognition of the hypocrisy in yelping for liberty while denying it to others, served to break down the old controls that held slavery in place, even as it emboldened bondmen to free themselves by tramping north—or by picking up a musket in the name of King George.

The pervasive language of liberty and equality, which reached its rhetorical peak during the overheated partisan warfare of the late 1790s, could not help but politicize black Virginians. This was particularly true of urban slaves and freemen who labored alongside stalwart white artisans, many of whom were members of the Democratic-Republican societies of Richmond and Norfolk. Most urban bondmen lacked a sophisticated understanding of the political issues they overheard, but that is hardly the point; popular revolutions often arise from conjunctions between the aspirations of the disenfranchised majority and the demands of the politically conscious minority. Only when Gabriel's plan is placed against the turbulent political background of 1800 does the logic of his conspiracy emerge.

By taking advantage of what he believed to be an impending civil war between Republicans and Federalists, Gabriel hoped his urban followers could force the Federalist "merchants" to yield to his simple demands for justice. It was not merely that the conspiracy developed during a time of division among whites; it was that artisan Gabriel, sharing the same small-producer ideology of many urban Republicans, hoped to join in and exploit that division. His faith was that white mechanics would see in his own struggle for liberty and economic rights grounds for accepting his support—and that of his soldiers. The remaining chapters of Part 1 chronicle the collapse of the plan and the execution of most of Gabriel's followers.

Part 2 carries the story beyond Gabriel's death; history, unlike literature, invariably fails to tie together all of its loose ends. The narrative moves through a second plot, an even more widespread—if less coherent and politically conscious—attempt to bring down the peculiar institution. Organized in late 1801 and early 1802 by Sancho, a minor recruiter who stood on the periphery of the earlier conspiracy, the Easter Plot, as it came to be known, finally grew so unwieldy that it snapped into three semiautonomous schemes, thus diminishing its chances for success.

The final chapters examine the unhappy legacy of the two near revolts. Between 1801 and 1805, the Virginia Assembly, terrified by the recurrent specter of true revolution, quietly debated the possibility of gradual emancipation—albeit with the qualifying tie of colonization. Following the failure of President Thomas Jefferson to implement its recommendations, the state legislature decided against any further plan of reform and chose instead to restore the old colonial instruments of control in order to better discipline a troublesome labor force and crush its rebellious spirit.

Although this book is the product of research conducted in ten repositories spread across five states and the District of Columbia, the fundamental source was the voluminous trial records stored in the Virginia State Library, in Richmond. Depositions and confessions taken by white authorities in courtrooms and jail cells are, of course, hardly neutral or objective documents. But a careful reading of these sources clearly indicates that Virginia jurists were honestly determined to get to the bottom of the affair. If they were terrified by the specter of black revolution, they were also tough, pragmatic men who wished to discover precisely what had happened so they could prevent its recurrence. Much of the courtroom testimony corroborates information supplied by other accused insurgents during pretrial questioning, yet there is no indication that white authorities asked leading questions. Slaves were questioned in isolation and (with only a few exceptions) without beatings. None of this is to imply that the accused received anything approaching a fair trial—or that they were indeed guilty of any crime. But it does indicate that the court records provide a generally sound window into the southern past and are not the wild transcripts of a witch-hunt organized by frightened planters determined to manufacture a slave conspiracy where none existed. When possible, I have supplemented the trial sources with material drawn from turn-of-the-century African American autobiographies and the Virginia slave narratives.

Because I wish to convey a sense of the time in which Gabriel lived, I have made no attempt to modernize or correct the spelling and grammar found in the trial records and correspondence relating to the conspiracy. I have also avoided the admonitory "[*sic*]" except when quoting recent historians. All additions within quotation marks appear in brackets.

In the writing of this book I have incurred more debts than mere acknowledgments will allow me to repay. Robert McColley, Graham R. Hodges, and Sylvia Frey provided detailed comments on the early portions of the work; Professor Frey also kindly allowed me to read portions of her then unpublished *Water from the Rock*, from which I profited enormously. Ronald Hatzenbuehler and Robert Paquette read Chapter 3 and supplied me with information about the political and international context of the conspiracy, and Clifford L. Egan caught more than one error in my discussion of the diplomatic consequences of the plots. Philip J. Schwarz read much of the manuscript in one form or another and generously shared some of his research with me. Jeffrey J. Crow and Bertram Wyatt-Brown read the material on the Easter Plot before it was presented to the Southern Historical Association and supplied me with pages of wise suggestions.

Most of all, I wish to thank those who have lived with this project the longest. Alan Gallay and Carolina Coleman waded through the entire typescript one chapter at a time, encouraging me in my work yet taking me to task for poorly defined ideas and even poorer prose. Richard R. Duncan, with unfailing good humor, set aside his own work on the last valley campaign to read yet another manuscript by his former pupil. The many references to Marcus Rediker in my footnotes are but small indications of the extent to which I have plundered his ideas on the Atlantic world in the Age of Revolution; his ready support and judicious counsel are ever appreciated. I am grateful also to Henny and Dave Yaworsky for the use and abuse of their Richmond home, and to my colleague Edward Judge for helping me to understand the complexities of WordPerfect. Peter Schroth supplied the excellent maps. Sarah Huggins, of the Virginia State Library, aided me in my efforts to locate the streets of turn-of-the-century

Richmond, and Billy G. Smith performed a similar kindness in helping me identify the alleys of late-eighteenth-century Philadelphia. John Langdon proofed the galleys, a task that he also performed, regrettably unacknowledged, on a previous occasion. Lewis Bateman and Pamela Upton have my thanks for their support and patience with my chronic disregard for deadlines. I am grateful also to Jan McInroy for her help in transforming a manuscript into a book. As always, my greatest debt is to my wife, Linda. As recompense for her love, support, and sharp red pen, I hereby promise to stop living in Gabriel's century.

Parts of Chapter 3 appeared in the *Journal of Southern History* under the title "Gabriel's Conspiracy and the Election of 1800." Chapter 8, in a slightly different form, was published in the *North Carolina Historical Review* as " 'Fly across the River': The Easter Slave Conspiracy of 1802." This material is reprinted with the kind permission of editors John B. Boles and Jeffrey J. Crow.

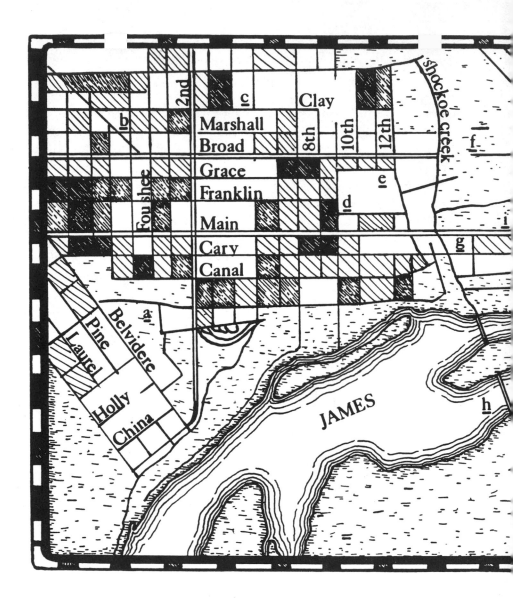

A. Penitentiary
B. Road Toward Brookfield
C. Thomas H. Prosser's Townhouse
D. Capitol Building
E. Governor's Palace
F. Gallows Where Gabriel Died
G. Byrd Tobacco Inspection Warehouse

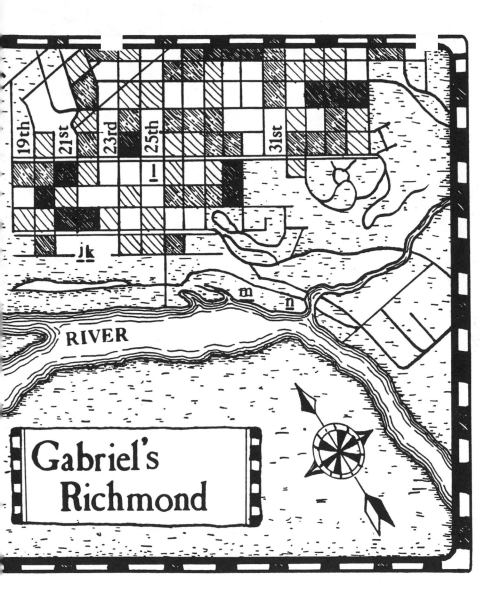

H. John Mayo's Bridge
I. City Market
J. Henrico County Jail
K. Henrico County Courthouse
L. St. John's Church
M. Rocketts Tobacco Inspection Warehouse
N. Rocketts Landing

Principal Centers of Rebel Activity
1800 & 1801

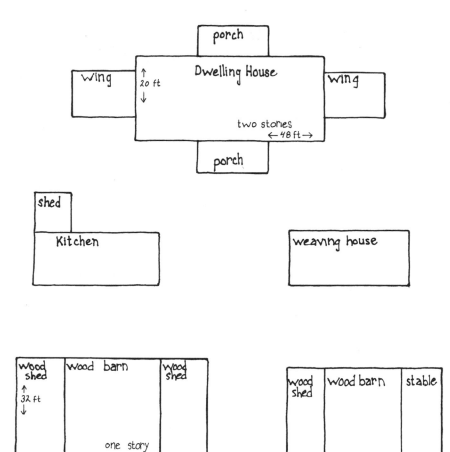

not shown: blacksmith shop and slave cabins

RICHMOND 1800

To be born in a free society and not be

born free is to be born into a lie.

JAMES BALDWIN

1

The Revolutionary Storm

Among the many events of the contentious and critical year of 1776, certainly the least noticed was the birth of a boy born into a lie. In that year Thomas Jefferson, a leading white Virginian, pronounced a self-evident truth: that all men were created equal and were endowed with certain natural and inalienable rights, among which were "life, liberty, and the pursuit of happiness." But the boy born on the Henrico County plantation of Thomas Prosser was of slave parents and so was heir to none of these rights. A young bondman who believed otherwise was headed for a life of trouble, and the slave midwife who cut his umbilical cord and predicted the child's fate by feeling the shape of his head might have guessed that this boy would become a bold man, doomed to a singular fate. His parents may have agreed. They named him Gabriel, after the divine messenger.[1]

Gabriel was born into a unique social environment in eighteenth-century Tidewater Virginia. The Tidewater was the low and often marshy land that bordered the Chesapeake Bay, and its tobacco planters controlled the commonwealth. These men set the social tone, provided the political leaders, and dominated the state's tobacco-driven agrarian economy. It was here that the large plantations and ancestral manors existed, and it was here that the first families of the state resided.[2]

The planter families reigned over a society that attached considerable importance to rank. The Virginia gentry accounted for about 10 percent of the colony's population. Class distinctions needed no explanation in this world. There were, as Patrick Henry observed, four classes: the "well-born" planters, the hearty yeomen (who worked their own farms), the "lower orders" (the landless poor whites), and finally the slaves, who numbered roughly 40 percent of Virginia's population. Although Henry's crude classifications did not admit of it, many of those on top had only recently arrived in the ranks of the gentry. More than a few middling planters—the sort of striving, ambitious men with but a dozen slaves and a small brick home—might be more accurately characterized as rising yeomen than as true aristocrats, and whatever their ancestry, the petty planters were far more numerous than were the "well-born" gentry. Yet birth was important, and if Henry would publicly recognize the new men as members of his political rank, he would privately resist the notion that many of them were his social equals.[3]

This well-defined social world was supported by the state's emerging political framework. The state constitution of 1776 was a profoundly conservative document that made no break from the colonial act of 1736 that had established conditions for voting. One had to own either fifty acres or twenty-five acres and a house, a qualification that could be met by only about half of the adult white males. The constitution also allowed men who owned land along the smaller Tidewater counties to vote in more than one district. It was a document designed to favor the interests of the large planters over those of the small farmers, those of the Tidewater over those of the western counties, and those of the rich over those of the poor.[4]

Wealth and family name provided the means for political power, but the form and tenor of elite rule found expression in an austere code of patriarchalism, through which the elite both defined and understood the social order and their place within it. In the early eighteenth century, when the slave regime was yet in its infancy, colonial leaders had been forced to incorporate feudal legal elements into their common law background as a way of protecting their labor system. In the process, the planters began to move away from their capitalist, bourgeois origins—even as they continued to participate in the capitalist market of the Atlantic world. At the same time, an indigenous slave labor class began to appear in this oldest of English colonies. The result was a mode of production that can accurately be characterized as seigneurial, in which the dependent slave labor force held some claim to the means of production and the planters' claims on the agricultural surplus were met by payment in kind. Like the feudal lords of old, the gentry came to regard their plantations as their manor and their labor force as a kind of extended family.[5]

In Virginia, the harsh patriarchal ethos was already giving way to the gentler ideal of paternalism, in which some masters spoke of their responsibility to docile and happy slaves. But patriarchalism, with its emphasis on order and authority, was still the dominant belief among the planter class. If it was harsh, it was also less constricting and claustrophobic for the working race than paternalism was. Eighteenth-century planters harbored no doubts about their slaves' unhappiness with their lot, and this grim knowledge made them frighteningly dangerous men to cross. But it kept most of them from believing the fiction that their disgruntled labor force was submissive or contented. Though they kept a sharp eye on their workers, they did not presume to intrude into the private lives of their slaves.[6]

In such a world, the planters, unlike the slaves, expressed few qualms about their assigned roles. Raised in a culture that had long found patriarchalism to be the norm, young members of the gentry automatically internalized notions of class distinction and responsibility to one's social "inferiors," white as well as black. More to the point, various forms of unfree labor existed in all parts of the Atlantic basin; if the Virginia master class felt any sense of guilt or shame over its labor system, there is little evidence of it.[7]

Hence when the safe world of the gentry began to crash down around them with the coming of the Revolution, the clamor seemed all the more frightening. But disharmony was indeed introduced when in April 1775, one month before the meeting of the Second Continental Congress in Philadelphia, Virginia's royal governor, Lord Dunmore, ordered the barrels of gunpowder in the Williamsburg magazine removed to a ship under cover of darkness. Townsmen frantically demanded the powder back, on the grounds that the lack of ammunition made the capital an easy target for rebellious slaves. Dunmore gave substance to the fears when he swore to a nervous physician that "by the living God he would declare Freedom to the Slaves and reduce the City of Williamsburg to Ashes" if patriot disorder continued. A number of slaves were prepared to do just that and eagerly presented themselves at the governor's palace. But Dunmore was as yet unwilling to back his words with action, and the bondmen were sent away.[8]

The passage of two months, however, only made it increasingly clear to the governor that his position in the capital was untenable. On June 8 Dunmore quit Williamsburg and took refuge near Yorktown on the sloop of war *Fowley*. Realizing that the majority of the gentry stood against him, Dunmore at last decided to make good on his threat. "Lord Dunmore sails up and down the river," wrote a horrified Norfolk resident, "and where he finds a defenseless place, he lands, plunders the plantation and carries off the negroes." In early November, Dunmore's roving flotilla became larger when he declared martial law and announced that he would free any slave who would bear arms in the loyalist cause. The English promise of black freedom was deflated somewhat the following month when Dunmore's black forces, most wearing sashes boldly proclaiming "Liberty to Negroes," were routed by patriot troops. But even as Dunmore fled from his defeat, he was trailed by waterborne slaves "flying" to his standard.[9]

The disruption only grew greater after 1778, when the British forces turned their full attention to the South. On June 30, 1779, General Henry Clinton publicly warned that any black who stood with the patriots was subject to sale "for the benefit of their captors." But those who joined the English would be granted freedom at the war's end. Like Dunmore's proclamation, Clinton's announcement was more a military than a humanitarian gesture, but black Virginians made the most of it. Royal certificates of service were widely regarded as permanent grants of emancipation, and by the end of the summer five hundred slaves from Norfolk alone had crossed into British lines. In fact, the announcement worked almost too well. An overwhelmed Clinton wrote to Lord Cornwallis begging the general to "make such arrangements as will discourage their joining us."[10]

Cornwallis had no intention, however, of stopping the flood tide of humanity. Every disrupted plantation was another blow to the patriot war effort. In late 1780 large-scale British depredations in Virginia were renewed when a force of 1,600 under the command of turncoat general Benedict Arnold sailed past Hampton Roads for Richmond. As the army made its way up the James River, slaves, according to one dismayed planter, "flocked to the enemy from all quarters, even from very remote parts." The rapidly swelling force, leaving in its wake burned homes and empty slave quarters, even raided as far north as Alexandria.[11]

Yet the War of Independence did not ultimately lead to black freedom. Bondpersons did the best they could to emancipate themselves, but the options at hand—even for those along the rivers—were not impressive. It quickly became clear that the British forces were liberators only by necessity. Word hummed along the slave grapevine that Cornwallis frequently allowed white owners who were neutral in the contest to retrieve their runaway property. Slaves from the Rappahannock River who had fled to the royal warship *Surprise* were even returned by force when it was discovered that their masters were Tories. Those who were not returned fared little better. British officers permitted few blacks to bear arms. Instead, slaves served the English cause much as they had their rebel masters: with hoe, axe, and pick. They were quartered in segregated huts and, when sick, cared for in segregated camp hospitals. That many British officers openly bought slaves as personal servants made the rationale for Clinton's proclamation all too apparent.[12]

Had the British truly held out the promise of unqualified black freedom and equality, the patriots might have been forced to make a counteroffer in the name of military necessity. As it was, they did nothing. Virginia allowed free blacks to serve in the army but prohibited the enlistment of slaves, even during the severe manpower shortages of 1780. As a result, fewer than one hundred slaves received freedom by serving in the militia, and those only because many gentlemen who preferred to sit out the war in the safety of their homes sent a slave in their place. The state rewarded these acts of loyalty with freedom at war's end.[13]

Yet the impact of all this turmoil was far greater than simply the small number of slaves freed by the British or the even smaller number freed by the planters in exchange for personal service. The combined proclamations of Dunmore and Clinton told the slaves that the possibility of freedom existed, especially when white elites were split. Moreover, by their very actions, the patriots created a climate of social insubordination and violence. The very real possibility of liberty, absent before 1775, combined with the incessant white rhetoric of liberty and equality, emboldened the slaves and gave them hope. However much white revolutionaries might try to limit the implications of their words, the significance of 1776 was not lost on black Virginians. This a Williamsburg gentlewoman discovered when a black man "insulted" her by failing to yield the sidewalk and forced her to step into the muddy street. Upon being reprimanded, the bondman spat out, "Stay, you d[amne]d white bitch, till Lord Dunmore and his black regiment come, and then we will see who is to take the wall."[14]

Such instances of black confidence were a genuine cause for white alarm. But there were other causes as well. Even as the war damaged patriarchalism and control, gentry authority came under fire from another quarter: the pulpit, or more accurately, the stump. In colonial Virginia the established church upheld the authority of the government, and the government upheld the authority of the church through taxes assessed on all free white males. Local church affairs were typically controlled by vestrymen, who were usually wealthy slaveholders. But even before the church was disestablished in Virginia following the Revolution, the evangelical movement known as the Great Awakening had been noisily challenging the religious, and hence the social, order. Baptists and Methodists especially preached their gospel not only to large crowds in the backcountry but also in the older, settled Tidewater.[15]

Anglican ministers—who were forced to travel all the way to London for ordination—complained bitterly about the untrained lay exhorters, who defied their religious monopoly. But planters were the most concerned of all. The "new light" preachers not only reached out to the humble orders, they implied that the simple people were more godly than the smug, ostentatious gentry. Baptist minister William Fristoe even promised one Virginia crowd that wealth hindered a man's entry into heaven. "[F]reed from hard labor, by having slaves to labor for them," Fristoe insisted, the planters had leisure to contract sinful habits and live the "high life." Preacher David Barrow elaborated on this point. Christ himself "had no slaves," he thundered, bearing down upon each point, "but *wrought* for his *livelihood* at the *business* of a carpenter."[16]

On occasion, dissenting preachers did more than simply criticize the fashionable and impious lifestyle of the gentry. Many of the lay preachers were uneducated farmers or self-taught artisans. Known for their fiery stump preaching rather than their devotional scholarship, they cared little whether their audiences were white or black. Emphasizing emotional experience and conversion over formal Christian education, Baptists and Methodists not only welcomed slaves into their meetings but even invited them to speak. As one Virginia Anglican caustically observed during the Revolution, the "most illiterate among them are their Teachers [and] even Negroes speak in their meetings." Slaveholders were further outraged in 1780 when the first Baptist church in Richmond opened its doors to all who would enter. One publisher alternately dubbed its white minister, who bravely mixed antislavery sentiments with the gospel, "Negro George" and "Haranger among negroes."[17]

Reduced to its purest form, Christianity carried a subtle political message that was at odds with a class-based society. When "Negro George" preached to the slaves and called them "brother," he implied that all people were equal in the sight of God. The unstated but natural consequence of such a view was the belief that a world that held fast to racial and class distinctions was a world manifestly not in keeping with God's will. For their part, blacks had little trouble incorporating this simple message of fellowship into their own religious traditions, especially since those traditions had already been altered by life in the new land. In the Baptist faith, slaves found a religious ethos familiar and flexible enough to allow them to integrate their African values, in the process creating a coherent cosmos that both preserved African usages and allowed for a Christian understanding of individual salvation. There is no way of knowing how many of the 150,000 slaves who lived in Revolutionary Virginia heard the message of God's fellowship, but for those who did, the message penetrated deeply.[18]

As it was, with the political atmosphere full of talk of liberty and equality, it was not difficult for this mood of evangelical fellowship to evolve into open and outright hostility to slavery. In 1774 English Methodist John Wesley published his *Thoughts upon Slavery*. If Wesley's work breathed hostility toward African "superstition" and promoted bourgeois virtues of thrift, social peace, and hard work (which should have pleased the gentry, who of course wanted none of those things for themselves, only for their labor force), it did denounce human bondage in no uncertain terms. Some Virginia Methodists went even further and put Wesley's words into action. In King William County a small band of white "Paterrolers" enforcing local curfew laws broke into a meetinghouse late one night, only to find themselves rudely "thrown out of the window and obliged to leave [by a mixed] gathering of whites and blacks."[19]

The high-water mark of dissenter antislavery in Virginia came during the Baptist General Committee meeting of 1790. The conference engaged in a lively debate on the "equity of heredit[ar]y slavery" but could reach no conclusions. Finally the matter was turned over to a committee under the control of William Fristoe and David Barrow, both ardent critics of gentry mores. The select group agreed upon a resolution prepared by John Leland and reported it back to the larger assembly. In its final, approved form it read: "Resolved, that slavery is a violent deprivation of the rights of nature, and inconsistent with a republican government; and therefore recommend it to our Brethren to make use of every legal measure, to extirpate the horrid evil from the land."[20]

This rather promising declaration was canceled out by the qualifying reference to legal measures; it asked members of the church in good standing to work within a legal system that defined people as property. Black Baptists had never recognized the legality of their enslavement and so were less concerned with such legal proprieties. Slaves who stole themselves and fled across English lines certainly were not prepared to restrict themselves to lawful remedies. Consequently, slaves and free blacks slowly broke free of the parent body. "[S]laves," noted one concerned official, began "to assemble in considerable numbers at meeting houses and places of religious worship, in the night." Autonomous black churches sprang up in Williamsburg under the guidance of a black exhorter named Moses, and in Petersburg on Harrison Street under the leadership of a free black named John Benn. By the last decade of the century, black Baptists outnumbered white congregants in Richmond. In Norfolk in 1796, Baptist Jacob Bishop even attempted to establish a church more in keeping with African traditions.[21]

Like the Revolutionary theory that fueled a sense of mission, the dissenting faiths created a new climate of black insubordination. Emboldened by the words of white and black preachers alike, religious slaves occasionally decided to carry their egalitarian faith to its logical conclusion and emancipate themselves in this world, just as they expected to be free in the next. Christianity freed their souls and told them they were worthy of physical freedom as well. A fugitive slave advertisement for forty-year-old Titus, whose back "retain[ed] the mark of the whip," observed that he was "uncommon[ly] sensible and artful for a negro, fond of preaching and exhorting, being, as he says, of the Baptist persuasion."[22]

It was for this reason, among others, that the gentry began to fight back. Farmers and artisans relied on their wealthier neighbors as markets for their foodstuffs or finished crafts, and in the absence of banks, planters, in the grand tradition of country patrons, also provided loans and even legal favors to their properly deferential social inferiors. When all else failed, planters appealed to racial solidarity. In the face of such pressure dissenters began to backtrack. In 1793 the Baptist General Committee voted to make the issue of slavery a "legislative" question, thus turning it over to the gentry-controlled Virginia legislature. But from the planters' perspective, the damage was done. Itinerant preachers and black congregations continued to fire the slaves with a sense of their self-worth, which kept them from becoming the passive labor force their owners wished them to be. "I believe it is from some inculcated doctrine of those [new light] rascals," grumbled Landon Carter, "that the slaves in [Virginia] are grown so much worse."[23]

The new lights were only one source of concern for Landon Carter. Another was his more progressive planter brethren, who were deeply affected by either Revolutionary or evangelical rhetoric, and sometimes by both. For the first time in their lives, at least some Virginia planters began to perceive the hypocrisy of yelping for liberty while denying it to others. The political order they had recently fashioned was based on the consent of the governed, a mutual contract of the men who formed political society. While this Lockean notion was not intended to include slaves— or women—it posed an obvious problem in a patriarchal society, at least for those few who pondered the logical conclusions of their political creed. This was not the sin of gentry indolence so often denounced by the new lights; it was something far worse—guilt.[24]

Not all of the gentry felt a sense of guilt over slavery. Lockean theory cut both ways, strengthening the bonds of slavery almost as much as it severed them. Locke had argued that humans possessed a "property" both in themselves and in their physical possessions, which in the Jeffersonian context included slaves. If the idea of the social compact damaged the concept of owning humans, it was equally true that forced abolition would trample the natural property rights of the master class. This view was particularly comforting to planters who found their consciences tweaked by both the new lights and their own Revolutionary speeches but who could not maintain their aristocratic habits without a cheap labor force. Patrick Henry, for one, willingly conceded that slavery was "repugnant to humanity" but could not imagine freeing his bondmen, because of "the general inconveniency of living without them."[25]

Clearly, English theories of social contracts fit none too neatly into a slaveholding society, and white Virginians struggled mightily to qualify Revolutionary thought and reserve it to themselves. Race could be used to explain why some people were not endowed with certain natural and inalienable rights such as liberty and equality. Because such God-given rights were taken for granted in a republic, patriot leaders found it necessary to be precise in their language. When George Mason's Declaration of Rights was introduced into the Virginia convention of 1776, many delegates complained bitterly about its preamble, which held that "all men are by nature equally free and independent." More than a few planters saw in those words a later basis for judicial emancipation. The declaration was saved only by the inclusion of the words "when they enter into a state of society," as whites insisted that blacks had done no such thing. Bondmen who had made clear their view on natural rights in the sashes they wore as they marched into battle the previous winter of course had no use for fine theoretical abstractions.[26]

As it happened, the potential for many planters to assuage their guilt did exist. Independence fostered fundamental change in the Chesapeake tobacco-based economy. British depredations in Virginia and attacks on the seas damaged the ability of planters to produce and export their crops. Just as the region was growing out of its economic slump, the outbreak of war between France and Britain in 1793 again wrought havoc on the ability of Virginians to market their tobacco profitably in Europe. Tobacco prices plunged again—and this time did not recover. More than a few desperate Chesapeake planters turned to wheat and corn, crops far less labor-intensive. Many slaveowners suddenly had a labor surplus on their hands, and some realized that supporting a large number of field hands now worked against them; if they were to retain their aristocratic pretensions they needed fewer, not more, laborers.[27]

This knowledge allowed the planter-controlled Assembly to give in to Quaker and new light demands that the law be amended to make manumission easier. In short, economic change allowed the gentry to solve the problem posed by the logic of their own egalitarian rhetoric. They forged a compromise between the natural rights interpretation championed by black Virginians and the property rights view held by most ruling-class white Virginians. In 1782 the old colonial restriction on private emancipation without petition to the governor was lifted. Thereafter, planters could free their slaves by deed, provided they were not in debt. A number of gentrymen promptly did so, although more acted as did George Washington, who wished to retain his extravagant lifestyle yet rid himself of guilt. The squire of Mount Vernon desired "to liberate a certain species of property which [he] possess[ed] very repugnantly to [his] feelings." But he did so only upon his death.[28]

If many slaves were emancipated only after their master had no further use for them, the fact remains that the rapidly rising number of freed blacks gave new hope to those who saw the law of 1782 as only the first step toward a general emancipation. The limitations of the act were obvious, yet it was an accurate barometer of gentry unease with a suddenly peculiar institution. Slaves—especially healthy young males—still sold for a good price in Virginia and the rest of the South, even if tobacco did not, and planters could have sold their surplus laborers to planters in the fresh lands of the lower South. Given that the typical Virginia master inherited his black property, as opposed to buying slaves at current prices, any sale outside of Virginia would have netted the often financially strapped planters a substantial profit. Yet many planters avoided this avenue and emancipated some or all of their slaves.[29]

For planters who were too burdened by debt to emancipate their slaves outright, there was a second possibility, which allowed planters to assuage their consciences *and* turn a tidy profit. More than a few Virginia bondmen were granted the opportunity to buy their own freedom. By laboring on their own time—evenings and Sundays—and carefully putting away their earnings, some slaves gradually accumulated enough money to purchase their liberty. Allowing a slave to purchase his person was hardly a ringing declaration against the system, but squeamish slaveholders found it preferable to selling their surplus workers south. "[I]n time past when Americans did not think so philosophically & justly as at present," sighed David Meade, "I was so unfortunate as to be under the necessity of selling Slaves."[30]

David Meade's slaves doubtless thought themselves to be somewhat more ill-used than their hard-pressed master, but it was this general sense of planter unease that inspired a handful of Virginia progressives to consider decisive action. In 1783, when it appeared that Virginia might call another constitutional convention, Jefferson drew up a draft document to present to the Assembly. Included in his model constitution was a plan for the gradual abolition of slavery. All children born of slave parents after 1800 would be trained in a skilled craft and then be emancipated upon reaching adulthood (the age of twenty-one for men, eighteen for women). Because Jefferson could not envision large numbers of free blacks living in perfect harmony beside their former masters, his plan also called for immediate deportation of those emancipated. The constitutional convention never materialized, but the draft nonetheless appeared in print four years later as an appendix to Jefferson's *Notes on the State of Virginia*.[31]

Other aristocratic critics of the peculiar institution were even more forthright. George Wythe, Jefferson's former tutor, handed down a decision from his perch on the Virginia Court of Chancery that mirrored the celebrated 1783 Quok Walker decision in Massachusetts (which held slavery to be in violation of the state constitution). Wythe argued that

Mason's Declaration of Rights had done precisely what its detractors feared it might: allow for immediate emancipation by judicial fiat. If all men were born free and equal, the justice reasoned, slavery could not legally exist in the state. "[W]henever one person claims to hold another in slavery, the *onus probandi* lies on the claimant." It was the responsibility of the master to prove that he could own another human, and not the duty of the slave to prove himself free. Wythe's decision was promptly overturned by a higher court, but his action—and Jefferson's far more moderate plan—revealed the extent to which the Revolution and the evangelicals had introduced guilt into the gentry mind, and how far some influential elites might go in trying to rid themselves of it.[32]

An even clearer sign of white disaffection with slavery could be found among some nonslaveholding farmers, tradesmen, and especially urban artisans. All three groups had developed a reciprocal relationship with their gentry neighbors, but each occasionally chafed against the aristocratic pretensions of the master class. By the 1790s subtle class animosity began to surface in the creation of small abolitionist societies, although the tenets of these societies, like the new light critique of planter idleness, were as much antigentry as they were antislavery. Still, it was clear that some whites dreamed of forging coalitions with blacks that would substantially alter Chesapeake society. These were men like John Simmons, a wheelwright, who had recently cursed the gentry, saying: "[I]f I had a few more White people to join me I could get all the negroes in the county to back us, and they would do more good in the night than the white people could do in the day." Freedom suits initiated by the abolitionist societies occasionally liberated small numbers of slaves; by 1796 nearly thirty suits were pending in Virginia courts.[33]

Individual freedom suits were small steps against a massive institution, but even when unsuccessful they served as a warning to the shocked gentry defenders of slavery that there were many among them of their own class and race who now decried human bondage as immoral. Evidence of cracks in the system were everywhere. In 1785 the College of William and Mary bestowed an honorary degree on antislavery activist Granville Sharp, an act that all but endorsed his cause. And in 1792 the Manchester, Virginia, antislavery society publicly denounced the peculiar institution as "not only an odious degradation, but an outrageous violation of one of the most essential rights of human nature."[34]

It was against such a background that in 1796 St. George Tucker, scion of one of the first families, penned a detailed and elaborate plan for ridding the state of slavery. *A Dissertation on Slavery* ran to more than one hundred pages, and while it was not the kind of plan that many blacks would embrace, it *was* nonetheless *a plan*. Tucker proposed that every black woman born after "the adoption of the plan [would] be free," as would be all of her children, male or female. The children, upon reaching age twenty-one, would "voluntarily [bind] themselves to service for a year before the first day of February annually," or it would be done for them by the "overseers of the poor." No freed blacks would be allowed to vote, hold office, or obtain "any estate in lands or tenements, other than a lease not exceeding twenty-one years." Neither could they bear arms, marry whites, serve as an attorney, nor prepare a will.[35]

What set Tucker's plan apart from other post-Revolutionary gradual emancipation proposals was its specificity—down to what sort of blanket black women would be given at age twenty-eight—and the fact that, unlike Jefferson's vague proposal, it did not require the freedmen to be colonized outside the United States. Although the state might encourage blacks to move to the Spanish colonies of Florida or Louisiana, colonization, Tucker insisted, was both cruel and financially impossible. His assumption was that most would remain in Virginia as a landless and politically powerless agricultural working class. In part, this was a frank recognition that most planters would never permit an end of slavery unless they could somehow retain their black labor force. The very abundance of land that kept the planter class an open and growing group mitigated against turning the white farmers into landless tenants. Under Tucker's proposal the "earth cannot want [black] cultivators." In short, his plan would allow the gentry to end slavery while retaining their class prerogatives.[36]

Although Tucker was loath to admit it, his plan was predicated upon white fear. Like many whites adrift in a time of rapid change, Tucker suspected that those on the bottom would attempt to carry the Revolution on to its logical conclusions. Certainly he never accepted the notion that blacks were his natural inferiors. "In this vast march of the mind, the blacks, who are far behind us, may be supposed to advance at a pace equal to our own," warned his cousin George Tucker, "but, sir, the fact is, they are likely to advance much faster." Thomas Jefferson doubted the native ability of blacks to improve to the level of white males, but he harbored no doubts that slaves could be rebellious. "[I]f something is not done, & soon done," he informed St. George, "we shall be the murderers of our own children [for] the revolutionary storm, now sweeping the globe, will be upon us."[37]

St. George Tucker respectfully laid his plan in the lap of the General Assembly. There, with little fanfare and even less discussion, *A Dissertation* was "ordered to lie on the table." Whether or not the gentry knew it, the Assembly's decision marked a turning point in Virginia history.

Refusal to implement—even to seriously consider—Tucker's gradualist scheme was tantamount to a collective, though certainly unconscious, decision to retain slavery. The Assembly acted in a quiet fashion, but in Richmond few events that related to slavery remained secret for long. Surely enough bondmen heard of the failure of the Tucker plan to understand that if freedom was to be theirs, they would have to take matters into their own hands.[38]

Tucker's plan was tabled in December 1796; thereafter it was almost as if a line had been crossed and even the tentative moves toward reform ended. The moves had been hesitant indeed, and often the Assembly had stumbled one step backward for every two forward. But now the steps marched only toward restoring the slave controls that had been allowed to lapse in the wake of the Revolution and the evangelical challenge. During the following year Virginia made it a capital crime to "advise slaves to rebel and murder the citizens of this commonwealth." In early 1798 the Assembly moved to cut off the growth of the free black caste by attempting to end freedom suits. No admitted abolitionist would be allowed "to serve as a juror in the trial of the said cause." In short, the state imposed an ideological test upon jurors, and only those who demonstrated the proper fealty toward the master class would be allowed to decide the fate of black claimants.[39]

After the near decision to retain the forced-labor system, moving against free blacks was a plausible expediency. The growth of this caste since 1782 had made it far easier for runaway slaves to elude their owners. Before the Revolution, it was a safe assumption that every black stranger on a lonesome road was a slave on the run. But by the end of the century nearly 10 percent of Virginia's black population was free. At the very least, the sudden appearance of free blacks gave those still in bondage a powerful model of human freedom. The "publick danger proceeding from this [type] of persons is daily encreasing," groused James Monroe, especially given "the contrast in the condition of the free negroes and slaves [and the consequential] growing sentiment of liberty in the minds of the latter."[40]

At century's end, no serious discussion of gradual emancipation could be heard in the halls of the Assembly or around the tables in the manor houses. "[I]n truth the emancipation fume has long evaporated," David Meade observed in the fall of 1799, "and not a word is now said about it." Meade, of course, was speaking only of whites. What discourse did occur was hence relegated to the slave quarters, and there the emphasis was not on gradualism.[41]

It was the quarters, and especially the families within them, that supplied Virginia blacks with the autonomy that the state was now almost daily laboring to restrict. Ironically, one of the same factors that led to the rise of patriarchalism before the Revolution continued to sustain bondpersons even after that concept was badly damaged by political change: the growth of a large native-born slave class. By the early 1760s the importation of Africans into Virginia was in decline; the Chesapeake Bay accounted for only 15 percent of slaves arriving in the English mainland colonies. By the time Virginia patriots halted human importation as part of the boycott of English goods, the flood of Africans had dwindled to a trickle. Just over four thousand souls had been brought into the colony during the previous decade.[42]

At the same time and attributable partly to natural increase, the typical Virginia plantation grew in size, which allowed more slaves to find a partner and build a family. As a result, by the mid-eighteenth century the vast majority of Virginia slaves—unlike their lower South counterparts—were strangers to the psychological and physical miseries of the middle passage and were able to rebuild the family structure that had so often been denied to their parents and grandparents. Chesapeake plantations increasingly allowed for settled and often lifelong marriages, and young children typically lived with both their parents. Thus even as the Virginia legislature attempted to reimpose some of the controls that had been allowed to lapse, the black family continued to provide psychological independence from gentry authority.[43]

Over time, as the black families of midcentury grew older and their children found partners on their own or neighboring plantations, a vast kinship network arose. This extended community, like the smaller family unit, granted slaves a measure of freedom from white dominance. Despite the fact that the quarters, typically organized by the slaves in the style of a West African compound, provided a separate source of authority, most planters tended to encourage the growth of a stable black community. Masters tried to keep parents—or at least mothers—and children together, or in the worst case, if financially pressed, to sell or transfer family members within their own neighborhood. Families provided a form of social control and peace on the plantation, and an extended network of agrarian laborers appealed to the patriarchalism of pre-Revolutionary gentrymen.[44]

With the onset of the Revolution and the rise of planter discomfort with the system, the slave community became even stronger as planter controls became even more haphazard. Many Tidewater growers required only that their bondpersons be in the fields when the conch shell blew at sunrise; if they chose to visit family members on nearby plantations after nightfall—"negur day-time"—few owners could bring themselves to object so long as the men were back at work in the morning. Slaves worked only half a day on Saturday and were at liberty on Sunday. Rare was the master who made much of an attempt to keep his slaves on the plantation grounds. Dick, a Virginia bondman, told one surprised visitor to the state that though his wife lived more than twenty-five miles away, he visited her at least once a week. A "negur never tire when he go to see his sweetheart," Dick patiently explained, "and after work on Saturday night I would start for Elk Ridge." Most likely, Dick's master would have been equally surprised to know exactly where his property went on the weekend.[45]

This breakdown of planter authority, mixed together with Revolutionary theory and religious egalitarianism, made for an explosive substance. As an institution, slavery was in a dangerous state of chaos by the end of the eighteenth century. Economic change, combined with the impact of the Revolution, had weakened the grip of the peculiar institution on the state and forced complacent masters to confront the hypocrisy of their own rhetoric. Gentry guilt had resulted in changes in the law, such as the act of 1782, which in little more than a decade had led to the emancipation (or self-purchase) of approximately ten thousand slaves.

The rise of this free black caste, however, did not indicate that most gentrymen envisioned an end of slavery. Rather, it indicated only that *some* planters either had no use for as many hands as they once had or had had their consciences tweaked by the Revolution, or both. When St. George Tucker proposed to do something more than simply engage in vigorous handwringing, the Assembly hesitantly examined the consequences of individual guilt and moved in the opposite direction. Still, guilt died hard, and masters found it personally difficult to do what appeared to be legislatively simple: reimpose control over their labor force. Having decided to maintain slavery, many owners simply could not bring themselves to do what was necessary to protect it. Even when they tried to do so, they came up against a vigorous slave community that provided black Virginians with the sustenance needed to maintain their own autonomy. In short, white Virginians were in danger. Emboldened by Revolutionary theory and radical Christianity, black Virginians had tasted just enough freedom to want more, and if after 1796 it was clear that the Assembly would not give it to them, some among them dared take it for themselves.[46]

2

An Upright Man

Slave controls were in a state of collapse in Virginia at large, but in the capital city of Richmond they were almost moribund. Although it was the political center of the state, Richmond, situated just below the falls on the north side of the James River, presented an unpromising face to visitors. Travelers from the south had to cross John Mayo's toll bridge, part of which teetered precariously upon fifteen large flat-bottomed boats, all held in place by a haphazard system of rusty chains and bent anchors. Riders lucky enough to make it across soon found themselves on Main Street, an unpaved ditch dusty in the summer and "hub deep" in mud during the rainy season. A dark cloud of coal smoke hung over the town almost year-round.[1]

Most of the town hugged the James. Although the city numbered barely seven hundred houses, most were new and of brick, a concrete symbol of the new wealth accrued from commerce in the Old Dominion's rapidly expanding capital. Gaslights had yet to make an appearance, but lanterns lit the avenues at night and flickered like fireflies in the dark. The city was an increasingly thriving port by the end of the century; tobacco, the region's chief cash crop, flowed out of Richmond even as manufactured goods of all description flowed in. Northern visitors who eyed the dung-ridden streets with distaste were nonetheless pleasantly surprised by the bustling business tone of the town, for the wharves were crowded with schooners, square riggers, flatboats, and scows.[2]

The massive capitol building gave the town whatever elegance it had, but even the capitol square betrayed signs of the recent move from Williamsburg. To one side stood the "Governor's Mansion." The majestic title hardly fit the structure. Built in 1798, the "mansion" consisted of a simple wood building of two floors. Nearby sat the squat guardhouse, an equally shabby frame house, topped by a belfry, which served as headquarters of the Public Guard. As the square itself had no fence, cattle grazed and pigs rooted in the tall grass. Dilapidated horse racks placed on either side of the capitol were used by legislators and soldiers to dry their wet laundry and sodden uniforms.[3]

Most of all, Richmond was a slave town. Slaves and free blacks numbered just above half of the roughly 5,700 residents in 1800. In nearby Henrico County, out of which Richmond recently had been carved, 4,600 more bondpersons toiled in the tobacco and wheat fields; there too, even without counting the more than 500 free blacks, whites were a minority. In the city, blacks loaded cargo and tobacco aboard the schooners and with oar and pole drove the flatboats around the falls. Standing at the heart of Richmond itself was the "public Whipping post," where squeamish whites could send their human property to be disciplined.[4]

About six miles due north of Richmond, across the stone bridge over Brook Creek, lay the Prosser plantation of Brookfield. The primary dwelling was a long, two-story frame house with single-story wings on either side and large porches front and rear. Rectangular kitchens and weaving houses sat behind the main house on the left and right. Further back lay two large barns, both flanked by long sheds and stables. A blacksmith shop stood some distance apart from the other wood structures.[5]

In the years after the war, Brookfield was the home of Thomas Prosser, a successful tobacco planter. But Prosser had one foot in the urban world, for he was one of the two partners in the Richmond trading firm of Alexander Front and Company. Evidence for his considerable standing in the community was his membership in the Episcopal St. John's Church on Richmond Hill, where he served as vestryman with businessmen like Daniel Lawrence Hylton. Yet, like many rough eighteenth-century planters, Prosser was a man of some temper, and in the 1760s either his tactics or his harsh words had gotten him ejected from the House of Burgesses. Hiring the services of Patrick Henry, Prosser won reinstatement to his seat. Henry, in turn, won the undying loyalty of the master of Brookfield.[6]

In time, Prosser married, and his wife, Ann, gave birth to two children, Elizabeth and Thomas Henry, the latter presumably named after the elder Prosser's recent counsel. Thomas was born on November 5, 1776, and was much younger than Elizabeth, who in the following year, 1777, married Thomas Goode, the son of Robert Goode of Whitby, in Manchester County.[7]

Considerably larger than his white family was Thomas Prosser's black family. At the war's end there were 3,925 slaves in the county and city combined. In that year Prosser owned 53 bondpersons. The black population of Brookfield was large by Virginia standards; only three other Henrico planters possessed more slaves.[8]

Among the families in the Brookfield quarters was a couple with three sons. The identity of the parents is lost to history, but the sons are not: Martin was by far the oldest, Solomon was the middle child, and the youngest, born in 1776, was named Gabriel. Bond parents generally named their own children—the Prosser slaves were free of the classical names that often indicated that the master had presumed to help name his black children—and by the age of Revolution black evangelicals increasingly used biblical names. That all three boys bore religious names demonstrated that their parents had been influenced by the new lights. But though the children were raised by a religious mother and exhibited a sound understanding of the Bible, they did not grow up to be slave exhorters. There is absolutely no truth to the popular myth that as an adult Gabriel was a messianic figure who wore his locks long in imitation of Samson. (Neither is there documentation to support the notion that Martin was a stump preacher.) As far as the extant evidence indicates, freedom would be his only religion.[9]

If Brookfield was a typical Chesapeake plantation, Gabriel and his two brothers probably lived in a small cabin with one or both of his parents. Most cabins were crude affairs, built of rough boards. Few had plank floors, and small holes in the walls were used for ventilation. The chimney was pasted together from mud and sticks. "As to the furniture of this rude dwelling," remembered one bondman, "it was procured by the slaves themselves." Straw-filled ticks under thin blankets provided the only comfort and warmth at night. Next to the cabins, Virginia slaves planted small gardens, which they worked in their off-hours.[10]

As Gabriel grew older, he surely found companionship in the quarters, but it is also likely that some of his time was spent in the company of Thomas Henry. Gabriel was among the youngest of the slaves on Brookfield, and as childhood often transcended the color barrier, it would have been odd if the two boys, both born in the same year, did not play together. Still, Gabriel could not have helped but notice that their fates were somehow different. Unlike Thomas, he wore no pantaloons, only a tow-cloth shirt that fell to his knees.[11]

Perhaps it was young Thomas, perhaps it was Ann Prosser (for the plantation mistress occasionally watched over the slave children as their parents worked in the fields), or perhaps, although less likely, it was his father—but *someone* on Brookfield taught Gabriel how to read. If Ann Prosser was the teacher, it was a foolhardy gesture, for a slave who could read and write was a slave with access to information and hence the world at large. Only about 5 percent of slaves were literate, and so Gabriel's education marked him as an unusual child. Yet his simple education was typical of a region that wished to maintain slavery yet engaged in practices often at odds with that wish.[12]

If Gabriel was in fact a pampered favorite of Ann Prosser's, that status began to undergo a distinct change as the boy approached the age of ten. Thomas Henry, groomed by his parents to become the young master, perhaps began to exhibit an attitude of superiority toward his former playmate. At about the same time, black children were sent to the fields to do light work. Several, however, were chosen to learn a craft. Gabriel and Solomon were among the privileged few.[13]

Every plantation of considerable size required a number of highly skilled laborers. An enterprise as large as Brookfield needed more than merely field help, and given the number of his human holdings Prosser enjoyed the luxury of training several slaves as artisans. Carpenters built and repaired barns, stables, and slave cabins, and coopers assembled the huge hogsheads that carried tobacco to market. The large weaving house at Brookfield indicated the presence of skilled weavers, who probably were trained at several other crafts as well. Slave blacksmiths shod horses and forged simple tools and sharpened the long scythes used for cutting wheat and grass.[14]

Most likely, Gabriel's father was a smith, the craft chosen for both him and his brother Solomon. (The much older Martin, for unknown reasons, was taught neither a trade nor how to read. Martin may have had a different father, which would have made him but a half brother to Gabriel and Solomon.) In Virginia, the children of skilled slaves commonly inherited their parent's profession; daughters of house servants became house servants, and sons of artisans became artisans. Slaves typically were not allowed to acquire property beyond the odd chair or quilt, but they could pass on to their offspring their most valued possession: the skill that kept them out of the fields and provided them with prestige in the quarters. Especially among the skilled craftsmen, such intergenerational training allowed for the preservation of African culture. Pots, pipes, and even metalware displayed signs of a former heritage.[15]

Status as a craft apprentice provided Gabriel with considerable standing in the slave community—as did his ability to read and write. As the boy blossomed into an unusually tall young man, even older bondpersons looked to him for leadership. "At fifteen years of age there were few who could compete with me in work or sport," recalled a similar Chesapeake slave. "All this caused my master and my fellow slaves to look upon me as a wonderfully smart fellow, and prophesy the great things I should do when I became a man."[16]

Certainly masters and slaves prophesied different fates for such men, but there was little doubt that Gabriel was no typical bondman. By the mid-1790s, as he neared the age of twenty, he stood "six feet two or three inches high," and the strength in his chest and arms betrayed nearly a decade in the forge. Like most smiths, Gabriel wore an osnaburg shirt—a heavy, coarse cotton of a plain weave—and buckskin breeches at his labors; away from his shop he likely sported a cotton waistcoat with elaborate cuffs and pockets, cotton breeches, and plaid hose. A white linen shirt and shoes with polished steel buckles would be reserved for special occasions. Aside from his clothes, rather fine for a slave, people noted Gabriel's unusual gaze. A long and "bony face, well made," was marred by the loss of his two front teeth and "two or three scars on his head." His hair was cut short and was as dark as his complexion. Whites as well as blacks regarded him as "a fellow of courage and intellect above his rank in life."[17]

During these years Gabriel met a young bondwoman named Nanny and fell in love. Probably Nanny was one or two years Gabriel's junior. Chesapeake women typically married young; most bore children soon after reaching sexual maturity and settled into permanent relationships by age twenty. Some slave women married the father of their first child shortly after its birth, as West African custom held that a marriage would be consummated only after a woman had demonstrated her ability to bear healthy children. Masters often recognized slave unions, primarily for reasons of plantation stability and labor control, but the state did not. "When yer married," sighed one woman, "yer had to jump over a broom three times. Dat wuz de licence."[18]

Little is known about Nanny, including the identity of her owner and whether she bore Gabriel any children. (Her name does not appear in the 1783 tax rolls of Thomas Prosser.) If she lived on Brookfield, she was either purchased after that date or was born after 1784. That would be possible, but improbable, as she would then have been no more than sixteen in 1800. More likely, she lived on a nearby farm or tobacco plantation. If Gabriel did take a wife from a neighboring farm, he surely did not marry "abroad" for the usual reason: the desire to be spared the misery of having to watch a spouse being beaten, raped, or overworked. Discipline on Brookfield, at least under the old master, appears to have been lax, and Prosser knew Gabriel well enough not to test a slave of his size and worth by openly abusing his young bride.[19]

In the fall of 1798, change came to Brookfield with the death of Thomas Prosser. The old master died quietly in his home on Sunday, October 7. The end was not unexpected; the previous year Prosser had completed a will. At the young age of twenty-two, Thomas Henry became the lord of Brookfield and the master of approximately fifty men, women, and children.[20]

The elder Prosser had always stood between the urban and rural worlds. His earlier partnership in a Richmond trading company had kept him solvent in a time of falling tobacco prices. But the new master was even more ambitious. Within months of his father's death, Thomas Henry Prosser purchased Watson's Tavern, a bustling public house just north of the city. Shortly thereafter he diversified his holdings further by entering into "an extensive auction" and real estate business with V. M. Moncure. All of this additional enterprise was accomplished without cutting back on his plantation operation.[21]

To conduct his thriving urban affairs more effectively, Prosser purchased a handsome Richmond townhouse on the corner of Fourth and K (also known as Clay) streets. The two-story brick building was forty-six feet long and nearly as wide. Shingles covered the roof. So well did Prosser do in his new life that by the summer of 1800 only two men in Henrico County paid more in taxes.[22]

Another sign of his urban prosperity was the surname of the woman Prosser began to court: Hylton. Born in 1746 into a New York family with an estimable shipping empire, Daniel Lawrence Hylton had moved to Henrico County shortly before the Revolution. From his Fifth Street townhome—separated from Prosser's only by a vacant lot—Hylton ran a lucrative trading business with Jamaica and New York City. But planters, not businessmen, set the social tone of Virginia, and so for reasons of status it was necessary for Hylton to purchase a home in the country— Windsor, which sat high above the James. The ownership of humans was not new to Hylton; slavery was still legal in New York, and he had brought several house slaves with him on his move (two of whom promptly "attempt[ed] to get [back] there"). His wife, Sarah, bore him two daughters, Mehitable, and Lucy Bolling, who caught the eye of their ambitious young neighbor.[23]

This connection would not be settled for several years, and there is evidence that Hylton had doubts about the ambitious young man who called on his daughter. (Hylton's will kept control of his daughter's inheritance safely out of Prosser's clutches.) But in Richmond Thomas Henry was well known and widely regarded as a man to watch. That did not mean he was widely admired. The patriarchal ethos of the region frowned on those who overly bestirred themselves in the cause of financial advancement. Disquieting rumors held that Prosser, unlike his benevolent father, pushed his laborers too hard and "behaved with great barbarity to his slaves."[24]

If the rumors were true—and, given Prosser's feverish interest in maximizing his profits, they probably were—they explain why the new master did not put a stop to a common practice that was at once both dangerous and lucrative: the hiring out of surplus slaves. Even the largest and most efficient plantations could not keep their bond artisans fully occupied year-round, and so many owners occasionally hired their craftsmen out to neighboring farms or town dwellers. Even with all the potential work to be done at Brookfield, Gabriel, and to a lesser degree, Solomon, spent more than a few days each month smithing in and around Richmond. Though no less a slave in the eyes of the law, Gabriel therefore enjoyed a rough form of freedom. Indeed, his ties to his owner became so tenuous that numerous historians have identified him as a free man.[25]

A typical period of hire was fifty weeks, beginning on the first day of January and stretching to just before Christmas. But owners could legally lease their slaves out for as little as a few days, and a bondman as necessary to a plantation as Gabriel was never long absent. Richmond had several hiring sections, including the steps of the Henrico County Courthouse on Twenty-second Street. There prospective employers could find "crowds of servants, men, women, boys and girls, for hire." The spectacle, which was common to all Virginia towns of considerable size, especially Norfolk and Petersburg, horrified visitors to the Chesapeake. Most compared it to buying animals. "[I]t is not at all uncommon for a White to keep Blacks to let out as horses are in England," observed one Briton. Slaves "are hired & let, bought & sold like herds in the stalls," gasped another.[26]

Over time, a body of law arose to meet this new variety of unfree labor. A standard contract specified the time of hire and required the lessor "to pay taxes & doctor bills [and] Clothe him during said time & return him [with] good substantial cloth or Janes shoes and socks and a blanket." Should the slave run away, the temporary owner had to pay full cost; if he died through no fault of the tenant, the owner had to bear the burden. Highly skilled bondmen, not surprisingly, brought the best prices. In 1796 Miles King paid a record $54.95 to lease Tom, an adult male, for one year. Even so, that princely sum was considerably cheaper than hiring white laborers, many of whom demanded more on account of their allegedly superior pigmentation.[27]

Nor were black artisans the only slaves to be hired out. Female domestics, butlers, and coachmen were leased to elegant townhomes for balls or holiday gatherings, and unskilled farm laborers were rented to small farmers who needed an extra hand during planting or harvesting time. The executors of Washington College hired out sixteen slaves willed to the school for an entire year; one "small boy" was hired out in exchange for "victuals & clothes" and training as an artisan. On one level or another, the practice was so widespread that during 1791, Robert Carter, the largest slaveholder in the state, hired out more than two-thirds of his 509 slaves. As a result, as Gabriel moved about the region, he inevitably came into contact with other young men who shared his quasi freedom. One of these men was Michael, the property of Prosser's brother-in-law, Thomas Goode, who preferred to be hired to Richmond so he could be near his wife, a slave of Joseph Mosby. Other new associations were Sawney and Sam Byrd, Jr., both of whom were leased to William Young of Richmond.[28]

Sam Byrd, Jr., a young mulatto owned by Jane Clarke, a widow of Henrico, was as bright, strong-willed, and independent as Gabriel. But one man Gabriel met during his labors was all that and more, and that was Jack Ditcher. If Gabriel was an imposing figure, Jack was even more so. Four years Gabriel's senior, Jack stood six feet five inches tall, was "stout made, and [was] perhaps as strong a man as any in the State." His unusually long hair was tied back in a queue, and an ugly scar ran over one eye. Although illiterate and a mere ditcher by trade, Jack possessed prodigious strength, which made him a valuable commodity. Like many of those who hired out, Ditcher was the slave of a recently deceased owner—William Bowler, a petty slaveholder who died in 1797. That meant that men like Ditcher and Byrd were the property of unsettled estates or were owned by women or children (Jack's new masters were two infant boys), a tenuous tie in a society built upon patriarchalism. Even if a conscientious trustee guarded the estate, as an absentee supervisor he was apt to be a lax master.[29]

Worse still, from the point of view of control, many masters found it convenient to allow their skilled slaves to hire their own time. The documentary record does not reveal just what sort of arrangement Gabriel worked out with his new owner, but the typical method in the upper South allowed the bondman to contract out his labor, then pay his master a share of the wages. Provided Gabriel was able to come up with the agreed-upon sum at regular intervals—and fulfill his Brookfield responsibilities—he was free to spend whatever he earned above that amount. The arrangement held out obvious benefits for both lord and slave, for it put cash in Prosser's pocket without requiring any attention on his part and it allowed Gabriel, in effect, to choose his own master. Gabriel thus moved ever more into the twilight world between slavery and freedom, a hazy status shared by many of his new acquaintances. Sam Byrd, Jr., was routinely allowed to hire "his own time for the greater part of [the] summer," and George Smith, property of the recently deceased Jacob Smith, had the ability "to hire his time of his mistress" and seek employment not only in Richmond, but around the region as well.[30]

The lack of supervision in such arrangements worried many authorities. Given the lax standards of slave discipline in Virginia, that self-hire was such a matter of concern testifies to the extreme freedom and autonomy inherent in the practice. One alarmed Henrico planter insisted that it caused "great discontent [among] other Slaves who are not allow'd such Indulgencies." To put an end to the practice, so common in urban areas, the Norfolk Borough Council approved an ordinance in 1786 prohibiting slaves from "hiring their own time." In 1792 the state also acted. "If any person shall permit his or her slaves to go at large, or hire him or herself out," read the law, "it shall be lawful for any person to apprehend, and carry every such slave before a justice of the peace [who] shall order him or her to jail."[31]

The law was unenforceable and unenforced. Ironically, because of the competition posed by the relatively cheaper slave hirelings, many white artisans fled north to free cities. White artisans amounted to only 6 percent of the population in border South urban areas, a figure far smaller than in the north. This chronic shortage of skilled workers in Virginia towns meant that most white employers routinely had to bend the law. The most sought-after skilled slaves even "shopped" about for employers and checked on the reputation of those who offered them work, a practice, according to an enraged Norfolk editor, that rendered the slaves "insubordinate and vicious." Gabriel's frequent change of masters also nibbled away at patriarchal command.[32]

The freedom granted to skilled slaves by the practice of self-hire was only one point at which the urban slavery system began to disintegrate. More dangerous was the cash that became available to men like Gabriel. Though the economy of agrarian Virginia could be described as seigneurial, a crude form of capitalism—a mode of production characterized by free wage labor, or here, semi-free, and the separation of the labor force from the means of production—had begun to appear in the towns and cities. On the plantations, master and slave forged a nearly feudal bond. There the relationship between the two, despite the fact that the blacks were engaged in forced labor, was primarily social rather than economic. But the kind of self-hire that allowed a slave to shop for owners and retain a share of his wages was a relationship based largely upon market considerations.[33]

Cash was, therefore, introduced into a labor relationship that was supposed to be based upon patriarchalism, a concept already weakened by the dislocation of the Revolutionary era. Thus the sound of hard money clinking in the pockets of slaves for hire was also the sound of paternal authority being torn asunder. Most of Gabriel's hard-earned salary went to Prosser, but some of it did not. What remained conferred a degree of psychological and social independence on the wage-earning bondman. For a man raised to believe that the acquisition of any sort of property was impossible, cash was a new and potent symbol of liberty and power.[34]

By allowing their slaves to profit and prosper, masters like young

Prosser unconsciously encouraged activity that frequently led to numerous forms of clandestine marketing. Some white shopkeepers welcomed cash regardless of the buyer, but many discouraged black patrons from crossing their thresholds. Respectable businessmen, in any case, were loath to sell slaves the kind of items—such as rum or small weapons—that they often wished to purchase. As a result, hired slaves with extra cash increasingly turned to free black shopkeepers and even to "slave factors," shady agents who kept caches of illegal goods in hidden spots. Some "factors" even dealt in forged passes or carried stolen items to neighboring counties for resale. This underground economy damaged property rights little enough, as only small amounts of goods and cash changed hands. But as an illicit network of communication available to shrewd slaves it had the potential to prove disastrous to white control—provided a leader arose who wished to use it for purposes other than trading.[35]

On many occasions plantation artisans hired themselves out to white artisans and tradesmen in Richmond who found themselves long on orders and short on apprentices, especially as more and more skilled whites abandoned the South. The hiring of skilled bondmen was nothing new in Virginia. Indeed, several of the more prosperous artisans owned bondmen as apprentices or assistants. According to the census of 1782, three Richmond carpenters owned twenty-eight slaves, five tailors possessed fourteen, and two smiths owned seven more. Ambitious men many of these white mechanics were, and in their haste to pull themselves up ever higher, more than a few of them worked the slaves they hired much harder than country squires like old Thomas Prosser ever had.[36]

When men like Gabriel had a choice, however, they sold their services to workingmen who were veterans of the abolitionist movement or who spoke from stumps on God's fellowship. Particularly in small shops, the workday was organized by the number of tasks at hand, and here could be found the least separation between notions of "work" and "life." Unpretentious white craftsmen drew no line of demarcation between labor and social intercourse and enjoyed the stories and jokes that made the work go more swiftly. In this casual atmosphere black and white mechanics labored side by side and in the process often developed strong bonds that cut across racial lines. In the early national border South, such forms of labor solidarity were not supposed to exist, but they invariably did.[37]

Ultimately, Richmond-area artisans—slave or free, black or white—dealt directly with urban merchants. Artisans did not produce for a free market but labored almost exclusively on specific orders from clients or merchants—"bespoke goods." The mechanics were paid by the piece according to a "fair" price established by the various trades. In exchange, merchants provided craftsmen with credit and materials. The relationship was a reciprocal one, but it was far from equal; merchants dominated the flow of marketable goods as well as raw materials. Although they could not dictate the price of finished goods, they could pressure the artisans to lower their prices by shutting off the stream of raw materials or threatening to take their business elsewhere. In a region with a weak tradition of craft organization, such tactics often worked.[38]

For slave artisans like Gabriel, the power of the merchants could be even more devastating. Unscrupulous businessmen often underpaid or even openly cheated bond hires, as blacks could not take them to court or testify against them. Word would eventually get around that such men were miserly employers, but in a system in which the failure to pay one's master a fixed sum could cost a slave the privilege of hiring out, even a single encounter with a dishonest businessmen could doom a bondman to life on the plantation. Evidently Gabriel found himself in this situation at least once. Perhaps also the white artisans with whom he labored were the victims of unfair practices. But Gabriel, according to the story later related by Ben, another of Prosser's slaves, came to see the "merchants" who dominated the city, and not whites in general, as his chief antagonists. Caught between the financial demands of his owner and the strange new power of merchant capital, Gabriel increasingly sought a way to pull both down at once.[39]

Nor were whites the only skilled laborers that Gabriel came into contact with in Richmond. The city was also home to large numbers of free blacks, bondpersons who had been emancipated in the two decades since the law of 1783 and who had drifted toward the favorable economic opportunities of the town. Many were skilled and helped to fill the ranks of the trades as white artisans moved north. It is unlikely that Gabriel would hire out to such men, as few of them did well enough to afford his services. But he came to know many of them well. Already in the possession of a crude quasi freedom, the bond smith gained from these associations new ideas of upward mobility that allowed him to indulge in realistic dreams of true freedom.[40]

The growing number of prosperous free blacks and bondmen with money in their purses gave rise to a small number of black urban entrepreneurs. Most ran small groceries or grog shops, having usually learned the necessary skills in bondage, for virtually every tavern in Richmond was staffed by both male and female slaves. The law frowned on black saloons, which doubled as pawnshops and gaming houses, and authorities made every effort to close them down; such establishments did, after all, play a leading role in the underground economy. But enterprising freemen secreted their shops away in basements and back alleys and protected them from prying eyes with hidden doorways and secret passwords. As white tradesmen fled the cheap competition, blacks moved into an ever-widening range of occupations. Slave or free tailors set up shop in Virginia, and two Richmond newspapers used—and trained—slave printers. Slaves like Mary Jones's John were even hired to help build the Richmond penitentiary.[41]

Virginia authorities were concerned more with black control than they were with acknowledging the economic realities of their capital city, and they made every effort to hinder free black prosperity. Potential employers were encouraged to accept free black laborers only on the basis of yearly contracts. These contracts ran from Christmas to Christmas and were little different from the standard agreements governing bond hires. In an attempt to monitor the movement of the freemen, the state required "every free negro or mulatto, who resides in, or is employed to labour within the limits of any city" to seek out the town clerk and "be registered and numbered in a book kept for that purpose." The clerk would record "his or her age, colour and stature." Most freemen risked considerable fines and actively evaded both laws.[42]

These restrictive laws were designed to do more than merely retard the growing economic autonomy of blacks. They were created to curtail the dangerous labor relations between bond and free, black and white. But they failed utterly. Just as interracial friendships occasionally flowered between politically conscious white artisans and the literate slaves they hired, close ties were forged between free and unfree blacks—and even unskilled whites—under the pressure of common discrimination.[43]

More disturbing from the perspective of control was that such associations persisted long after the day's work ended. Laboring together in a small city that was far more integrated than northern urban centers, artisans and unskilled day laborers of both races fell into the natural habit of retiring together to dine and drink. (Indeed, most of those who went in search of a mug or a bottle of rum were only intent on continuing what had begun during the innumerable breaks during the day.) Many grog shops were infamous, according to one Virginia authority, "for the equality which reigned [between] the blacks and whites—all is hail fellow well met, no matter what the complexion." Over time, a working-class subculture emerged. Apprentice boys, servant girls, bond hirelings, radical whites, free blacks—and in Norfolk especially, more than a few sailors—banded together in a common cultural domain of street fairs, May Day celebrations, and disorderly houses. Here could be found stable relations between skilled blacks and white servant women, a union that was far less common on the plantations. Well-heeled urban dwellers were horrified by the "negro den[s] where white, yellow [mulatto], and black congregate[d] to eat, drink and be merry."[44]

This back-alley culture was not in itself revolutionary, in that it did not consciously challenge the established political order. But black artisans who shared a tankard with a white craftsman or sailor or, more seriously, entered into a solemn relationship with a poor white servant girl, surely flouted Virginia social conventions. Planter lawmakers rightly feared that the decidedly undeferential discourse heard in cramped drinking cellars threatened their hegemony, and they labored as hard to cut apart these interracial gambols as they had to define citizenship in the first place. From the early 1780s free blacks and slaves were prohibited from congregating at night to play at cards, dice, or ball, and from joining whites at cockfights and horse races. The few police that there were constantly raided back-alley taverns and grog shops, but when one was closed another quickly opened. The testimony of travelers made it clear that such gambols continued.[45]

Given Gabriel's tenuous grasp on prosperity and quasi freedom, it was hardly odd that his notions of right and justice took on a uniquely urban flavor. The mood of the city was far removed from that of the countryside. Surrounded by an atmosphere of business enterprise—and driven by a need to stay solvent—the black artisan was hardly impervious to the claims of money and property. (Money could, after all, purchase his freedom and that of Nanny.) It was natural that Gabriel was influenced by the bold words of the white workers he encountered in the forge and the tavern. More than a few insisted that as laboring men they were far superior to those, like the merchants, who squeezed profits from the sweat of those who worked with their hands. As a result, Gabriel increasingly adopted the dominant values of his urban world, for his association with radical white artisans hastened his already-underway cultural transformation. He dreamed of overturning the central class relationship in his society, but not that society itself. He was too much a part of it. And so Gabriel came to dream not only of freedom but also of an equally inestimable treasure: the right to his earnings. All of them.[46]

Above all, Gabriel was a Virginian. Raised amid the heady talk of liberty and natural rights and fueled by the words of his Richmond fellows, Gabriel surely began to ponder what the Revolutionary legacy of his state meant to him. Like the men of 1776, he desired freedom—personal and economic—although in a far less rhetorical way. Like the artisans and free blacks among whom he labored, he found that his dreams stood him on the radical edge of a democratic movement that was securely rooted in bourgeois ideology: his wish was to pull down "the merchants"[47] and "possess ourselves of their property." As an artisan he was a radical, but as a slave artisan he was a revolutionary.[48]

It was one thing to dream, but perhaps his dreams also emboldened him to challenge more openly the white authority he had never recognized and obviously no longer feared. In September of 1799 he moved toward overt rebellion. Probably Gabriel commonly engaged in pig stealing. Slaves found it necessary to supplement their diet with beef and pork; equally important was the pig as a symbol of a master's authority. Slaves did not regard the raiding of a pen as theft. Stealing was defined as theft from other slaves, or Prosser's demands for a portion of Gabriel's cash earnings. Taking food from a planter was merely the transference of property, the payment for labor performed. But this time Gabriel was caught. Absalom Johnson, a former overseer who rented part of Nathaniel Wilkinson's neighboring plantation, discovered Gabriel, his brother Solomon, and Jupiter, a bondman of Wilkinson's, removing a pig from his farm. Furious, Johnson began to berate the three men. His words must have cut deep, for suddenly Gabriel launched himself at the overseer's legs. They fell in a thrashing tangle of limbs, Johnson yelling blue murder, while Solomon and Jupiter danced about, shouting encouragement to their friend. Gabriel got the best of it. Johnson lost his pride and, somewhat more seriously, the better "part of his left Ear."[49]

Pig stealing was a minor crime. Attacking and biting a white man was quite another matter; it carried a capital penalty. Under Virginia law, slaves were not tried as whites were but instead were prosecuted under a 1692 statute that set up special segregated county tribunals known as courts of oyer and terminer. The courts were composed of five justices of the peace. There was no jury and no appeal except to the governor. The legalistically minded authorities did, however, supply the accused with counsel, for whose services the slave's owner paid five dollars. An amending act of 1792 mandated that the trials take place no later "than ten days after the offenders shall have been committed to jail." Decisions had to be unanimous.[50]

Jupiter was the first to appear in court. On September 23, 1799, he "was set to the Bar in Custody" and charged with "Hogstealing." As was custom, Jupiter "said he was in no wise Guilty of the Crime." Prosecutor George William Smith examined several witnesses, one of whom was Absalom Johnson. Jupiter was "fully heard in his defence" by his counsel, but to no avail. The court unanimously voted him guilty and ordered "that he receive [the biblical] thirty-nine lashes on his bare back well laid on at the public Whipping post." With his sentence performed, the sheriff was instructed to "discharge him out of Custody." If convicted again of the same crime, Jupiter would be sentenced to "stand two hours in the pillory, with both ears nailed thereto, and then cut loose."[51]

Solomon followed Jupiter to the bar. Although not accused of hog stealing, Solomon had verbally threatened Johnson during the fracas with Gabriel, and Johnson brought a formal complaint against the slave on "an apprehension that the said Solomon will destroy him or his property by Fire or otherways." Johnson repeated his concerns, but Solomon wisely calmed the fears of the justices. The "Complaint [was] dismissed and the said Negro man Slave Solomon [was] discharged out of Custody."[52]

On October 7 Gabriel was finally "set to the Bar [and] charged with Maiming Absalom Johnson." Before the accused sat the five justices: William Foushee, Hezekiah Henley, Gervas Storrs, George Williamson, and the improbably named Pleasant Younghusband. The counsel assigned by the court was Charles Copland, a member of the House of Delegates with a lucrative legal career. Gabriel pleaded innocent and was examined "in his defense" by Copland. But the evidence—the word of Johnson and the absence of his ear—was overwhelming, and Gabriel was found guilty. He escaped the gallows, however, through an odd loophole that, ironically, was denied to white offenders. Under a 1792 statute, Gabriel had the option of "benefit of clergy." If he could recite a verse from the Bible—as well he could, thanks to the religious faith of his Baptist parents—he had the option of being "burnt in the left hand [by] the Jailor in Open Court." He would then be released. Like the lashing of Jupiter, branding before witnesses was a form of public humiliation as much as punishment. Moreover, if Gabriel were again convicted of a felony, the brand would mark him as ineligible for a second reprieve. Until the date of his punishment, Gabriel was "remanded to [the Henrico County] Jail" in Richmond.[53]

Released shortly thereafter from jail, with his spirit somehow intact and his resolution unimpaired, Gabriel returned to his wife and his labors in the city. But that was not the end of it. Johnson was not appeased by the branding or the whipping. He remained convinced that his assailant was determined to "injure him either in person or property," and on November 4 Gabriel again found himself in the Henrico County courtroom. A new complaint lodged by Johnson insisted that his life was still in danger, and he now demanded assurances from Prosser that the huge blacksmith would be controlled. Younghusband and Williamson, who had heard the case the previous month, found Johnson's fears to be justified and again remanded Gabriel to jail until Prosser could post bond "for the good behavior of the said Gabriel." The next morning Prosser was back. A promissory note of "one thousand Dollars of his goods and chattels Lands and Tenements" won Gabriel's release, but on the condition that the slave "shall be of good behaviour and keep the peace towards all the good people" for the next twelve months. Prosser could not have been pleased with the incident and the trouble it caused him, but Johnson, the former overseer, was of dubious background and new to the area besides, and a skilled bondman in jail netted the young master no income.[54]

By the fall of 1799, Gabriel, now a branded criminal, stood on the edge of rebellion, and not simply the kind of rebellion that represented the personal victory of stealing a hog or overcoming a white neighbor in a bloody fight. His court appearance and his days in the Henrico jail were the final blows in a long chain of assaults upon his person. In a different world, Gabriel would have prospered. His intelligence, his physical size, and his skill would all have marked him as a man on the rise. But this was not a different world; Gabriel was a black man in Jeffersonian Virginia. For all of his advantages, his race kept him down and would forever do so. In a way, his assault on Johnson was an assault on the system that bound him at every turn, but he then discovered that the state would step in to do what his master had failed to do: tighten the chains of bondage.[55]

At the same time that the state machinery labored to crush his independence, other forces worked to restore his spirit. His wife and brothers, especially Solomon, were a source of strength. The artisans he sweated beside in the city, with their talk of a laboring brotherhood, were another. But his family and fellows could provide him with only a hazy form of freedom; his nights in the dank Henrico jail reminded him of that. He now wanted true freedom and the right to his just earnings. Ordinarily the achievement of such desires was to be had only by running away, a course that would force him to abandon his family and his ties to the city. The alternative was rebellion. All he needed was an opportunity, and by the final days of 1799, as he listened to the heated political arguments raging over the forge and the table, it appeared that such a moment was at hand.

3

The Year 1800

The last months of 1799 witnessed two kinds of irrevocable decisions. In November, following his second incarceration, Gabriel moved toward open rebellion. Resolved not to further surrender his rights to his owner and the state, he began to plan for his freedom. In December, the Virginia Assembly resolved not to further surrender its rights to an oppressive federal government, and the nation stumbled toward the precipice of civil war. The timing of these seemingly disparate events was no mere coincidence. The connection between them was later observed by William Vans Murray, a young diplomat then in Europe. "Certainly there are motives sufficiently obvious," he informed John Quincy Adams, "to account for an insurrection of the slaves; but I doubt not that the eternal clamour about liberty in V[irginia] and S[outh] C[arolina] both, has matured the event which has happened."[1]

Vans Murray was correct. The opportunity that Gabriel sought lay in the divisive political climate of Virginia. From start to finish, the shadow of politics hung over the affair. Spending many of his days in Richmond and laboring beside politicized artisans, Gabriel could hardly fail to notice that white elites were badly split along partisan lines. His literacy provided him with access to political affairs, although his ability was probably such that reading a newspaper was a chore. But though he understood the issues imperfectly, he understood them well enough to know that the Union appeared to be coming apart. John Adams, who had become president in 1797, had inherited not only George Washington's office but also the problems of the European war, French attacks on American shipping, and the question of how the new minister, Charles Cotesworth Pinckney, would be received in Paris. The French Directory confounded Adams by giving a hero's send-off to the recalled minister, James Monroe, while refusing to receive the reactionary Pinckney. The Directory also announced that all American sailors found on British vessels, even if they were the victims of impressment, would be hanged as pirates. Adams decided to follow the example of his predecessor and send a special mission to France.

Elbridge Gerry and moderate Virginia Federalist John Marshall joined Pinckney in Paris on October 4, 1797.[2]

The long-anticipated dispatches from the three envoys arrived in Philadelphia on March 4, 1798. Far from solving the outstanding problems, the negotiations had broken down completely. The Americans had been met by agents of Charles Maurice de Talleyrand, the French foreign minister, who informed them that they would not be received until they repudiated Adams's public criticism of France, paid a bribe of fifty thousand pounds sterling, and agreed to a loan of twelve million livres. The indignant diplomats refused, and when Adams laid their correspondence before Congress, substituting the letters "XYZ" for the names of the French agents, the nation was electrified. Federalist extremists called for a declaration of war. The Republicans, including Vice President Thomas Jefferson, who were correctly perceived as being soft on France, were in a state of disarray and panic.[3]

On May 27, 1798, the Federalist majority in Congress—dubbed "the tories" by the acidic Philadelphia *Aurora*—forced through several measures that stopped just short of declaring war on France. They empowered American naval vessels to capture all French cruisers in American waters and created a ten-thousand-person army to augment the regular army of three thousand. A provisional paper army of another fifty thousand was created in case of actual invasion. The bills passed along party lines and came, interestingly, not from a recommendation of President Adams but from private citizen Alexander Hamilton, the leader of the reactionary High Federalist faction.[4]

Congress did not stop there. "Victory has given more confidence to the [pro] British [Federalist] Party," observed one young English visitor to Richmond. "[T]hey think nothing of wishing [the opposition] destroyed." In the summer of 1798 the Federalists enacted four laws, dealing with naturalization, friendly and enemy aliens, and, most of all, "the Punishment of Certain Crimes," a sedition act that made all criticism of the president or Congress, even private criticism, illegal. The Alien and Sedition Acts were nothing less than a blatantly partisan attempt to outlaw the Republican party, as was evident in the provision continuing the sedition act "in force until March 3, 1801," the last night of Adams's term.[5]

Given Virginia's position as a Republican stronghold, it was not surprising that the great partisan counterattack, the Virginia and Kentucky Resolutions, anonymously authored by James Madison and Thomas Jefferson, originated in that state. On December 21, 1798, the Virginia Assembly formally denounced the sedition act as a "palpable and alarming infraction of the constitution." The resolution, which passed along strict party lines, called upon the other states to join with Virginia "in maintaining the authorities, rights, and liberties, reserved to the states." Although Madison, unlike Jefferson in his Kentucky Resolution, backed away from the logical conclusion of his position, the warning to Philadelphia was unmistakable. If the government did not desist in the sedition trials, Virginia would fall back on strict construction and use the Tenth Amendment to interpret the Constitution and nullify the sedition law within its boundaries.[6]

No other state but Kentucky followed Virginia's lead, and most, including South Carolina, formally condemned the concept of single-state nullification. But with their very right to exist as a legal opposition under fire, the Republicans stubbornly refused to back down. During the following session the Virginia Assembly, again voting along strict party lines, endorsed Madison's *Report of 1800*. It reaffirmed the principles of nullification (although Madison refrained from using that explosive word), stating that when Congress presumed to pass a law so openly in the teeth of the Constitution, the states had the right to "interpose [and] arrest the deliberate, palpable, and dangerous exercise of powers not granted" to the federal government. Two weeks later, Virginia Republicans, no strangers themselves to devious political combat, passed a state law designed to destroy *their* enemies. Confident of statewide victory in the upcoming presidential contest but unsure about their strength in important districts, the Republicans devised the "general ticket" law, which was designed to submerge Federalist regional strength under a flood of Republican votes.[7]

If the general ticket law struck Virginia Federalists as more than a trifle underhanded, Republicans could respond that the liberties of the country were at stake and that no recourse was unjustified. Indeed, in desperation, Jefferson even provided financial support to notorious scandalmonger James Thomson Callender, who had recently moved to Richmond. Evidently believing himself to be safe within the sovereign confines of Virginia, Callender began work on a new pamphlet. Proof sheets of the work were sent to Jefferson, and although its rhetorical excesses were extravagant even by the standards of the decade, the vice president pronounced himself pleased with the attack upon Adams. "[S]uch papers cannot fail to produce the best effect," he informed Callender. "They inform the thinking part of the nation."[8]

Even the patronage of such a personage as Jefferson, however, could not shield the polemicist from the federal courts. When the finished work, titled *The Prospect before Us*, was published in the early spring of 1800, the author was charged under the sedition law "with intent to influence the coming election of President." Supreme Court justice Samuel Chase, a staunch Federalist, heard the case while conducting the Richmond circuit court. Chase was determined to convict Callender. Whether he indeed instructed the federal marshal to strike from the jury list "any of those creatures called democrats" is unclear, but the final twelve were all sound Federalists. The jury promptly found Callender guilty and sentenced him to nine months' imprisonment.[9]

If the two parties united on any issue, it was on the fear that the election was likely to result in civil war and disunion. Certainly the overheated partisan atmosphere of Richmond could grow no more incendiary. The "extreme acrimony," observed one visitor to the state, and "the grossly abusive language which prevails everywhere is quite disgusting." Rumors were rife that if Jefferson was victorious the Federalists would not relinquish power. The Fredericksburg *Virginia Herald*, a Federalist journal, predicted an "ultimate appeal to arms by the two great parties," and Republican leader William Branch Giles was even heard saying in the crowded Swan Tavern that he hoped "to see a separation of this state, from the General-Union."[10]

How serious Giles was, or even whether the charge was true, is unknown. The Federalists hoped to use the claim that the Republican leadership was plotting violence, a terrifying prospect in a slave society, to discredit their opponents. But the charge was widely believed, and with good reason. The appalling lack of justice in many of the sedition trials—including the imprisonment of a Republican congressman for comments made in a private letter and the jailing of a drunkard for refusing to stand as the president rode by—made it all too clear how far the federal government would go in crushing any opposition. Certainly the Republicans in the Assembly conceived of no organized resistance other than their formal protestations, but equally certainly more than a few individual Republicans considered picking up a gun—or began to evaluate the worth of the Union.[11]

In the midst of these rhetorical rumblings of civil war Gabriel apparently came to believe that if the slaves could ever revolt successfully, the time had arrived. But William Vans Murray, who attributed this belief to the Republican talk of liberty and freedom, was only partly right. The desire to breathe free had never been absent, and the Revolution had fired the slaves with a sense of their natural rights. The divisive election of 1800, rather, provided the slaves with an opportunity that had been lacking since Dunmore's decree: a split among white elites. Yet it was not simply that Gabriel hoped to exploit the discord. Like the bondmen who had fled to British lines and carried a musket for King George, Gabriel hoped to throw his lot in with whichever side would do the slaves the most favor in the coming civil conflict.[12]

From Gabriel's urban vista, it was simplicity itself to choose between the two sides in the impending struggle. But the cities masked what was in fact a very complex political picture. The Republicans may have controlled the countryside, but the merchants and middling businessmen, and hence the Federalist party, held sway in the cities. Even after the spring elections of 1800, in which the Republicans were victorious almost everywhere else in the state, the thriving commercial towns of Richmond, Petersburg, and Norfolk remained stubbornly Federalist. Charles Copland (the young Federalist who had defended Gabriel the previous fall) was "again elected a Member of the House of Delegates." Visible signs of political allegiance were everywhere for Gabriel to witness; most Federalists donned black cockades. And the Federalists, almost to a man, were merchants.[13]

Gabriel and most other artisans—black and white alike—already regarded the merchants with animosity and fear. For their part, the Federalists employed heavy-handed electioneering tactics that all but incited urban blacks to revolt, or that at least appeared to clarify the positions of the two parties. Playing upon white fears, the Federalist press spread the rumor that "Jefferson would liberate all [the] Negroes if elected." Fuel was thrown on that fire by George K. Taylor, who denounced the Virginia Resolutions on the grounds that resisting federal authority would leave the state open to black revolt. Taylor moved many delegates to tears with his vivid description of the potential rape and murder of their wives and daughters at the hands of slave rebels. Even their figures of speech, meant to terrify white moderates, only made the meaning of the election all the more clear to urban bondmen. "Shall we then embark," queried the Federalist Richmond *Virginia Gazette*, "with [Jefferson], on the tempestuous sea of liberty?"[14]

Many in Richmond were prepared to do just that. Chief among them were the artisans, who in the mid-1790s had formed themselves into Democratic-Republican societies and who composed the backbone of Jefferson's urban support. By the turn of the century at least seven artisan clubs existed in the Chesapeake region; Richmond and Norfolk acted as host to several. Always far more radical than the planter leadership, urban Republicans adhered to an egalitarian interpretation of the American Revolution, which is to say they took Thomas Jefferson at his word. In the process, the craftsmen brought other, less-politicized, laborers— white and black alike—into the political maelstrom. That many of these lowly white workingmen lacked the requisite property requirement for the franchise hindered their participation in political discourse not at all;

their vision of the coming political order was more important to them than their present humble status. And that many urban bondmen lacked a sophisticated understanding of the political questions of the day mattered not at all either; popular revolutions often arose from such conjunctions between the aspirations of the disenfranchised majority and the demands of the politically conscious minority.[15]

If the merchants' rhetoric served to portray them as the enemies of freedom, the artisans' speech tied the bond hirelings ever closer to them. Without challenging basic property rights, a position that would not have sat well with slaves who were demanding a more equitable share of the wealth of society, the Democratic-Republicans did suggest that those who made their living from the toil of others—merchants, speculators, and bankers—had less right to their enormous property than those who had mastered a productive trade. Such men, they argued, had failed to live up to the egalitarian meaning of the Revolution and abdicated any right to govern society.[16]

Because the merchants and artisans inhabited the same small urban centers, political rivalry in Virginia cities was especially intense. The merchants, because of their economic hegemony and a truncated political system that disenfranchised many white males, held the whip hand, but the growing network of artisan clubs challenged that control. One Philadelphia journal dubbed the capital city "Sans-culotte *Richmond*, the metropolis of *Negro-land*." In Fredericksburg, following a public dinner sponsored by the Federalist party, John Marshall was driven from the town's theater by a hearty chorus of boos and catcalls emanating from the back balcony.[17]

Although denied the ballot and held in bondage, slaves like Gabriel well knew of this growing urban division. Indeed, in this atmosphere political discussion could not be avoided. Gabriel could read, but for those bondmen who remained illiterate, there were always those who would read to them; in election years working-class taverns all but became Democratic societies, with literate craftsmen reading the latest journals from table-tops. "Even the peaceful fireside," complained one visitor to Richmond, "is disturbed by political fanaticism." None were immune to its effects. "The surface—the great men of every nation—were once the only part of the mass really interested," continued the disgusted traveler. "[But t]he present storm is so violent, that the ocean is moved to the very depth."[18]

Even those unskilled slaves who had little contact with the politicized artisans had plenty of chances to hear of the upcoming contest and the threats of violence. Rumor and gossip passed freely among white and black during the evening revels, as servant girls and sailors and illiterate bondmen congregated in the gaming houses and back alleys. Sailors in particular were a common source of news about events in the Atlantic basin, and slaves like Gabriel had every opportunity to hear their stories. Illicit grog shops were "always full of a set of idle low-lived fellows, drinking spirits or playing cards," noted one visitor to the state. "Perhaps in no place of the size in the world is there more gambling going forward than in Richmond."[19]

The area around Brookfield plantation, no less a Federalist stronghold than the nearby city, was equal witness to fiery political talk. The political affiliation of either Thomas Prosser is uncertain, but close family friend Patrick Henry, whose dramatic "liberty or death" speech was already famous around the state, won a seat in the Virginia Assembly as a Federalist in the spring of 1799, the year of his decease. Prosser neighbor Mosby Sheppard was undoubtedly a Federalist; in 1798 he contributed money for a "barbecue for John Marshall." Gabriel knew Sheppard, a moderately prosperous farmer, through two of his slaves, Tom and Pharoah, who were close enough to their master to know his political leanings.[20]

Whether the angry words that Gabriel overheard actually foretold of violence between the agrarian Republican leadership and the urban business community is doubtful. But more than a few radical artisans were ready enough to back their words with muskets. From Gabriel's limited urban perspective, it appeared that the white mechanics he labored alongside were preparing to do battle in a political cause, and that cause was his as well. It would not be the first time that class would supersede race in a political quarrel; in 1767 a mob of armed blacks and whites battled redcoats in a press riot in Norfolk. Bondmen once more did not intend to stay above the fray, and for one moment in time the Virginia working class stood on the verge of overcoming its crippling internal division of race. "We have as much right to fight for our liberty as any men," Jack Ditcher told Prosser's Sam.[21]

The failure of Gabriel was not one of logic; it was one of information. The unusual economic contours of the city masked the complex political realities of the countryside. Unknown to Gabriel, the typical Virginia Republican was not a rebellious craftsman but an agrarian. The important division in the state was not between merchants and artisans but between the rising business class and the slaveholding planters. The egalitarian rhetoric that pledged to make good the promise of the Revolution was aimed only at white males; indeed, aristocrats like Jefferson could more safely preach equality in a slave society than in a free one, for in Virginia the labor problem was solved. The middle-class yeomen had economic and racial ties to the gentry, and the very poor—the blacks—were enslaved.

This Gabriel did not understand. It appears that the Republican planters played no part in his thinking, for he never identified them, or even whites in general, as his enemies. That term was reserved for the "merchants."[22]

Gabriel's faith was that white mechanics would see in his own struggle for liberty and economic rights grounds for accepting his support in the upcoming civil war. Had it been as simple as that, he would not have been far wrong. As to one point, he was correct: The hostilities with France and the resulting political upheaval provided him with a rare opportunity. Nervous whites agreed. The "unrighteous, impolitic & distracting [Quasi] war," wrote Virginian David Meade, "we here think will prove fatal to the Union [and] must bring evils upon the three or four Southern States, more terrific than Volcano's [or] Earthquakes."[23]

The undeclared naval war with France was indeed a danger to white control, and not only because it rendered a division among Virginia elites. The political allegiance of the slaves to the Republican party was reinforced by the role that France played in American domestic politics. Since the early 1790s, Republicans had favored France in its contest with Britain, at least in part as southern planters craved the widest possible markets for their export crops. Proponents of liberty—and slaveholding society was full of those who professed to love the common man, so long as the common man was not of African ancestry—also saw the French Revolution as the next chapter in the saga that had begun in 1776. The rise of the Directory and the Napoleonic coup of 1799 dampened their ardor somewhat. But fears that an English victory in Europe would reduce the United States to a British vassal governed by corrupt "Anglomen" and self-serving Hamiltonian capitalists—bankers and merchants—made it difficult for most Republicans to voice hidden doubts about France. Even after Talleyrand's duplicity became known, John Randolph opened his letters with the Gallic salutation "Dear Citizen."[24]

The ties to revolutionary France were especially strong among the artisans. The Democratic clubs were almost fanatically anti-English and pro-French. As the decade wore on, many artisan societies dubbed themselves Jacobin clubs, in imitation of the radical political groups of Paris; one southern club, in a salute to the community of liberal republics, went so far as to formally apply for membership in the Jacobin club in Paris. (Its application was accepted.) For artisans who were fighting for their economic and political rights at home, France appeared to be the symbol of antiaristocratic resistance.[25]

In the final months of 1799, about the time that Gabriel was released from jail for the second time, the ties between the Virginia Republicans and France were made explicit. James Monroe, who as minister to France had publicly denounced his government's attempts to appease imperial Britain in Jay's Treaty, announced that he would stand for election as governor. Federalist critics vowed to make his conduct in Paris a major election issue and charged that he sought to revolutionize the world in alliance with Bonaparte. In December the legislature, in a strict party vote of 116 to 66, chose Monroe over James Breckenridge, the Federalist candidate.[26]

Monroe's fondness for egalitarian France was honestly arrived at, but it was based upon Francophilic passion, not true ideological communality, and so it meant nothing. Gabriel's failure to grasp the essential hollowness of the new governor's political convictions would have tragic consequences. Judging from the rancorous election rhetoric, however, Monroe appeared to be a man who supported French ideals, and for the slaves, that was all to the good. It was no secret in Richmond that in 1794 the French Convention had abolished slavery throughout its Caribbean empire. French nationals in Philadelphia and elsewhere formed abolition societies, most of which were in contact with each other through committees of correspondence. At the political heart of a state that had passed a bill for gradual emancipation in 1780, Philadelphia became the center of American abolitionism and, because of its location, a mecca for runaway slaves.[27]

The very existence of a Philadelphia or a Paris served as a beacon of hope for bondpersons trapped in a state that had ceased to make any further movement toward black freedom. Oppression of the variety practiced in Virginia functioned most efficiently when feelings of inferiority existed in the minds of the oppressed. The rhetoric of the American Revolution had badly damaged the patriarchal authority of the plantation by infusing the slaves with a sense of their own worth. Now "the French system of fraternity" reinforced that sense, even as it further tied the slaves to a party whose rhetoric appeared to make it an heir to the promise of 1776. "If the modern doctrines of liberty and equality and the rights of man have obtained a general currency among the slaves," worried one Virginia slaveholder, "they cannot be eradicated."[28]

That the "Adamsites," who were denounced as "British subjects" even in private correspondence, publicly insisted that the French were preparing to join the Republicans in the expected election violence served only to clarify the role of the two parties for the slaves. Like some white voters, a few naive urban bondmen evidently believed the Federalist claim that "Jefferson would call upon France and Napoleon's veterans [to] invade the country to aid in his planned civil war."[29]

A far greater concern than French troops in France, from the point of view of the Federalist party, was the remnants of French troops in

America. Following the Franco-American treaty of 1778, troops under the command of Count de Rochambeau arrived in the United States to undertake a combined land-sea operation with the patriots. With the defeat of the British at Yorktown, most of Rochambeau's forces abandoned the Chesapeake for the fighting in the Antilles. A small number of regiments remained in the region, where they waited for the transport ships that never returned.[30]

Even in the last days of the war, the French troops had acquired the reputation as a safe harbor for runaway slaves. Rochambeau's troops, not unlike those of their enemy, Dunmore, required laborers, and the French were none too careful in investigating the background of the blacks who arrived within French lines and announced themselves to be free-born men. Exasperated planters could do little but entreat their unwilling allies to return their property or to try and recover their runaway property before the bondmen could pass beyond the French pickets. An "artful black Guinea Negro Man, named George, a good Waggoner," read a typical advertisement, was "attempt[ing] to join the French troops . . . under the command of Rochambeau."[31]

Some of the soldiers abandoned by the French drifted north toward Philadelphia, where they were joined by a rising tide of émigrés fleeing the Terror. But many chose to remain in the Chesapeake, and they congregated in the Tidewater cities and towns. One visitor to Petersburg was surprised to discover that the town was largely composed of "foreigners," especially Irish and French. There they quietly continued to push for abolition, even before the Paris Convention acted in 1794. More than a few became passionate advocates of the Republican party and saw the Jeffersonians as potential partners in the cause of advancing Atlantic revolution.[32]

It was in Richmond, perhaps in a back-alley grog shop, perhaps in the shop of a white artisan who had hired his time, that Gabriel met one of these veterans, a man named Charles Quersey. The Frenchman had evidently arrived with Rochambeau, for Gabriel believed him to have been "at the siege of Yorktown." Almost nothing is known about the shadowy Quersey, but as an abolitionist he was well known to area bondmen. He "frequently advised [them] to rise and kill the White people, and said he would help them & Shew them how to fight." If Gabriel was already contemplating just such an uprising and was eager for aid, Quersey's bold talk convinced the blacksmith that the Frenchman, knowledgeable in the ways of soldiering, was a man he could use.[33]

Quersey apparently had no permanent domicile, and given his taste for haranguing the slaves about their liberty, it was wise that he did not.

But Gilbert, a slave of William Young's and an acquaintance of Gabriel's, first met Quersey around 1797 when the Frenchman was "living with Mr. Francis Corbin in Caroline [County]." Corbin had been a Federalist in his politics, but he was already turning against the Adams administration for its attacks on "the State Sovereignties" when he formally broke with the party in a fit of rage after being denied an officer's commission in the Quasi War. Corbin would have been a likely candidate to take the Frenchman in, provided that Quersey kept his views on abolition to himself. County tax records indicate that in 1797 an unidentified white male resided with the disaffected Federalist.[34]

As a foreign national who was constantly on the move, Quersey evidently enjoyed a number of contacts in the French neighborhoods of urban Tidewater. One of them was Alexander Beddenhurst, who was known to slaves in Petersburg and Norfolk. Gilbert identified Beddenhurst as a Frenchman, although his name implies that if, like Quersey, he arrived with Rochambeau's forces, he was a member of the German-speaking Fourth Regiment under the Duke of Deux-Ponts. Beddenhurst, even more than Quersey, remains a mysterious figure. Though often in Virginia, he had either business or political contacts in Philadelphia. While in the North, he rented a room from John Boulanger, the proprietor of the "French Boarding-House." The establishment sat on the corner of Coats' Alley, a street heavily populated with artisans and French nationals; as a part of the Sixth Ward, it was also in a section of the city that was the traditional home of Philadelphia blacks.[35]

The documentary record does not reveal precisely when Quersey and Beddenhurst first became involved in the yet imprecise conspiracy. Most likely, Gabriel, already considering revolt, was drawn to Quersey's daring talk of black freedom, and the Frenchman then contacted Beddenhurst— whom Gabriel apparently never met —even before any definite plans had been laid. But the evidence does indicate that both whites were early conspirators. Jack Ditcher later believed "that the two White Frenchmen [were] the first instigators of the Insurrection," although that is unlikely; Gabriel needed no convincing. And the roles the two men would play are clear. Should Gabriel move beyond talking of revolt, "[t]he man from Caroline was to be [a] commander" in the rebel army, and Beddenhurst "would furnish [them] with [guns and] all things needful."[36]

All planning was still in the future. What remains clear is that as Gabriel's angry talk metamorphosed into action, the two Frenchmen became equally active; Beddenhurst's tracks to Philadelphia demonstrate that their contribution was more than merely supportive words. Whatever their motivation, they were taking their lives into their hands. "Every free person who shall hereafter advise or conspire with a slave to rebel, or make insurrection," read an unequivocal 1798 Virginia statute, "shall be adjudged a felony, and upon conviction thereof by due course of law, shall suffer death without benefit of clergy." Most likely they were political radicals and staunch antislavery men who were willing to forfeit their lives in the effort to achieve the kind of liberty and equality of which the Jeffersonian leadership only spoke.[37]

Tragically, the involvement of two white Frenchmen served merely to simplify further what was in fact an extremely complex political situation. Quersey, though he was a man dedicated to universal revolution—this was a man, after all, associating with slaves and urging them to rise up—could only have been anti-Federalist in his domestic persuasion. That meant he represented the extreme left wing of the emerging Republican coalition. Gabriel, however, understanding nothing but the urban dimensions of the Jeffersonian party, would have seen Quersey as a typical Republican, and so reinforced his perception that the coming political warfare was a contest between merchants and those common people who wished to dramatically restructure the social order.

This dangerous misperception was further confused by the role that Saint Domingue played in the unfolding drama. The western half of a Caribbean island shared with Spain, the sugar colony had been the most valuable of all French possessions. In 1789 the population stood at nearly six hundred thousand persons, five-sixths of whom were black bondpersons. Of the others, about half were free mulattoes, who made up the middle caste; the remaining fifty thousand persons were French planters and colonial administrators who formed the aristocracy of the island. When in 1789 France exploded into revolution, the oppressed mulattoes— many of whom were slaveholders—seized the moment to advance their claim for political equality. The resulting division between the mulattoes and the whites paved the way for black liberty. In 1791, the slaves, under the leadership of a huge bondman named Boukman, rose in revolt. A *commandeur de plantation*, Boukman was the equivalent of a head driver; like Gabriel, he was a bondman of some importance and a man to whom other slaves listened. After his death in the fighting, a second slave, Toussaint Louverture, took charge of the uprising. By 1793 the slaves controlled most of the colony.[38]

For several years, as Louverture struggled to establish his control over the colony, internal convulsions racked the war-torn island. Spain and Britain both attempted to add the colony to their Caribbean empires, and so, faced with the inevitable, the French Convention, which hoped to keep Toussaint loyal, abolished slavery in February 1794. Although the decision did not come without dissension, the convention had little choice; the slaves had made it for them. But France's grip on the colony continued to slip as the war in Europe drained naval resources. Rewards were thus heaped upon Louverture, who in 1797 was named general-in-chief with command over the entire island. Southern Federalists played the part of nervous spectators. They were already opposed to France on ideological grounds, and the specter of a black general not far from American shores seemed to them a sign that the French cry of universal liberty was more than mere cant. The Fredericksburg *Virginia Herald* chronicled Toussaint's spectacular rise and uneasily noted his "fealty to the French Republic."[39]

To all of this there was an interesting corollary. As was appropriate for a loyal citizen of France, General Louverture professed to be an enemy of the United States; Federalist journals in Virginia spoke of his hostility to the Adams administration. Southern Federalists even discovered that this example of black rebellion was a useful political tool. Robert Goodloe Harper warned his constituents that one of Toussaint's officers, on orders of the Directory, "was preparing to invade the Southern states from St. Domingo, with an army of blacks." But in point of fact most of this hostility was illusory. Louverture wisely suspected that his position and the freedom of his countrymen would last only as long as the war in Europe did. It was imperative that he obtain aid from other sources. In the same way, John Adams, embroiled in an undeclared naval war with France, was eager to seduce the former slave away from Paris. The mercantile-minded president was also interested in encouraging trade with the Caribbean. Brushing aside the qualms of the southern branch of his party, Adams quietly sent envoys to the island and even encouraged Toussaint to declare Saint Domingue's independence.[40]

This was not to imply that sympathy for the black revolutionaries was widespread within the Adams administration. In addition to considerations of diplomacy and trade, Secretary of State Timothy Pickering believed that an independent Saint Domingue would be "incomparably less dangerous than if [the former slaves] remain the subjects of France." His fear, shared by the president, was that "France with an army of those black troops might conquer all the British [Caribbean] Isles and put in jeopardy our Southern States." Far better, Pickering argued, to negotiate with Louverture now than deal with his "Negro revolutionary agents" later.[41]

Of such delicate and secretive diplomatic maneuvers, Gabriel could have known nothing. For him, the struggle for freedom in Saint Domingue was a source of inspiration. Toussaint Louverture demonstrated that black liberty could be won and that black rebellion could be successful, especially if those on top were bitterly divided. By fighting for the principles of liberty that Jefferson had proclaimed and Dunmore had delivered, the Dominguan slaves reminded their Virginia brethren that the struggle to fulfill the promise of 1776 was far from over.[42]

With Dominguan planters fleeing in all directions, news of the revolt—which in any case the Virginia press thoroughly covered—could not be kept from mainland bondpersons, especially those in the cities. As early as 1793, the first wave of white refugees broke on Chesapeake shores. One visitor to the region claimed to find as many as three thousand Frenchmen huddled in Norfolk, most of them "from the West Indies, and principally from St. Domingo." A few made their way back to France, but most remained in the American South. "[T]hose who staid in the town opened little shops of different kinds."[43]

The refugees, however, brought with them more than merely the news of Toussaint's victories. When they could, they brought their human property as well. By 1795, as many as twelve thousand Dominguan slaves had entered the United States. Southern authorities regarded them as slaves who had been infected with the malady of insurrection, and most states promptly enacted laws barring the entry of bondpersons from the island. Virginia, however, neglected to take this step and so became a popular haven for French planters and their slaves. The island slaves naturally mixed with Virginia bondmen and passed on word of the world being remade just off the coast. "The scenes which are acted in St. Domingo," worried Governor Monroe, "must produce an effect on all the people of colour in this and the States south of us, more especially our slaves, and it is our duty to be on our guard to prevent any mischief resulting from it."[44]

The governor was absolutely correct; the "refugee negroes" were "disseminating the results of their experiences" among Virginia slaves. But Monroe's task was an impossible one. What was required was not greater white vigilance but the suppression of information about the Atlantic world, and that could not be accomplished. As word of the successful island uprising spread like ripples in a Caribbean pond, so too did black determination to be free. In the last decade of the century, slave revolts erupted in Puerto Rico, Venezuela, Curaçao, and Grenada. Major conspiracies were detected in the Spanish colonies of Cuba and Louisiana, and armed bondmen in British Jamaica battled to establish an inland maroon sanctuary. Perhaps no better example of the movement of subversive ideas among American slaves—as well as the connection between popular revolts in the Age of Revolution—exists than that of a runaway slave who was captured in Kingston. When asked his name, the defiant bondman spat out "John Paine."[45]

Word of black victories in Saint Domingue provided John Paine with a high level of political self-respect, and Toussaint's impact was no different in Virginia. Slaves who believed themselves to be rightful participants in the political order, even if participation was denied to them, could not be intimidated by white authority. Combined with the heady rhetoric of artisan republicanism and what appeared to be the coming conflict between Federalists and Republicans, the island symbol of black victory informed Virginia bondmen not only that they had a right to govern themselves but also that victory was possible. It is not surprising that one scholar has identified Gabriel as a Dominguan slave brought to the mainland. The fact is wrong, but the logic is impeccable.[46]

Sometime during the first days of spring in the election year of 1800, Gabriel began to formulate a more precise plan for his freedom. He did not rebel because he was a slave; he had always been a slave, but only in recent months had he achieved a level of psychological autonomy that empowered him to break free from what he had borne for so long. His incarceration in the Henrico brig was the first step. His jailing and the public humiliation of his branding reminded him that whatever his status in the Brookfield quarters, neighboring whites and the machinery of the state were determined to hold him down. The violent political rhetoric of 1800 played an equally important role in Gabriel's personal development. As the public debate grew more clamorous, those on the bottom of society were drawn into the discourse, and they were drawn to the side of the stouthearted mechanics and unskilled whites beside whom they labored and supped. The challenging words of Quersey inspired Gabriel and helped him to choose sides in the coming conflict. Finally, Saint Domingue served as an inspiration to Gabriel and completed his development. Like Quersey, the distant figure of Toussaint, still publicly loyal to France, seemed to clarify the domestic situation and told him that if he dared, success might be within his reach.[47]

Richmond was the key. As well as being the political heart of the state, it was also a predominantly black city and the home to countless bondmen who might be willing to join Gabriel's crusade. In northern cities, a discernible gap separated the politically conscious artisans and the unskilled laborers, who commonly expressed their grievances through sporadic crowd activity. But Gabriel stood at the top of a distinctly compressed southern urban class structure. White artisans were few in number, and skilled slaves were politicized by the election debates and radicalized by the news from Saint Domingue. As his vague plan began to emerge, Gabriel hoped to rely on a form of popular protest to achieve essentially political ends. His following would assume the form of an urban mob; they would rise up not merely in protest over a single practice but because they expected to achieve something lasting by it. They expected to attain their freedom and a place in the political order.[48]

The violence anticipated during the fall election would provide the right timing, for it might gain allies for him. When the slaves rose in demand of their rights, Gabriel told Ben, another of Prosser's slaves, "he expected the poor white people" and "most redoubtable democrats" in the city to rise with them. Their revolt need not be the prelude to a race war; the black and white insurgents he expected to recruit would spark a class struggle that had a recognized purpose and might force specific concessions from the state authorities. "Quakers, the Methodists, and [all] Frenchmen . . . were to be spared," Gabriel insisted, on account of "their being friendly to liberty." The blacksmith "intended also to spare the poor white women who had no slaves."[49]

There can be little doubt of the role that partisan politics played in Gabriel's thinking. In mid-April, just one day before notifying Jefferson of the Republican victories in the preliminary spring elections, James Monroe informed the vice president of odd rumors that had surfaced "of a negro insurrection." But whatever news had leaked to authorities quickly died down, and the governor thought no more about it.[50]

4

The Preparation

By the early spring of 1800, as white Virginians found their way to the polls, Gabriel's determination to be free had gone beyond being just so much bold talk and had become a carefully considered plan. At the age of twenty-four, the huge blacksmith had decided that he, his wife, Nanny, and his brothers would cease to live as slaves—or they would cease to live. The election was his moment, and he meant to seize it.

At a conference in the blacksmith shop at Brookfield, Gabriel revealed the now precise plan to Solomon and to Ben, another of Prosser's servants. He clearly doubted the abilities of his far older brother, Martin, an unskilled field hand, for Martin was not immediately brought into the conspiracy. Richmond and Henrico slaves, Gabriel explained, would gather late one night at either "Prosser's black smith's shop in the woods" or the nearby Brook Bridge. As Charles Quersey helped to organize the insurgents, Gabriel would see to it that Thomas Prosser, his boyhood playmate, and Absalom Johnson, the neighbor who had caused Gabriel to be branded and returned to jail, paid for their crimes with their lives. The group would then "move on to Richmond." By the time the rebel army reached the city, Gabriel promised, his forces would be "1000 men" strong.[1]

That figure represented but a small proportion of the nearly eight thousand slaves and free blacks who lived in Richmond and Henrico County. In fact, he needed not even that many. All that was necessary to carry a rebellion was a small army of determined soldiers. Once the fighting was under way, other African Americans, both those who had heard of the plot but remained noncommittal and those who heard of it for the first time when the small band fought its way into the city, could be counted upon to join up. In a slave rebellion there could be no neutrals.[2]

As Gabriel's army neared town, it would split into three groups. "The centre [column], well provided with cutlasses, knives, pikes, and muskets," would move on Capitol Square and seize the guns stored in the building. James Monroe, sleeping in the adjacent Governor's Mansion, would be taken hostage but left unharmed; it was expected that, as an advocate of French liberty, he might be brought, by persuasion or force, to consider the slaves' demands. The other two groups would set fire to the warehouse district as a diversion and then hold Mayo's Bridge and fortify the city. While they awaited "reinforcements" from the other Virginia towns, the rebels would "take the treasury, and divide the money amongst the soldiers." Enough townspeople would die, or be taken hostage to force the town leaders to grant concessions. "[I]f the white people agreed to their freedom they would then hoist a white flag, and [Gabriel] would dine and drink with the merchants of the city on the day when it should be agreed to."[3]

What would happen next, Gabriel declined to say. Surely he believed that his revolt would bring about more than just the freedom of his soldiers; the young husband did not intend to risk his life so that his wife and family could remain in bondage. The seizure of the capital city must mean the end of slavery in Virginia, and perhaps beyond. But his desire to humble those on top, and then live among them, was clear enough. Gabriel understood that simple liberation was not sufficient. He wanted the fully acknowledged position of equality with the master class—political, social, and economic—that was the antithesis of human bondage.[4]

The political dimensions of the conspiracy were equally clear. Gabriel warned that "Quakers, Methodists, and French people" were not to be harmed. The "poor white people," those who had no more political power than did the slaves, he assured Solomon, "would also join him." As he marched into the city he planned to carry a flag inscribed with the words "death or Liberty." Gabriel's banner was designed to appeal to his broad coalition. West African armies marched under unit flags that presumably made them invincible in battle. The banner would remind older bondmen of Dunmore's regiment, and by turning Patrick Henry's famous phrase on its head, it would also remind whites that they too professed to believe in freedom.[5]

By reversing Henry's words, Gabriel expected to inspire urban slaves who already spoke the language of artisan republicanism. But turning Henry's phrase around would not be enough to inspire the less-politicized rural bondmen and white Baptists who instead spoke of God's fellowship. Here, in his failure to bend evangelical Christianity to his own ends, the blacksmith all but alienated much of his potential support. The new lights had laid the groundwork, but Gabriel, despite the religious training of his youth, failed to build upon it. Stump preachers had shouted that the powerful and the greedy were not fit to rule on earth, but Gabriel, unlike Nat Turner, neglected to cast his appeals in messianic terms or to imply that he was the man chosen to bring on the day of jubilee. Perhaps his own lack of faith ruled out such an approach. But his failure to adopt this strategy, or to portray his far more devout brother, Martin, as a modern Moses, revealed the limits of his pragmatism. Contrary to popular myth, Martin was no preacher. But Martin believed that if Gabriel's followers would "worship [God] five of [them] shall conquer an hundred, and a hundred a thousand of our enemies." Gabriel, whose association with politicized white artisans pulled him away from the religious traditions of the quarters, evidently believed no such thing.[6]

Nor did Gabriel deign to cast his appeals in terms of West African religion. By 1800 only a few elderly slaves in Virginia could remember Africa, but many first-generation American blacks retained African religious beliefs, even though they often merged them with the Christian traditions of their new land. George Smith knew of these "out landish people" and understood the necessity of using folk magic in reaching out to them. Magic was an integral part of African religious life, for talismans or amulets could protect individuals and preserve spiritual health. The "witches and wizards" who understood the use of charms, Smith argued, could prove useful in raising men, for rural slaves believed they could "tell when any calamity was about to befall them." As African religious leaders often represented political as well as spiritual authority, the influence of one of these men would have been considerable. Yet here, too, Gabriel refused to listen. Not believing in such things, he failed to grasp their appeal to those who did.[7]

Despite his lack of faith in folk religion—or perhaps because of it— Gabriel obtained the willing consent of Solomon and Ben, and the conspirators quietly began to spread the word among those slaves whom they knew well enough to trust. It was no accident that most of those contacted early on were skilled men who hired their own time. Such slaves would have few if any ties to their owners, and their skills meant that they would be in the best position to benefit should true freedom come. Sam Byrd, Jr., readily agreed, as did Jack Ditcher and Jupiter, Gabriel's partner in hog stealing. Martin soon heard the whispers in the quarters and sought out his younger brothers. He insisted that he was ready to fight, but Gabriel shook his head. He was "too old." Martin, who lacked both literacy and a skill, angrily retorted that "he would [make] bullets and keep them in bullets." Doubting Martin's ability to live up to this promise, Gabriel nonetheless resigned himself to his sibling's involvement and allowed him to become a soldier.[8]

Gabriel had no intention, however, of endangering his dream by revealing too many secrets to field hands like Martin. He established a kind of "free-masonry" (a term already identified with intrigue) and recruits "were made acquainted with the plot, wholly or in part, according to their rank." As neighborhood slaves joined, they were sworn to a strict oath of secrecy and fidelity. At one typical early meeting, Ben and Gabriel attended a Sunday "Barbecue" and then casually asked George Smith and William Burton's Isham to accompany them home. "[A]fter being some time at Gabriel's house," the blacksmith "explained to [Isham] and George, for what purpose he [had] asked them to join him." Both eagerly agreed to serve, "and each shaking the other by the hand exclaimed, 'here are our hands and hearts, we will wade to our knees in blood sooner than fail in the attempt.'"[9]

In forming his inner circle, Gabriel chose no women. Nanny knew of the plot, and if she lived with her husband on Brookfield she would have been a shadowy presence at many of the early meetings. But women of African descent inhabited a separate, domestic sphere in the New World just as they had in the old. (Most West African secret societies excluded women.) Motherhood structured their lives, and if Nanny had any children their care would have occupied most of her spare time. As a result, fewer women than men hired out. It was more than probable that Nanny, unlike her artisan husband, did not stand between the agrarian and urban worlds. She would have had less opportunity to leave her master's farm or plantation, and her very lack of mobility would have placed her only on the periphery of the increasingly urban conspiracy.[10]

If women were excluded, by conscious decision or merely because traditional sexual roles kept them from the ranks of the mobile hirelings, there were many men willing to join, and Gabriel knew how to find them. Just as many of the slave artisans learned their craft from a parent, they in turn often trained other slaves. That meant that Gabriel and Solomon knew numerous other plantation smiths in southern Henrico. Travel around the county was hardly difficult for the brothers. Gabriel routinely hired out away from Brookfield, and even when he did not, Virginia patrollers operated only periodically; on weekends, when the patrollers were on duty, most slaves simply avoided the roads and traveled through the woods.[11]

On Saturday evenings and Sundays, a host of activities, sanctioned by time and approved by benevolent masters who wished to keep their black servants happy and passive, presented the conspirators with ample opportunities to recruit followers. Henrico blacks traditionally assembled near the Brook Bridge on Sunday afternoons for picnics and religious services. Ben especially found the Sunday "preachment[s,] Fish feasts and Barbecues" at William Young's spring a perfect pretext "to concert the plan of Insurrection." The small groupings and earnest conversations of men after the services occasionally bothered more cautious black exhorters. One aged preacher told white authorities that "he never preached up any doctrine but that they should serve God and their masters faithfully." But "as for others who preached," he conceded, "he knew they did not advise the same thing."[12]

From then on, the conspiracy, at least in the region around Brookfield, was less a question of recruiting soldiers than it was of swearing in those who heard the rumors and came forward to volunteer. After one service Michael, the slave of Prosser's brother-in-law, Thomas Goode, approached Ben and said "that he understood Gabriel [intended] to take the country, and that [Ben] was one of the party." A skilled hireling who spent much of his time with his wife in Richmond, Michael was more than prepared to fight. So "soon as the boys on this side got to the capitol," he promised Ben, "he would be there ready." Roger Gregory's Charles also sought out the leaders. He proudly announced that he wished to join as a captain. Gabriel laughed that "he might be a Sergeant—he was too trifling a fellow." Charles "cursed mightily" but was so anxious to join that he eagerly promised to steal guns.[13]

A few especially mobile or bright bondmen, however, were more sought out than enrolled by the insurgent leadership. Ben Woolfolk, an eighteen-year-old mulatto who hired out to William Young, caught the eye of George Smith. Woolfolk had not been raised by Paul Graham, his current owner, had no ties to any master, and checked in with Young so infrequently that he was virtually free. Gabriel hoped to obtain followers outside of Henrico County, and Woolfolk, born a slave of Paul Woolfolk of Caroline, would thus make an excellent recruiter. One spring evening, while he was cutting wood at Young's, Woolfolk was approached by Smith, who asked him "if he would join a freemason society," a "society to fight the white people for their freedom." Woolfolk demurred. But Smith soon returned in the company of Sam Byrd. Together they urged him "to come over to their houses on Friday night." There they would talk more.[14]

Perhaps he sought only friendship, or perhaps it was curiosity, but Friday evening found young Woolfolk poking about the darkened quarters in search of the two men. George Smith's wife pointed him toward Byrd's house, and from there he was taken to meet Gabriel. The rebel leader, together with Martin and a handful of other slaves, sat in council around a small table. Woolfolk was not again asked whether he wished to join, but "an oath was administered to [him], by which he was bound not to discover the secret to man, woman, or child, nor to any person whomsoever that he suspected had not genius or strength enough to support the plan." Woolfolk stammered that he was willing to make cutlasses. But Gabriel had other plans.[15]

The techniques used to draw the young mulatto into the web demonstrated Gabriel's keen understanding of other men. Woolfolk, who was anxious to please his new companions, was not given a second chance to refuse participation. Instead of again being approached in the familiar surroundings of Young's home, he was taken to the house of the rebel leader and virtually besieged by men who spoke of strength and courage. Other recruiters often relied on the same tactics. Several appealed to masculinity. Charles, who himself had been derided by Gabriel as weak, tried to shame Patrick into joining by asking "if he was a man." Many of those who volunteered relied upon similar rhetoric. When Woolfolk told Woodfin's Jacob "that he looked so poor and weakly that he could not kill a man," Jacob angrily demanded that Ben "not take me by my looks, [for] I can and will kill a White man as free as eat." Not long after, Williamson's Lewis boasted to Woolfolk that "he would cut off the heads of his master and Mistress." Both were allowed to join.[16]

Gabriel welcomed brave talk, but more than sheer numbers he required weapons. Slaves who had access to guns or swords were eagerly sought out. Men who promised to provide the rebels with weapons were not turned away. Gabriel and Ben approached Gilbert, a hired man who belonged to William Young—Byrd's current renter—and asked him "if he had studied on the business." (The "business," a common slang term for the insurrection, was a term Gabriel's men perhaps picked up in the waterfront taverns, for it was widely used in the Atlantic world to refer to any sort of revolutionary activity. Indeed, revolution was their business.) Gabriel then "asked him if he had a Sword." Gilbert "replied that his Master had one hanging up in the house, which he would get." Other slaves, like Roger Gregory's Billey, said they would join only "if Gabriel would find [them] arms."[17]

A handful of slaves with access to their masters' rusty sabers would not be sufficient. Gabriel planned to seize the guns in the capitol, but his rebels would first have to fight their way into the building. As yet he had "received [only] six guns." A slave rebellion led by unarmed men would be doomed to failure, and the young husband did not intend to die. Part of the dilemma was solved by Will, who brought Gabriel two scythes he had stolen from his master. Wheat was grown on many of the farms in the region, and the heavy tools used to harvest the grain were long enough to be formed into two blades each. Will's suggestion was brilliant, and it was odd that the rebels had not thought of it before; as smiths, Gabriel and Solomon routinely worked with such metals. The artisans set to their task. They produced a good number of swords by "breaking the blade of a scythe in the middle." The short, heavy weapons were hammered and sharpened and "well fastened in proper handles and would have cut off a man's limb at a single blow."[18]

As the numbers of the conspirators grew, it became necessary to maintain some rough form of organization. Gabriel suggested that leaders keep a list of their recruits and take responsibility for maintaining contact with those under their command. Gabriel and Solomon, both literate men, began to keep "lists of the names" of their contacts, as did Sam Byrd. Jack Ditcher could neither read nor write and so he kept no record of his followers; during the spring and for much of the summer, Ditcher in any case was not a member of the rebel inner circle. By the date of the insurrection, there were at least six such lists of names. It was a practice as necessary as it was dangerous.[19]

Equally perilous was the rapidly growing number of bondpersons who knew of the plot. Gabriel realized that he walked a dangerous course. A handful of Henrico slaves could not take the city, but as more recruits joined, the chances grew that someone who could not be trusted to maintain silence would hear of the plan. Gabriel simply had no choice. His hope was that his followers would have the sense to seek out only the right kind of men and that an oath of silence would suffice to keep his plan a secret. And so with many of his Henrico neighbors signed on, Gabriel decided the moment had come to recruit in Richmond. Spending many of his days in the city, the blacksmith already had more than a few potential contacts in mind. Certainly the city, like the Sunday gatherings at Brook Run, offered ample opportunities for gaining followers.[20]

Gabriel spoke to slaves who sweated in the tobacco storehouses along the James River, especially those in the vast Rockett's Warehouse on the dock below Twenty-ninth Street. As a frequent denizen of the back-alley taverns, he was able to tap into the illicit network of communications—the underground economy—that free blacks and slaves used to move stolen goods and news. But it was a measure of the confused state of slavery in Virginia, as well as an indication of his confidence that his political goals cut across racial lines, that Gabriel did not restrict his recruiting to bondmen. He spoke with similar abandon to Lucas, an unskilled white laborer, and to Thomas Jordan Martin, a freeman of the city. Both joined. Lucas even promised to help "lead them" if there was money to be gained.[21]

Gabriel was not alone in his labors. Sam Byrd and Ben Woolfolk both made numerous forays into Richmond. Their job was to approach those they knew to be brave souls and to observe others carefully. Late in March, Woolfolk journeyed into town. On his way he fell in with King, who had recently been purchased by Philip Nicholas. The two men stopped near a stream to share some grog. Suddenly Nicholas appeared on horseback and reprimanded his servant for "not having gone to wait on dinner at Mr. Randolph's, as he had been directed." Nicholas rode off, with King trailing behind. King soon returned, complaining bitterly of his new master. King's anger encouraged Woolfolk. "Are you a true man?" he asked.

"I am a true-hearted man."

Woolfolk ventured on, but he was concerned about King's reputation as a drunkard. "Can you keep a proper or important secret?"

King was now alert. "Yes."

Woolfolk decided the moment had arrived to be plain. "The negroes are about to rise and fight the white people for our freedom."

"I was never so glad to hear anything in my life," crowed King. "I am ready to join them at any moment. I could slay the white people like sheep."

Ben warned King to tell no others but "sound or true-hearted men" and not to mention the business "in the presence of any woman." King's name was added to one of the lists. The conspiracy had grown by one.[22]

Most of those who joined in the city were cut from the same cloth as the Henrico rebels. Many enjoyed a skill, some were literate, and few had any attachment to their masters. When Gabriel spoke of the slaves' receiving a fair share of the wealth of society, these men implicitly understood. As men who grasped the power of wealth, the destruction of property required by the diversionary fire was troubling. George Smith, a slave for hire who had long known Gabriel, told Gilbert he "was not for burning the [ware]Houses, as he observed they would want the Whole of them for their own use." Bob, a "big Man" who loaded hogsheads at Rockett's, was, however, of quite another mind. When the word was given, he promised the leaders, he would set fire "to his own warehouse."[23]

A movement that called for the radical restructuring of the social order held a special appeal for those on the bottom of society, and if George Smith was concerned over the disorder and incendiary terror necessary to accomplish that change, others were less squeamish. Free blacks were bound by laws that differed little from those that chained urban bondmen, and it made sense that Thomas Jordan Martin was not the only freeman to join. One of the most important recruits in Richmond was Matt Scott, an acquaintance of Byrd's. Upon joining the conspiracy, Scott was given the job of contacting men in the free black community. Probably on Byrd's advice, the literate Scott began to keep a list of those who enlisted under his command.[24]

There was one Richmond freeman whose participation was even more crucial than Matt Scott's, and that was Robert Cowley, an educated mulatto reputed to be the son of one of the most prominent white men in

Virginia. Ever since the Revolution Cowley had served as doorkeeper to the capitol building and was entrusted with the keys. Whites in the city knew him on sight by his "court-dress," a suit of "black velvet, ample in skirts and flaps," and respected him for his unassuming demeanor. Yet Cowley was still a black man in a city that equated color with class, and the old doorman had ties to the slave community. Jupiter suggested to Gabriel that Cowley might be persuaded to "let them into the capitol to take the arms which were there." Still short on weapons, Gabriel decided it was worth the risk.[25]

It might seem doubtful that a man so circumstanced could have entered into rebellion. Cowley's annual salary was the princely sum of two hundred dollars. His patrons—like his paternity—were white, and he might be as likely to turn the conspirators in as he was to join their cause. But rumor held that Cowley was already more than one hundred years old. Perhaps Gabriel hoped that a man so close to the shades would have little to fear from white authority and might be willing to help free those of his mother's race. Jupiter and Gabriel called at Cowley's home, and they later told Gilbert they "had viewed the arms" stored in the capitol. That may have been a boast, but the insurgent leaders were clearly determined to bring Cowley into the fighting; Jupiter assured Gabriel that Cowley would "be at the Capitol on the night they were to rise & have all the arms in readiness."[26]

By April, Gabriel spent "every Sunday" in Richmond trying to procure ammunition and discover "where the military stores were deposited." Several times, he insisted, Cowley had given him the keys so he could examine the muskets. This declaration may could have been little more than brave words to calm the fears of his followers. Most likely, Cowley knew of the plot but was noncommittal. Several slaves, including Judith Owen's Michael, refused to join the conspiracy but allowed that "should [they] see the business progress well [they] would afterward join" the fight. The ancient doorkeeper may have made a similar pledge. Gabriel, in all events, was confident that if the rebels successfully made it into town, Cowley would have little choice but to "hand him arms out."[27]

From the perspective of the leaders, their recruitment technique was flawless. Using their relative freedom, they contacted only those whose talents and skills made them self-sufficient and nearly free in their unique urban world. The Henrico and Richmond conspirators were the most likely to demand total freedom and were in the best position to benefit from that freedom should it come. But in order for their plot to include enough blacks to assure success, the rebels had to reach beyond the urban elite to the slaves on nearby farms and plantations. Having few cultural or economic ties to the "out landish" plantation field hands—as George Smith called them—many of whom were Africans or their less assimilated children, the insurgents failed to persuade the rural slaves to join their ranks. Gabriel believed that he had at least the tacit acceptance of "nearly all of the negroes in town," but when asked "how he come on in the country," he simply shook his head sadly. Until the last moment Gabriel's conspiracy was completely urban, the only plot of its kind in southern history.[28]

Petersburg was an altogether different story. As it grew increasingly clear that few agrarian slaves would join Gabriel's ranks, it became imperative to seek numbers among bondmen in other Virginia towns. The Dinwiddie County town just twenty miles below Richmond was his next goal. "[A]ll the negroes from Petersburg [are] to join [me]," Gabriel confided to Ben, "after [I] . . . commence the Insurrection." To convert this hope into reality, Sam Byrd was ordered to head south. Byrd agreed. He told Woolfolk that he "intended hiring his own time" from his owner, Jane Clarke, "for the greater part of the ensuing summer, which would enable him to go about and engage a number of men [in] Petersburg." The trip would not be difficult; slaves were allowed to travel by stage, provided they carried a pass, and by 1800 coaches made daily round trips between Petersburg and Richmond.[29]

If Richmond presented visitors with a dilapidated appearance, the hamlet of Petersburg wore an even more woeful expression. Located just below the falls line on the Appomattox River, the town housed 3,521 souls. Three hundred buildings crept along the river for more than one mile. Streets ran only two blocks deep, and the crude frame houses were "built without any regularity." Petersburg, however, conducted a "very flourishing trade" with the lower counties and even with North Carolina. Vessels of sixty tons shared the wharves with smaller craft. Like Richmond, the city had a black majority; indeed, Petersburg had the highest percentage of free blacks of any Virginia city. Many prospered as barbers, caterers, blacksmiths, or boatmen. Most free blacks clustered together in the old suburb of Pocahontas.[30]

Among those residing in Pocahontas were Reuben and Jesse Byrd, "two free men of colour" who were also Sam Byrd's uncles. Both were light-skinned mulattoes, and Reuben, a successful mason and carpenter, was alternately listed by the Petersburg tax assessor as "Free black" and "white." Both men evidently did well in their trades and were respected by the black community, but neither prospered enough to acquire taxable property. They listened intently to what their young nephew had to say and promised "to inlist men" in their neighborhood.[31]

Others stepped forward to join, although the record leaves obscure whether the later recruits were contacted by Sam Byrd or his two uncles. Perhaps the answer is both. Sancho, a riverman who hired his time from his owner, John Booker of the neighboring county of Amelia, agreed to fight and "tried to induce others to join the insurrection." Jacob Blandum and John Pidgeon also agreed to serve. Both were free men and so were probably contacted by Reuben or Jesse Byrd.[32]

In some cases, the surnames of white owners provide clues as to how word of the conspiracy spread. Virginia gentry families tended to intermarry, so much so that one visitor to the region expressed surprise to discover that "[h]alf the Gentlemen of the county seem to be married at least to second or third cousins." As white families united and divided by marriage, so did black families, who often accompanied young ladies as dowry gifts. That meant many slaves had an extended network of friends and relatives who had been dispersed across the state; most likely, Sam Byrd was frequently told by one rebel whom he should contact upon arriving in another county. One of the men who joined in Petersburg was Peter, a slave of the recently deceased William Claiborne. Among those who had married into the extensive Claiborne family was the Lipscombe clan of Hanover, a family who also provided the insurgent ranks with several rebels.[33]

Under the guidance of Byrd and his two uncles, a considerable number of Petersburg slaves and free blacks joined the conspiracy and formed a "union of plan" with the Brookfield leaders. John Scott, a literate slave who hired out to Alexander McCrea, was given final command of the city. His job was to rally his men when the time came and either seize the city or move north and help Gabriel's wing hold Richmond. Scott was important enough to be put in contact with Beddenhurst, and either he met the mysterious Frenchman or he was given the Coats' Alley address in case the conspiracy should collapse, leaving him in need of refuge.[34]

In spite of their apparent success in Petersburg, the conspirators evidently did not yet feel confident in their numbers. Probably without consulting Gabriel, one of the Petersburg leaders—most likely John Scott—decided to carry the word down the James to Norfolk. An "illbuilt, unhealthy" seaport town built largely of wood, Norfolk was unusual for a Virginia city in that it had a white majority: 3,850 whites and 3,076 blacks in the year 1800. Some free blacks had prospered, but most freemen and slaves lived huddled together in the narrow alleys that ran in irregular paths from Water Street and Loyall's Lane. Even more so than in Richmond, working-class revels were interracial affairs, with white and black seamen gathering in "licentious dance cellars" to drink and love and squabble.[35]

Communication between Richmond and Petersburg was not especially difficult, but maintaining contact with Norfolk was something else again. Not surprisingly, Scott turned to the black rivermen who carried cargo, information, and, as rumor had it, more than a few runaways, downriver to the Chesapeake. After making several discreet inquiries along the docks sometime in June, Scott was pointed in the direction of Jacob, a skipper for hire whose ties to his owner, William Wilson, were virtually nonexistent. Jacob often sailed as far west as Petersburg, although most of his trips carried him up the bay to Gloucester County. Whatever it was that Jacob ferried north, he clearly wished to avoid prying white eyes, for "he always went & return'd in the Night." The skipper agreed to run messages and papers between the two lower cities, and to recruit men around Norfolk and Gloucester. So confident was Jacob of his ability to avoid detection that the papers he carried were not hidden but used as a "jugstopper" in his cabin.[36]

Despite the best efforts of the black skipper, however, Norfolk never produced many insurgents. Communications remained a problem, and Jacob, a slave who was accustomed to using his considerable talents to remain hidden from other men, lacked the standing in the Norfolk black community that the Byrds enjoyed in Petersburg. He did, however, convince John, who had previously been owned by Thomas Buckner of Gloucester, "to inlist the Negroes" there, and John was often "seen in different parts of the County [having] lengthy conversations" with slaves. Several literate bondmen, including Frank, also labored mightily to recruit soldiers, and a number of slaves in the village of Suffolk, twenty-five miles southwest of Norfolk, willingly signed on to fight for their liberty. Yet in the end Norfolk, the most populous of Virginia's urban areas, produced the smallest number of recruits.[37]

At the same time that Sam Byrd, John Scott, and Jacob were passing word of the rising south and east, so did word of the business begin to inch its way north. Most of the counties near Henrico had black majorities, and Gabriel was still determined to reach out to at least several of the neighboring slave communities. During a Sunday meeting at Prosser's Spring, Gabriel, George Smith, and Ben decided to send Ben Woolfolk to the Tidewater county of Caroline, two counties north of Henrico. The following Friday the three men, accompanied by William Lewis's Sawney, went "to Mr. Young's to see Ben Woolfolk whom they found in bed." Gabriel shook Woolfolk awake and "gave him money to buy liquor to treat with in Caroline" to persuade "the negroes there to join in the Conspiracy."[38]

Woolfolk's task was to speak to the men after services at Littlepage's Bridge in southern Caroline. Saturday morning found him well on his way through Hanover. There he stopped at the courthouse, where he encountered Thornton, a bond artisan of Paul Thilman's whom he had known for some time. The young mulatto ventured that he was going north to the preaching, and Thornton replied "that if he would wait a little time he would accompany him." On the road the conversation finally turned to the conspiracy. A surprised but game Thornton growled, "[I'm] damned glad to hear it." Arriving in Caroline, the two men found themselves too early for the meeting, and so Woolfolk proposed "to go to Ellis's Tavern to buy some liquor to treat their men with that day." From there they wandered up to the bridge and waited for the singing to end.[39]

The decision to recruit along the border of Hanover and Caroline is worth pondering. Gabriel knew few if any slaves in the region—although it is clear that Woolfolk did—but perhaps the rebel leader had heard fireside tales of the slave plot that had matured in Hanover around Christmas of 1769. The conspiracy had been found out, and when the leaders were seized a bloody battle ensued between some forty whites and an equal number of blacks. Among those involved in the plot were some of the slaves of Charles Carter, the grandson of Robert "King" Carter. Possibly Gabriel suspected the presence of a revolutionary tradition among Carter's slaves and hoped that recruits were to be found in those quarters.[40]

His hope was fulfilled. The preaching ended, and most of the slaves began to drift home, but a small number of bondmen lingered at Littlepage's Bridge. Among them were Thornton and two other slaves of Paul Thilman, George and Scipio; Carter's Jack Gabriel, Bristol, Ben, John, and John Fells also remained behind. Woolfolk lowered his voice. The Caroline slaves leaned forward, and Woolfolk explained the plan in detail. Several recruits "enquired about the business and how they were to get arms." Satisfied by his answers, most of those present joined. But Bristol would have none of it. If Thornton "did not desist," Bristol pleaded, he might have to "inform the White people." The timid Bristol was shouted down, and the group agreed that Jack Gabriel should be "captain" of the Caroline men and bring them to the rendezvous on the yet-to-be-appointed date. Should he be unable to travel, "he would send his men by John Fells," a boatman, "who was to be a Colonel upon that occasion."[41]

Other recruiters made forays into Hanover. The indefatigable Sam Byrd, Jr., upon his return from Petersburg, agreed to travel north to Hanover Town, a Tidewater hamlet on the south bank of the Pamunkey River. The town did not promise to yield many soldiers. Some fifty blacks resided in the town, whose entire population stood at only seventy-five. "There is only one miserable brick store," observed a visitor to the town, "the rest of the buildings are of timber and excepting one or two, much out of repair." But among the few blacks was Sam Byrd, Sr., a freeman of some means. (Sam Junior's mother was a slave.) The older man promised his son he would enlist men in town and along the river.[42]

From there, Byrd hurried on to Louisa, a slave-heavy Piedmont county due west of Hanover. Upon his return Sam told Ben that he "had enlisted a good many men there," but most likely that was a sad boast to cover his failure. Louisa had few towns of any size, and Byrd had no more success than had Gabriel in recruiting among plantation slaves and black farm hands. In fact, only a few joined, and they were men who already knew Byrd. Among them was Ben, a slave of Charles Smith's, who joined the ranks of the conspirators on June 16.[43]

But Sam Byrd was not a man to be easily discouraged. From Louisa he pushed on west toward Albemarle, where he spoke to slaves in the growing town of Charlottesville, a burg sixty-five miles northwest of Richmond. The resourceful young man also recruited a black mail carrier to be the regular courier between Richmond and Charlottesville; Byrd found the slaves of that town "very willing to join" the revolt, but it was necessary to find a method of passing increasingly detailed information among the conspirators of the several urban areas. The mail service, he hoped, would meet this need.[44]

As the spring turned into summer, the rebel leaders made two final attempts to bring outlying regions into the business. George Smith agreed to spend several Sundays raising followers. A trip to the Hungary meeting-house was a success and resulted in several dozen new soldiers; the following Sunday found him quietly talking among the men of Manchester after services. That village, he insisted in what had to be an exaggeration, supplied them with "50-odd men." Rather more promising was the offer made by Watt, an old Brookfield slave, to travel west out of Henrico into Goochland, where he "had several sons [who] he knew would readily engage." Together with his sons, Watt assured Ben, "he could at any rate raise the number of men required of him."[45]

And yet the number of men required was still far more than had enlisted; Gabriel understood that his white artisan brethren might not support his cause unless forced to do so by sheer numbers of black insurgents. For that, he needed to try again to reach the less-politicized rural slaves. It was a dangerous gamble. On most farms the tie between master and slave was far closer than in the cities or on the larger plantations, and Gabriel feared that one of the "out landish" slaves might reveal the plot to his owner. But the need for men finally outweighed the concern with caution. On Sunday, July 20, Gabriel and Ben determined to openly recruit followers at the Sunday revels held near the Brook Bridge. The leaders even let it be known that the purpose "of the barbecue was to concert measures for raising an insurrection." Gabriel arrived to find slaves and free blacks fishing and "gaming with quaits pitching." He shouted for them all to gather and listen.[46]

The Brook Bridge was not far from Brookfield, and so most of those present, including those in attendance from Richmond, knew and trusted the huge blacksmith. Gabriel obviously felt it unnecessary to outline his plan in detail. It was enough to say that he had a plan "for their liberty." Gabriel called for those "who were to join to stand up." Ben moved among those on their feet and "enlisted a considerable number who signed a paper by making their marks"—an indication that most of those at the meeting were illiterate field hands. A paper replete with rough marks was useless as an organizational list. Instead it was a way for the rebels to express a collective resolve; in scratching on a paper they had given their word to fight and could not easily back away. Gabriel then announced that a second meeting would be called "at Young's Spring afterwards to confer on the same subject." To keep the Caroline men informed of events, the blacksmith ordered Mary Jones's John north to pass the word of the second meeting.[47]

Perhaps Gabriel had no firm date in mind for the next meeting, but Sunday, August 10, presented a unique opportunity. William Young "had given leave to one of [his slaves] to have a funeral over his child on that day," and Young then obliged the conspirators by riding for Sweet Springs. Gabriel, Solomon, and Ben arrived early and were appropriately dour during the service, but with the end of the funeral "Gabriel gave an invitation to some of the Negroes to drink grog down at the Spring." There he announced—significantly—that he had a plan to fight not just for black freedom but also "for his Country."[48]

Gabriel was too pragmatic a man to believe that his fellows would wager their lives on a dream, and so he revealed the details of his now-sophisticated plan. After killing Prosser and Absalom Johnson, the Brookfield slaves, bringing their scythe swords with them, would meet with the Henrico, Hanover, and Caroline soldiers at the bridge. "One hundred men were to stand at the Brook Bridge, [and] Gabriel [would] take one hundred more and go to Gregory's tavern and take the arms which were there." The small but well-armed band of insurgents would then move on Richmond in the dead of night.[49]

As they approached town, they would split into three groups. Fifty soldiers would descend on Rockett's, where in conjunction with the hired men who labored there they would fire the warehouses "in order to alarm the upper part of the town and induce the People to go down there." In the meantime, a second group would march on the relatively unguarded penitentiary, where Monroe had recently established a powder magazine. The last group, led by Gabriel, would move on the capitol building, where they expected Robert Cowley to hand out guns to the city slaves who met them in the streets. There they would await word that Norfolk and Petersburg also had been taken. Strangely, Gabriel did not mention taking Monroe hostage. Also left unsaid was his determination to cut a deal with the merchants. Perhaps he thought it unwise to burden his new recruits with the political complexities of the urban milieu.[50]

The black Jacobin did, however, go as far as to say that he fully "expected the poor White people [to] join him, and that two Frenchmen had actually joined." Out of concern for their safety Gabriel refused to divulge their names, although he promised that the other leaders knew who they were and that at least one would join them on the night of the rising. Hoping that other foreign nationals might take their side after the fighting began, Gabriel warned that no "Frenchmen . . . were to be touched." Surely, he shouted, when forced to choose, the rebels could count on the aid of "every free negro and mulatto," and more than a few "of the most redoubtable democrats in the State."[51]

The crowd fell silent while the assembled pondered Gabriel's words. One slave then demanded to know how soon this uprising would take place. Gabriel suggested the night of Saturday, August 30. Slaves typically worked only half the day on Saturday and then headed for the city; Richmond whites would not think it suspicious to see large numbers of bondmen moving toward town. George Smith argued for the following Sunday evening on the grounds that the Caroline men could not join them "without trouble on Saturday after quitting work," although "they might travel on Sunday without suspicion." Gilbert spoke up to say that the summer "was almost over, and he wished them to enter upon the business before the weather got too cold." Gabriel's brother Martin, who had played almost no part in the recruiting, obviously wanted to play a role at the end. "[T]here was this expression in the Bible," Martin insisted, that "delay breed[s] danger; at this time . . . there was no patroling in the country." Gabriel nodded. August 30 it would be.[52]

Many at the spring still had their doubts. One slave demanded of Sam Byrd, Jr., who stood near Gabriel, how many men he had enlisted. The chief recruiter, like all of the leaders, had been keeping a list of conspirators, but instead of producing it, he insisted he had a firm commitment from "five hundred" men. Doubtless Byrd was exaggerating to calm the fears of the insurgents, but Gabriel, who had just outlined his plan using far more realistic figures, shouted, "[We have] hands enough to execute the project." He again promised that many in town, black and white alike, would rally to his banner once they had made their stand, and "their brothers from other counties [will] come and join them."[53]

Here, as at the July meeting, Gabriel called on those who would follow him "to stand up, and those who would not"—for most of the excited bondmen were already on their feet—"to set down." The vast majority of men cast their lot with the extraordinary man at the front and moved toward him, professing their support. Laddis solemnly swore "to stand by [Gabriel] 'till the last." Charles and Billey, two slaves of Roger Gregory, stood quietly, signaling their assent, as did Prosser's Peter. Others, like Sam Graham, promised to be at the bridge and bring as many others as he could. "He said he would certainly attend at the time appointed if [his] life lasted."[54]

Suddenly Jack Ditcher shoved his way to the front. As an unskilled laborer for hire, Ditcher was well known to Gabriel, and he had long promised to join the rebels when the time came. But Ditcher had not been a member of the leadership group. Most likely his lack of literacy and a trade had led Gabriel to regard him less highly than he did men like Sam Byrd. But Ditcher's size and prodigious strength marked him as a man to be reckoned with in the slave community. Ditcher challenged Gabriel's leadership and "applied to the many who had agreed to engage in the insurrection, to give him the voice for General." The slaves, who had learned more than a few lessons in politics in that singular year, decided to settle the matter by holding their own election. Preparing to undertake a possibly suicidal venture, the slaves wisely preferred Gabriel's brains over Ditcher's brawn, and "upon the votes being taken, Gabriel had by far the greater number."[55]

The meeting was almost at an end, and by any measure it was a success. But before any final decisions could be made, the soldiers were "interrupted by the appearance of Mr. Young's overseer." The crowd dispersed. As the men and women moved away, driven by the angry voice of white authority, Gabriel quietly spread the word that the rebel leadership should meet again at "Mr. Moore's school-house, where a final conclusion on the business should be had."[56]

Those who were present at the school on Thursday, August 21, had little need for the kind of theatrics Gabriel used to cajole the field hands. Instead, final organizational plans were drawn. Young's William handed passes to Gilbert and to Ben Woolfolk, who was ordered to return to Caroline and inform his contacts there of the date of the rising. Also present was George Smith, who gamely agreed to set out again for Manchester on the following Sunday. Gabriel, Sam Byrd, Jr., and Jack Ditcher completed the circle. The seven men "conversed untill late in the night on the subject of the meditated war."[57]

Woolfolk reached Caroline by Sunday morning. On his way through Hanover, the young mulatto again sought out Thornton, who "worked [there] as a blacksmith." Thornton informed Woolfolk that the Henrico rebels "need not provide arms for his men, for he would do that himself, and pointed to some scythe blades in the shop." Together the two men ventured on to Caroline, where "after the preaching" the small band of men congregated at Littlepage's Bridge. "Ben informed [them] of the time and place of meeting, and that arms would be provided for them." John Fells and Jack Gabriel again swore their loyalty. Thornton guessed their strength to be "about 20 or 30 men," including the slaves from Charles Carter's plantation. All agreed to meet on "Saturday night [at] Gists' old field and proceed to Richmond."[58]

Just as Woolfolk and Thornton began to leave the bridge and return south, "two Negroes who were at the meeting" denounced the plan as foolish talk and "threatened to communicate the insurrection to the white people." Nancy Leftwich's Randolph and several other bondmen surrounded the two and threatened them with "death" if they broke the silence. Blacks could join or not as they saw fit, Randolph snarled, but any who turned on their brothers would die.[59]

Final instructions also sailed south, some evidently ferried downriver by Jacob. Somebody—perhaps Gabriel—posted letters to Beddenhurst "in Philadelphia, as well as [to] the towns of Petersburg [and] Norfolk." Though Beddenhurst was back in Pennsylvania by the end of August, he had recently, according to Gilbert, been deeply involved in the Norfolk end of the plot. Several slaves informed Gilbert "that two Frenchmen have been very active in [Norfolk]"; he assumed the other was "Charles Quersey."[60]

Given the geographic size of the plot, it is surprising that it remained hidden from the view of white authorities as long as it did. In mid-August, however, a hint of the plan surfaced in Petersburg. "[S]ome whispers have been heard here within a few nights past indicating some plan of insurrection among the blacks," a white postmaster informed Augustine Davis, "intended tonight or some Saturday night." Davis hurried the news to Richmond mayor James McClurg, who in turn reported the rumors to James Monroe. "It appears to be vague and uncertain," the mayor conceded, but it was prudent "to put the citizens of Richmond upon their guard, as the scheme might extend to this place." McClurg quietly strengthened local patrols, but the governor, accustomed to white paranoia and chronic fears of slave conspiracies, took no action. Surely he made no connection between this rumor and that of the previous spring. Besides, a slave plot with branches in two cities sounded preposterous.[61]

On the night of Monday, August 25, a final meeting was held in Prosser's blacksmith shop. All the lieutenants reported back to their general. Wilkinson's Daniel promised that "the boys in town [were] ready to do the business." Sam Byrd, Jr., armed with "a pass as a free man," prepared to leave for Petersburg, where he would join his two uncles and John Scott in leading the slaves of that city toward the capital. Watt agreed to return to Goochland on Friday evening and guide his recruits east. Woolfolk had not yet returned from Caroline. Although Gabriel expressed no doubts that Ben had accomplished his mission, he instructed Simon (like Thornton the property of Paul Thilman) to head north and tell Thornton "to bring his recruits down on the [next] Saturday night."[62]

All was in readiness. In the following days, Gabriel quietly distributed the swords that he and Solomon had been making "since the harvest." Counting the Richmond slaves and the ten counties into which the conspiracy had spread, Gabriel estimated "his associates to the number of 5–600." That figure included bondmen who had heard of the plot and voiced support, although many of them would surely fail to rise when the time came. Others, however, would be swept along in the fighting. Given the number of bondmen in the towns and counties where recruiters had been active, as well as the tradition of slave militancy reaching back to Dunmore's regiment, it was not a bad estimate. Toward the end of the month approximately 150 men, including 20 from Norfolk and at least a few whites, gathered near Whitlock's Mill, close to the Suffolk border. All they awaited was word that the uprising had begun.[63]

Saturday, August 30, dawned at last. Those close to Gabriel noticed no special apprehension on his part. Together with his brother Solomon, his wife, Nanny, and Jack Ditcher, the rebel leader waited for night to fall. Looking up, he noticed the sky was overcast and gray and rapidly growing darker.

A Plot Discovered

Just as all was in readiness, nature took a hand in the affair. Watching the sky darken, Gabriel grew increasingly concerned; late summer storms in the Chesapeake could be both sudden and dangerous. Also watching the clouds, which extended far to the east, were inhabitants of Norfolk. Slaves moved toward Whitlock's Mill and their expected rendezvous with the Suffolk bondmen, while white theater patrons crowded to see the popular tragedy *A Plot Discovered*.[1]

So too did James Callender, peering between the bars of his Richmond cell, notice the sky. "[J]ust about Sunset," he observed, "there came on the most terrible thunder Storm, accompanied with an enormous rain, that I ever witnessed in this State." Walls of water brought travel to a halt. Creeks rose, washing away fragile wooden bridges and cutting off communications between Brookfield and the city. Observant whites noticed slaves "going [away] from the town," whereas it was normal for rural bondmen to crowd into Richmond on Saturday night. But these potential soldiers were unable to reach the Brook Bridge. Even if Quersey had been as good as his word, he could have made no progress coming from Caroline.[2]

Only the insurgents in the immediate vicinity were able to reach the appointed meeting place. Jack Ditcher was there, favoring the sky with a baleful glare. So too was Michael, who "obtained his sword" and quietly stood waiting. George Smith arrived soon after and demanded to know "why they did not start." A quick council assembled. Clearly their numbers were too few. Only a bare handful of slaves, all of them soaked and muddy, stood ready to march on the city. The Richmond men could not get out of the city, and even if a few forged the stream, the water was rising so quickly that the larger body would not be able to make it back into town. Quersey was nowhere to be found, and Woolfolk and the Caroline soldiers had not yet arrived. In desperation, Gabriel and Nanny passed the word as best they could for his followers "to meet at the tobacco house of Mr. Prosser the ensuing night."[3]

The chances of success, while diminished, yet existed. If order could be restored, enough men could still be organized to march on the city. Contact between urban centers had always been imperfect; the Petersburg and Norfolk wings waited less for the night of August 30 than they did for news that Richmond was besieged. Whites would not think it any more odd to see so many bondmen moving about on a Sunday than a Saturday night. But the chaos of the storm gave pause to more than a few potential rebels. Among them was Pharoah, who lived on Meadow Farm, a small tract near Brookfield. Pharoah had "joined the party" only within the last few weeks, and he was now startled to hear Solomon insist that "the insurrection had so far advanced that they were compelled, even if discovered, to go forward with it."[4]

Then "twenty-seven years of age," Pharoah had been the property of the Sheppard family at least since the age of seven; most likely he always had been. Owned in 1782 by William Sheppard, Pharoah was later purchased by William's nephew, Philip Sheppard, for the considerable sum of $432.90. Together with three other slaves, Pharoah worked the 165-acre farm with his new master and Philip's brother, Mosby. Philip's widowed mother, Elizabeth, and several younger sisters completed the family.[5]

Over the past years Pharoah had become "an expert scythesman" and was highly valued by the Sheppard brothers. During the harvest season he cut more than his share of hay, and "in the winter [he was employed] in such business as his Master prescribe[d] him." Despite his skill, Pharoah inhabited the rural more than the urban world. Unlike many of the Henrico rebels, he never learned to read or even to sign his name. Instead, when he was allowed to hire his time he would scrawl "his Mark," an "X," next to his name.[6]

Despite the fact that he occasionally hired his time, Pharoah was the kind of recruit that Gabriel typically wished to avoid. (Probably it was impossible to keep the conspiracy a secret from neighboring slaves after the meeting at Young's Spring.) Small farms did not develop a racially based division of labor as did larger plantations like Brookfield. Bondmen and master often labored side by side and established an easy familiarity, perhaps even eating or drinking together while in the fields. Although indeed slaveowners, the Sheppard brothers were not harsh masters, and Mosby's account book revealed gifts to Pharoah of cashmere and muslin waistcoats, cloth and down vests, and silk stockings.[7]

Even so, Pharoah's ties to his masters did not prevent him from keeping the conspiracy secret for several weeks before August 30. Perhaps he feared the Sheppard brothers less than he did Gabriel and Jack Ditcher. Perhaps only the fury of the storm and Gabriel's desperate attempts to rally his men brought Pharoah face to face with the prospect of failure and death on the gallows. The account books of Mosby Sheppard also reveal that Pharoah had a wife and son. Like Gabriel, he had much to lose, and now he began to consider his options.[8]

Pharoah's decision was not an easy one. West Africans believed that the souls of traitors could not return home or communicate with the spirits of relatives and ancestors. Yet there was also this world to consider. Four years earlier, Mosby Sheppard had allowed a then-forty-two-year-old slave, also named Gabriel, to purchase his freedom for the exceedingly low sum of £30—roughly $100. The sale indicated either that the younger Sheppard brother harbored some guilt over his human inheritances or that Gabriel had been allowed to buy his freedom so cheaply as a reward for some signal service rendered. As the soaking-wet Pharoah pondered his future and that of his young family, it must have occurred to him that he was in a position to grant his owners an extraordinary favor that could win him—and perhaps also his wife and son—his freedom, and for much less than the older Gabriel had paid. And it would come at no risk to his life—only his soul.[9]

Returning to Meadow Farm, Pharoah hastened to speak with Tom, another of the Sheppard servants. Thirty-three years old, Tom was the property of Elizabeth Sheppard, Philip's and Mosby's mother. Unlike Pharoah, Tom had never been involved in the conspiracy, and those who were deep in the business were wise not to have told him of it. Although "very bright," he "had not obtained some profitable mechanic trade." Tom was especially close to his white family. When the Sheppard brothers "were frequently absent from home," they had no qualms about leaving "the care of the [farm] entirely to Tom." Pharoah quickly told the older slave of the evening's events, and Tom suggested that they see Mosby Sheppard.[10]

The young farmer was up late in his tiny office—he grandly called it his "counting room"—when the two slaves timidly knocked on his door. Making sure no one else was about, Tom and Pharoah entered and pulled the door shut behind them. The slaves were preparing "to rise," they whispered. Prosser, Absalom Johnson, and another Brookfield neighbor, William Mosby, were to fall first. The insurgents would then march on the capital. "Here they stopped, appearing much agitated."

"When [is] it to take place?" Sheppard stammered.

"To night."

"Who is the principal man?"

Giving the conspiracy away was one thing. Giving up the leader to certain hanging was quite another. Both men paused, stared at their feet, glanced at each other. "Prosser's Gabriel," one of them finally said quietly.[11]

Sheppard rushed first for the home of William Mosby, reaching his door around eleven o'clock. "[M]uch alarmed," Mosby, himself on the list of those to die, galloped toward the plantation of militia captain William Austin. A cooler head, Austin promised to take his "troop of horse" to the brook and sent word to Dabney Williamson to do likewise. Sheppard rode on to spread the word and get what help he could, but the downpour kept him from going far. The rain also kept Mosby from making his rendezvous with Williamson, but at Priddy's Tavern he rounded up Roger Gregory and a few others. Mosby's contingent rode "as far as Mr. Prosser's," and then waded up the brook. They "made no discovery." Weary and drenched to the core, the horsemen returned to the tavern by Sunday dawn.[12]

Sipping rum in the warmth of the tavern, Mosby began to suspect that there was nothing to the story. Despite the weather, a few patrols had been out and had seen nothing, although they thought it odd that "all of the negroes [they] passed on the road, in the intervals of the storm, were going away from the town," contrary to custom. Cursing Sheppard's fears, Mosby rode for home and bed. But even before he could fall asleep one of his house servants entered his room, saying, "You must not tell." She asked him if he had heard of the conspiracy. Mosby nodded. She confided they were now to meet on Sunday night and numbered "300 or 400, some from town and some from the country." At virtually the same moment, a second slave, far to the south, also revealed the plot. A frightened Petersburg slave informed his owner, Benjamin Harrison, "that the slaves, free negroes & Mulattoes did intend to rise" and that "two white men," whom he named, "were concerned."[13]

Only then—about noon on Sunday—was word of the conspiracy hurried to the governor in Richmond. Because the General Assembly was in recess, Monroe had been at his home in Albemarle and only recently had been called back to the capital to deal with a yellow fever quarantine in Norfolk. Monroe now saw the earlier hints of an uprising in a different light, and he took no chances. Although determined to avoid a public scare and "keep [the information] secret . . . till [he] saw the extent of it," he promptly took measures to protect the town. Scratching his signature on a hastily prepared order, Monroe removed the "publick arms" from the capital and placed them in the penitentiary, which was still unfinished but easier to defend. Perhaps expecting a fight, the governor—who fancied himself a military tactician—also appointed three aides-de-camp.[14]

The bustle of the city was matched by the Sunday calm of the countryside. At Brookfield, Gabriel labored to restore order and awaited word from Caroline or Richmond. Ben found Gabriel in the company of Ditcher and Solomon, neither of whom had seen or heard the small band of armed whites the night before. Together with Frank, Ben walked to the nearby home of Joseph Mosby in search of Michael, a slave for hire owned by Prosser's brother-in-law, Thomas Goode. Michael insisted that the rain had kept him from Brookfield the previous night, but pulling a gun from his belt, he swore to meet them that evening. Before Ben could spread the word further, an unknown slave arrived with the grim news that "the insurrection had blown" and that several roving patrols were apprehending blacks along the brook.[15]

As yet these small groups of armed whites had no official sanction, but white men needed no legal authority to detain blacks during times of potential insurrection. Based upon what Tom and Pharoah had disclosed, a large number of Henrico whites converged upon Brookfield. But Ben reached the plantation first. Gabriel and Jack Ditcher vanished. Isaac was not as lucky. Returning empty-handed from Gabriel's cabin, William Gentry and a Mr. Glenn saw Isaac just as he fled into the woods. Taking up the pursuit, the two whites rode the bondman down. Isaac put up a game "battle" with his scythe sword but finally was overpowered. By the end of Monday, September 1, six slaves were captured and quietly committed to the Richmond jail.[16]

Even though the cordon drew tighter and tighter as more armed whites took to the roads, many rebels were able to get away—at least at first. Gabriel and Ditcher were nowhere to be found. Watt, who had left for Goochland the Friday before the intended rising, initially made good his escape simply by not returning to Henrico. Some of the leaders, being especially bright and able men, eluded authorities by virtue of their skills. Upon being told that Ben had been taken, Gilbert "commenced measuring himself [paper], and began to write himself a pass." For a time, such tactics worked.[17]

As word of the failure hummed along the slave grapevine, bondmen in other counties also began to plan their escape. The conspirators at Whitlock's Mill remained at their post until word arrived that "the Richmond plan had failed." Most left for their cabins, bravely promising "to enlist more [soldiers]," although few seriously believed that to be possible. In Caroline, Paul Woolfolk fell in with two blacks who were armed with crude blades. Ordered to surrender, the rebels bellowed for Woolfolk "to come on, they were ready for him—[and] they would go where they pleased." Helpless, Woolfolk watched as they disappeared into the plantation of Charles Carter. Far to the northwest, in Albemarle, four black men were seen carrying "Muskets & bayonets [and several] large knapsacks." It "is suspected they are flying from Justice," a nervous white informed the governor.[18]

Escape was more complicated for slaves in Richmond. King and another rebel, most likely Brutus, the property of William Anderson of Caroline, packed their bundles but found it difficult to flee the city unmolested. "[A] man can't go out of his house now but he is taken up to be hanged," an inebriated King unwisely told a female shopkeeper. "We are doing what we can. What we can't do with our guns we will do with our bayonets."[19]

Even as many conspirators tried to flee the region, several bondmen courageously tried to hold the plan together—or to free those already taken. Lewis, a slave of Dabney Williamson, who had been one of the first to form a patrol on August 30, wanted to fight on. Upon his return from Caroline, Ben Woolfolk found Lewis demanding the rescue "of the negroes confined in Jail, and insist[ing] that one hundred of them could effect this business." As late as September 20, one upriver rebel wrote to Jacob, the black skipper, and warned him that the conspiracy had collapsed. "To all you in gloster [County]," he wrote, you "must keep still yet—brother X," perhaps Gabriel, would come "and then you may [k]no[w] more about the bisiness." The more prudent Jacob, however, did not wait. Then "laying in Ware River," the pilot promptly "sail'd in the Night for Norfolk."[20]

In spite of all this activity on the part of terrified conspirators, Virginia authorities as yet had no real idea of how extensive the plot was. Word from Benjamin Harrison of Petersburg had not yet reached Monroe, and so as far as the governor was concerned, the rising was limited to a small number of slaves in southern Henrico. The few slaves captured stubbornly said nothing. Then came the break the authorities needed. Elisha Price's James (commonly known by the nickname of John) fell under suspicion because he often hired out to Hugh Shelton of Richmond, who occasionally employed the already-captured Michael. Several whites cornered John and demanded that he tell what he knew. By making "some important discoveries [he] might Save himself," one threatened, but if he did not he would "be Sent for trial." Gabriel and Ditcher were the leading conspirators, John sputtered finally. That much the impatient captors already knew. Threatened perhaps with more than a court hearing, the scared John then went on to implicate Gilbert, George Smith, Billy Chicken, Sawney, and Sam Graham, thereby indicating that the conspiracy extended at least to Caroline and Hanover counties.[21]

James Monroe now turned to manpower: the state militia. Each county had at least one militia company, composed of all able-bodied white men and led by a small officer corps, usually staffed by the most prominent planters in the region. Nominally created to defend the state in a national emergency, the Virginia militia, like that of all southern states, in reality existed to prevent slave insurrections. To better demonstrate white authority and military power, each company mustered several times a year.

Part of Richmond's company, under the command of Captain William Austin, had been in the field unofficially since the night of August 30. Now the governor called the body, known formally as the Fourth Regiment Richmond Troop, up to its full strength of forty-four men (one of whom was Mosby Sheppard). Calling out the Nineteenth Regiment to provide support, Monroe signed requisitions for 539 rations, including "Spirits," at seventeen cents each. The Fourth Regiment was to serve until September 15; a smaller force of three officers and eighteen privates would remain in the field until October 10. The governor clearly was taking no chances; the Ninteenth would stay on duty until the end of November.[22]

The arms had already been moved from the capitol to the penitentiary, and those that were not requisitioned by militia units were closely guarded by thirteen privates on special assignment from the Nineteenth Richmond. The contingent served until well into February of 1801 and were paid $6.66 each month. The soldiers had to be fed as well, and the ordinarily penurious governor was forced to sign payroll and ration receipts for a total of $246.04.[23]

In an agrarian state that could ill afford any expenditures, these disbursements were an unhappy burden. (The operating budget for the coming year stood at only $377,703.) And these bills were just the beginning. Far up the James, Cartersville demanded protection from "the batteaux men," the slaves who worked the inland waterways, and Monroe was forced to place "stationary patrols along the river." More bills came flooding in. John Harrison charged the state $47.29 for a few days' labor by seven patrolers, and the Nineteenth Regiment lived up to the governor's worst expectations by running up a liquor tab of another $75. "Colonel" John Mayo paid a handful of drifters to guard his toll bridge and then forwarded the bill to the government. Monroe, however, perhaps decided that this was money well spent when the militia, while searching for Gabriel, discovered "a number of rude arms" forged by the rebel leaders and hidden on the Prosser plantation.[24]

Militia leaders in other counties, most of whom were drawn from the planter class, thought little of the cost and demanded to be called into service. Lieutenant Samuel Weisner, of the Twenty-third Chesterfield militia, was most vociferous in his pleas to defend home and hearth. On September 4 the governor obliged. For the better part of the month, several hundred men, including a fine "drummer and fifer," crashed about the county harassing blacks but finding virtually no conspirators. Finally growing tired of this sport, the Twenty-third agreed to be mustered out and presented the astonished governor with a bill for $2,321.[25]

Equally active, but with considerably better cause, were the authorities along the lower James. The Suffolk militia was called out "upon request of the people" but was hampered by the lack of arms. Monroe agreed to provide the necessary muskets but then found himself unable to keep the promise. By the end of the month the arms still had "not arriv'd," wrote an exasperated official. "[T]heir arrival at this time wou'd be peculiarly pleasing." Even so, local whites organized themselves "into regular patrols, and perform[ed] their duty every night." Several bondmen who had been at Whitlock's Mill were swept up, as were "two white women" who lived with them. Floating posses even set sail in search of Jacob, and they too forwarded bills for their services to the governor, who watched in alarm as the state's contingency fund dwindled to nothing.[26]

To the north of Richmond, frightened whites in Caroline County searched for those implicated by the captured John. Guards surrounded the courthouse, as they would for months, and extra jailors were hired to watch over those unfortunates dragged in by the patrols and the militia. Receipts also arrived on the governor's desk from the militia called out to guard the "State Arsenal[s] in Goochland and Fluvan[n]a."[27]

At this suspicious moment, slaves were deemed to be suspects simply because they were slaves. Soon the Caroline County seat of Bowling Green boasted of "Seven slaves . . . committed to the Gaol." The weary governor signed pay warrants for another $289.71 to cover the cost of the extra guards and provisions. By September 14 the state had "about five Hundred Militia" in the field and devoutly hoped that the clamor would put an end to the rebels' "prospects of succeeding."[28]

The clamor also alerted terrified whites to the seriousness of the plot. Many Virginians, accustomed to living as if a slave rising were an impossibility, had initially shrugged off the rumors. "I laughed at the thing" at first, George Tucker confided to his cousin on September 1, "till some developments took place" to change his mind. Still, Tucker was confident that "it was the hasty scheme of one or two restless villians . . . and not a general or even an extensive conspiracy." The press also labored to avoid a panic. "The plot has been entirely exploded," the *Virginia Gazette* assured a nervous populace, "which was shallow; and had the attempt even been made to carry it into execution, but little resistance would have been required" to put it down.[29]

Soon flashes of sabre and wholesale arrests put the lie to such comforting deceptions. The extent of the conspiracy would not be known until the trials were well under way, but the sheer number of militiamen in the field made it all too clear that the plot was not the work of one or two disgruntled bondmen. Riding toward Richmond from Fredericksburg, John Minor was astonished to find the southern road lined with guards and the capital city swarming with soldiers. "The delusion of the poor Blacks has been much more extensive than it was at first apprehended," he reported home. "My heart bleeds for them, and yet this severity is necessary." Nerves were not much assuaged by the news from the lower James that a large number of blacks from Norfolk and Suffolk were involved. The consequences of retaining a system of bondage but doing little to uphold it began to become painfully clear. It appeared that no part of the state was untouched by the conspiracy.[30]

Few urban whites, as the enormity of the plot was revealed, harbored doubts that the rising would have been a success—or at least would have led to enormous bloodshed on both sides. The rebels "could hardly have failed of success," the still imprisoned James Callender bleated to his favorite correspondent, Thomas Jefferson. "[F]or after all, we only could muster four or five hundred men of whom not more than thirty had Muskets." John Randolph agreed. Randolph, then in the capital city, believed the plan to be perfectly feasible. The "execution of [Gabriel's] purpose was frustrated only by a heavy fall of rain which made the water courses impassable."[31]

Living in the eye of the storm, Richmond whites were obviously the most anxious. But urban dwellers across the state had just cause to be concerned, and panic spared few towns. Sailing down the James, Norfolk mayor Thomas Newton "received the most alarming accounts of Insurrection at this place." Newton was gratified to hear that the militia had already been called out, but he complained that "they have not arms, and are on that account only equal to the slaves except in numbers." So too did John Bracken, the mayor of Williamsburg, beg the beleaguered governor for muskets. Although there was no hint that slaves in the old capital were involved, the town fathers well remembered the days of Dunmore and hastily adopted a resolution calling on Monroe for "the loan of 25 Stand of Arms & the necessary Accoutrements." Having no evidence to link Williamsburg with the plot, the governor decided that the town was on its own and filed the request away in his desk drawer.[32]

News of the intended rising even crossed the Atlantic, where it worried those who had friends or relations in Virginia. Bristol merchant George Braikensridge read of the "Insurrection" in the London press and promptly sat down to write to Francis Jerdone, his American agent. "I fervently hope that it was discovered before any Violence had been committed by them," the jittery merchant prayed, "& shall be uneasy untill I hear from you."[33]

As other uneasy whites began to come to grips with their narrow brush with revolution, they found the leisure to ponder what this upheaval would have meant, had it succeeded. Most white men were sure of one thing: the slaves had planned to "take possession of the houses and white women." Although the first concern was right enough, the second fear was utterly without foundation. Several rebels had built stable unions with white women, a not-uncommon relationship among the urban working class. But those relationships were marriages in the eyes of all but the state. What white men feared, rather, was that having turned the world upside down, black men would behave toward *their* wives as they long had toward the wives of black men. It would require too much for the planter class to understand that what Gabriel demanded was freedom and a rightful share of the benefits of society; it was more natural for troubled consciences to believe that the bondmen wanted not justice but retribution: their wives and their daughters.[34]

This assuasion of white guilt by imputing impure white sexual desires to black men had long ago found its way into Virginia statutes. When the legal code was revised in the wake of the Revolution to bring it more into accord with the Age of Reason, laws pertaining to black sexual misconduct retained their ancient flavor. Under a 1792 statute it remained lawful for any court "to order and direct castration of any slave [if] such slave shall be convicted of an attempt to ravish a white woman." This benevolent law did hold, however, that if a clumsy surgeon should kill a bondman during his lawful "dismember[ment]," the owner of the property would be compensated in full. White authorities were now confident that many of Gabriel's men would share that necessary fate.[35]

No evidence exists, of course, to support these racist fantasies. Had Gabriel succeeded in altering the legal structure of his state, surely a few interracial couples would have hastened to county courthouses to legalize their de facto marriages. But if anything, the end of slavery would have decreased, not increased, sexual contact between the races by emancipating black women from the lusts of their white owners. Slavery provided both the authoritarian environment and the close contact that encouraged interracial relations. Had Gabriel's army carried the day, the patriarchal structure of the state would have been broken.[36]

White lawmakers refused to concede this point, and so it was against this background of white fear and sexual paranoia that the Virginia courts of oyer and terminer—the special slave courts—prepared to begin their deliberations. By September 9 nearly "30" slaves, including Solomon, Martin, and Frank, who had all been captured near Brookfield, were "in prison" in Richmond alone. Monroe thought it best to begin the trials as a sure method of "lead[ing] to further discoveries." The governor was quite positive, he assured Jefferson, "that the whole, very few excepted, will be condemned." In Virginia, the scales of justice were a precise instrument.[37]

"Monroe has been very active," John Randolph observed. It was not an understatement. No detail, no matter how insignificant, eluded the attention of the busy administrator. As the fall came on, the jailed slaves would grow cold, and so the governor secured an additional thirty bushels of coal and ordered "48 candles delivered to gaol." Anticipating a large number of trials—although not lengthy ones, for Virginia justice was also swift—Monroe signed pay warrants to Leigh Wood "for copying 29 pages of documents on the Subject of the Insurrection." [38]

Equally ready for an unusually busy fall was penitentiary keeper Martin Mims, the turnkey responsible for housing the accused who could not be crowded into the jail. Half expecting that the slaves would try to do what Lewis demanded—obtain the freedom of those already captured—Monroe acceded to Mims's request for additional guards. Although the "party of Recruits" would serve well into the following March, the investment was a sound one. The state paid only seventeen cents per ration for the men, the same amount spent on the "Maintenance" of each slave, who were accorded two rations daily. (Few of the guards would have been cheered by the knowledge that they ate no better than did slaves.) Still, the state had so far expended $5,431.90 of its meager budget, and as yet not a single slave had swung from the gallows or been castrated, exercises that would also cost money. [39]

As the judges donned their robes and wigs they—like the busy governor—were keenly aware that the three men they most desperately wished to hang were absent from the proceedings. The militia had scoured the countryside around Brookfield but with the exception of Solomon had captured few of the leadership cadre. Gabriel and Ditcher had not been seen since Sunday morning, and Sam Byrd, who had left for Petersburg the previous week, proved equally elusive. How Gabriel and Jack escaped Henrico remains a mystery, although clearly they separated to elude capture. Most likely Gabriel moved south along the swampy Chickahominy River. When the young blacksmith next appeared, two weeks had elapsed and it was Sunday, September 14. Four miles below Richmond, Gabriel crouched on the bank of the James. Offshore, the three-masted schooner *Mary* perched on a sandbar near Ward's Reach; Captain Richardson Taylor slept below as he waited for the tide to free his ship. Either the rebel leader recognized one of the blacks on board or he was simply desperate. Hailing the schooner, Gabriel launched himself into the river in a fine, flat dive. Strong hands pulled him aboard. Gabriel threw aside his scythe sword and calmly asked to see the captain. [40]

Cemeteries Take What Is Given Them

"Thirty or forty of the party have been arrested and confined in jail for trial," observed the Fredericksburg *Virginia Herald*, which, like most newspapers, now made little attempt to minimize the enormity of the crisis. As with Governor Monroe, the editor had no doubt that "nearly the whole of them [would be found] guilty." A "called court," the special court of oyer and terminer, was set to begin on Thursday, September 11.[1]

Sharing that grim assessment were the accused bondmen then awaiting trial. Housed in "separate apartments" to minimize the possibility of communication or escape, the captured slaves were remanded to the Henrico County Jail (which served also as the Richmond jail and the state public jail). Built before the Revolution, the simple two-story structure wore an expression of benign decay, but it was solid enough, with thick brick walls and a stone floor. It sat on Twenty-second Street, just below E Street. The turnkey was William Rose, a tall and cadaverous figure who habitually donned a dour suit of black silk smallclothes above immaculate white hose.[2]

Adjoining the jail sat the Henrico County Courthouse, a similarly dilapidated fifty-odd-year-old brick structure that was familiar to Jupiter and Solomon as the site of their trial the previous fall. Equally familiar was the special court of oyer and terminer, the segregated tribunal that had been created more than a century before to try slaves without benefit of jury. Composed of at least five justices of the peace, the court had absolute say over life and death; there was no appeal save to the governor. Authorities, however, flattered themselves as fair men, and "suitable counsel" was assigned to the "prisoners," for which the slaves' owners paid five dollars per trial. State law demanded that the trials take place no fewer than five days nor more than ten days after the offenders had been committed to jail. Decisions had to be unanimous.[3]

Insurrection trials, predictably, assumed a unique flavor, and bondmen who had appeared before the court in the past for lesser infractions would discover several crucial differences. For most capital crimes, the state required "thirty days at least between the time of passing judgement and the day of execution." This interval allowed for appeal to the governor. There were, however, three exceptions to this delay: "in cases of conspiracy, insurrection, or rebellion." While the possibility of appeal yet existed on paper, the court in fact had the power to order an immediate execution upon a finding of guilty, which in reality all but eliminated any chance of petition. As the justices in effect would be condemning property, Virginia compensated the owners for the full value of their executed assets. The state paid $333.33 (£100) for healthy but unskilled young bondmen; slaves who were literate or had been taught a skill brought a higher figure; older slaves and women were deemed to be worth less.[4]

Archaic loopholes in the criminal law that favored slaves also closed tightly in times of insurrection. Gabriel had lived to conspire for his freedom only because he had been allowed to claim benefit of clergy in 1799—an option no longer available to whites. But an act of 1792 specified that slaves who "conspire[d] to rebel, or make insurrection [should] suffer death, and be utterly excluded all benefit of clergy." For Gabriel, carrying a brand on his left hand, a second reprieve would in any case be out of the question. For those who appeared before the court for the first time, even this degrading and painful alternative was absent.[5]

In the eyes of the men who donned black robes to settle the fates of recalcitrant property, the system they had devised was eminently reasonable, even fair. Counsel for the accused allowed the prisoners to be fully heard in their own behalf, and as in the case of Solomon the year before, it was not impossible that a slave might be set free without punishment—especially if at least one of the justices found the slave's pleas to have merit. A written legal code accessible to all implied that when bondmen *were* found guilty, the decision was decreed not by individual men, nor even by "this Court," as the justices preferred to style themselves, but by law and justice itself.[6]

In the eyes of the men who appeared before the robed figures, however, the court was a fraud. Slaves had their own sense of justice, which in many cases was far superior to that of their masters; the injustice of their own condition was an effective teacher. Faced with an inequitable system that defined them as property and yet tried them as men in segregated tribunals, the slaves were hardly mystified by the robes and wigs and rituals of the court. The justices might view themselves as neutral arbiters upholding the law, but the accused did not. Slaves understood that the law upheld and defined rights, and in Virginia "rights" meant property in humans. The law and their masters were thus one and the same. (In some cases this was almost literally true, as several of the accused were tried by magistrates related to their owners by blood or marriage.) As one of the accused would defiantly state: "I beg, as a favour, that I may be immediately led to execution. I know that you have pre-determined to shed my blood, why then all this mockery of a trial?"[7]

If the partial and unjust nature of Virginia law was not clear enough, the point was made more so by the fact that the law was not color-blind. That slaves were not tried in the same courts as whites or free blacks was only part of the fraud. Enslaved blacks could testify against fellow slaves—indeed, given the nature of most slave crime it was often impossible to obtain a conviction without black testimony. But slave testimony was considered too untrustworthy to be introduced in the trial of a white man or a free black, a sign that the word of a bondman was legally degraded. Free blacks, of course, never became justices of the peace. That position was reserved for those who sat at the top of society, and that meant slaveholders. As such, the trial of a slave was never a trial by his or her peers. It was the trial of troublesome property by those who wished to retain an unjust system.[8]

Three days before the trials began, two justices who were prepared to uphold that system questioned several of the slaves scheduled for trial on September 11 to determine whether there was "sufficient cause to sustain" the charges of conspiracy and insurrection. Most of those brought before magistrates Gervas Storrs and Joseph Selden only glared at their tormentors. But Ben, one of the youngest of the Prosser slaves—and one of the earliest conspirators—"determined to save his life by any means possible." The record is unclear on this point, but evidently the justices fell back on the time-honored ploy of dividing slaves by rewarding those who turned against their fellows. They promised the frightened bondman that if he would "make a discovery of all he knew" and provide testimony in the upcoming trials, he would escape both the hangman and the terrors of court proceedings. His confession confirmed what authorities already suspected. "[W]e do not hesitate to say that Gabriel," they informed Monroe on September 8, "was clearly proved to be the main Spring and chief mover in the contemplated rebellion."[9]

Armed with this information, together with what Elisha Price's James had already told his captors, the governor issued two proclamations the following morning. Declaring both Gabriel and Jack Ditcher to be fugitives "from justice," Monroe promised a "reward of Three Hundred Dollars, to any person or persons who shall apprehend and convey" either man to the Henrico jail. Taking a clue from the tactics of Storrs and Selden, Monroe also guaranteed—although only in the case of the rebel leader—"a full pardon," plus the reward, to "any number not exceeding five of [his] accomplices, who shall apprehend the said Gabriel, and deliver him up" for trial.[10]

As more than a few white Virginians took up the chase, Thursday morning finally arrived, and the trials began. Fittingly enough, the first slave to be "set to the Bar" was Solomon. To one side sat a single clerk. The center table belonged to "gentlemen justices" Miles Selden, Bowler Cocke, Hezekiah Henley, Benjamin Goode, George Williamson, Pleasant Young-husband (whose cheerful name belied his second job as county coroner), and Prosser's prospective father-in-law, Daniel Hylton; the stern expressions of three of the magistrates indicated that they remembered the accused from the previous year. To the other side stood Ben and Pharoah, nervous but ready to testify. The court was otherwise closed to African Americans. Although the proceedings were not open to observers, the public benches were dotted with those who had somehow obtained admittance—all men, and consequential ones at that, listening intently and quietly spitting tobacco juice in the general direction of small boxes of white sand placed strategically around the room.[11]

Hylton began by calling Pharoah and Ben to the stand. Coming from a conspirator and a Prosser slave, Ben's testimony was especially damaging. Ben placed Solomon at all the organizational meetings and swore that he "kept lists of the names of the conspirators." Solomon was "fully heard in his [own] defense" by James Rind, his court-assigned counsel, but to no avail. "Solomon is guilty of the Crime with which he stands accused," intoned Hylton, "and for the same [is sentenced to] be hanged by the neck untill he be dead" on September 12—the next morning. In recognition of the blacksmith's special skill and intelligence, the count valued the condemned man at an impressive $500.[12]

Even as Solomon was hurried out of the chamber, John, a servant of Mary Jones, was dragged before the court. Ben provided no testimony, but the justices had arranged for information from another quarter: John Williamson's Daniel. Daniel meekly identified John as both a "captain" in the conspiracy—a rank that he applied also to Gabriel and Solomon—and a recruiter in Caroline County. James Rind collected another five dollars for pleading John not guilty, as was customary, but here too the cause was hopeless. The justices leaned together and spoke in hushed tones. John was found guilty. Although he had been hired out as a builder at the yet-unfinished penitentiary, the court valued him only at the average market value of £100 and sentenced him to die the next morning at "the usual place."[13]

Will and Isaac, the slaves of John Mosby and William Burton, were the next to approach the bar. Ben provided testimony against both. He insisted in turn that they had signed on as "soldiers" under Gabriel; John Holman's Toby and Burton's Dan corroborated his story and added that they had heard Isaac promise to be at Brookfield on August 30. The court wasted little time in finding both Will and Isaac guilty and sentencing them to hang "on Tomorrow being the twelfth Instant." [14]

The door crashed open and "Michael alias Mike," the property of Judith Owen, was brought forward. A long parade of witnesses spoke, including Ben, Pharoah, Owen's Ned, and William Gentry, who had helped capture the accused. Ben allowed that "on the Saturday evening appointed for carrying the plot into execution, the prisoner applied at the house of Gabriel and obtained his sword." The gavel fell. Michael was "guilty of the Crime with which he stands accused" and sentenced to hang the next morning with the others. Court clerk Adam Craig dutifully noted that the condemned was valued at "One hundred pounds Current money." [15]

The slave of another widow, Anne Parson's "Ned alias Nat," was "set to the bar" and "being arraigned of the premises pleaded not Guilty." Ben again spoke, as did Wiltshire, who swore that "he sold a sword to the prisoner, who informed him he wanted to stand guard at the warehouse where he then lived and had care of." As it was clear that Ned wished only to protect what he regarded as his rightful and future property, and not the interests of the company that had hired his time, the court was little impressed with this act of devotion and sentenced him to "be hanged by the neck" the following day "at the usual time and place." The widow Parsons was pleased to discover that her skilled bondman was valued at $400. [16]

The seventh slave brought before the court was Billey. By this time dusk was rapidly approaching, and the court decided it lacked the time to provide the kind of hearing that Roger Gregory's property deserved. It "adjourned till tomorrow morning ten O Clock." Still, it had been a full and fruitful day for the court. Six slaves had appeared before the tribunal. All six had been sentenced to die on the gallows. [17]

Returned to their cells, the condemned men slept little that night. Alone with his thoughts, Solomon began to ponder the fate of Ben. Although as deeply involved as himself in the "business," Ben had escaped trial through his willingness to implicate others. As the eastern sky began to glow, Solomon panicked and decided to follow the same path. Perhaps he comforted himself with the knowledge that much of what he had to say had already found its way into the court records. Perhaps also he promised himself that he would not testify against others. At daybreak he shouted for the jailor and insisted that if granted "a respite for a few days from [the] awful sentence which was been pronounced ag't him" he would "make numerous and important discoveries concerning the late" conspiracy. Selden and Storrs presently arrived. Solomon carefully laid the plot out in full and begged the magistrates to believe that his "brother

Gabriel was the person who influenced me to join him." Solomon also implicated Ditcher and briefly mentioned a mysterious white "man from Caroline who was at the siege of Yorktown." The justices scribbled madly as the condemned man spoke, but they made no promises.[18]

Just as the magistrates left the jail, the building exploded into religious chaos. Impromptu Afro-Christian services had been quietly held throughout the night, but when William Rose rang his "daylight Bell" to call his "Servants to rise to duty," he also "roused the unfortunate [slaves] to a sense of their approaching fate." The "whole jail" came alive with "Hymns of Praise to the Great God." Rose hoped that "true repentance" had begun; doubtless most of those about to die repented only that they had not been successful in winning their freedom. Slaves had long believed God to be on their side. Now they prayed only to have their souls set free.[19]

Seven blocks away, near Fifteenth and Broad, the hangman made sure that all was in working order. In a low spot surrounded by "tall pines and undergrowth" sat the city gallows. The hanging of the rebellious slaves, like all executions, was a public affair. Hangings were at once a form of entertainment and a potent symbol of the power of the state over the individual; for slaves, who were encouraged to attend, they were a bloody lesson of the futility of resistance to white domination. Nothing was more successful in inducing passive behavior—or proved more psychologically damaging to black men and women—than being forced to watch fathers and husbands and friends kicking at the end of a noose. Even such lessons, however, had their limits in an allegedly civilized society. In the 1776 revision of the criminal code the state had abandoned the ancient practice of leaving the bodies of the executed dangling from the gallows as a further rebuke to the deceased—"to rot like scarecrows on gibbets," as Jefferson characterized the practice.[20]

Soon after sunrise Will, Mike, Nat, and Isaac marched into a tumbril for their journey to the gallows. Expecting trouble from the black Jacobins still on the loose, the governor instructed several companies of "infantry and horse" to form a circle "around the gallows, to keep off the croud." The four men—perhaps tied and blindfolded—mounted the scaffold, the sound of their feet on the boards drowned out by shouts and catcalls from whites and "the singing of hymns and the wails of their fellow slaves and friends who were allowed to crowd the space outside the line of military." The trapdoor swung open. The heads of the four men snapped back and then were still.[21]

When at all possible, the families of the executed retrieved the bodies and carried them to the countryside for burial. All Africans believed that human spirits lived on after death in another realm (rarely in the sky) that was far better than this troubled world. Failure to properly send the deceased on their journey could hinder entrance into the land of the dead; those denied admittance were doomed to become the "wandering dead," restless spirits who haunted their old community and posed a danger to the quarters. As in Africa, the deceased were interred at night by the yellow light of flickering torches. Following a funeral feast and an all-night vigil, the families scattered white shells and broken crockery over the grave; the broken vessel symbolically freed the spirit, and the liquid within assisted the deceased in his long journey. "I don't guess you be bother much by the spirits," Sarah Washington sighed, "if you give 'em a good funeral and put the things what belong to 'em on top of the grave."[22]

Even before the bodies of the first four conspirators were taken to the countryside, the Henrico court of oyer and terminer began a second day of deliberations. Billey, whose case had been interrupted by sundown, "was again set to the Bar." The same justices sat as on the previous day, with the exception of William Mayo, Jr., who filled in for the absent Bowler Cocke. Again the magistrates made quick work of their business. Ben was the only slave to provide testimony against the accused, but his words were more than a match for the uninspired performance of defense counsel James Rind, who made little, if any, attempt to call witnesses favorable to his client. As Hylton droned out a verdict of guilty, Billey shook his head sadly but did not take his eyes off the floor. His life was to end on "Monday next," September 15.[23]

Nearly sick with fear, Martin then appeared before the bench. Gabriel's brother stuttered out a plea of not guilty and then watched helplessly as Ben, a man he surely thought of as a friend, testified that he had been involved almost from the beginning. At that juncture, even Ben was surprised to see Mary Jones's John, who had been condemned the previous morning, step into the box to testify against the accused. "When [Martin] was asked by Gabriel if he would join him to fight the white people he said he would," insisted John. This flatly contradicted Ben's testimony, who hinted that Gabriel had been approached by his older brother and was unenthusiastic about his sibling's participation. But Rind either failed to notice or lacked the talent to make use of it. Again the gavel fell. The "said Negro man Slave Martin is guilty of the Crime with which he stands accused," intoned Hylton, "and for the same [shall] be hanged by the neck untill he be dead" on September 15. Because of his age and lack of skill, the court valued Martin at a paltry $300.[24]

The guards prodded Charles forward. James Rind rose halfway to his feet and again called out a laconic plea of not guilty. Several slaves swore that Charles was deeply involved in the plot, although Ben testified that

Gabriel was unwilling to allow Charles to be a sergeant—"he was too trifling a fellow." The fact that he played even a supporting role in the extraordinary drama was enough for the court. The justices sentenced Charles to die with Martin "on Monday next" and valued him at "One hundred pounds Current money."[25]

And off Charles stumbled, hurried along by the guards, even as two more warders nudged Frank forward. Frank, another of the troublesome Prosser slaves, was "arraigned of the premises [and] pleaded not guilty." Although the prisoners were housed in separate cells, little information remained a secret in the jail, and so Frank was probably not surprised at finding Ben, a slave he had known for most of his life, "charged sworn and [ready to be] examined." Ben testified that Frank readily signed on to fight "for their liberty." Mary Jones's John spoke next. The condemned man insisted that he saw Frank leap to his feet at the July 20 Brook Bridge meeting, an indication that he had joined the conspiracy. "It [was] the unanimous opinion of the Court" that Frank was guilty. He too was sentenced to swing "untill he be dead" the following Monday.[26]

If John prayed that his testimony would lead the court to spare his life, he was to be disappointed. Just before noon John, together with Solomon, who confessed in full but stubbornly refused to testify against his fellows, was bundled into the cart and carried to the gallows. The crowd had no doubt thinned since the morning, but more than a few Virginians, white and black alike, were present when the trapdoor swung open. Ironically, it was Mosby Sheppard, who had first sounded the alarm, who certified that Solomon and John had "suffer[ed] death this day at 12 O'clock."[27]

That done, the court doggedly resumed its labors. Martin, like Charles a slave of Roger Gregory, was brought "to the Bar." Gregory's Billey indicated that Martin knew of the conspiracy—evidently Martin was at the Brook Bridge meeting—but had said he "believed he would not join" the plot. Ben testified that he knew Martin, but did not know whether he was involved in the business. Rind was now alert. The number of cases had allowed him little preparation, but he knew a weak case when he saw it, and now he called Moses to the stand. The old slave swore he had "heard the prisoner, after the plot was discovered, curse the black people for intending to rise." That kind of loyalty the court wished to reward. Martin was "acquitted and discharged out of Custody." Of eleven slaves tried, Martin was the first to be acquitted.[28]

September 13 fell on a Saturday, but with the militia arresting more blacks almost every hour the court had no leisure to cease its deliberations until Monday. At "ten O' Clock" the third day of trials began. William Burton's George, whose trial had been continued from the previous afternoon, "was set to the Bar." Several witnesses spoke from the box, as did George himself. Almost to his surprise, James Rind heard the court read a finding of not guilty. The evidence against Nathaniel Wilkinson's Frank was equally tenuous, and he too was "acquitted thereof and discharged out of Custody." As with the case of Martin, Rind had done little enough to obtain Frank's release, but if he wished to retain his standing in the community and his legal practice, he would have to be careful about winning the release of accused rebels.[29]

Sawney was not as fortunate. A smart, skilled bondman whose ties to his owner were so tenuous that the court never determined precisely who his master was (he hired his time to William Young but gave a share of his earnings to owner William Lewis), Sawney was not the kind of rebel the magistrates were willing to set free. Ben testified that he had been with the prisoner when he donated "six pence" to Ben Woolfolk to use in Caroline. If Sawney's defense counsel rose to challenge Ben's testimony or to call other witnesses in his behalf, the court scribe failed to report it. Sawney was found guilty and sentenced to hang on Thursday, September 12.[30]

Elisha Price's James proved equally unlucky. Ben Woolfolk, who had recently been taken and quietly had approached magistrates Storrs and Joseph Selden with promises of testimony, tied James to the plot. Lucy Riddell's Jack also spoke but did his best to prove Woolfolk's testimony wrong. The court believed otherwise. Estimating James to be worth $500, they sentenced him to hang "at the crossroads near four mile creek church." Since the justices chose to believe Woolfolk, it therefore followed that Jack "hath perjured himself." To make sure that other sympathetic bondmen would not try the same deception, the justices demonstrated that they could punish as well as reward. Jack earned "thirty nine Lashes on his bare back well laid on at the public Whipping post [and was] thence discharged out of Custody."[31]

Daniel was next. But it had grown late, and the court decided to continue the case "untill Monday next." Despite the large number of slaves still waiting to be tried, the next day was Sunday. Justice Daniel Hylton would be needed at St. John's Church, where he served as a vestryman. The fate of John Brooke's property would have to wait.[32]

For the next two mornings the town awoke to the sound of bells. On Sunday, the chimes called Richmond whites to church; on Monday, the bells reminded them that more Richmond blacks were about to die. As the crowd again gathered near the gallows, the cart nosed through the line of militia. Inside stood Billey, Charles, Frank, and Martin, the oldest brother of the still-missing Gabriel. Again witnessing the hangings was Mosby Sheppard, who certified that the four died together without incident.[33]

Noticeably absent from the hangings was James Monroe. The governor was preoccupied with his council, which decided that the situation was sufficiently under control to warrant a reduction in the "Guard of Militia" to 150 men for Richmond, 30 for Manchester, and 25 for southern Henrico. But the hangings were on his mind, and when the council adjourned, Monroe sat down at his desk and addressed a letter to Thomas Jefferson. The governor had long ago tied his career to that of the vice president, and now he needed the older man's advice. Ten rebels "have been condemned and executed," he informed Jefferson, "and there are at least twenty, perhaps 40 more to be tried, of whose guilt no doubt is entertained." Slaves were still being taken, and as several of the leading conspirators had yet to be captured, the death toll could reach well above one hundred. "When to arrest the hand of the Executioner is a question of great importance." The noble democrat was unable to say "whether mercy or severity [was] the better policy in this case," although he hastened to add that "when there is cause for doubt it is best to incline to the former." Monroe would "be happy to hear [Jefferson's] opinion on these points."[34]

As the governor's missive worked its way west toward Albemarle County, the trials resumed. John Brooke's Daniel was again brought to the bar. But either the two additional days had done nothing for the state's case or James Rind had used the time wisely in preparing an adequate defense. Despite several witnesses against him, Daniel was acquitted and allowed to return to a life of servitude.[35]

Prosser's Peter, "a Mulatto man Slave," and Wilkinson's Jupiter were next. As a Prosser slave, Peter was automatically viewed as tainted with the disease of liberty, and the court made quick work of his case. "Guilty," bawled Miles Selden. The court sentenced Peter to die "at the usual time and place of execution" on Thursday, September 18. Jupiter rose next, still bearing the thirty-nine scars from his last encounter with white justice. Ben testified that Jupiter was an early recruit, and the court harbored no doubts that Gabriel's old partner in hog theft was involved from the start. He too was sentenced to die on Thursday.[36]

Sam, another of the aged "Colonel" Wilkinson's slaves, followed Jupiter "to the Bar." Again, Ben was the state's sole witness, but his testimony was devastating: "Sam said that if they had men enough to fill up the Capitol Square they would drive all the White people in[to] the River." Ben's memory for conversations that took place more than seven months before was astonishingly good, perhaps too good. But the justices were willing to accept the gist of his testimony in this case, as in most of the others, and so Sam was found guilty of "Conspiracy and insurrection [and sentenced to] be hanged by the neck" with his allies on "Thursday next."[37]

Isham was shoved forward. Ben again provided testimony, telling the court that Isham, the property of William Burton, had joined the plot at the July 20 barbecue. "Here are our hands and hearts," Ben remembered Isham and his brother George telling Gabriel, "we will wade to our knees in blood sooner than fail in the attempt." Rind called a number of witnesses who were at the bridge yet had heard Isham say nothing, but as they all testified that the slave was at the barbecue, their words corroborated as much as contradicted Ben's claim. The court sentenced Isham to die with the rest.[38]

The sixth and last slave to be brought to the bar on the fourth day of deliberations was Daniel, another of Wilkinson's slaves. That fact alone made the court suspect his guilt, for it appeared that the aged planter, who had rented out most of his land, had lost control of virtually all of his servants. But the justices, who fancied themselves honest agents of the law, were trapped by the rules of their own making. Ben's testimony convinced them all that Daniel was guilty, but because of the slang that Gabriel and his followers had used, they could not bring themselves to convict him of a crime. Daniel had told Solomon that "the boys in town are well and nearly ready to do the business," Ben informed the court. "[F]rom Solomons usual way of addressing persons involved concerning the plot [he] supposed [Daniel] to understand the enquiry from Solomon as alluding to the insurrection." But Daniel had only used the term "business," and for legal men who did not speak the language of radical laboring people, that was not enough. The prisoner was "discharged out of Custody."[39]

Daniel's unusual case was the final trial of the day, but the justices were at the bench early on Tuesday, September 16, the fifth day of the hearings. The jail walls still groaned with prisoners, and the justices hoped to hear at least eight cases by sundown. One by one, William Young's Ned, James Allen's Isaac, and John Williamson's Laddis were thrust to the front of the room. The speed of the trials confused even Adam Craig, the court reporter, who several times referred to Ned as Gilbert, another slave of Young's whose trial had just been postponed. Rind spoke in behalf of all three, but Ben spoke also, and all three were found guilty and sentenced to die on Friday, September 19. (The harried clerk recorded that Isaac was to hang on September 18, "Friday next," but no one caught the mistake.)[40]

Hylton called a short recess of "half an hour," doubtless to get the proceedings better organized. Beginning again, the guards were instructed to bring forward Ned, Joe, and Harry, three "servants" of Thomas Austen of

Hanover. Again Rind allowed each to be "fully heard in his [own] defense," and this time Ben had no testimony to offer. With the state's central witness unable to implicate the three, there was nothing for it but to acquit the bondmen and "discharge [them] out of Custody." Billy Chicken was next, and he was equally fortunate in that the only voices against him were hearsay, inadmissible even in the trial of a slave. He too was found "not guilty of the Crime with which he stands accused."[41]

Afterward in the quiet courtroom, the justices pondered the central weakness in cases like those of Ned's and Billy Chicken's. Ben had proved to be an excellent witness, but his testimony was effective only against men that he knew from the region around Brookfield. All he knew of conspirators from other cities and counties was what he had heard from Gabriel or from the recruiters his brother had sent out. That information was secondhand, and Rind was at least deft enough to have such testimony ruled inadmissible. What the authorities required was another witness, someone who had actually heard slaves in Caroline promise to aid in the plot. The conversation turned to the upcoming trial of Ben Woolfolk. Woolfolk had already testified against James, at which time he had hinted to several of the magistrates that "he would make some important discoveries on conditions of having mercy extended to him." As a recruiter, Woolfolk's words not only would complement those of Ben but also would prove equally useful in the trials that had already begun in other counties. Moreover, the justices understood the importance of carefully selected pardons. Mercy, when applied to the right person, produced devotion and deference, concepts necessary for supporting the mental structure of human bondage.[42]

The next morning Gervas Storrs and Joseph Selden spoke at length to Woolfolk. The eighteen-year-old hired man described how he came to be involved in the plot, in the process implicating Sam Byrd and George Smith. He downplayed the extent of his own recruiting—although he provided a long list of the men he had enlisted in Caroline—and made it clear that he was a simple soldier, not a planner. That role was reserved for Gabriel and Jack Ditcher. Perhaps to make sure that Woolfolk lived up to his bargain, the young slave, unlike Prosser's Ben, was put on trial the next morning. Despite his confession Woolfolk entered a plea of not guilty. Ben and—in a curious case of revenge—Price's James, who had been condemned to death in part on the words of Woolfolk, testified against him and insisted he "was to have the title and command of Captain." The justices unanimously found him guilty and sentenced him to be hanged on Monday, September 22. Within the hour, Governor Monroe and his council voted to pardon Ben Woolfolk in full. To protect him from the wrath of his friends he was removed from the jail and housed with Ben in the still unfinished penitentiary on the slope of Oregon Hill.[43]

Elsewhere in Richmond, the morning of September 18 was more forbidding. Daybreak meant the start of the third round of hangings and the execution of five more men. Watching the scene from his jail window was James T. Callender, who despite his own incarnation showed little sympathy for the condemned; the journalist's early antislavery sentiments had not survived his move to Virginia, where most of his patrons were wealthy planters. "Three [slaves] were in the Cart and had got about half way to the gallows when they were intercepted by an order from the executive council," he informed Jefferson. The council acted in response to a petition presented "by some Ladies of Richmond who lived not far distant" from the gallows. "[P]erhaps you will suppose that the prayer of the petition was to save the lives of these wretches," Callender snickered, "but it was only that they might be hung *in some other place*, because the exhibition was offensive." In deference to the ladies, the cart swung north out of town. In a quiet spot above the city five more men—Peter, Isham, Sawney, Jupiter, and Sam—met their death.[44]

The gentlemen justices' decision to find a more secluded spot may have rendered the morning easier for genteel city ladies, but it also made for a crueler death for the rebels. Bondmen hanged at the town gallows at least experienced a quick death, as the fall from the trapdoor instantly broke their necks. But slaves who kicked at the end of a long rope hanging from a handy branch died slowly by asphyxiation. There was no long drop as the cart on which they had stood drove away; the hanged were simply "launched into eternity."[45]

The need to find a new place suitable for mass executions was only a tactical problem. The Henrico court of oyer and terminer had no intention of slowing its pursuit of justice. No sooner had the weary gravediggers put away their shovels than the justices convened on the morning of September 19 to hear the case of George Smith. This time the court had no doubts about the outcome; Ben Woolfolk described Smith's trips to Caroline and Manchester. "[U]p there the prisoner was a Colonel," Woolfolk assured the court. Rind called only Smith himself to the stand. The justices were not impressed with his vows of innocence and sentenced him to die on October 3 at the clearing near George Watson's Tavern, now the "property of Thomas Henry Prosser." Presumably that was where Isaac and Laddis were hanged later the same day; they were the sixteenth and seventeenth to swing from a noose.[46]

More than a few white Virginians, it seems, were not reassured by the rising body count. Among them was Thomas Jefferson. On September 22 his answer to Monroe's missive arrived in Richmond. The letter was carefully worded, yet unmistakable in its intent. "Where to stay the hand of the executioner is an important question," Jefferson agreed. He said it was true that those "who have escaped from the immediate danger, must have feelings which would dispose them to extend the executions." But the time had come to stop the killing. "[T]here is a strong sentiment that there has been hanging enough," he warned. "The other states and the world at large will forever condemn us if we indulge a principle of revenge." The warning caught Monroe off guard, and his answer was defensive. "The danger has doubtless passed but yet it wo[ul]d be unwise to make no provision ag[ai]nst possibilities," insisted Monroe. But the governor well understood the wishes of Monticello.[47]

Nor was the squeamish Jefferson the only planter to express qualms about the continued hangings. Seventeen men had already died, and "about 30 [were] yet in confinement" awaiting trial. Now that authorities had put Ben Woolfolk to good use, it was "impossible to foresee," said one troubled observer, "where this dreadful tragedy will terminate." John Randolph of Roanoke agreed. The conspiracy "has been quieted without any bloodshed," he informed Joseph Nicholson, "but that which has streamed upon the scaffold." Like most slaveholders, Jefferson and Randolph preferred seeing a few slaves writhing on the gibbet to having their plantation world turned upside down. But as men who harbored serious doubts about their peculiar institution, they were unnerved by the thought of dozens of men dying for the crime of yearning to be free.[48]

Yet only blocks from where Monroe sat reading Jefferson's words, the trials once more were under way. Gilbert, whose case had been continued three times since September 15, "was again set to the Bar." Ben, James, and Ben Woolfolk all testified against him. Valued at $366, Gilbert was sentenced to die outside of town on October 3. Gilbert stepped back and Prosser's Tom was nudged forward. Again Ben and Ben Woolfolk took the stand, and so Tom joined Gilbert in the ranks of those condemned to die "at Prosser's Tavern" on October 3. The choice of a tavern not far from Brookfield, owned by the master of the slave set to hang, had to do with more than merely a desire to please Richmond ladies who were offended by the wailing of bondwomen and small children. Slaves were encouraged to attend the execution of their fellows as a lesson in white hegemony, and hangings in the Henrico countryside allowed slaves who had not witnessed the Richmond executions the chance to view the power of white authority for themselves. But it was also a rebuke to young Prosser. Masters were supposed to control their slaves themselves. Prosser clearly had not done so, and his failure nearly resulted in revolution. The state now had to discipline his slaves for him. To make that point clear, it did so on his property. It is significant that William Young's William, who also was found guilty that day, was instead set to be executed "at the Cross roads near four mile Creek Church."[49]

The Henrico justices, notwithstanding Jefferson's admonition to avoid vengeance, had no intention of allowing the rebel leadership to escape punishment. On September 27 Sam Byrd, Jr., and Michael, the slave of Thomas Goode, Prosser's brother-in-law, were hauled into court. "[S]undry Witnesses," including Ben Woolfolk, were examined, as were both of the accused. The tribunal unanimously decided that both men were guilty of "Conspiracy and insurrection." Byrd and Michael were led back to their separate cells, not to meet again until the morning of October 3, when they were to be carried to Prosser's Tavern and "hanged by the neck untill [they were] dead."[50]

Sam Graham, whose trial was twice continued until September 29, suffered the same fate. He was scheduled to die at "the Cross roads near four mile Creek Church" on October 10. As Sam had been a leading conspirator and an important man in Hanover County (where his owner, Paul Graham, resided), his fate had long been sealed. On the advice of Monroe, however, the court began to deal less harshly with those who had enlisted in the plot but had done no recruiting or planning. On the same day that Graham was condemned, the court also pronounced Thomas Burton's Abraham guilty as charged. But "for reasons appearing to the Court they recommend[ed] Abraham to the Executive as a proper Object for mercy," and the governor agreed. Later that afternoon Jim Allen and Moses were both acquitted despite solid cases against them and the testimony of Ben Woolfolk.[51]

On the last day of the month the court still faced a full docket, but the will of Jefferson had been made clear, for the desire to shed more blood began to wane. Jacob and Dick, slaves of Thomas Woodfin and Jesse Smith, appeared in turn before the bar. Both were found guilty of conspiring to become free men and sentenced to death, but the court deemed them, like Abraham, "fit Object[s] for mercy." The governor pardoned both on October 2, well before their scheduled execution on October 10. The last slave to appear was Solomon, "the property of the Estate of Joseph Lewis." He too was found guilty and sentenced to hang. But all five justices who heard his case "respectfully recommend[ed]" that Solomon be pardoned. Again Monroe assented.[52]

For the justices it had been a busy month, and now it was nearly over. Yet one trial more, at least, remained. The "Villon" Gabriel had been captured in Norfolk on Tuesday, September 23, and had been returned "in irons" to the capital city.[53]

7

A Companion Picture

As Norfolk authorities took Gabriel to Richmond, the trials of his followers continued in the special courts of oyer and terminer in a number of counties. Slaves were tried in the county of their arrest, not in that of their master's residence; a number of those already tried in the Henrico tribunal, including young Ben Woolfolk, belonged to Caroline or Hanover slaveholders. As the far-flung conspiracy collapsed, rebels across the state were brought before the dock in several different towns and hamlets.

Strangely enough, some of the trials were separated from Henrico only by arbitrary lines of jurisdiction. Richmond City County had been carved out of Henrico, but the city still conducted its legal business in the old building on Twenty-second Street (which both municipalities shared with the Virginia's Supreme Court of Appeals). In normal times the state's justice was a sleepy enough affair, and the multiple use of the courthouse posed few problems. But in the hectic days of September, the Richmond justices waited impatiently for the Henrico magistrates to pause in their deliberations. On Thursday, September 25, such a break occurred. The Richmond magistrates, led by Mayor James McClurg, bustled into the temporarily empty chamber and shouted for King to be brought before them. Despite overwhelming evidence against him—both Ben Woolfolk, who had first recruited him, and Mary Martin, the shopkeeper who had heard King talk of fighting on after the rebellion collapsed, testified for the prosecution—his owner, Philip A. Nicholas, wished to retain the venerable rebel. Nicholas testified in King's behalf and even hired an expensive lawyer to conduct his defense. The justices, however, remained unimpressed and sentenced King to die with the other rebels on October 3. Still Nicholas persisted. His friend Larkin Stanard wrote in King's behalf to the governor, who was by now ready to embrace any argument that would spare a minor conspirator. "I always thought him to be much attach'd to his master," Larkin insisted, "Tho subject to drink. [A]nd when in a State of Intoxication would say things I do not believe he thought of when sober." That was good enough for Monroe, who decided to split the difference. King got his pardon but not his freedom. Until the governor could decide upon the fate of the likes of such men, he ordered the slave returned to his cell.[1]

"Brutus alias Julius," the property of the classically inclined but indecisive William Anderson of Caroline, was the next man to be brought before the bar. Brutus insisted "he was in no wise guilty," and either the evidence against him was weak or James Rind performed better than Nicholas's higher-priced talent, because the court found in his favor. Ralph, the property of Elizabeth Page, was the last slave to be tried by the Richmond justices. He too was found not guilty and "discharged."[2]

To the west, a court of oyer and terminer was sitting in Louisa County. Despite the boasts of Sam Byrd, who had passed through on his way to Albemarle, few in the county had joined in the business, but among those who had was Charles Smith's Ben. Now Ben, charged with "Feloniously and deliberately Conspiring to make Rebellion, and insurrection, &c against the peace & Dignity of the Commonwealth," stood and faced his tormentors. Ben knew he was likely to swing. Several witnesses even remembered the day—June 16—when Ben had joined the conspiracy. Worse still, his defense counsel was David Yancey, the cousin of Justices Charles and Robert Yancey, who both sat on the tribunal ready to decide his fate. But he had one chance. The most important witness against him, Sam Byrd, sat in a jail two counties away, and the recruiter was not a man to cooperate with the authorities. "[T]he Majority of the Court [was] of Opinion that the prisoner [was] Guilty but because the Court was not Unanimous Sentence Cou'd not be passed—and the prisoner [was] hence discharged from this prosecution."[3]

The magistrates of Caroline, two counties to the north of Henrico, faced brighter prospects. Virtually all of the soldiers there were recruits of Ben Woolfolk, who by now had replaced Prosser's Ben as the state's chief witness. Woolfolk had already implicated most of those he had met with at Littlepage's Bridge. Among those named were Thornton, George, and Scipio (all owned by Paul Thilman), as well as "One-Eyed Ben," John, and Jack Gabriel (these three the property of Charles Carter). Those named by Woolfolk were quickly apprehended by the Caroline militia. By mid-October "Seven slaves [had been] committed to the Gaol" in the town of Bowling Green. The trials were set to start on Wednesday, October 22, with Edmund Pendleton prosecuting. The seventy-nine-year-old jurist, who sat on the Virginia Supreme Court of Appeals and was considered to be one of the finest legal minds in the state, had served as legal mentor to Jefferson. But evidently he felt little of the squeamishness his former pupil evinced over the hanging of black revolutionaries.[4]

John Hoomes, one of the Caroline magistrates, had no intention of making the same mistake as his Louisa brethren. "Ben [Woolfolk] is the only witness against" the accused, he informed Monroe. "If the Governor could send him up" the trials could proceed. "[H]e may take the Stage in the morning and be here in time," Hoomes promised. Monroe took the matter up with his council, which agreed that Woolfolk could be sent "as a Witness" provided he was properly escorted.[5]

The result was all that could have been wished for. On the morning of October 22 "One-Eyed Ben" was brought before the court; Robert G. Robb served as his "council." In what Ben must have regarded as an ugly act of treachery, Ben Woolfolk told of recruiting the young slave after morning services. The hostile testimony of Bristol, who had threatened to inform his master of the plot, was more expected, if not more welcome. The justices wasted little time in arriving at a finding of guilty and sentenced Ben to be "carried to the Gallows between the Hours of ten and twelve o'clock in the morning of the twenty-ninth day of this month and there hanged up by the neck until he be dead."[6]

Virginia masters reacted to such verdicts with mixed emotions. Some, like Philip Nicholas, felt guilty enough about the institution to understand the desire of their slaves to be free, and these men worked to obtain pardons. Others, like Charles Carter, who lifted not a finger to save Ben or any of his accused bondmen, demonstrated little concern for their slaves beyond their monetary value. Condemned slaves brought ready capital, a rare enough commodity among the cash-poor Virginia gentry. The money paid out by the state could be used to purchase more slaves, or it could be invested in other ways. "[I]f all [of] your personal property in Henrico & Charles City were annihilated tomorrow you might derive more neat profit from your estate," Carter Berkeley advised his cousin shortly after the fact. "How much better it would be to convert *them* into money & draw from it a certain annual fee."[7]

If Carter was counting on further convictions to fill his purse, he was to be disappointed, at least for a time. His "John a Boatman" was the next to be brought forward. Again Woolfolk spoke against one of his own recruits, but several of the justices suspected that John had been a less than ardent rebel. "Upon hearing the Testimony of Ben Woolfolk a negro Slave the Court [was] of opinion that the said John a Boatmen is not Guilty." Acquitted on the same grounds was George, a slave of Paul Thilman of Hanover. Here too a majority of the magistrates believed George to be guilty, but at least one argued that the "testimony of the said Ben Woolfolk is not Sufficient to Convict." Like John, George did not swing, but he lived only to return to a life of forced labor. A fourth man who was tried that morning received a similar fate. The court found Scipio guilty and sentenced him to die, but Justice Hoomes informed the governor that as Scipio was but "a lad" he was "sorry he was not recommended for mercy." Monroe hastily scribbled out the pardon.[8]

For one week, the Caroline County Courthouse was quiet. But on October 29, the special court resumed deliberations. Again the magistrates sent for Woolfolk. "[I]t appears that a fair [successful] trial cannot take place without the attendance of Ben," Pendleton warned Monroe. "I hope it will be convenient for you to send him." Jack Gabriel, the ringleader of the Caroline branch and a slave of Charles Carter's, was the first to be dragged before the bench. Woolfolk testified, as did Edward Garland's Humphrey. "Guilty," barked John Hoomes. The prisoner was sentenced to die "on the second Friday in November next." Humphrey was next. But while Woolfolk's testimony made it clear that the slave was a willing participant in the plot, one of the magistrates thought Humphrey should be rewarded for testifying against the more dangerous Jack Gabriel, whom the authorities regarded as a "general." The vote stood at four to one, and so "the said Prisoner [was] discharged from Custody." So too was William Penn's Billy found not guilty.[9]

The following morning was October 30, and only two bondmen remained in the Caroline brig. Paul Thilman's Thornton was the first to be set to the bar, with Carter's John Fells close behind. Ben Woolfolk testified against both, telling of how the two had pledged their lives at Littlepage's Bridge. Now they would pay the price of following the wrong man. After a summation by Pendleton, the justices found both men guilty and sentenced them to die with Jack Gabriel on November 14.[10]

One county away, in Hanover, similar trials ensued, and two men, evidently including Paul Thilman's Holmy, "were condemned to death & confined in the Gaol of Hanover." But with only two rebels to watch over, the jailors grew careless. They did note that as the weekend approached the prisoners grew increasingly "riotous & ungovernable," although they attributed it only to the natural surliness of men who had nothing left to lose. But the following Saturday when one of the guards entered the cell with food, the two men, who had been "handcuffed & chained to the floor," knocked him to the floor and raced for the door. A number of blacks were milling about in the street and "pretended to follow them," shouting and pointing in all directions and generally getting in the way of white authorities' pursuit. The local justices assumed that the men had been passed a key by a number of blacks who had visited "the Gaol under the pretence of preaching &c the Week before." The condemned slaves were never retaken.[11]

Far downriver in Norfolk, authorities faced a very different kind of problem. Upon receiving word that the conspiracy had failed at its source, the black and white Jacobins who had met near the Nansemond County border at Whitlock's Mill drifted home. At almost the same time, Mayor Thomas Newton heard the news and called out the militia; numerous patrols also sprang to life without awaiting official sanction. One of these apprehended two white women who were married to black men (whether slave or free is unclear), but under "examination" the women sat silent. Patrols swept up a number of bondmen and "endeavour[ed] for several days by examinations and otherwise [beatings] to discover the promoters." But no Ben Woolfolks came forward, and with Jacob, the black skipper who provided the link between Norfolk and Petersburg, still at large the evidence against the men was inconclusive. "[T]here seems to prevail among them a determination to disclose nothing," grumbled one justice. Newton bound several over for trial, although he doubted the evidence would "be sufficient." [12]

In mid-October the trials began in the Norfolk Courthouse, a crude pile of boards on Main just east of Church Street—"a plain mean building," observed architect Benjamin Henry Latrobe, "with a meaner spire." But over the intervening weeks nothing had happened to help the prosecutor's case. More than a few bondmen were examined, but the slaves simply glared at their captors. Working-class whites were no more help. Under stern questioning several confessed that "they had heard of the assembling of 150 negroes at the mill." But when asked how they came by such information they "equivocate[d] and depart[ed] from the truth." Lacking even a single witness against those arrested, Norfolk authorities bowed to the inevitable and released the accused rebels. [13]

The city was deeply shaken by the affair, however, and for several months nightly patrols tramped the streets and outlying plantations. One nervous white man reported that as late as Christmas Day he had stumbled upon a "parcel of negroes" talking in hushed tones. Pretending not to notice them, he got near enough to hear one bondman insist that "the business only required a beginning, and that there never was, or would be, a better time than the present." Finally taking note of their observer, the slaves lowered their voices, but not so low that he did not catch one final word: "liberty!" [14]

Of all the Virginia towns, next to Richmond the city of Petersburg was the most haunted by the terrifying specter of revolution. Just south of Richmond on the falls line of the Appomattox River, the Dinwiddie city had a black majority, and when Richmond mayor James McClurg informed the town fathers that there was "an union of plan with the negroes about Petersburg," few of them were surprised. By September 9, six African Americans had been seized "on suspicion of being concerned and put in

Jail." Lacking instructions from the governor, the city "hardly [knew] what to do with them." The view expressed by Joseph Jones, a former state senator from Dinwiddie, was typical. "My opinion is that where there is any reason to believe that any person is concerned," he brayed at Monroe, "they ought immediately to be hanged, quartered and hung up on trees on every road as a terror for the rest. Slay them all." [15]

For less bloodthirsty and more legalistically minded Virginians, those arrested presented a special problem. Petersburg had a higher percentage of free blacks than any other city in the state, and while Sam Byrd had carried the news south, most of those contacted by his two uncles were like themselves—free men. Under the law, slaves could not testify against free men of any race. Former mayor William Prentis, acting upon information supplied by Monroe, "caused the arrest of Reuben and Jesse Byrd." Also taken were Jacob Blandum and John Pidgeon. Of all the captives, only Peter, a slave of the recently deceased William Claiborne, was human property, and it was possible that Peter had been contacted not by the Byrds but by a slave of the extensive Lipscombe family of Hanover, who had married into the Claiborne clan and furnished "the business" with several soldiers. Obtaining testimony against any of the accused would prove nearly impossible. [16]

As the weeks dragged by, the Dinwiddie magistrates pondered their dilemma. Prentis wrote again and again to Monroe, asking the governor to supply them with information explaining "what grounds there are for believing [the Byrds] to be connected in the plot." In fact, just such information had emerged in the Henrico trials, but under state law all of the evidence, supplied as it was by slaves, was inadmissible in the cases of the four free blacks. In a sense, the authorities were trapped by the rules of their own game. Although the laws existed to hold a system of human bondage in place, white Virginians told themselves they were fair men. Once the laws were in place, they could not easily be ignored. To do so would be an admission that their world was built not on law but on brute force. Bend the laws they could; break them they could not. And so in the end Reuben and Jesse Byrd, together with Blandum and Pidgeon, were released without trial. The number of those executed would have been much higher had it not been for the protection of the law, which, ironically, was a fraud from the point of view of those on the bottom. [17]

When deliberations finally began in the simple frame courthouse on Bollingbrook Street, a muddy, unpaved boulevard, Peter stood alone. Defended by Richard Claiborne, a kinsman of his deceased master, Peter was charged with conspiracy and rebellion and "not having the fear of God before his eyes." Several men—slaves all—testified against Peter. The justices found him guilty, valued him at a low $300, and sentenced him to swing on the morning of Friday, October 24.[18]

Nor were the Petersburg authorities the only ones to confront the peculiarities in working with a body of laws that had been designed to control an entire class of unfree people in a time of rising manumissions. To the north, in Hanover Town, Sam Byrd, Sr., "a free mulatto," was picked up and sent to Richmond for trial. After a few days in jail, the elder Byrd was released on Monroe's orders, "it being decided that people of his colour, in slavery, could not give testimony against him." Bob Cowley, the free black keeper of the keys, was not arrested, although he was sharply questioned by the Henrico justices. Finally they were satisfied that he was not an active conspirator. Cowley, unlike the elder Byrd, had been more circumspect in regard to the plot. But even if he had been more deeply involved the court could not touch him, and the frustrated magistrates knew it.[19]

In Henrico, the heart of the conspiracy, October began, and with it a second month of trials. The county court of oyer and terminer, now led by Miles Selden, prepared to hear the case of Dabney Williamson's Lewis. James Rind was back in his by-now comfortable role of lethargic defense counsel. Returning also as the state's chief witness was young Ben Woolfolk. Lewis pleaded not guilty, but Woolfolk was able to place the prisoner at too many of the meetings with Gabriel, and the justices unanimously found him guilty. Valued at an impressive $366, Lewis was sentenced to die on Friday, October 17.[20]

With most of the trials behind them, the justices finally began to slacken their pace, which is not to say that the accused slaves received any more cautious brand of justice. It meant only the end of the race to try a large number of slaves each day. Court clerk Adam Craig was happy about that. He needed time to sort out the next two cases. Brought before the bar were two slaves named Billy, one of them the property of Nathaniel Lipscombe, the other the servant of Lipscombe's deceased brother Ambrose, a Hanover resident. Both were found guilty and sentenced to swing, but Selden suggested that "for reasons appearing to the Court they recommend [them] to the Executive as a proper Object for mercy." The last man to be tried that day, Allan Williamson's Peter, was also found guilty but was recommended for pardon. In addition, Selden hinted that they had no objection to sparing Lewis. All four returned to the jail to join the growing number of convicted but pardoned slaves until Monroe could decide just what to do with them.[21]

Clearly the Henrico magistrates, unlike their Caroline and Dinwiddie counterparts, had finally grasped the message of Jefferson; surely Monroe was not slow in making the popular vice president's will clear to the court.

Perhaps the justices too had grown weary of the bloodshed, or perhaps the slumbering consciences of these old revolutionaries were awakened by the political nature of much of the testimony. Too many of the accused, reported observer John Randolph, displayed a proud "sense of their [natural] rights, [and] a contempt of danger." One insurgent, speaking at his trial, made the political and revolutionary nature of the conspiracy all too evident. "I have nothing more to offer than what General Washington would have had to offer, had he been taken by the British and put to trial," he patiently explained. "I have adventured my life in endeavouring to obtain the liberty of my countrymen, and am a willing sacrifice in their cause."[22]

Declarations of that sort were merely disquieting. The magistrates could live with their own hypocrisy. Rather more troubling, at least for the Republicans sitting on the bench, were the odd hints of French involvement that kept surfacing in the testimony. As early as September 11, the first day of the hearings, Prosser's Ben had testified that Jack Ditcher had spoken to him of "two white Frenchmen" who were involved in the plot. Later that same day, during the trial of Will, Ben had again claimed that no French nationals "were to be touched" on the night of the rising. During his confession, Solomon had confirmed these statements by mentioning a mysterious "man from Caroline" who was to help lead the men the first night. These statements were easily dismissed, at least in part because of Ben Woolfolk's naive insistence that "the french [had] landed at South Key, which they hoped would assist them." During the Age of Revolution desperate insurgents around the Atlantic world often hoped that France would somehow sail to their aid, and Woolfolk's assertion that the "french would join them" was easily dismissed as a foolish dream. But in ignoring this testimony the magistrates failed to note that the young mulatto had been recruited by Gabriel to serve as contact with Caroline County; he lacked the access to the inner sanctum and its secrets that Solomon enjoyed.[23]

Evidence of a very different and unwelcome kind, however, surfaced with the capture of John Scott, one of the leaders of the Petersburg wing. Alexander McCrea had been "privately informed" that his servant might try to escape by boarding the Norfolk stage and so "attended at the stage office to seize him." When Scott appeared and demanded a ticket as a freeman, McCrea and several others grabbed him from behind. Scott fell to his knees begging for mercy, but when McCrea released his grip the slave suddenly "darted between his master's legs" and fled out the door. With a pack of bellowing whites on his heels, Scott raced across a short bridge. Finding his way blocked by the approaching stage, he flung himself over the railing, only to be stunned by the smooth rocks just below the shallow water of the Appomattox. Scott was just coming to his senses as white hands roughly dragged him to his feet. Found in his pocket were ten dollars, Beddenhurst's name, and his Philadelphia address. The paper appeared to "have been written but a little time before."[24]

Scott's evidence, with its enormous implications, was a very real threat to the Republican ascendancy. Already perceived as soft on France, Monroe's party was at that moment facing charges that Jefferson, if elected, would call upon France to "invade the country" to aid in a planned civil war. Evidence that two Frenchmen, even acting strictly on their own, were involved in another kind of civil war could devastate the Republicans in their southern political base. Woolfolk's peculiar comments had been shunted aside. The Beddenhurst letter was not so easily ignored. But the governor was in luck. Selden and Storrs, the examining magistrates on the special board of inquiry, took the slaves' depositions before their perfunctory appearance in the court of oyer and terminer (where Selden sat as well). From their judicial posts the magistrates could contain most, if not all, of the damaging information. The two magistrates were not only good and true Republicans, but Storrs and Selden's brother, Joseph, were members of the six-man party committee that named the state electoral ticket. Monroe knew that the implications for the Republican party of French involvement in the plot would be minimized by these faithful party members. Unhappily, however, a Richmond slaveholder, displeased with the way the plot was initially hushed up for fear of alarm, was an early spectator at the trials. As a proslavery ideologue, he was determined "that the origins of this great evil should be known." And he had caught wind of the Beddenhurst letter.[25]

Evidence pointing to the involvement of two Frenchmen continued to grow in proportion to the number of leaders captured. At the time of John Scott's capture, Gabriel was still at large, but Solomon and Sam Byrd, Jr., had long since been taken. It had been important for these men to keep lists of the names of those they had recruited. Trial testimony indicated that Solomon, Byrd, Gabriel, John Scott, and Matt Scott all kept lists, as did Jacob, the black skipper who had yet to be arrested. There is no evidence that Ditcher, who probably could not read, kept a list, although he knew the names of the two Frenchmen. One white court observer told the Fredericksburg *Virginia Herald* that correspondence from Philadelphia, Norfolk, and Petersburg had all been captured.[26]

All of these documents were rushed not to the Henrico County Court but to the governor, from whose office most of them simply disappeared. For those who wanted access to the information contained in the documents, Monroe's behavior was perplexing. Mayor James McClurg, a staunch Federalist who had acted as foreman of the grand jury that indicted Callender for sedition, increasingly found himself left in the dark about the ongoing investigation. William Prentis, the former mayor of Petersburg, which was also a Federalist stronghold, heard that Monroe had "a list of a number" of conspirators and wrote to him in an unsuccessful attempt to obtain a copy. When no answer was forthcoming, Prentis tried again, telling Monroe he had it on good authority that further documents had fallen into the governor's hands. "I presume," he hotly observed, "an enquiry into them would avail nothing, otherwise you would have sent them here."[27]

Despite efforts by Monroe and the two magistrates to suppress evidence, information concerning the two Frenchmen began to leak out. William Young's Gilbert actually named Charles Quersey, whom he had known in Caroline, on September 23, and the pesky Prentis accused the two magistrates of interrupting the confession of a condemned slave. About the same time, John Mayo, who was not involved in the legal proceedings, took it upon himself to ask several slaves just before they were hanged about the rumors of the Frenchmen. Warned not to "die with a lie in his mouth," Judith Owen's Michael admitted that "there was a white man more concerned [than] them." When asked for a name, Michael "collected himself" and went to his death silently.[28]

Late in the month of September, Monroe's mind was rendered more uneasy yet by the news that Gabriel had been arrested in Norfolk. Having boarded the schooner *Mary* on Sunday, September 14, Gabriel asked to see the captain, Richardson Taylor, who was asleep in his cabin. The blacksmith insisted that he was a freeman bound for Norfolk. But when asked for his freedom papers, Gabriel "did not shew any, saying he had left them" in town. One of the sailors on board was Billy, a slave for hire owned by Miles King, late of Elizabeth City and now a resident of Norfolk. Billy had hired out to Richmond in the past, for he recognized Gabriel and told Taylor that this was the man "the reward was offered for." Hoping to bluff his way out of the trap, Gabriel admitted that he was called by that nickname but insisted that his real name was Daniel. Isham, a former slave of Taylor's, sided with Billy. Taylor listened intently to his crewmen and then quietly ordered them to set sail for the lower Chesapeake.[29]

Even if Taylor doubted that his crewmen were correct, he was taking an enormous chance in spiriting an unfamiliar black man downriver. A former overseer and a longtime resident of Norfolk, Taylor well knew the rules governing the movement of African Americans. The law not only required all blacks to carry free papers, it also called upon ship captains to "produce" before a local magistrate, at the risk of a $500 fine, "any negro or mulatto" he intended to carry out of the state. Taylor had fulfilled none of these requirements. Logic told him that the huge man who had arrived on his ship in so peculiar a fashion was the leader of the vast conspiracy, yet he did nothing. Certainly he had ample opportunity to take action. Billy and Isham appeared more than willing to seize Gabriel, and as the *Mary* pushed downriver it passed a number of vessels and docks "where [Taylor] could have obtained force to have secured him."[30]

Taylor's behavior thus invites speculation. Although a former overseer, the skipper evidently changed his ways along with his career. Atlantic watermen, not unlike urban artisans, had a rough egalitarian streak that placed greater emphasis on ability than on color. Africans and black Southerners composed a significant part of ships' crews during the late eighteenth century. Naturally the members of this interracial nautical proletariat were early and vocal advocates of abolition. Perhaps the tars he encountered while sailing the Chesapeake had provided him with a new perspective on black liberty. As Billy's presence on board indicates, Taylor still hired bondmen, but he had freed his only slave, Isham, some time before, while he was in Williamsburg. Taylor, moreover, was a recent convert to Methodism. Perhaps, too, his contact with rugged new light preachers or a reading of John Wesley's *Thoughts upon Slavery* led him to understand that a world based upon racial distinctions was an ungodly world. Either way, there can be little doubt that Taylor knew precisely who Gabriel was, understood the magnitude of the risk he was taking, and yet willfully tried to spirit the slave rebel to freedom in Norfolk or beyond.[31]

As the *Mary* approached Norfolk on the morning of Tuesday, September 23, Taylor and his strange cargo began to notice that the seaport was still a city in fear. Just below town a small skiff pulled up beside the schooner, and a Captain Inchman scurried aboard. Inchman demanded to know where Taylor had been and if he had seen anything unusual. The captain calmly shook his head, and Inchman moved on to the next craft. Around noon Taylor and his crew put in at the wharves along Water Street. The docks teamed with men—slave and free, black and white—sweating in orderly chaos. Most were too busy to take note of the unexceptional schooner, but if they had they would have seen only Taylor and his two crewmen. Their mysterious passenger was nowhere in evidence.[32]

Taylor made one miscalculation. As the skipper of his own vessel, the former overseer had done well for himself. Three hundred dollars, the reward offered for Gabriel's capture, meant little enough to him, especially when weighed on a scale beside his conscience. But for a slave like Billy, the sum was not only more money than he would probably ever see in his life, it was nearly enough to purchase his freedom from Miles King. Surely

Billy had thought much about this over the last week, and when Taylor sent him into the city around two o'clock, he saw his chance. As he walked toward Water Street, Billy saw John Morse, a black "apprentice boy" of his acquaintance and told Morse that the rebel leader was on board his ship. Perhaps Billy promised his friend a share of the reward, for Morse "immediately" ran for the homes of constables Obediah Gunn and Robert Wilson. Grabbing their muskets, the two men raced for the docks. At the same moment Billy told Sheriff John Moss that Gabriel was on board. Moss "gave other[s the] Information for fear he Should Make his escape" and also dashed for the ship.[33]

Moss and the two constables reached the *Mary* almost simultaneously and rushed up the plank. "Without delay the Villon was arrested." Trapped below deck, Gabriel "manifested the greatest of firmness and composure, shewing not the least disposition to equivocate or screan himself from justice." For more than a year, since his attack on Absalom Johnson, Gabriel had lived with the possibility of death; he would not beg now. The authorities then turned their wrath on the captain, who stammered that he was just then "going to Secure" his passenger. Gunn and Wilson saw no evidence of that and arrested Taylor "on suspicion of intentionally aiding and assisting in [Gabriel's] escape." Until matters could be settled, Billy and Isham were also taken into custody. Billy, however, had little to fear. The governor, Moss quietly assured him, "knows best how to Compensate [a] Negro Man for his good Conduct." Perhaps nothing could better illustrate the strange ambiguity of the times than the fact that Gabriel was spirited away by a white man and betrayed for silver by a slave.[34]

While Gabriel was placed "in irons," Taylor was taken before Mayor Thomas Newton. Again the captain pleaded that he had just begun to write a letter to the authorities "to know what he was to do with [Gabriel]." The mayor no more believed this explanation than had Moss. "I confess I think Mr. Taylor knew much better than he acted," Newton confided to Monroe, "what to do in such a case." Still, the mayor had no desire to imprison a white man for aiding a black rebel; such interracial class alliances were safer left ignored. He would leave the decision to others. Taylor was thus "bound over" to appear before Richmond mayor James McClurg "to answer for his conduct." In the meantime, the captain was released on his own "recognizance."[35]

Billy's fate was altogether different, if perhaps more fitting. Shortly thereafter James Monroe and his council unanimously consented to grant Billy his reward: fifty dollars. Upon consideration, the governor discovered that Billy did not qualify for the entire reward. Monroe had made a promise of three hundred dollars, or three hundred dollars and a full pardon, if the man who turned Gabriel in was one of his followers. Although a slave, Billy was not a conspirator, and so did not require a pardon. But as a slave uninvolved in the business, Billy could hardly expect to receive the full amount. Virginia law and society did not recognize all men as equal but drew distinctions based upon birth, property, and race. It made little sense—indeed, it smacked of anarchy—to ignore such carefully crafted distinctions when dispensing rewards. Billy would receive his prize, but it would be too little with which to buy his freedom. Ironically, Billy would have fared better had he been a conspirator.[36]

On September 24, Gabriel, still in chains, appeared before Thomas Newton. Rumors already held that when captured, Gabriel had "letters in his possession from white people." Newton, a Federalist, wanted to know about the names on those missives. The unrepentant slave replied that he would reveal nothing. Perhaps believing he would receive a more sympathetic hearing from the man the Federalist press painted as a Francophile and a radical, Gabriel insisted he would "confess to no one else" but Monroe. "Gabriel says he will give [only] your Excellency a full information," Newton sighed to the governor.[37]

Later that afternoon a small posse hurried Gabriel through the streets and placed him aboard a ship bound for Richmond. "[C]harged with the delivery of Gabriel" were constables Gunn and Wilson, who kept the huge slave below deck in chains and under heavy guard. "Should the wind continue as it was yesterday," laughed the editor of the *Norfolk Herald*, "he will have a short, if not pleasant passage."[38]

Even as the tiny ship sailed north, the governor was planning for the complete isolation of the prisoner. Like all of the conspirators, Gabriel was to be placed in solitary confinement, but Monroe gave additional orders that the guard should hold "no conversation with him on any subject or permit any other person to do so." The penitentiary keeper also was instructed to dismiss the "extra guard" and to allow no whites to speak to the prisoner "without order from the Governor."[39]

The governor, however, was unable to keep Gabriel from speaking to his captors on his voyage from Norfolk. While the black Jacobin admitted that "he was to have had the chief command," he insisted that there were four other persons as deeply "concerned in the business" as he was. Gabriel said he could "mention several in Norfolk—but being conscious of meeting with the fate of those before him he should make no confession." Of the slaves, only Jack Ditcher and Sam Byrd, Jr., were as deeply involved. The other two—those in Norfolk—had to be Quersey and Beddenhurst.[40]

By the morning of Saturday, September 27, the ship carrying Gabriel passed the point where he had boarded the *Mary* nearly two weeks before. For the prisoner, the last part of the journey was all too familiar. In midafternoon the ship landed. Word flew along the docks that Gabriel was on board, and "an immense" crowd quickly formed. Pleased with the attention, Gunn and Wilson eagerly paraded their prize across town toward Capitol Square. Hearing the mob even before they rounded the corner, Monroe stepped out on the porch—and stood stunned. A "great cloud of blacks as well as whites gathered round" Gabriel, more than enough to free him from the grip of the constables. The governor fought to clear his head. The health of his infant son, always delicate, had taken a turn for the worse a few nights before, and Monroe had not slept for days. The doctors now held out no hope for the child, who would die the following evening. Monroe snapped at William Giles, who stood nearby, telling him "to form a guard of 15 or 20 of the Citizens he could collect on the ground, [and] to take [Gabriel] under its care to the Penitentiary." Shouting above the din for assistance, Giles succeeded in wrenching Gabriel from the grip of the startled Norfolk men before the crowd could react.[41]

For more than a week Gabriel sat isolated in the penitentiary. It does not appear that Monroe, distraught over the death of his son and concerned with the broken health of his wife, paid the prisoner a visit or had Gabriel brought before him. Finally, on October 6, the Henrico trials began again. Outside the courthouse the streets were crowded with men and boys who wished to see the trial of the slave general. Whites, jostling for position, came to jeer; slaves, free blacks, and the odd white mechanic stood quietly as they awaited word on the man who had tried to make liberty and equality more than mere slogans. To the dismay of all, other men preceded Gabriel to the bar. Randolph, the property of Nancy Leftwich of King William County who hired out to Paul Thilman, was the first to be tried. Randolph was found guilty, but like Thilman's Dick, who followed him "to the bar," obtained a recommendation for mercy. Guards shoved Thilman's Bristol forward, but the evidence against him amounted to little, and he was "acquitted and discharged out of Custody." Thomas Jordan Martin, a freeman, was the fourth man to be tried. As was by now customary, Prosser's Ben and Ben Woolfolk stood ready to testify. This time, however, the usually taciturn Rind jumped to his feet. Martin's counsel observed that Martin, like the elder Sam Byrd, was not a slave, and "under the existing Laws of the Land" neither Woolfolk nor Ben could testify against him. The justices grudgingly agreed and released Martin, but not before demanding a bond of one hundred dollars to ensure "his good behavior." Martin's mother, Macky, "a free mulatto," promptly posted the bond.[42]

Finally, just as the sun was slipping away, "the property of Thomas

Henry Prosser" was brought forward and "charged with Conspiracy and insurrection." Standing before the bench, Gabriel listened impassively as the charges were read but then turned to glare at Woolfolk and Ben; Rind entered the requisite plea of not guilty. Ben was the first to speak. His testimony left no doubt that the blacksmith had instigated the vast conspiracy, but many of his words shook the magistrates more than they did the accused. Gabriel did not expect protracted and bloody fighting, Ben insisted. It was true that Thomas Prosser was to die, but "if the white people agreed to their freedom they would then hoist a white flag, and [Gabriel] would dine and drink with the merchants of the city." With the justices sputtering beside him, Ben elaborated. Gabriel "expected the poor White people would also join him, and that two Frenchmen had actually joined." No doubt to the relief of Miles Selden, Ben sadly allowed that the leadership had stubbornly kept the names of the Frenchmen from him.[43]

From the uneasy perspective of the Republicans on the bench, the testimony of Ben Woolfolk, the next man to speak against Gabriel, was not much easier to hear. Woolfolk discussed the conspiracy in detail, making clear that at every meeting it had been Gabriel who took the lead in organizing "the business." But like Ben, the young mulatto eventually—and innocently—turned to the political dimensions of the plot. No "Quakers, Methodists, [or] French people" were to be harmed, as they were the friends of freedom. To the audible sound of uncomfortable revolutionaries squirming in their seats, Woolfolk explained how Gabriel was to carry their flag on the night of the rising. It was to bear the oddly familiar slogan of "death or Liberty."[44]

Had it been the intention of the state's two chief witnesses to point out to the magistrates the hypocrisy of their actions, they could not have done a more effective job. But they had not intended to; they simply told the truth. It was the truth that laid bare the falsity of the Jeffersonian cry of liberty and equality. One way to put a halt to the agony was to pass sentence. "It is the unanimous Opinion of the Court," snarled a red-faced Miles Selden, "that the said Negro man Slave Gabriel is Guilty of the Crime with which he stands accused and for the same that he be hanged by the neck untill he be dead and that execution of this sentence be done and performed on him tomorrow at the usual time and place of execution." The court valued the condemned man at $500, an inadvertent admission of his intellect and ability. Suddenly Gabriel's stony demeanor broke. The justices observed "that much anxiety and trouble seemed to hang on his countenance" and thought perhaps he wished to confess. He "would make no discoveries," he snapped, but he had one request. He wished to have his sentence delayed for three days, until October 10, so that he might hang on the same morning as George Smith and Sam Byrd and his brothers. Agreed, growled Selden, rather sourly.[45]

Two days later Jack Ditcher turned himself in. The news that Gabriel had been taken and sentenced to die seemed to crush the resolve of the man who once had challenged Gabriel for leadership. The giant slave, believed by some to be the strongest man in the state, now felt very small. Ditcher had been hiding in the home of Peter Smith, a free black. Smith perhaps wanted to rid himself of his dangerous guest and, seeing his opening, advised Ditcher to give it up and beg for mercy. "On Wednesday evening," October 8, Ditcher simply walked into town and "surrendered himself" to Gervas Storrs. Like the luckless Billy, Peter Smith petitioned the state for the promised reward of three hundred dollars. But the governor's council saw fit to pay him only fifty dollars "for his services in the surrender of Jack Ditcher."[46]

The last leader of the conspiracy who remained at large was Jacob, the black skipper who worked the river between Petersburg and Norfolk. But in early October, he too was taken, hunted down by a floating posse of five ships and captured near Norfolk. Jacob was found to have in his possession letters dating as far back as "June 1800." On hearing this promising news, the determined William Prentis tried one final time to pry information out of the governor. "As the names of a number [of rebels] who I am informed are on the list, are now living in this town," wrote the former Petersburg mayor, "probably the writing might be traced." Prentis was little surprised when no reply was forthcoming.[47]

As Jacob was being taken back upriver, the morning of October 10 arrived—and far too soon it did, for the seven men waiting in the Henrico jail. In an attempt to minimize the event, the court decided that the rebels would not die together. As the sun broke over the town, two men—Young's William and Sam Graham—were packed into a wagon that headed not for the usual place of execution but for the crossroads near Four Mile Creek instead. Goode's Michael had already swung on October 3, and so the death toll, as carefully recorded by Benjamin Sheppard, now totaled an even twenty.[48]

At almost the same time a second cart, driven by Samuel Mosby, rolled away from the jail toward the clearing near Prosser's Tavern. In the wagon stood Prosser's Tom, George Smith, Sam Byrd, Jr., and Gilbert, a minor conspirator who had been foolish enough to blurt out Quersey's name during his confession. The tavern was close enough to Brookfield for the families of the condemned to witness the execution of their husbands, sons, and fathers. Four ropes were thrown over a high branch. Suddenly Mosby roared a command to his horses, and the wagon jerked forward.[49]

The last of the seven to go was the man who had planned it all. Standing alone in the back of the tumbril with his hands bound behind him, Gabriel was driven to the town gallows near Fifteenth and Broad. A considerable crowd had gathered, but probably his wife was not among them. Because he was hanged in Richmond, it was unlikely that Gabriel was able to say good-bye to Nanny, and because he was hanged alone, he was denied the small comfort of being executed by the side of one of his fellows. A myth later arose that as he mounted the steps Gabriel "lost all firmness [and showed] nothing but abject fear," a legend for which there is absolutely no supporting documentation. Given the way he lived his life, there is every reason to believe that he died with quiet composure before a horde of vengeful whites. The trapdoor fell open, and Gabriel, at long last, found sweet freedom. "I do hereby certify," scribbled a pleased Mosby Sheppard, "that the within mentioned Slave [Gabriel] was executed agreeably to the within Centance of the Court."[50]

Virginia authorities hoped that would be the end of it. Many slaves believed otherwise. Black Baptists retained enough of the West African worldview to believe that a restless soul who died unnaturally would not pass into the spirit world but instead would find a home in the body of a newborn child. Eight days before, on the Southampton County plantation of Benjamin Turner, a boy had been born to slave parents. The couple called their son Nathaniel, an Old Testament name meaning "gift of God." The Henrico magistrates had only hanged the man. They could not kill the dream.[51]

But hang the man they had, and with the death of Gabriel the Henrico deliberations entered a final phase. So far, twenty-five slaves had died at the hands of the courts, and because the law demanded that their owners be compensated in full, the death toll amounted to a staggering $8,899.91. Still more slaves awaited trial, among them Jack Ditcher, whose size alone would win his child-owner a healthy sum. Militia duties totaled another $5,431. Prison warden Martin Mims was busy preparing yet another bill to present to the governor for "Sundry Persons [who still stood] Guard at the Jail & Penitentiary." For a state with an annual budget of only $377,703, the most effective brake on further hangings was the financial impact of the killing. The governor had to find an alternative.[52]

Monroe had long since lost all stomach for more executions. His refusal to visit Gabriel in jail surely had as much to do with his disinclination to face a defeated revolutionary as it did with the death of his son. He never doubted that Gabriel would have to die. The public demanded it, and besides, the artisan's tales of French radicals posed a political threat to Monroe's party. But just before Gabriel was hanged the governor suggested to his council that "those less criminal in comparison" with the leaders "sho[ul]d be reprieved [so] that their case[s] might be submitted [to] legislative consideration." What to do with those who were pardoned presented a problem. But Jefferson, ever interested in the idea of colonizing blacks outside of the country so long as he did not have to take the lead—"I should be unwilling to be quoted in the case"—provided a suggestion. "Surely the legislature would pass a law for their exportation, the proper measure on this & all similar occasions?"[53]

For the troubled governor, the suggestion was manna from heaven. Always concerned with his reputation as a virtuous Republican, Monroe was uneasy about hanging men who compared themselves to George Washington. In later years he virtually refused to discuss the event; when pressed, he finally told one young correspondent that "several of the conspirators were hanged." The term "several" was vague enough, but it hardly indicated the twenty-seven men who would eventually pay for their desire to be free with their lives. The governor had no vote in his own council—a flaw in the state constitution that all strong governors despised— but at length he persuaded the body to suspend further executions until "the opinion of the Legislature can be had on the subject." At that point, the Assembly could discuss Jefferson's recommendation. Given the "immense numbers who are implicated in the plot," one editor suggested, failure to stop the hangings not only would bankrupt the state but also would "produce the annihilation" of Virginia's black working class.[54]

Best of all, if slave rebels were transported outside the country, Virginia would suffer less of an economic loss. Owners of bondmen removed from their service would still receive compensation, but if condemned blacks were transported rather than hanged they could be sold to a trader. The proceeds could be placed back in the state treasury, and if Monroe bargained wisely, the state might break even. For those rebels still awaiting trial, as well as for those condemned but not yet hanged, the rumors that no more would swing arrived as but a mixed blessing. They would live, but they would remain slaves. Moreover, they were sure to be sold far away from friends and family, perhaps even to the steamy lands of Spanish Louisiana, where they were sure to die young. Jack Gabriel, John Fells, and Ben, all belonging to Charles Carter, were "Reprieved for Transportation," as were Lewis and King. Ned, believed to have a "very weak mind" and to have been drunk when he was enlisted, was pardoned outright and returned to William Young. Elisha Price's James also received a pardon.[55]

Following the decision to transport those still to be tried—the question of where they were to go awaited the December meeting of the legislature—the court proceedings, now entering their third month, became a tired charade that held little interest even for those whites involved. Few Richmond dwellers wandered down to the courthouse to try to gain admittance. For the accused, it was another matter altogether. Their hearings meant the difference between remaining in Virginia or dying in a faraway place. On November 3, three more slaves were dragged before the bar: Absalom, Emanuel, and Watt. Instead of hearing the cases, the bored magistrates, led by Daniel Hylton and Joseph Selden, adjourned until the following morning. At that juncture Absalom and Emanuel, owned by William Price and Drewry Wood, were found not guilty. Watt, an aged slave of Thomas Prosser's, was not as lucky. Ben testified that Watt was a willing if infirm participant in the plot. The court quickly found him guilty, placed his value at a paltry $150, and sentenced him to die in early January. But in keeping with the council's decision, the court recommended that he instead be transported out of the state.[56]

Even Jack Ditcher was allowed to live, although it would most likely be in the harsher plantation world of the Gulf South. Just days before, on Wednesday, October 29, "Slave Jack," owned by "William Bowler's Estate late of the County of Caroline deceased," was "set to the Bar [and] Charged with Conspiracy and insurrection." Three slaves, including Ben and Sam, one of the few Prosser slaves uninvolved in the conspiracy, spoke against the broken lieutenant. Ben testified that Jack was a frequent guest at their forge, where he "mentioned [the plot] at repeated times." Ben also placed Jack at Brookfield on the night of the rising and the morning after the storm. The jurists found Ditcher guilty, valued him at $400 (an impressive figure for an illiterate and unskilled bondman), and sentenced him to hang in mid-November. He too, however, was recommended for transportation.[57]

It would be only Peter, the Petersburg slave owned by the estate of William Claiborne, who would die after the decision was made to hang no more slaves. Although close enough by stage or boat, Petersburg was far removed from the advice of Jefferson and the deliberations of the governor's council. Peter swung on Friday, October 24. He was the last hanged. But he was not the last to die. That would be Jacob, the black skipper. According to William Wilson, his master, Jacob "killed himself" while being brought back upriver for trial. It was certainly possible that Jacob, a man so mobile that most contemporaries thought him a freeman, could not imagine a life of chopping sugarcane. Or perhaps he had not caught wind of the rumors about transportation and thought he was already a dead man and so decided to deny the court its victory. It was equally possible that his captors went too far in their questioning and that Jacob, like Stephen Biko, had more than a little help in his suicide. Either way, the death toll now stood at twenty-seven.[58]

Only the persistent political rumors surrounding the conspiracy refused to die. Given the partisan leanings of the Virginia townsfolk, it was not unexpected that terrified Federalists did their best to turn the conspiracy into a partisan issue. What was surprising was that the subsequent debate remained largely ideological. Conservatives from Fredericksburg and Norfolk insisted, quite correctly, that the Republican cry of "Liberty and Equality has been infused into the minds of the negroes." The "amis des noirs [the friends of the blacks] in Pennsylvania," one Federalist bleated at Monroe, "are exciting our negroes to cut our throats."[59]

The self-evident hypocrisy of the Virginia Republicans also attracted the full fire of the embattled New England Federalists, who hoped the threat of revolt would bring the southerners to their senses. "If any thing will correct & bring to repentance old hardened sinners in Jacobinism," prayed the Boston *Gazette*, "it must be an *insurrection of their slaves*." With this, Robert Troup agreed. "In Virginia they are beginning to feel the happy effects of liberty and equality," he laughed to Rufus King. More creative Federalists even charged that the revolt had been planned "by the noted Callender in prison."[60]

To this the busy Callender returned fire. Writing from his Richmond cell, Callender insisted that only one "white man" in the nation was evil enough to conceive of "such a project" and that man was "Alexander Hamilton." Yet the truly dangerous charges, at least to James Monroe, were not the theoretical ones but the persistent rumors of French involvement. The conspiracy was "quite a domestic one," Monroe assured John Drayton, the lieutenant governor of a terrified South Carolina. "If white men were engaged in it, it is a fact of which we have no proof."[61]

In fact, Monroe had plenty of proof, as he knew all too well. Late in September some of the stories about Quersey and Beddenhurst finally found their way into print. But for Federalist election hopes it was too little and too late. Picking up the Virginia rumors, a Boston newspaper, *Russell's Gazette*, reported that "*two Frenchmen*" were involved in the conspiracy and that "a correspondence was kept up between those villains and some others in Philadelphia, Norfolk, [and] Petersburgh." Even this small leak gave pause to Virginia Republicans. "Our federalists have endeavored to make an electioneering engine of it," complained John Randolph.[62]

The issue assumed national proportions when William Duane, the editor of the Philadelphia *Aurora*, took up his quill and fired back. Duane was then free on bail while he awaited trial for seditious libel, and so few understood better than he the importance of killing the rumors before the election—rumors that he did not believe in any case. "The insurrection we are told, was organized upon the French plan," he editorialized. "It appears to us to be organized upon the British plan," for only Albion could be so perfidious. Two days later he returned to the topic. The story of the two Frenchmen was a Federalist "good joke," he laughed, a jest not meant to be taken seriously.[63]

Duane need not have worried. In a very real sense Monroe was right: there was no longer any proof. All that remained was the nearly unanimous testimony of the conspirators that two Frenchmen were involved. Any corroborating and specific testimony or hard evidence—such as the lists kept by the leaders or the correspondence captured with Scott, Gabriel, and Jacob—all of which was sent directly to Monroe, never was turned over to the court. It was not included in the pertinent records that he relinquished upon leaving office. And with good reason. Evidence that two Frenchmen, even acting strictly on their own, were involved with black revolutionaries would have devastated the Republicans in their southern political base.

Gabriel had hoped to use the election to the advantage of not just himself and his followers but also, as he said, "for his Country." His conception of the "revolution of 1800" went far beyond even the dreams of white artisans. Gabriel's revolution was one of property relations, beginning with the death of slavery and the substitution of a system of free and fair-wage labor. Indeed, his vision of political change was to the Republican agrarian leadership the world turned upside down. If Gabriel had intended to treat hostage Monroe with leniency, such magnanimity was not returned, especially from Republicans who were startled to discover that their slaves believed they had a common enemy in the merchants. And so in the end Joseph Selden congratulated himself on the victory of his party over "the Adamsites & British subjects," while Gabriel and Solomon and Martin and twenty-four of their followers went to their deaths.[64]

HALIFAX 1802

Great men make history,

but only such history as it is

possible for them to make.

C. L. R. JAMES

Recalled to Life

Gabriel was dead, as were Solomon and Martin. Jack Ditcher languished in a cold cell, while Monroe and the Governor's Council pondered his fate. Quersey was nowhere to be found; most likely he had gone underground or fled north to the corner house on Coats' Alley. But if Virginia authorities thought that would be the end of it, they were wrong. Even as Peter, the last slave to be executed in 1800, swung from the Dinwiddie County gallows, other slaves in and around Petersburg began to whisper that the dream of liberty and equality should not be given up. Chief among them was Sancho, a bondman of John Booker, who had urged his fellows to fight for their freedom beside Reuben and Jesse Byrd. Now he was willing to try again.[1]

Sancho had been only on the periphery of the 1800 plot, for one central reason: he was not an artisan but a ferryman. Like thousands of other bondmen, he worked along the extensive river system that bound Virginia and the Carolinas to the Atlantic market. Virtually all southern towns—indeed, virtually all large plantations that hugged the waterways—employed large numbers of slaves trained to perform maritime tasks. Ship carpenters, pilots, sailmakers, riggers, and caulkers, as well as simple sailors who doubled as dockworkers, could all be found toiling in shipyards and plantations along the Chesapeake. In a region built upon both human bondage and the export of staple crops, most of which were carried east by river, it was hardly unusual for slaves to be trained for a myriad of shipping occupations. In short, after the hangings of 1800, the plot, now taken over by a different kind of leader, acquired a new constituency: black watermen.[2]

Sancho's age is unknown, but he was at least as old as Gabriel, which means he came of age during the Revolution, a conflict that greatly increased the number of black watermen, bond and free alike. During the war the Chesapeake Bay states relied on black rivermen, who knew the rivers and inlets well, to pilot their navies. In the process, plantation workers who had long plied lighters—small boats used for moving people and goods short distances—found themselves promoted to a position of responsibility in the patriot military. Lord Dunmore, in response, used runaways for the same purpose. But since Britain held out the promise of liberty, Dunmore had more recruits. Upon arriving in Virginia, General Cornwallis discovered that his army of "above 7,000 men" included "thousands of poor blacks." On the day of his surrender, the general recorded that his force of five thousand seamen admitted of only eight hundred white "man of war sailors." The rest were black mariners who had sailed to his standard.[3]

With the return of peace, many of the runaways fled with the British, but more than a few remained behind and worked the waterways as free men. To replace those who fled abroad or remained uncaptured, plantation owners—or more commonly, those unlucky slaves who had not made it to British lines—trained yet another generation of watermen. That simple term, however, masked an occupation with a distinct hierarchy. Inhabiting the lowest rank were the common laborers, men who had little to recommend them but their good hearts and stout arms. These bondmen worked the docks, loading and unloading the ships; when all the cargo was aboard, they manned the vessels as well. At other times, their muscles were hired by the town or state to repair wharves and bridges. In 1802 the Virginia Assembly allowed the Potomac Company to "employ slaves for [the] purpose [of] rendering the said river navigable." As always, most, if not all, of the pay went to the slaves' masters, and the legislature was careful to add that "the slaves so employed shall not be entitled to freedom or any other advantage which they might derive from [their labor]."[4]

Above the unskilled laborers stood the trained rivermen. These were the slaves and free blacks who sailed the bateaux—light boats nearly sixty feet long and only four feet wide—and the flatboats—larger craft capable of transporting eighty hogsheads of tobacco—up and down southern waterways. Three men could manage a bateau; working a flat required at least double the number. Moving the hogsheads safely downriver was tricky work and required years of training. Returning the boats, laden with tools and other goods, back up the rivers demanded a strong back; rivermen often had to force their reluctant vessels along with oar and pole. The voyage was typically a long one. Slaves pushed into the heart of the state on the James and Appomattox rivers. Cargo from southwestern Virginia was brought down the Roanoke (Staunton) River into Albemarle Sound.[5]

At times, bond rivermen hired on as sailors with larger vessels, much as Miles King's Billy had signed on with Richardson Taylor. So many slaves and free blacks took jobs as sailors that by the turn of the century they had all but monopolized the occupation. "Besides those [ships] having entirely colored crews," complained one Virginia newspaper, "nearly all the larger vessels and some of the small ones, (schooners, &c.,) have colored cooks and stewards."[6]

On occasion, exceptionally able (and lucky) sailors found themselves captains of their own vessels. Most probably had been pilots before. A few freemen caught the eye of a wealthy patron, usually a merchant in need of goods or materials, who admired their industry and set them up in business. Such arrangements were unusual, but merchants with a keen eye for talent were occasionally willing to overlook race, especially when white skippers were a rare enough commodity. Somewhat less common were bond skippers. But since most large plantations trained several men to work the rivers, it was not surprising that a few slaves, like William Wilson's Jacob, found that they were sailing farther and farther downriver on behalf of their masters. In time, they became nearly autonomous and worked for themselves as much as for their masters.[7]

Many of the rivermen, regardless of their place in the labor hierarchy, were slaves for hire. As with their bond artisans, planters short of ready cash thought it wise to occasionally hire out the men who worked their docks and sailed their bateaux. Finding temporary masters was not difficult. White captains, merchant shippers, and shipyard employers all created a fluctuating maritime job market for hired labor. Masters pocketed most of their bondmen's earnings, but a part of the cash went into the slaves' purses. The most skilled watermen traditionally held the right to contract out their labor and in effect to choose their new masters. Certainly slave skippers earned an impressive wage, even if they were forced to turn over the lion's share to their owners.[8]

By necessity, black rivermen were absent from their masters' homes for long periods of time. Both those who hired their time and those who worked only for their owners found it convenient to live away from their masters. Bondmen sought their own resting places in the towns and hamlets that dotted the waterways. Unlike hiring out, living out was illegal, but as the economy demanded it, Virginia authorities fell into the habit of looking the other way. In effect, many rivermen lived much as free blacks did. Although they were still slaves in the eyes of the law, those who lived out remained unmolested so long as they surrendered most of their annual earnings to their distant owners. For all the economic benefits to the master class, such arrangements, as Gabriel and his chief lieutenants so aptly demonstrated, posed a threat to stability in a slave society. Patriarchal obligations were eroded by the hired slaves' frequent change of owners, and the depersonalized nature of the monetary wage introduced a dangerous foreign element into the organic relationship of master and slave.[9]

Worse still, from the perspective of control, labor along the rivers allowed for a rough form of upward mobility. Learning the ways of the bateaux or flat—and especially a larger craft—meant the acquisition of not only a skill but a profession. In theory, ambitious property that wished to better its lot was a form of property that had lost much of its usefulness to its owner. But a slave who rose to the rank of pilot was a man of position and was respected as such by his black and white crewmen alike, particularly since maritime culture was far more egalitarian than landed society was. Atlantic mariners denounced slavery in the saltiest of language, in part because their own lot often resembled human bondage. Impressed into service, paid an unjust wage, and disciplined by the cat-o'-nine-tails, white seamen (like Richardson Taylor) saw themselves as just another slave beholden to the authority of merchant capital. Using these white allies as a base of support, Chesapeake bondmen seized upon the opportunities that the rivers and port cities offered to better themselves financially and socially.[10]

Many of the watermen who achieved a high level of physical and intellectual autonomy sought to turn their quasi-free status into true freedom by slipping away during the long voyages downriver. Indeed, it says much about the crucial role that bond rivermen played in the economy of the border South that the master class made little effort to crack down on their relative freedom despite the fact that they escaped in alarming numbers. Highly skilled and wise in the ways of white society, they already knew how to peddle their arts in a free labor market. Billie, for example, escaped from Virginia in a stolen "schooner's boat." His disgruntled owner, John Tayloe, assumed that as a skilled "ship carpenter," Billie would try to find work with "some ship builders to the northward." With their knowledge of southern geography, many bond hires, who knew large numbers of friendly free blacks and white laboring men along the rivers, simply never returned from a lengthy excursion. One by one, and acting as individuals, they disappeared from sight. Between 1736 and 1801, watermen made up 14 percent of all skilled Virginia runaways. Typical was Bristol, who vanished with his daughter, Sally, in the late fall of 1800. According to the advertisement placed by his new owner, Bristol's "clothes are a sailor's, being accustomed to work on board of ships at City Point. [He] is a sensible artful fellow, and I believe was concerned in the late conspiracy, and procured a forged pass."[11]

More to the point, whites continued to allow these practices to exist despite their fear that the river craft might be vehicles of discussion, that is, subversion. If plantations fragmented the black labor force by isolating one group of slaves from another, the rivers and maritime centers did just the opposite. News and ideas passed as freely as goods in the cities, where literate black artisans dealt with their less-acculturated brethren on a daily basis. Rivermen, moving from town to town, served as a vital link between port towns like Richmond and Petersburg and Norfolk; black boatmen also played a crucial role in Virginia's underground economy. White fears about the transportation of knowledge and stolen goods grew so intense that in 1784 the General Assembly passed a law mandating that no more than one-third of the crew of any river craft could consist of slaves. The law was unenforceable and unenforced.[12]

Perhaps ruling-class trepidation was somewhat assuaged by the vague perception that skilled Virginia-born slaves, unlike their African ancestors who had been brought to the Chesapeake in the early eighteenth century, fought back or escaped as individuals. Billie and Bristol were typical in that they ran away on their own or, at best, with their families. But if that was the case, white Virginians failed to perceive a crucial point and demonstrated that they had learned little from the singular events of August 1800. Even as assimilation into the white world broke down the African tradition of collective resistance, the occupation of some slaves gave them a new basis for collective rebellion. Skilled bondmen for hire had their own unique list of demands: they wanted not only their freedom but social equality and the right to all of their earnings as well. As Gabriel made clear, Chesapeake rebels in the Age of Revolution did not challenge bourgeois property relations. They demanded the right to the property that their hard labor had acquired for others. Gabriel conspired to overturn the central class relationship in his society, but not that society itself; he sought not to flee from Virginia but to join it on equal terms. From the perspective of the slaves, their demands were simple justice; from that of their owners, who did not draw such a fine distinction, their demands constituted a truly radical proposition. And now highly mobile watermen had the means to set the conspiracy afoot once more.[13]

Ever since the hangings in 1800, more than a few of those who had survived the first conspiracy hoped to rekindle the business. But the memory of white brutality and the all-too-vivid images of young men kicking at the end of a rope kept the plan from evolving into action for nearly a year. Then in the fall of 1801 Sancho emerged as the newest progenitor of slave rebellion. His master, John Booker, lived in Amelia but owned a ferry several counties away, on the Roanoke River, which formed the border of Halifax and Charlotte counties. There, in the western portion of the two counties, the latter of which had a black majority, the "plot was most matured." Sancho ran the ferry for his owner, who wrongly believed him to be a docile and loyal slave. A year before, at a time when he evidently was living in Amelia, Sancho had joined the widespread Petersburg wing of the plot and "had tried to induce others to join the insurrection under Gabriel."[14]

The obstacles that lay ahead of Sancho were nearly insurmountable, and he knew it. But he had learned a few hard lessons from the earlier plan, and he clearly intended to avoid what he guessed to be the errors of Gabriel. Instead of trying to enlist as many men as possible, he worked to recruit a small but dedicated band of followers who could raise men quickly at the appropriate time. Such an approach would diminish the chances that a less-courageous slave—like Pharoah or Tom—might hear of the plot and pass the word to his master. "[W]e shall most certainly Suceed without difficulty if our Schem is not betrayed, beforehand," wrote one literate conspirator, "as there is but one in a Family to know of it untill the time is but Actually arrived."[15]

The date of the conspiracy was a closely guarded secret. Only those at the very vortex of the plan knew it as either "good fryday" or Easter Monday of 1802. Like Christmas, Easter was "a general holiday" for the slaves, who were typically "disbanded till [the following] Wednesday morning." Whites would not think it unusual to see so many slaves moving about or heading for the nearest town. The "sound of a horn, Trumpet, &c" would signal the leaders to begin raising men. Sancho also avoided the risk of trying to make or stockpile swords or muskets. Anticipating Nat Turner's plan, the insurgents instead would "be furnished with them" as they moved from house to house.[16]

As for the plan itself, it was as simple as Gabriel's was complex. In place of careful planning and strategic calculation Sancho substituted a flexible framework for meeting unexpected situations. Once his immediate followers had each recruited a handful of men, they were to meet "at Daniel Dejarnett's [public house] and Jamison's store." The "destroying [of] the White people" would begin, but how long it would continue was undetermined. Evidently the leaders assumed that the authorities would quickly offer concessions. Only then would the rebels formulate their final demands, which certainly would include their freedom, the right to their earnings, and an equitable distribution of property.[17]

Like Gabriel, Sancho never explained—at least in any extant document—what his conspiracy held for slaves who did not join in the fighting. One bondman close to Sancho—Frank, a slave of Archer Robertson—told a potential recruit that they were "going to take the Country." Surely Sancho believed that his plan would precipitate the collapse of slavery in the region. As mobile as he was, Sancho had at least some ties to the agrarian community. Skilled rivermen had wives, cousins, friends, and parents on the plantations and farms that dotted the riverbanks. After all, many bond watermen were little more than plantation slaves who on occasion carried their masters' goods on short trips. The leadership nucleus could not have envisioned a plan that would leave so many of their friends and relations in bondage.[18]

One significant difference between the conspiracies of 1800 and 1802 was the striking absence of political discourse in the latter plot. With the election of Jefferson, the heated partisan debate that led Gabriel to believe that the state stood on the brink of civil war had diminished considerably. Perhaps, too, the brutal actions of James Monroe made the depth of Republican hypocrisy clear to literate Virginia bondmen. Whatever the reason, Sancho's men made no plans to march forth under a banner emblazoned with political slogans. They simply planned to march.

Both Gabriel and Sancho built upon the assumptions that the fighting would be brief and that they were not precipitating an all-out race war. Gabriel had "expected the poor white people [to] join him." The conspirators of 1802 were not as sanguine in that hope, but they did count upon "the poor [white] sort that has no blacks" at least to remain neutral in the contest. The "great Conflagration of Houses fodder Stacks &c," insisted one rebel, "will Strike such a damp on there Spirets that they will be . . . willing to Acknowledge, liberty & Equality." Since white seamen were among the most radical parts of the Chesapeake population, it was not odd to find such hopeful assumptions among black watermen. Because, as one observer marveled, "The good will of 'old salts' to negroes is proverbial," it was hardly irrational for Virginia authorities later to suspect that a few white laborers were actively "connected in [Sancho's] plot [and would] give aid when the negroes should begin."[19]

On the whole, however, Sancho put most of his faith in slave watermen, especially those who hired away from their owners, to give him the force he needed. He approached Humphrey, who promptly signed on. Together they "persuaded [Abram] to do so" as well. By November "about Sixty [men] had inlisted." But not every man whom they approached was willing. Hailing Bob, a hired man who operated William Royall's ferry, as "a valuable fellow," Sancho challenged him "to join me to raise against the White people." Bob stammered that it "was impossible." Remember "what was done at Richmond," he cautioned, "they all rose there [and] were destroyed." But Sancho replied only that "he reckoned it could be done."[20]

With the conspiracy well under way in Halifax, news of the rising began to ripple down the river arteries that bound the region together. Absalom, a member of Sancho's inner circle, told several slaves "that he had been over the [Roanoke] river to the county of Charlotte" in an attempt to enlist potential leaders. Cautiously following Sancho's admonition to contact only the kind of daring, defiant men who could be counted on, if not to join, at least to keep silent, the slave cadre kept in close contact with written notes. "[W]e have intellegence from almost all parts," observed one rebel, "that our intentions have successfully spread with the greatest Secrecy."[21]

This cautious state of affairs could not last for long; Charlotte County touched upon several smaller rivers that fed into the Appomattox, itself a major route to Petersburg. As Sancho was a bond hire who occasionally traveled home to surrender most of his earnings, it is probable that some of his days in late 1801 and early 1802 were spent with his master in Amelia, directly on the Appomattox. Even if he did not return home, the river connected the southwestern portions of the state to Petersburg. One traveler, noting that the "streets of Petersburg were crowded with hogsheads of tobacco," was told that the wagons and scows were "coming eighty or a hundred miles from the interior." As cargo passed from hand to hand, so did word of the conspiracy.[22]

The inclusion of the Dinwiddie town in the scheme was both a blessing and a burden. Two years earlier, Gabriel had reached out to the skilled bondmen of Petersburg, a connection that had cost Peter his life. Remembering Peter's fate, as well as that of Sam Byrd, Jr., who had spoken in behalf of the Richmond rebels, those involved before were noticeably absent from the second conspiracy. None of the Petersburg men arrested in 1800, including Reuben and Jesse Byrd, were implicated in the Easter plot. Instead, new men came forward. But the larger the new conspiracy grew, the more likely it was that word would pass to a slave who could not be trusted to keep the secret. News of this second attempt at "the business" became so general that on Christmas Day 1801, Grief Green's Ned overheard three unfamiliar slaves speaking openly of the plan. The next day, as he walked back toward his home in Nottoway County, Ned was approached by yet another slave who "said he wished him to join [and] help him kill all the White people."[23]

Ned insisted he would have nothing to do with the plot, but bolder men were willing to listen. In Nottoway, which bordered on both Amelia and Dinwiddie, a second nucleus soon formed around Joe and Bob, slaves of Batt Jones and John Royall. Joe became involved sometime in December. "[T]he white people had so much more liberty than [we] had," he told one young recruit, "that [we] could not do as [we] pleased unless the White people were destroy'd." In keeping with Sancho's basic strategy, they would rise suddenly and "commence the business" in Nottoway, then march on Petersburg, "killing and robing as they went." There, armed with whatever "they got from the Country Inhabitants," they planned to move "on to [a] General Rendezvous" with the Halifax insurgents.[24]

Had the conspiracy spread no further, it might have stood a chance of success. But the more it carried down the rivers, the more control of it slipped from the grasp of Sancho and the Halifax men. Even with their relative freedom of movement and their ability to pass written communications, the conspirators were unable to guide a vast group of rebels who would have to rise quickly and at nearly the same moment. The decentralized nature of the conspiracy rendered it possible, of course, for one isolated revolutionary group to continue to plot even if the plan was discovered in another county, but that may have been more by accident than design. Once white military power was alerted, the prospect of unarmed blacks' achieving their freedom would be considerably diminished. Thus there is good reason to believe, as did white authorities in Halifax, that the conspiracies around their county were connected to the one "in Notoway," but if Sancho's plan were to spread much farther, ties of communication would surely snap.[25]

Snap they did when word of the conspiracy flowed out of the mouth of the Appomattox into the James, washing both upriver toward Richmond and downriver toward Norfolk. Carrying the news north was Lewis, a Goochland slave who worked "at the Manakin town ferry," some twenty miles above Richmond on the James. Lewis was the property of John Brown, but as a hired man he habitually traveled to Petersburg "under a free pass written by himself." There he fell in with several rebels, including Rochester Jumper, a free black. Jumper told Lewis of the plot and promised him that he would fight to "free you all." Pleased to be taken into the confidence of a free man, Lewis gladly swore to return north and recruit "among the Negroes and prepare them for a General insurrection."[26]

Upon returning to Manakin, Lewis preached about the business in Goochland, as well as across the James in Powhatan. There he contacted Franke Goode, Roling Pointer, and Jacob Martin, literate slaves who volunteered to guide the conspiracy in their county. "We have agreed to begin at Jude's Ferry," Goode promised, "and put to death every man on both sides of the river to Richmond." Goode, weary of seeing the better part of his hard-won wages disappear into the pocket of his master, hoped they would "get a Bundance of money and also men enuf." Goode got his men. In early January a patrol of armed whites "was abused and insulted by a [single] negro man," who defiantly shouted that "they had already been permitted to go on too long but that it should not be long before a stop should be put to them." Other "instances of insolence of the same nature" so concerned Powhatan residents that perplexed authorities saw fit to report them to the governor.[27]

Lewis moved on to Richmond, where he spoke around the docks "and on the South side of [the] James." Most likely he revealed this new plan to black seamen and to the slaves who labored along the recently completed canal that allowed light craft to proceed above the falls. Perhaps also he spoke to some of the "hundreds" of black fishermen, "most of [them] working for the benefit of their owners," who skimmed for chad in the churning waters just below the falls. But Lewis found few who cared to listen. The sound of sad hymns wafting from the city jail was still too loud in their ears. The brutal lesson administered to the conspirators of 1800 had cooled their ardor.[28]

But events were by now flowing too fast to be dammed by the hesitancy of the Richmond slaves. Down the James sailed news of the plan. Several craft carried the volatile cargo; one of them was a "free negro's vessell." The captain, like many freemen who became skippers, was a shadowy figure who lived by his wits, as was his mate, an "Irish" seaman who kept messages from the Petersburg rebels "as a stopper of a jug." Two years before, Jacob had paid for similar involvement with his life. Now another black captain was acting as the link between potential conspirators in Norfolk and "the negroes of the upper country."[29]

News of the second attempt to do "the business" found a receptive audience in Norfolk. Home to roughly three thousand blacks, most of them slaves, the port city had a white population of just under four thousand. Many slaves and free blacks crowded into Loyall's Lane and Water Street, a dockside tenement section only slightly more ramshackle than the rest of the unsightly wooden town. As word moved along the docks, slaves like Will were given to understand that the time of the rising was to be "on [Easter] Monday Holy day night." But if most of the slaves who got word of the rising understood themselves to be a part of a larger conspiracy, there is scant evidence for it. The Halifax leadership had lost control of their plan.[30]

And yet it is clear that word of the conspiracy was reaching slaves strikingly similar to Sancho's group. Will's owners, Mary and William Walke of the neighboring county of Princess Anne, were both deceased. The estate was yet unsettled, and the Walke heirs continued to allow Will to hire his time around the region. The Norfolk insurgents, whose number was never estimated by either black or white sources, also expected working class whites to join them after the fighting began. A few even believed that several white men "had arms concealed for the purpose." Should it appear that the rebellion stood a chance of success, white tars, they hoped, would come to their aid, just as Norfolk blacks once had battled British press gangs shoulder to shoulder with white seamen.[31]

In any event, word of the conspiracy did not stop in Norfolk. Once more it took to the water. Norfolk handled much of the commerce of North Carolina, which is to say that much of North Carolina's commerce was handled by black dockworkers and sailors. Numerous black skippers ferried passengers and mail between Norfolk and Elizabeth City. One of them, perhaps the same man who carried word downriver from Petersburg, became the "emissary" to North Carolina. Soon "a correspondence [was] held by [Norfolk] meetings and similar ones in North Carolina."[32]

But that was only one way that word of the rising reached North Carolina. The news also arrived via a second path. At the same time that the secret made its way north out of Halifax to the Appomattox, it also flowed south from Booker's Ferry down the Roanoke to Brunswick County. There the message found a willing recruit in Isaac, a skilled slave of the recently deceased Joseph Wilkes. As were all of the conspirators, Isaac was through with allowing others to control his time and purse. "[I will] not serve the Wilkes [family anymore]," he groaned, and "[will] kill or be killed first." Isaac told several Brunswick slaves that he in turn had recruited Hagood's Phill "to raise a company" when the time came. More fearful slaves, like Isaac's own mother, begged him not to join, for the authorities "would raise a company [of militia] and take him." Isaac merely "nodded his head." He "would raise a Company too."[33]

From Isaac's home on the Roanoke, it was only a short distance downriver into North Carolina. Perhaps Isaac worked on the river, for apparently the widow Wilkes allowed him to hire his time. He told his friend Ransom "that he had been in No[rth] Carolina a doctering and raising men." When the business began, his recruits would quickly raise companies of their own and join the insurrection. For his part, Isaac intended to make sure that the yet unsettled Wilkes estate stayed that way. Potential heirs Thomas and Burwell Wilkes were the first "that was to be killed."[34]

Isaac probably ventured no farther than the town of Roanoke Rapids, but his words of black liberty spread much further. South of Brunswick, the Roanoke ran through Halifax County, North Carolina, a region that was in almost daily contact with Virginia. The upper counties of the Old North State had been settled largely by Virginians who drifted below the border, and most transplanted agriculturalists found it easy to remain in their old economic patterns of trading with Petersburg. Slaves and free blacks carried much of the upriver "produce" north to Virginia, observed one foreign traveler, "where [farmers and planters found] a better market than they Could Expect in any part of their own province." As cargo passed back and forth across the state line, so did "letters [and notes] to, and from [the rebels in the] lower counties" of Virginia.[35]

Those who joined the conspiracy in North Carolina understood themselves to be part of a far larger group. Bearmas's George "said the negroes were going to rise in Virginia & would carry it on here." One literate rebel, Ashbourne's Davy, claimed that "they could get encouragement from Virginia." The "head negroes" live there, he insisted. Even those who had no idea "where the plan originated or how far it extended," agreed that "a negro man somewhere in Virg[ini]a," probably Isaac, "was at work under the ground [and] that when the fight was begun all the negroes were to join those who commenced."[36]

Despite enormous difficulties and dangers, the upriver rebels maintained at least minimal contact along the Roanoke throughout the life of the conspiracy, for the plan in North Carolina was a mirror image to that of Sancho. As in Virginia, only those men "noted for their secrecy, were intrusted with the plot, and not more than one or two in a family." Few bondmen knew the actual date of the rising, and those who did refused to tell their contacts "until the night before." Neither did they make any attempt to gather and store arms. Instead, like the Halifax leadership, they planned "to furnish themselves with Arms [taken] from those who were first killed."[37]

Clearly too, the men who joined in North Carolina were cut from the same cloth as those up the Roanoke. Many were rivermen, and some hired their time. Several had recently deceased owners. They had tasted just enough independence—physical and economic—to want more of both. Typical was Salem, who recruited in the "ship yeards." He was fighting, he told his fellows, for the right to control "*their time*" and reap the full fruits of their labor. United, he boasted, they "could do anything"; they could "fly across the river." Surely "after killing the Whites sufficiently," agreed Gain, they would be granted "their freedom & live as White People." It says much about the aspirations of these revolutionaries that they did not plan to flee the state but to live and labor among southern whites—if not their former owners, many of whom would lie dead.[38]

Despite all of their similarities and ties to Sancho's followers, however, the North Carolina wing of the conspiracy inevitably took on a life of its own. Unlike the Norfolk insurgents, they always understood themselves to be a branch of a far larger group. But in the end the lower Roanoke part of it, like Norfolk, essentially evolved into a separate group. Given the distance the news had traveled, it is surprising that the plot remained as cohesive as it did. When this wing of the conspiracy snapped free, its own leaders rose to the fore. "Captain" King Brown and Frank, a slave of David Sumner, both literate bondmen, quickly seized control. Ignoring the Easter timetable, the Carolina blacks chose instead the night of Thursday, June 10, as the moment for rising. That evening would be the quarterly meeting of several Kehukee Baptist associations, a time when most whites would be neither armed nor on their guard. The rebels would begin, as Gabriel's men would have, by setting fire to "the Houses of Windsor," a small hamlet north of the Roanoke. By the next day they hoped to "receive considerable reinforcements from up and down the river." Bolstered by these new recruits, they would march toward "Virginia and help the blacks there." Slaves who did not join, Brown warned, "should not live among them [and] they wou'd kill them."[39]

Mid-spring arrived. King Brown and Frank by then had recruited "about 28 or 30" leaders, each of whom agreed to raise a band of men "the night before" the business was to begin. At that point they would "go to every man's house, set fire to it," and kill those inside who did not readily agree to black freedom. The leaders also labored to stay in touch with their contacts upriver. Dick Blacksmith instructed Davy "to contrive a letter [to] Virginia, [a] letter concerning a request to negroes to come forward and assist in destroying white people."[40]

The decision to burn the houses in and around Windsor revealed much. It indicated that the conspiracy had come all the way down the Roanoke to the Albemarle Sound. Windsor was in Bertie, a county that shared the river with Martin, two counties that had already gotten word of the insurrection by way of the Norfolk conspirators. The plot had thus come full circle. By May 6, King Brown told a rebel "that all up the [Roanoke] River were joined & ready." As former governor Richard D. Spaight later wrote, "I am decidedly of Opinion that it was to have been General through out the State, at least the Sea board part." The conspirators waited for the word from King Brown and Frank—or news that the lower counties of Virginia were aflame.[41]

The Footsteps Die Out

The word would never come. Even as news of the conspiracy flooded down the James and Roanoke rivers, the plan began to unravel at its source. It is unnecessary to speculate as to whether the revolt, had it taken place, would have been anything but a bloody failure. Sancho's inability to attract large numbers of urban bondmen meant that the conspirators could not count on taking more than a few hostages. The fighting would have to take place in the countryside, where blacks—and their well-armed adversaries—were more dispersed. Sancho's failure to limit the conspiracy geographically meant that it would never have a chance to be even a hopeless battle. Long before Easter arrived—even as early as December of 1801— hints began to surface around Petersburg that a new conspiracy was afoot. While many white authorities at first did not believe the rumors, most, like William Prentis (by now a veteran at putting down black rebellion), were shrewd enough to call "the Patrolls" back into active duty.[1]

Living upriver in northern Halifax, Sancho did not hear of the alarms. Isolated from his downriver followers, the rebel leader was unable to provide direction at this critical juncture, or to move the timetable up. As a result, his followers in Nottoway continued to wait for Easter Monday, serenely unaware that white vigilance once more had been awakened. On January 1 "the Patrollers [in Nottoway] caught them in the business." Crashing directly into the midst of a midnight rendezvous, the patrol swept up Bob and Joe and three other lieutenants. Joe only glared at his captors, but Bob lost his nerve. "[I] told York and Brister that it would come to this," he cried out bitterly as the patrol herded the men toward jail. Major Richard Jones rushed news of the arrests to Prentis, back in his former post of mayor of Petersburg. "We have at present five [men] in our Gaol," Jones reported, "and hourly expect more."[2]

Furious at his exclusion from the governor's confidence two years before, Prentis nonetheless understood that the safety of his town required far more than a few patrols sweeping the area. On January 2 William Martin of Petersburg hurried an account of the affair to James Monroe and begged the governor to call out "the Petersburg and Prince George Light

Horse." Two days later Prentis, who clearly did not consider subtlety a distinguishing feature of his character, wrote to express his fears and assure the governor that he would "communicate to you every information on the subject." Within two weeks, Monroe passed the information along to the General Assembly. "An alarm of a threatened insurrection among the slaves took place in Nottoway County, which soon reached Petersburg," Monroe warned the legislature. "A variety of causes contribute to produce this effect," he added, among which were "the growing sentiment of liberty" among the slaves "and the inadequacy of the existing patrol laws." Slavery, according to the governor, was not itself a cause of slave unrest; the problem instead consisted of finding a way to qualify and contain white notions of liberty and equality.[3]

With gloomy tidings of a second conspiracy being bandied about the halls of the statehouse, Virginia planters in the region around Petersburg prepared for the worst. Once more, white vigilance paid off. In mid-January the overseer on John Harris's Powhatan plantation noticed two bondmen talking in hushed tones. Unable to make out most of what was whispered, the overseer did hear one slave promise "that the event would shortly take place." His companion agreed. "[I]t would certainly take place very shortly, and would create a great change in affairs."[4]

The two slaves said no more, and their muttered promises implicated no leaders. A few days later, however, white authorities found out all they needed to know when they barged into Jacob Martin's grog shop. Martin squirmed through a rear window and fled into the woods, but in his haste he left behind several incriminating documents. Among them was a letter from Franke Goode to Roling Pointer. Powhatan leaders forwarded the documents to Monroe, who passed them along to the Assembly. While Goode had made no reference to another county, the governor had long been cured of his old assumption that Virginia bondmen were a simple lot incapable of devising a statewide conspiracy. He wasted no time spreading the word that "strong and active patroles are [to be] kept in motion" and that militia regiments should "be in readiness to act in case of an emergency at a moments warning."[5]

Like the fleet-footed Martin, Goode and Pointer were nowhere to be found. But their correspondence, coming on the heels of the capture of the Nottoway leadership, set off a new wave of panic in Richmond and Petersburg. For the second time in two short years the capital resembled a city under siege. The Richmond Nineteenth Regiment took to the streets armed with "four hundred and twelve stands of publick Arms." "[N]ine great guns" stuffed with grapeshot shone in the winter sun at strategic corners about the city, while "continued and active patroles" crashed about the Richmond countryside, looking for massive insurgent armies but, of course, finding none. As was his practice, Mayor Prentis begged Monroe for "powder and ball; there being none [in Petersburg] except powder, and that is private property." Prentis prayed that the governor would see fit to provide him with "a field officer" to establish order and organize the city's defenses. "[E]verything is in a measure of confusion," he worried. Surely his city would collapse should "an insurrection absolutely to commence and [the rebels] make a stand."[6]

As Monroe pondered the fate of his own city, he recalled Gabriel's plan and the role that burning the warehouse district was to play in diverting attention away from the main thrusts into the heart of Richmond. "If the people get into confusion, unarmed, running in different directions," he now fretted, "they may become a prey to a very small force." Should "alarms of fire" be given, he warned the militia, "a certain portion of the regiment" should not head for the fire but automatically move "on the Capitol Square." Monroe instructed fifty more men to stand "on the east side of the bridge, near the Jail." Still another fifty should race for "the height[s]." Such careful instructions, however, could not prevent drunken sentinels from firing their muskets in the dead of night, a droll joke that "gave much alarm to the citizens on account of what was reported relative to the Slaves."[7]

After this kind of renewed panic, there was little chance that Bob and Joe would get a fair hearing, a rare enough event even in moments of white contentment. Once more the oyer and terminer courts sprang into action. On January 7, 1802, the two bondmen appeared before the court; the appropriately named Edward Bland entered the requisite plea of innocent in their behalf but otherwise exerted himself not at all. Five justices, including James Jones, a distant kinsman of the late Batt Jones (Joe's owner of record) heard the case and found little reason to doubt that the two slaves were guilty of "insurrection." The justices hurried the transcripts to Monroe. The governor believed "the charges to be clearly proved" and so "thought it proper to let the law have its course." On the third Saturday of the new year, Bob and Joe swung together from the Nottoway gallows.[8]

That the executed slaves were clearly not the organizers of the conspiracy bothered area authorities. "We have been very assiduous," Richard Jones of Nottoway promised William Prentis, "but find much difficulty in discovering their full design." Still, patrols increased in size and frequency, and slaves found themselves the subjects of harsh, random questioning. Although the extant record is unclear on this point, several fingers evidently pointed across the border into Brunswick. They singled out the highly mobile Isaac, the slave of widow Henrietta Wilkes.[9]

In early February Isaac and Phill, a bondman of Randolph Hagood's, were arrested. On the third day of the month the two rebels, pale and sweating despite the cool weather, appeared in the dock. Three slaves—George, Adam, and Jeffrey—the last of whom was also owned by the late Joseph Wilkes, insisted that Isaac had traveled into North Carolina to recruit men for the plot. Their stories varied enough to indicate that they had not been coached by anxious authorities. Edmund Cooper, the defense counsel for both men, ventured a laconic plea of not guilty. The gentlemen justices thought otherwise. "[B]eing moved & Seduced by the devil" to commit conspiracy and rebellion, Isaac and Phill were found guilty and sentenced to hang on February 12. Once more Monroe declined to intervene, and so, like Bob and Joe, the two Brunswick conspirators died together.[10]

Up to this point, Virginia authorities had thought that the conspiracy was confined to a few counties. The testimony against Isaac, however, raised the specter of a plot that encompassed two states. Frightened whites all across Virginia now feared—with good reason—that word of the rising had reached their town. "For some weeks past," Norfolk mayor John Cowper confided to Monroe, "it has been rumoured that an insurrection of the Negroes was to take place on the Night of [Easter] Monday." The mayor doubted the rumors but urged area whites to be especially vigilant.[11]

This vigilance paid off on April 15, the Thursday before Easter, when Will, a slave of the Walke family, was overtaken outside of Norfolk by Caleb Boush and a companion named Jarvis. Jarvis, who was much "in liquor," grabbed the Princess Anne hireling by the collar and shouted that he was "of bad character." When Will was unable to show his captors a pass, Jarvis insisted that he was one of the "sons of bitches" who was involved in the conspiracy and was probably about on the business.[12]

Unlike the cloth-headed Jarvis, Boush was sober enough, but there was something about Will's noisy protests that he "was not one of them" that seemed to admit of more information than an innocent man should have. Together Jarvis and Boush dragged Will back to the Norfolk home of John Floyd, who had hired the slave for the year. Floyd told Jarvis that Will had left his house that morning, which contradicted Will's claim that he was coming *from* Princess Anne. Caught in a lie, Will remained quiet for some time. "[N]o threats [were] made" by either man, but finally Will spoke. He admitted hearing of the plan "to burn Norfolk" on "Monday Holy day night" but insisted "that he refused to join." Will claimed he had been contacted several times by John Ingram's Ned, John Cornick's Jeremiah, and Ned, a fellow slave of the legally troubled Walke estate. Before allowing

Will to sign the statement, Floyd sternly reminded him "that the lives of the persons he had informed against depended upon his evidence." Will stubbornly maintained it was all true.[13]

Now convinced of the conspiracy's reality, Mayor John Cowper wasted no time in sweeping up those named by Will. A "strong patrole of the citizens" scoured the area nightly. Easter night found the city nervous, but except for a furious thunderstorm reminiscent of the gale that destroyed Gabriel's plan, the town was quiet. By Tuesday morning "six negroe men [had been] taken up and confined in gaol."[14]

The military power of the terrified whites was more than effective. Boarding several vessels owned by free blacks, Norfolk authorities discovered in one boat papers stuffed in a jug that confirmed the "suspicion that communications [were] being held with the negroes of the upper country." General Thomas Mathews, in charge of the Norfolk militia, took measures to "apprehend" a bondman he believed was acting as "emissary" to the rebels in North Carolina. From Richmond, James Monroe encouraged the militia to remain out as long as necessary to protect "the town and its inhabitants," but remembering the still-unpaid debt incurred in rounding up Gabriel's men, he also prayed that "the patriotism" of the militia companies would "induce them to charge nothing which they can avoid, [so] that the publick may not be improperly burdened."[15]

Certainly the Norfolk Borough court of oyer and terminer did not intend to tax the purses of anxious whites by prolonging the trials. Within a week of their arrest, Walke's Ned and Jeremiah were declared guilty before "a numerous audience [of] about 300" people and sentenced to hang. Will was the only witness against either; he testified that he had encountered both men outside of Norfolk "above the Town Bridge," where they tried to recruit him for their plan of "setting the town on fire on Easter Monday night." The court, which included the mayor, set the value of Jeremiah at four hundred dollars, well above the standard market price for a young bondman, an indication of literacy or some marketable skill.[16]

The court's verdict was not acceptable to all local whites. George McIntosh, a Norfolk merchant and small planter who had married into the intermingled Walke-Cornick families, rushed evidence to Monroe that suggested that Will had implicated innocent men. McIntosh argued that Ned could not possibly have been at the Town Bridge when Will claimed to have met him, for he was visiting his pregnant wife half a mile away. Almost before the governor could act, indignant letters supporting the decision of the justices arrived from Cowper and former mayor Thomas Newton, who had been instrumental in crushing the conspiracy two years before. Cowper insisted that both men were guilty and that another slave had provided supporting information—although not testimony. Newton agreed with Cowper on this point but conceded that Ned was simple-minded and "easily brought to any measure proposed to him." Perhaps, Newton suggested, the governor might consider transporting the slave instead of allowing him to die on the gallows. Of Ned's guilt, however, Newton promised, there was absolutely no doubt.[17]

On May 8, Monroe brought the matter before his council. Most of its members indicated their utter indifference to the fate of the two slaves, but Monroe, who was again becoming uncomfortable with the growing body count of black revolutionaries, argued that McIntosh's arguments should be carefully considered. As was his habit, the governor spoke slowly and paused often as he gathered his thoughts. But his words finally had the desired effect. Letting Jeremiah and Ned go free was out of the question, but at length a consensus emerged to grant a reprieve until Friday, May 28. Both Cowper and Newton were informed of this decision and encouraged to submit—and to allow others to do likewise—further documentation on "the character of those slaves or the Witness." At the same time, Monroe released a circular to the various county courts, reminding them of a new law of January 15, 1801, which mandated that copies of transcripts and testimony "for and against" slaves tried for capital crimes be forwarded to the governor so that the executive could consider the bondmen for the alternative punishment of transportation. "[I]t is presumed that the obligation which is imposed on them so to do," Monroe huffed, without mentioning the Norfolk court by name, "has escaped their attention."[18]

The reprieve was met without enthusiasm in the finer white neighborhoods of the crowded port town. Newton assured Monroe that while he welcomed an open hearing, he sincerely hoped the two men would "never again be permitted to go at large in this place." Cowper was more blunt. McIntosh's arguments, he thundered, "if not absolutely false, [were] certainly partial." More to the point, Cowper warned, Monroe was risking his political future. "Much discontent has been caused by the indulgence which the Executive has granted the condemned negroes." The Norfolk press chimed in as well. The "unexpected interference of the executive," one editor agreed, "has thrown a damp on the laudable exertions of the inhabitants in keeping a nightly watch." So great was the outcry that even a New York journal expressed surprise that Monroe would protect slaves "found guilty on the clearest evidence."[19]

The clamor brought Monroe up short. Concerned though he might have been about the "encreas[ing] number" of corpses, Monroe had never been a politician to swim against the tide, and the mood of the city demanded at least one more body. And so in the end the council decided to spare

Ned but allow Jeremiah to meet the fate decreed by the court. Jeremiah, Monroe explained to Cowper in a letter of May 25, appeared to be "of bad character." The hope of the council was that "his example will prove an useful admonition to the slaves his accomplices, and totally suppress the Spirit of insurrection." Ned was an altogether different matter. "He is represented to be almost an idiot, little capable of acting for himself." The decision was designed to please almost everyone but the two recalcitrant bondmen. Norfolk authorities would get their revenge, and McIntosh could tell himself that Ned had been saved, although only to be "removed to the penitentiary for transportation" and resale (a task that was certified accomplished by Daniel Hylton).[20]

Despite appearances, the desperate entreaties of George McIntosh had carried little weight. That Jeremiah and Ned were guilty of wishing to be free was never in doubt in the minds of the council. Will's testimony against Ned, as McIntosh suggested, was indeed dubious, as it was almost a mirror image of the evidence he had provided against Jeremiah. Yet Jarvis only accused Will of being a conspirator; it was Will who provided the date of the uprising. Surely then, Monroe reasoned, Will had at least heard of the plot, and if he was involved, why name innocent men? Moreover, the three men that Will implicated all belonged to recently deceased owners, a situation common to conspirators across the state. The governor might also have been warned that McIntosh's interest was partly economic. If Ned should be hanged, that would represent a financial loss to the five Walke heirs, one of whom was married to McIntosh. Finally, the merchant was new to the region and harbored doubts that African Americans could be rebellious. "[T]he Negro population in this section of the State," McIntosh later asserted, "are too intelligent to enter into a combination to effect any measure by force." Having come face to face with Gabriel, Monroe knew that view to be utterly fallacious. Ned was spared only because the governor had long grown sick of the bloodshed and had no stomach to allow a simpleminded rebel to go to the gallows.[21]

For Ned, the letter working its way from Richmond nearly arrived too late. Cowper did not intend to delay one moment beyond the end of the reprieve. Just past sunrise on Friday, May 28, several jailors hastened Jeremiah and Ned into the tumbril and raced for the gallows. Jeremiah "took leave [of his] wife and two children," shouted a final "declaration of his innocence," and went calmly to his death. Somewhat to the disappointment of the assembled throng, a tired and sweaty rider, holding aloft the governor's letter that spared Ned's life, nosed his horse through the crowd.[22]

The sight of Jeremiah swinging from the gibbet appeared to appease the bloodlust of the Norfolk leaders. Monroe guessed correctly, all they wanted was one "example" to dampen the ardor of other black rebels. As a result, only Jeremiah would die in Norfolk. On June 20 the other Ned, a bondman of the widow Ingram, appeared before the bar. Will and several other witnesses were "fully heard" and cross-examined by Samuel Marsh, Ned's counsel, but only five of the six justices believed him guilty. The oyer and terminer courts required unanimity, and so Ned was released. The final three slaves remaining in jail had "but hearsay evidence appearing against them, [and] they [too were] discharged."[23]

During the same week that the Norfolk rebels were swept up, the conspiracy finally collapsed at its source. Halifax authorities always had assumed a connection between the conspirators in Nottoway and the rivermen of neighboring counties. On May 1 Monroe directed that the "plot and parties to it should be traced [upriver]." And the plot stopped at Booker's Ferry. A large number of slaves were "taken up." Those seized were questioned "at a considerable distance from each other" so that they could not make up a common story. Without prodding and without beatings several confessed a "concurrent tale" and, tragically, implicated each other in the process.[24]

As had been the case two years earlier, one slave did more than implicate his fellows in a moment of terror. Abram, a skilled bondman of William Smith's, cynically determined to save his life by turning informer. By doing so, Abram illustrated an important point. Privileged slaves who stood on the edge of freedom were often the most likely to instigate slave rebellions. As literate or hired bondmen, they were close enough to liberty to risk a bold move that might succeed in shedding their quasi freedom and earn them the real thing. But when faced with defeat, some privileged slaves eager to save what few privileges they possessed—as well as their lives—promised to turn informer. "[Y]ou are hereby commanded to receive into your custody Abram," James Dejarnett instructed the jailor of Halifax County, "[h]e being a witness in behalf of the Commonwealth." Dejarnett assumed the jailor would take the appropriate precautions, although he felt compelled to add "that the above witness [should] be kept separate from the prisoners he is a witness against."[25]

On April 23, Sancho, appropriately enough, was the first rebel brought before the bar. Abram took the stand and made clear that the Easter plot was the work of the ferryman, who promised him "that there were to be two companies of negroes collected and at Mr. Jameson's store" on the night before Easter. In case that evidence was not enough to guarantee Sancho's death, Bob, whose owner lived in nearby Charlotte County, swore that Sancho claimed to have been involved in Gabriel's conspiracy but somehow had escaped the gallows. The justices wasted little time in arriving at a verdict of guilty. The court valued Sancho at an impressive $400 and sentenced him to swing three weeks hence, on Saturday, May 15.[26]

In a curious turn of events, Phebe, a house servant of Daniel Price's, was pushed forward and formally charged with conspiracy and insurrection. She was the only woman to be so charged in either conspiracy. Abram spoke against her, but the court either found his testimony doubtful or, what is more likely, lacked the will to hang a woman for a crime that had cost no white lives. Not that slave women were not habitually beaten, overworked, and sexually abused. But the sight of a woman kicking and twisting at the end of a noose was one that the squeamish Virginia gentry desperately wished to avoid; their pretensions to being civilized men would be all but shattered. Phebe was released.[27]

Their masquerade as moderate men intact, the justices could now address the matter at hand. On April 26, Absalom appeared in the courtroom. Several slaves identified him as one of Sancho's lieutenants, and William Martin, one of his captors, testified that "no threats or promises were used to frighten him or persuade him to a confession." The justices conferred briefly and sentenced him to die with his leader on May 15. Two other bondmen, Frank and Martin, received the same sentence.[28]

On May 1, Abram, who had testified against three of the four men sentenced to death, confidently strode into the dingy courtroom. Perhaps he had been led to believe that a fast trial and an even faster recommendation of clemency awaited him. But the testimony against him demonstrated that his involvement in the plot was far deeper than what he had led his captors to believe. Bob swore that Abram had actively recruited around Halifax and that he "intended to kill his master William Smith" on the "fryday night before Easter." Following the murder, he was to "join the other conspirators at the Seven Islands." Robin added that Abram routinely "went over the river Stanton" to speak about the business. Placed upon the scales of white justice, these damning words outweighed any vague promises that James Dejarnett had made to a mere slave. To his horror, Abram heard a finding of guilty pronounced. The justices calculated his value at $400 and sentenced him to die alongside the men he had helped to send to the gallows.[29]

In all, thirteen slaves were tried in Halifax. Of those, five were sentenced to die. Most local authorities, like John Scott, assumed that still greater numbers of slaves "were concerned" in the plot. But "probably for the sake of humanity," he informed Monroe, "tis well to stop here." The governor, who flinched at bloodshed beyond making the obvious point of white domination, readily agreed. But the leadership, he warned his council, "shou'd be neither reprieved or pardoned." And so on Saturday morning, May 15, Sancho, Absalom, Martin, Frank, and Abram, their betrayer, all swung together from the Halifax gibbet.[30]

The last of the Virginia conspirators taken was Lewis, the Goochland ferryman who had traveled toward Richmond just before Easter. In late April the literate hireling was picked up in Nottoway, several counties from the home of his owner, John Brown. His captors demanded that he reveal "verry fully the whole Scheme." When he did not, he was "repeatedly and severely whipped." Finally Lewis gave the names of the few contacts he knew in Petersburg, Arnold and a free black named Rochester Jumper. "[T]hreatened with immediate death if he did not disclose [all of] his partizans in the conspiracy," the bleeding Lewis gasped out the name of a Richmond slave carpenter, Arthur Farrar, whom he had not seen in years. With that his tormentors were satisfied.[31]

While anxious authorities in Nottoway, Dinwiddie, and Richmond labored to apprehend the slaves accused by Lewis, the ferryman was held "in prison as a runaway until all the information he possesse[d could] be obtained." Jumper was taken, as was a confused and astonished Arthur, who remembered Lewis only as a small boy. But since none of these men, guilty or innocent, offered a confession or implicated his fellows, Lewis, like Ben Woolfolk before him, would have to be escorted from county to county so that "advantage may be taken of his testimony," extracted though it was under torture.[32]

As James Laughlin took Lewis to Richmond, the nervous capital again forced itself to consider the awful possibility of black revolution. James Monroe, who knew nothing of Arthur Farrar beyond the upsetting rumors that he allegedly had been heard to say "he had once gotten clear of the gallows," forced himself to consider the worst: more bondmen who reminded him of his own hypocrisy by comparing themselves to George Washington. The governor placed Arthur "in cell by himself" in the penitentiary. Lewis too was isolated. Strict orders allowed "no one to confer with them but Mr. Storrs and Mr. Selden the Magistrates."[33]

Having been tortured into providing partially false information, Lewis discovered that he could not safely change his story now. But Arthur was only a name from his past, and he had no other names to provide, for few Richmond slaves had proved willing to give the business a second try. When the Richmond court of oyer and terminer sat on May 17, Lewis's story grew even more elaborate and sounded suspiciously like what he had heard of Gabriel's plan. "[A]ll of the free blacks, and a great number of the poor white people were to join in it," Lewis assured the court. Arthur had recruited "a great number of men towards Hanover, who would meet near the Brook bridge" before marching on the town. There the poor whites would supply them with arms from the magazine.[34]

The gentlemen justices were impressed. Hezekiah Henley and George Williamson, who had presided over many of the cases two years before, listened especially carefully. Since the plan of attack mirrored one that they too well remembered to be true, they readily believed Lewis's story. That it mirrored Gabriel's plot a bit too closely, including the preposterous notion of assembling at the bridge near Prosser's plantation, apparently did not occur to them, and defense attorney Samuel McGraw was far too dull a wit to point out these absurdities. While Farrar floundered about in the dock, the gavel fell. Sentenced to die on Friday, June 18, Farrar was valued at $500, as "the prisoner is a Carpenter."[35]

While McGraw collected his fee of ten dollars for services rendered, Farrar frantically dictated a letter to the governor, his only hope for pardon under the oyer and terminer system. The slave pointed out that Lewis was the only voice against him, that the testimony was tainted with torture, and "that when he last saw [Lewis] in Goochland he must have been a boy." Monroe believed the words. At the very least he was uncomfortable with testimony taken during a brutal whipping. But remembering the storm of criticism that settled upon him when he deigned to question the wisdom of the Norfolk court, the cautious man proceeded cautiously. In early July he suggested to his council that Farrar's sentence be reduced to transportation. Until then, Farrar could remain in the penitentiary.[36]

In the meantime, Lewis's mention of Hanover set off a new and equally unfounded alarm in that quarter. Since the story that Lewis spun was based upon what he had heard of Gabriel's plan, it followed that those slaves upon whom suspicion now fell were those who had been on the periphery of the earlier plot. Among them were Tom and Glasgow, two slaves of the recently deceased Paul Thilman, three of whose servants had been involved with Gabriel. In early May the two men were brought before the Hanover court. James, a mulatto slave, insisted that he had heard Glasgow say he would join a plot "to kill the whites." As was Arthur Farrar, Glasgow allegedly was another of Gabriel's men who were willing to try again. "Yes," James insisted Glasgow had sworn, "I have rose for my freedom [once before], and I have never got it; but damn it, I will either die or be free." Tom, a cook, was simply accused of hearing this conversation and doing nothing. Several other slaves testified that they were present during the conversation but heard no revolutionary talk. The court found the sentiments remembered by James to sound authentic. Despite a decided lack of evidence that a plot existed in Hanover, they sentenced the two slaves to die. Again Monroe moved slowly, but he moved, especially when Paul Woolfolk (the original owner of Ben Woolfolk) assured him that James was a man of "bad character." Tom and Glasgow escaped the noose but joined Farrar in the penitentiary while they awaited news of their ultimate destination.[37]

From Monroe's perspective, the trials in Nottoway and Dinwiddie proved equally disastrous, though for altogether different reasons. By the end of his stay in the Richmond penitentiary, Lewis had had enough. Enough beatings. Enough coerced testimony. Enough lies. In early June commissioners from Nottoway escorted him out of Richmond. The plan called for him first to testify in the county of his capture, then to make a detour by his master's home in Goochland, and finally to be heard in Petersburg at the trial of Jumper. But somewhere outside of Richmond— his hapless warders never wished to explain just where or how—Lewis made good his escape and disappeared from sight. With no witness, the Nottoway trials collapsed. Jumper, in the Dinwiddie jail, saw his trial "postponed" indefinitely, although he did not obtain immediate release. As late as October, embarrassed authorities feared explaining the situation to Monroe, who wondered what the delay was all about. John Brown, Lewis's master, also began to worry that his property was lost. "I have to request," Monroe thundered to Peterson Goodwyn, that "you will be pleased to cause him to be delivered to the bearer."[38]

For Virginia rebels, the successful escape of Lewis meant little compared with the grim fact that Sancho was dead. For North Carolina rebels, the execution of the Halifax leaders meant that they were now on their own. If black watermen carried news about the collapse of the Virginia rebellion down the Roanoke, their warning rode alongside a letter from a former governor of North Carolina to the current chief executive, Benjamin Williams. William R. Davie warned of a major slave plot up the river, extending perhaps to the frontier town of Roanoke. Virginia justices of the peace, Davie claimed, had reason to believe that the plan reached downriver into North Carolina. Indeed, at that moment "nightly meetings" were taking place in Bertie. There the leaders stayed in touch by passing letters from hand to hand and waiting for June 10.[39]

Given the need to rise rapidly as a group, that the literate rivermen stayed in touch through letters was not surprising. The generally poor state of roads and communications in the region was the reason the plot had fragmented into three smaller conspiracies. But the use of correspondence, even when it was carried by other slaves, presented dangers as well as opportunities. Should even one letter be captured, the names of the cadre so necessary to the scheme would be known to authorities. On June 1, Fed, a Carolina bondman, encountered several slaves on a road near Colerain in Bertie County. One of them was David Sumner's Frank, who gave Fed a letter to carry to King Brown. Fed obviously knew of the plot, for Frank felt free to remind him that on "the 10th June they were agoing to make a Start & come down to the Ferry [and] then come to Mr. Hunters Store & Break it open & get what powder was there." But when Fed reached the home of Jude (perhaps King's wife) the next morning, he gave the letter to "her little Girl [and] told her to give it to her mother."[40]

At the same moment, Davie's letter of warning had scared the patrollers into action. Since late May they had been searching the cabins of blacks along the rivers for arms, but of course had found none. Sometime around midday on June 2 they forced their way into Jude's home, where they found not guns but the letter "containing the names of about 14 negro men." The terrified woman confessed that it had been "left with her that morning by Fed," who had promised "to carry [it] to [Joseph] Brown's King."[41]

The capture of Frank's letter destroyed what little remained of the Easter conspiracy. Anxious patrollers apprehended the insurgents "named on the paper." Riders hurried word of the plot to "the adjacent counties" of Hertford and Martin. By June 10 large numbers of slaves had been picked up and confined near Jamestown. A howling mob of whites wanted to shoot them "on the spot," but several justices of the peace instead urged that a "Committee of Enquiry" be formed "to examine and take down the depositions of the prisoners." The committee separated the slaves and had "the youngest and most foolish lad" brought before them. They told him that his name was on Frank's letter. If he would confess, "he should be forgiven." Like some of the terrified men of Halifax, Virginia, he agreed.[42]

A second young slave was thrust forward. Again crafty magistrates, well versed in the theory of divide and conquer, promised a full "pardon"; "the lash" was not necessary. The young bondman agreed to "discover the whole plot," and he knew a great deal to tell. As an "officer" he had been involved for some time, although he had not been given the final date of the rising until June 1. Because of the cautious method of recruitment, he could not name every slave involved, only those "belonging to the same company." Those names he revealed. Over the course of two days nearly thirty more slaves were all examined separately. The authorities insisted that the accused were not coached and that there was no way for them to know "what had been previously declared by others." After giving testimony some were whipped or had their ears cropped and then were released. Those who were implicated as the leaders were taken to the town of Windsor for trial. Sent with them as evidence were Frank's letter and a missive from Virginia "also found at Colerain."[43]

If anything, the North Carolina authorities were even more legalistically minded than their Virginia brethren. Since 1790 a number of reforms in the slave code had been implemented. Unlike slaves in Virginia, North Carolina bondmen enjoyed the right of trial by jury and appeal to the state supreme court. The suspicion that white artisans and unskilled laborers lacked the desire to uphold their unique domestic institution, however, had led the framers of these laws to stipulate that the jury, if the case involved a crime "the punishment whereof shall extend to life, limb, or member [penis]," must be composed only of slaveholders. In the Bertie trials, "six or seven" slaves testified on behalf of the state against "the officers." Nine men, including King Brown, were found guilty and executed on Wednesday, June 16. Two more eventually followed them to the Windsor gallows.[44]

At the same time, trials were being held in the neighboring counties. In Hertford, to the north of Bertie, ten slaves were tried. But only Frank, whose case was heard in the county where his master resided, was executed. The other nine, "who did not appear equally criminal with Frank and King [Brown], were punished by [the] cropping [of their ears], whipping, and branding." Two slaves swung in Martin, a county that shared the Roanoke with Bertie, and Mrs. Foord's Sam was hanged in Halifax on June 27. In all, twenty-five men from Virginia and North Carolina paid for their demand for liberty and the just fruits of their labor with their lives. The Easter conspiracy was over.[45]

The conspiracy may have been over, but the terror it inspired among the ruling race was not. As in Richmond and Hanover, the number and might of the insurgents were wildly overestimated. Published accounts insisted that slaves were "embodied in large companies, armed, and in the Great Swamp" or that massive risings were taking place in the counties of Perquimans and Hertford. One paper even reported that the slaves had captured "the town of Windsor, and had committed great havock." A rider from Winton galloped toward Windsor "to ascertain the truth of the report," but he met only a lone rider coming from that town to discover whether rumors that Winton was under attack were true. It was not until early August that the state settled down to the fact that the alarm was "generally allowed to have been greater than the occasion warranted."[46]

While the corpses were buried in North Carolina, the four reprieved Virginia slaves, including Ned, awaited word on their transportation. They could not know it, but the debate on their ultimate fate then taking place in the Virginia General Assembly promised—for one all too brief moment—to do what Gabriel and Sancho had been unable to do: bring about an end to human bondage in the most important of all southern states.

10

A Place of Asylum

In the fall of 1800, even before Sancho began to plan for his freedom, the white Virginia conscience, bewildered and vengeful though it was, belatedly made its appearance, and the hand of the hangman was at long last stayed. Jack Ditcher, Watt, King, Jack Gabriel, and a handful of other conspirators escaped the gallows, but only in exchange for the treacherous sentence of transportation. The question was where to send them. On that thorny matter Governor James Monroe hoped to solicit the advice of the General Assembly.

In that year the legislature met on December 1. All was disorder as old and new delegates pushed through the dilapidated barnyard that was Capitol Square. Perched on a gentle rise above the city, the capitol building nonetheless appeared majestic to the largely rural delegates. Some foreign travelers thought otherwise. "This building is finished entirely with red brick; even the columns themselves are formed of brick," Isaac Weld snorted. The outside was painted "with common whitewash" to make it appear to be marble. "[I]t proves to be a clumsy ill shapen pile."[1]

The first few days of the session were occupied with the selection of a speaker and committee assignments. By December 5 both houses were prepared to receive a special message from the governor on Gabriel's plot. As the clerk droned out Monroe's lengthy message, most delegates sat in stunned silence, for the magnitude of the danger, as Monroe told the tale, was far beyond what all but the most dramatic journalists had described. Even Benjamin Harrison, whose slave had told him of the Petersburg rebels, and Charles Copland, who had defended Gabriel in 1799, sat with mouths agape. Only Gervas Storrs, one of the two representatives from Henrico, knew the full story, including those details regarding the Frenchmen, which the governor now declined to reveal. Monroe's missive concluded with a request that the Assembly provide him with any "recommendations" it might think proper "on the issue" of the near revolt, as well as advice on the matter of transportation.[2]

The governor did not have a long wait. On the last day of the month Edmund Harrison of Amelia, chairman of the committee to which the matter had been referred, issued his report "on the subject of the late conspiracy." Recommendations drawn up by a group could not be expected to suggest a unity of mind, but even by the disorderly standards of government by committee, the seven resolutions produced by Harrison's committee were a chaotic blend of liberality and repression. They reflected the confused state of gentry thinking that had reigned since the Revolution, for they demonstrated a determination to maintain slavery—a view particularly prevalent since 1796. But enough reformist elements lingered to indicate that many planters still harbored more than a few doubts about their peculiar labor system.[3]

The desire to maintain human bondage by repairing the tattered system of controls that had lapsed in the two decades since the Revolution was especially apparent in the first three resolutions, all of which were promptly proposed as legislative measures and brought before the House. The first law streamlined and strengthened the state militia. As the first line of defense against rebellious slaves, the militia, with its local sources of authority and archaic organization, had proved woefully inadequate. As they pondered the revelations of the official correspondence—with its endless pleas for powder, guns, and guidance—committee members quietly thanked the heavens that a providential thunderstorm had done the militia's work for it. The second law called for a similar strengthening of the patrol system. Both laws passed by January 17, 1801.[4]

The third resolution went even further. Monroe's report indicated that several free blacks had been involved with Gabriel. Even had there been no Reuben or Jesse Byrd, the danger that such models of black freedom and prosperity posed in a slave society was all too evident. In 1782 an earlier legislature, in trying to narrow the gap between revolutionary rhetoric and rough reality, had allowed for private manumissions. Now, having seen the consequences of such liberalism, another legislature considered overturning that law. But to return to the days of colonial restrictions on individual gentry action disturbed many representatives. "Among the good laws talked of, is one to repeal the law empowering Slave holders to emancipate them," Thomas Brooke fumed to Congressman Levin Powell. "[H]ere is liberty for you." Evidently many agreed. On January 12 the third resolution, formally entitled the "free black" bill, was postponed until after the session, an action that effectively killed it.[5]

More assured of passage was the sixth resolution, which called for the freedom of what must have appeared to the Assembly to be the only two slaves in southern Henrico who had declined to fight for it. This resolution too fell under the category of control. As "sound policy dictate[d] that rewards should be held out to those who have rendered essential service to our country," the legislature called on the governor "to purchase and set free" Pharoah and Tom. Rewarding bondmen who informed on their fellows had long been a way of dividing the slave community. Pharoah had guessed that he would be generously recompensed for his treachery, and now, without his having had to raise a sword for his freedom, his liberty was at hand. On January 12 the resolution was turned into a bill and passed by the House; the Senate concurred three days later.[6]

The Assembly offered only to purchase the two loyal bondmen, however. It was left up to Monroe and the Sheppard family to arrive at a fair price, and here the unhappy governor soon found himself mired in the typically convoluted world of southern family finance. Monroe discovered that Elizabeth Sheppard, matriarch of the clan, had long resolved to sell Tom, her faithful family retainer, upon her death and divide the proceeds among her heirs. The heirs included her two sons, Philip and Mosby, four married daughters (whose husbands had a say in the affair), and one unmarried daughter. All parties agreed that Tom "shou'd now be sold and emancipated," but Elizabeth would not hear of taking less than five hundred dollars for him. Even that, she insisted, was "far short of a compensation." Her son Philip was "immovably decided to take nothing less" than the same amount for Pharoah. Monroe correctly regarded these demands as robbery and grumbled aloud that slaves who had "acquired no trade" were worth far less than skilled artisans like Gabriel. But the Sheppards proved to be accomplished negotiators. In the end Pharoah and Tom left the Sheppard household as free men, and a disgusted Monroe signed warrants totaling one thousand dollars.[7]

The seventh resolution, on the other hand, qualified as a progressive measure, at least when judged by the standards of the Virginia gentry. Bloodthirsty though planters could be, many shared Jefferson's antipathy for further executions and agreed wholeheartedly with Monroe's decision to transport most of the rebels tried or taken after late September. Selling convicted bondmen out of the state seemed a perfect solution: dangerous rebels would be removed from the region, and if the governor bargained wisely, the financially pressed state could recoup its losses by selling the slaves to a soul trader for the same amount it paid the slaves' owners for the loss of their property. The slaves might die in the harsher climate of the tropical South, but if so, their blood would be on the hands of others. By January 12 the resolution had been transformed into statute. The governor was granted the power to contract for "the sale and purchase of all those slaves who now are or hereafter may be under sentence of death." The buyer had to agree to carry the rebels "out of the United States." Any slave returning to see family or friends would be immediately "apprehended and executed." County courts bore the responsibility of forwarding copies of trial testimony to the governor before hanging convicted rebels, so that the council could decide whether to fall back on the less severe alternative of transportation. This measure in effect terminated the ability of courts to try a bondman one day and execute him the next.[8]

The Assembly must have been pleased with Harrison's handiwork, as the House of Delegates passed the transportation bill later that afternoon. Three days later the Senate agreed. The small band of powerful men huddled in the crowded capitol chambers feared, surely incorrectly, either that the public opposed this supposed leniency or that their slaves would see a retreat from executions as a sign of weakness, for the matter was discussed behind bolted doors and shuttered windows. The clerks of both chambers declined to record the names of those voting, or even the margin by which the bill passed. Passage of the act, like that of all the others, went unmentioned in the Richmond press.[9]

Word of the impending law had not yet reached the bondmen waiting in the penitentiary; but they had long understood that for reasons they could not fathom, they were not going to die. Now it was clear that their destiny was at hand. In late January, Jack Gabriel, John Fells, and Ben (all belonging to Charles Carter) arrived in Richmond "from the Jail of Caroline." John Holmes and a small army of fourteen guards pocketed $116.73 for conveying the "Criminals" to the capital, although an annoyed Monroe deducted $6.00 for a "musquet lost" by an irresponsible guard. Another $64.62 went out to nine new men to stand watch at the penitentiary—one guard for each of the eight condemned slaves awaiting transportation.[10]

This extreme caution was most unnecessary. Escape from the small penitentiary, which stood on the western edge of the city, was all but impossible. Thick "outter walls 20 feet high" surrounded brick dormitories laid out in a semicircle. If Jack Gabriel caught a glimpse of Ditcher as his carriage rumbled through the gate, he probably did not recognize him. Convicts wore garments of "course material, uniform of colour and make." And Ditcher's shaggy locks and queue were gone. Inmates had their "heads and beards close shaven at least once in every week" and donned "caps of various colours." Their meager diet consisted of bread, Indian meal, and "other inferior food," although "course meat" was served twice a week; warden Martin Mims dutifully recorded that this inelegant diet cost the taxpayers "sixteen Cents per head for each day."[11]

The Caroline rebels did not have to endure these indignities long. Even as their carriage rolled south toward Richmond the industrious governor was already discussing the sale with potential buyers. Only eleven days after the transportation law passed the Senate, a deal was struck with well-known traders William Morris and John G. Brown. For $2,917.34—precisely the figure that the various courts of oyer and terminer had demanded paid to various owners—the two men purchased the entire lot of eight black revolutionaries and a ninth slave, Jane Hornett's Billy, who was uninvolved in the plot but guilty of a capital crime. The slavers requested that the coffle be delivered to the town of Staunton, "from which place," Brown insisted, "we think we can take them on in safety." Evidently Ditcher and the others would be driven overland to the Ohio River and then ferried by water to the port of New Orleans. That would satisfy the state's demand that the convicts be removed from the country. The Gulf city, despite the recent secret treaty of San Ildefonso, which called for the transfer of the Louisiana territory to French control, still remained in Spanish hands. Although Brown and Morris paid a steep price, they would have little trouble in making a tidy profit in the newer lands of the Gulf South. The nine slaves would in all likelihood be worked to death in sugarcane fields, but Monroe and his council could flatter themselves as liberal men who had spared the lives of condemned bondmen.[12]

That left only the fourth, and potentially the most significant, resolution. Dated December 31, 1800, the Harrison committee's most ambitious plank called upon the governor to correspond with the president of the United States "on the subject of purchasing land without the limits of this State, whither persons obnoxious to the laws, or dangerous to the peace of society may be removed." The line between this resolution and the one that called for mere transportation was a fine one, and one that at this juncture went unexamined by the Assembly. It may be assumed that transportation was a temporary expedient, meant to be applied only to the remainder of Gabriel's followers. This resolution, on the other hand, was a permanent remedy. Instead of hanging "dangerous" slaves, the state would simply ship them to lands purchased by the federal government. Harrison's recommendation was a peculiar proposal for a state wedded to localism and strict construction, and so it indicated how truly sick of bloodshed the gentry was.[13]

The idea of somehow exporting recalcitrant property from the state was not a new one. Jefferson had broached the issue in his September 20 letter to Monroe. Whether his reference to the "exportation" of slaves in this private missive pertained to transporting rebels to New Orleans or obtaining land as a sort of benign prison colony was unclear. But a legislature weary of hangings clearly gave it the latter interpretation, and if the letter had not been shown around Richmond, certainly Jefferson's views on further hangings and removal had become common knowledge around the city.[14]

The most detailed inspiration for the Harrison committee, however, flowed from the pen of George Tucker. As early as the previous November, Tucker had "committed [to paper] some crude thoughts on the subject"; no doubt this southern liberal was not shy about quietly raising the deportation issue with like-minded men. By early January his descriptively titled *Letter to a Member of the General Assembly of Virginia, on the Subject of the Late Conspiracy of the Slaves with a Proposal for Their Colonization* was ready for publication. No name graced the title page, but around the city the authorship was hardly a well-kept secret. "Considering that it is a mere skeleton of an argument intended for the thinking few," Tucker gushed to his cousin St. George Tucker, "it has been more favorably received than I dared expect." So popular was it that in March 1801 a second edition appeared.[15]

Readers of the pamphlet who were also members of the Assembly could have harbored no doubt that more than a little consultation had taken place between Tucker and the Harrison committee. Like the resolution, Tucker called for cooperation between state and federal governments. The purchase of land, he insisted, was far beyond the meager resources of an agrarian realm, especially one already groaning under the financial burden of having put down a vast uprising. The most striking difference, however, between Tucker's plan and Harrison's brief resolution was that Tucker openly prayed that the end result would be the abolition of slavery in Virginia. Tucker spoke not of a homeland for rebellious slaves but of an asylum for "400,000" bond men and women. A likely place would be Spanish holdings on the "Western side of the Mississip[p]i [River]."[16]

In a sense, Tucker's proposal was less realistic than his cousin's more elaborate 1796 plan, which had not envisioned the colonization of the black labor force. St. George Tucker had correctly assumed that most members of his class would never consent to free their slaves unless they could maintain them as low wage, politically powerless laborers. But the author of the *Letter* hoped that a legislature terrified by the specter of black revolt would boldly adopt his scheme of gradual emancipation and colonization, even if "the public mind [was] not *prepared* for a remedy which shall strike at the root of the evil." He was to be a disappointed spectator. Instead of turning the Harrison resolution into a bill, as it had with the other six, the Assembly merged Tucker's ambitious dream with Jefferson's succinct proposal. The state simply approved the resolution and agreed to ask the federal government for assistance, but only to buy land for bond "criminals," not as a homeland for all black Virginians.[17]

The stubborn refusal of the Assembly to undertake Tucker's grand scheme made it all too clear what it was *not* willing to do. But by merely approving of Harrison's vague, one-sentence resolution, the Assembly had also failed to make clear precisely what it did wish to be done. Thomas Jefferson, now in the executive mansion in Washington City, was one of those confused by the brief statement. On November 24, 1801, he returned the document to Monroe and requested a clarification as to who exactly was covered and where exactly they were to be sent. One month later this request, along with all of the correspondence between the governor and the president, was laid before a "closed" door session of the Virginia Assembly. Monroe repeated Jefferson's plea. "As soon as its sense is declared on those points," he informed the speakers of both houses, "I shall hasten to communicate the same to the President." It was Jefferson's "wish," Monroe hastened to add, "that the communication be considered confidential."[18]

At this juncture, as the Assembly labored to clarify its will, Sancho and his followers intervened. The center of the plot was as yet undetected, but by mid-January of 1802, the Easter revolt was beginning to unravel at the edges. On January 16 the governor informed the legislature of this new danger. "An alarm of a threatened insurrection among the Slaves took place in Nottoway County," Monroe announced to the Assembly in a private letter, "which soon reached Petersburg." This warning, brief though it was, fundamentally altered the course of the discussions on Jefferson's query that were then reaching a final stage. The Assembly had no way of knowing how serious or widespread this new conspiracy was. But for gentlemen who already harbored secret fears of the men and women who worked their lands and prepared their dinners, this unwelcome news made it appear that such revolts threatened to become biennial events. Suddenly the Assembly began to consider a more serious remedy.[19]

Later that afternoon the speaker of the House of Delegates ordered the doors closed. Abraham B. Venable, to whose committee the question had been referred, rose unsteadily and began to read a two-part resolution. Section 1 clarified the meaning of the original House resolution of December 31, 1800. The question of colonization, Venable insisted, was not intended "to embrace offenders for ordinary crimes, to which the laws have been found equal, but only those for conspiracy, insurgency, treason, and rebellion." The legislature only envisioned removing the kind of bold slaves who had "produced the alarm in the fall of 1800." The committee again called upon Monroe to appeal to the federal government to purchase lands on "the continent of Africa, or any of the Spanish or Portuguese settlements in South America."[20]

Venable moved on to Section 2, which had been hastily drawn up only moments before, after the receipt of Monroe's letter. His voice faltered briefly and then rose again as he found his courage. "Resolved, also," he read, "that the Governor be requested to correspond with the President" on obtaining a homeland "to which free negroes or mulattoes, and such negroes or mulattoes *as may be emancipated*, may be sent or choose to remove as a place of asylum." Venable read on, but his voice now had to compete with those of the startled delegates. Although his committee had not openly endorsed Tucker's colonization proposal by name, it had all but adopted his vision of a free and white Virginia. Badly shaken by the news of this second conspiracy, many in the Assembly now went considerably beyond the original resolution. Venable's hope was that many guilt-ridden (and frightened) planters would consider emancipation if the result of their action would not be adding to the allegedly dangerous caste of free blacks in the state. Virginia would remove not only slave rebels but, over time, slavery itself the root cause of these near revolutions.[21]

A good many delegates agreed with Venable's recommendation. The resolution in its entirety passed the House of Delegates later that evening. One week later, on January 23, the Senate concurred. The upper chamber added a brief preamble, which emphasized that Jefferson should choose a spot for settlement in Africa or South America. The Spanish colonies in central or western North America, the uneasy Senate insisted, were too close a location for dangerous bondmen. As with the earlier resolution, neither house recorded a roll call vote. Even the resolution itself went unprinted in the regular journals of the House and Senate.[22]

On February 13 a pleased Monroe forwarded the resolution to President Jefferson. Although the lengthy document was self-evident, Monroe felt the need to ensure that this time there would be no confusion. The first section pertained only to men like Gabriel, not to common bond criminals. Colonization to a foreign land, Monroe added, "was deemed more humane" than selling and transporting "such offenders beyond the limits of the State." The second part, he conceded, was new. His state now also wished to find an "asylum" for already-"free negroes and mulattoes," as well as for those who might be emancipated by their masters with removal specifically in mind. The second part of the resolution would therefore solve two problems. Free blacks, who were believed dangerous models of black liberty, would have a homeland should they wish to emigrate. As the years passed, the colony would allow for the gradual extinction of slavery in Virginia.[23]

The president found the proposal intriguing—and oddly familiar. Over the years the master of Monticello had assuaged his embattled conscience on the question of owning humans by convincing himself that Africans and their offspring were intellectually inferior to Europeans and their descendants. Scientific evidence, he doggedly argued, demonstrated that blacks and whites could never coexist as equals. Therefore, if slavery were swept away, as he consistently prayed it would be, the colonization of blacks to another country would be necessary. Jefferson's antislavery stance was therefore qualified, as it was limited by his pronouncements that he would act only if the time was right. In 1779, for example, Jefferson had drafted a "Bill Concerning Slaves" with George Wythe and Edmund Pendleton. Although the bill was never introduced—the three men judged the time not yet propitious—it called for the emancipation of slave women at age eighteen and slave men upon reaching twenty-one. At that point the former slaves would be forcibly "colonized to such place as the circumstances of the time should render most proper." Now, nearly a quarter of a century later, a similar proposal was at hand, a proposal with the protective endorsement of Virginia's legislature and chief executive.[24]

For one all-too-brief moment, this potent tripartite alliance of president, governor, and legislature proposed to achieve what Gabriel and Sancho had been unable to bring about: the extinction of slavery in the state that was home to 40 percent of the nation's black population. There was ample reason for optimism. Although slavery was sound enough economically, the aristocratic will to continue human bondage had weakened due to Revolutionary ideology, evangelical Christianity, and, most of all, two widespread conspiracies that threatened to take numerous white lives. But this progressive frame of mind was born of fear of the black working class. As a result, emancipation, should it come, would not come on Gabriel's terms. It would be gradual. It would be left to the will of individual planters. And it typically would be contingent upon removal to a strange land.[25]

Because the Assembly's tentative steps toward emancipation dovetailed with Jefferson's insistence on colonization, the president "entirely concur[red]" with the new resolution. But he had his own idea as to a suitable asylum. The "British establishment at Sierra Leone," he informed Monroe, "at once presents itself." Founded in 1791 by Thomas Clarkson and Granville Sharp as a homeland for many of the Chesapeake slaves who had fled with Lord Dunmore and afterward found themselves starving on the streets of London and Halifax, Nova Scotia, the colony was, Jefferson understood, quite "prosperous." Edward Thornton, the British chargé d'affaires in Washington, in response to Jefferson's inquiries, thought there would be "no objection on the part of the company to receive" more black settlers. Thornton warned that since slavery was illegal in Sierra Leone, American blacks would have to be sent as "free persons." Almost without thinking, Jefferson promised the young Englishman that doing so would present no obstacle.[26]

Seeking additional assistance, the president next turned to Rufus King, the American minister in London. King's instructions were to approach the directors of the colony and persuade them to accept slave rebels, including those now being swept up as the Easter conspiracy collapsed. In a peculiar admission that many of these convicts were indeed the black counterparts of General Washington, Jefferson urged King to impress upon the directors that these were "not felons, or common malefactors, but persons guilty of what the safety of society . . . obliges us to treat as a crime." Nor would the slaves who might be freed hereafter, he assured the New Yorker, "be a selection of bad subjects." King, a man of abolitionist sympathies, was enthusiastic about the plan. Equally pleased was his aide Christopher Gore, who praised Jefferson for "the wise, and humane plan, you have so benevolently contemplated, of opening a path for the emancipation of the Blacks."[27]

King and Gore were more than a little dismayed, therefore, to discover that the white directors of the black colony failed to share their enthusiasm. "The idle and disorderly Character of the Negroes who deserted their masters and joined the Br[itish] army in America," King sighed, "has produced an unfavourable opinion of our Slaves." Moreover, Sierra Leone recently had accepted African rebels who attempted to establish a free maroon society in the British sugar colony of Jamaica. The "maroons" had proved troublesome, and the company was obliged to apply to Parliament for financial aid and military assistance "to keep in check the restless, and disturbed spirits already there." The directors were thus little interested in taking on more rebellious slaves. As a result, King did not press for a decision. As he informed the president, he had "reason to believe it might be in the negative." Instead he asked only that the directors consider the matter. Perhaps, King politely urged, they might try it "as an Experiment, & upon a small scale."[28]

The first word of these unpromising developments reached Governor Monroe just as the Virginia General Assembly prepared to convene on December 6, 1802. Jefferson was not entirely without hope of a definitive answer by way of King "before the rising of the legislature." But the delegates were in no mood to wait. On December 9, Monroe reluctantly turned over to them his correspondence with the president. For the moment, he informed the Assembly, "the attention of the President is directed at the Sierra Leone establishment." As the negotiations were yet "in train," Monroe promised an update should a final decision be forthcoming.[29]

The legislature, having come this far, was displeased with the delay. But for the four "condemn'd Slaves" huddled in damp cells in the penitentiary, the stalled negotiations had rather more tragic implications. Since there was as yet no place of asylum for convicted rebels, the state would have to fall back on the harsher penalty of transportation. Although the law of January 15, 1801, had been meant only as a temporary expedient for Gabriel's followers, it remained on the books. And so Monroe, faced with the limited options of execution or transportation, again found himself in the distasteful business of trafficking in souls.[30]

The first trader to step forward was George Goosley. Although tactful enough to acknowledge that the sale was not a "matter of traffic" but an alternative to hanging, Goosley had not made his fortune by acting the kindhearted tradesman. He offered only "three hundred dollars" for each of the black convicts, well below what the county courts had adjudged their worth. Certainly he anticipated an ample profit in exchange for his public service. After conveying the bondmen "*by water*, to Norfolk & from thence *by Sea*" to the South American country of "Surinam, or the [city of] Havanna," Goosley expected to obtain "good prices" for his cargo.[31]

Chagrined at losing money on the transaction, Monroe had no choice but to accept. But the sale promptly foundered. Goosley discovered that he could find no market for his cargo. As a result of the rising tide of black revolution in the Atlantic basin, Madrid suddenly shut its Caribbean ports to "slaves from any other quarter than Africa." Rebellious black Americans who had been infected with the disease of liberty were quite unwanted. And Spain's former colony of Louisiana no longer presented a solution. Since its "cession to France," Monroe sighed, the further importation of slaves "has been prohibited." Nor were the British sugar islands open to Goosley's human freight. The English consul in Norfolk had caught wind of the sale. "[F]earing that [the slaves] might promote insurrection in the countries where sent," the consul posted hasty warnings to British authorities on Jamaica and Grenada. No island would allow the cargo to land. At length the miserly trader conceded defeat and informed Monroe he would "be gladly released from the engagement."[32]

Despite of these seemingly insurmountable troubles, a second trader, William Fulcher, proved willing to try his hand. On July 3, 1802, Fulcher offered to purchase the slaves in the penitentiary for the extremely low price of $266.40 each, "payable in one year from the time I receive them." The state would lose a considerable amount of cash in the transaction, but since Fulcher agreed to buy all seventeen slaves then being held—thirteen men convicted of various capital crimes, as well as the four alleged rebels—Monroe advised his council to accept. Fulcher sailed downriver to Norfolk to obtain the latest news on conditions in the Caribbean. In the meantime, the black convicts remained in the penitentiary, where warden Martin Mims put them to work as manual laborers. This turn of events dismayed Monroe, who feared the slaves might use the opportunity to "brake" out. "You may safely employ them in any business in the Cells," he warned Mims, "but when you take them out you do it at your hazard."[33]

Mims was the least of the governor's concerns. Once more problems arose. None of the Caribbean islands would open their ports to the Virginia slaves, who were "suspected of being the worst kind." To further complicate matters, three French warships cruised the Gulf waters in an attempt to sell "a number of renegade negroes." Monroe feared that the frustrated captains might eventually try to "dispose of them along the Southern coast in a clandestine manner," which would mean he would have more, not fewer, unwanted slaves to sell abroad. By early September, Fulcher had "yet failed to comply" with the agreement. No other traders were foolish enough to step forward, and so Monroe was forced to await the trader's return.[34]

Fulcher had not been idle in Norfolk, and he caught wind of one small possibility. On October 17, the trader returned to Richmond and announced that he was ready to accept delivery of his seventeen pieces of property. Among them were the simpleminded Ned, Glasgow and Tom, and Arthur Farrar; the last three surely were innocent, and probably Monroe knew it. Fulcher and his small but heavily armed band chained the men together into a coffle. Most likely they were marched south across the Carolinas and Georgia to the mouth of St. Mary's River in Spanish Florida. There they were resold to Jack Cooper, a trader who routinely dealt with Spanish planters. From there the slaves disappeared from the sight of history.[35]

The problems encountered by the governor and his slave-trading partners had a very significant consequence. They brought to Monroe's attention a previously unnoticed contradiction between the Virginia resolution for transportation and that which called upon the federal government to buy land as an asylum for future rebels. On June 11, 1802, Monroe explained the problem to Jefferson. In thinking of Africa as a refuge, both the legislature and the president unconsciously assumed that the rebels "should be free when landed there, as it is not known that there exists any market on that coast for the purchase of slaves from other countries." But Monroe now noticed a flaw that had escaped the attention of the Harrison committee. If black insurgents were freed upon reaching Sierra Leone, "it wou'd put culprits in a better condition" than that in which they had been. The hard fact was that the fourth resolution, which had never been codified into law, was in "violation" of the seventh resolution, which had been turned into the "transportation" act of January 15, 1801.[36]

Actually, transportation had been but a temporary expedient until a colony could be established. Monroe was resorting to legal subterfuge. The renewed resolution of January 23, 1802, which included slaves who might be freed in the future by their owner, made it clear that the legislature did not intend to purchase a penal colony. But Monroe was right enough on one score. Neither did the Assembly mean to reward slaves for sharpening scythes by freeing them in the land of their ancestors. A contradiction existed, and the governor stumbled upon it. Monroe privately hinted to the president that he would be wiser to "seek an establishment" in the "Portuguese, Dutch or Spanish settlements in America." The governor in effect was nullifying Venable's revised resolution and returning to the original idea of locating them in some sort of benign prison colony—a place where free blacks would not care to settle.[37]

In the meantime, Rufus King, blissfully unaware of these private missives between governor and president, continued to press English abolitionists to open Sierra Leone to black Virginians. He turned first to William Wilberforce, the preeminent abolitionist of his day and a member of the colony's thirteen-man board of directors. King insisted that the potential colonists would benefit the troubled settlement. Those slaves who might be freed, he promised, would "include our most meritorious Slaves," and the rebels would "not be the idle and the vicious, as these would not possess sufficient influence over their associates to become Leaders in Schemes of Insurrection." King also lobbied Henry Thornton, an evangelical member of Parliament and the largest stockholder in the colony. Opening the colony's doors to "the State of Virginia" would prepare the way for private manumissions leading to eventual "emancipa[tion]." Such a plan, King insisted, should "readily receive your approbation."[38]

Receive Thornton's approval, however, King did not. At that very moment Thornton was preparing to "Transfer the Chief authority of the Colony of Sierra Leone to the [British] Government." King was given to understand that in September 1800 and again in April 1802—almost at the same moments as the two Virginia uprisings—black settlers in the colony had risen up against oppressive white colonial control. The leaders of this revolution were the Chesapeake slaves who had fled with Lord Dunmore and arrived in West Africa by way of Nova Scotia. Such ingratitude astonished the board of directors, who, after all, had saved these "ungovernable" freemen from starvation and now thought it only fair that white investors be allowed to make a tidy profit off their labor. The "expense and trouble of maintaining the settlement [was] so great," King reported to Jefferson on May 12, 1803, "that the Company have determined to abandon their plan." Just days later, Parliament agreed to accept control of the colony as of January 1, 1808. Ironically, the political demands of these former Virginia slaves turned colonists would have doomed the hopes of present Virginia bondpersons—had Monroe not already scuttled the plan.[39]

Thornton urged King to discuss the situation with the British government. But the matter was destined to go no further. The New York Federalist had tired of his London post after eight years, and with the renewal of war between France and Britain, Jefferson desired to have a more trusted friend in that crucial position. He appointed none other than James Monroe to the post; resigning his present position, the former governor arrived in England in the summer of 1803. Negotiations would not continue over Sierra Leone—or anyplace else, for that matter. Jefferson always pronounced himself willing to terminate slavery if the conditions were right, but evidently they no longer were. Had the Virginia Assembly sought only to colonize free blacks, the president might have continued to search for an asylum. But he now saw matters as Monroe did. He had no wish to incite his own slaves to revolt by holding out the promise of freedom elsewhere should they fail. The resolution as it now stood was an invitation to revolution.

Neither Jefferson nor Monroe ever sought to explain this delicate point of logic to the legislature. The two men simply ceased their search for a colony. Unaware of this, the Assembly continued to press the matter. Almost a year later, on February 3, 1804, the House of Delegates churlishly resolved "that the governor be requested to continue a correspondence with the President of the United States upon the Subject."[40]

When no reply was forthcoming, the Assembly tried again. On December 3, 1804, the first day of the session, the House resorted to both a new tactic and tougher words. This fourth resolution on the subject "instructed" their representatives in Congress "to exert their best efforts for the purpose of obtaining from the General Government a competent portion of territory" in the now American-owned "country of Louisiana." Even had the president not already abandoned the plan, these new instructions would have served only to strengthen his resolve against it. Jefferson would not consider the West; that was to be the province of his white yeomen constituents.[41]

Later in the month, Jefferson responded to the persistent queries of the new governor, John Page. The president insisted that he was quietly continuing his search for a location. Sierra Leone was still in a state of flux but might prove to be a possibility in the distant future. "An attack during the war," he observed, "has done the settlement considerable injury." Equally hopeless was Saint Domingue. The embattled island was "too unsettled in the conditions of its existence to be looked to as yet for any permanent arrangements." This comment was more than a little disingenuous on the president's part. Much of Saint Domingue's "unsettled" condition was due to the actions of the president, who had done much to isolate the island economically. Louisiana went unmentioned.[42]

In early 1805, the Assembly made one final attempt to resolve the issue. Both houses renewed their previous four resolutions and begged that any further correspondence between *any* president and *any* governor be forwarded to them. The dismayed men in the two chambers could not fathom why their small efforts, so laboriously made, had been rebuffed by a Virginia president who previously had openly advocated colonization. This last motion was largely symbolic; the Assembly would have been surprised to receive a response. There would be no more resolutions.[43]

Typically, the president continued to insist that a policy of general abolition remained in the state's future. "[T]here are many virtuous men who would make any sacrifice to effect it," he confided to William Burwell, his private secretary. Certainly the drive for reform "will be goaded from time to time by the insurrectionary spirit of the slaves." But for Jefferson the time had not yet arrived. "I have long since given up the expectation of any early provision for the extinguishment of slavery among us," he sighed. Perhaps Burwell knew the story, for Jefferson declined to add that he played a leading role in seeing to it that slavery would not vanish from Virginia in the foreseeable future. Perhaps instead he declined to mention it because he did not blame himself. Self-recrimination was never the president's strongest character trait.[44]

And so it happened that the Virginia slavery debates of 1801–05, maundering and confused though they were, came to an end. These faltering discussions—and especially Abraham Venable's critical second resolution of January 23, 1802—have not been accorded the attention given to the celebrated Virginia slavery debates of 1831–32, which followed Nat Turner's unsuccessful struggle to bring about the day of jubilee. But in their haste to analyze the 1831 debates in search of antislavery tendencies, scholars have failed to grasp the larger point. By 1831, it was too late for an elite-led scheme of emancipation.[45] By that time a thriving interstate trade with the fresh lands of the lower South carried thousands of young slaves out of the state each year. In Gabriel's day planters with surplus laborers often allowed their servants to buy themselves at a low price or freed them outright. But with the rise of the cotton kingdom, greedy masters found it far more profitable to sell the young men and women they had little use for to the traders who approached their gates with offers of hard cash. If ever Virginia was going to move against slavery, it was while influential attorneys like the Tuckers were alive, while enough planters felt guilty about their labor system, and while leading politicians yet persisted in characterizing slavery as an evil, not a positive thing in itself. Jefferson spent his life insisting that he would act against slavery only when the conditions were auspicious. In 1802 they were, and he spurned the opportunity.[46]

As for the five resolutions, there was a curious revival of sorts. In early 1816, a young member of the House of Delegates, Charles Fenton Mercer, fell into a late-night political discussion with two of his colleagues. Suddenly Federalist Philip Doddridge, waxing voluble in the grip of alcohol, blurted out that Jefferson was "a consummate hypocrite." Dabney Minor, a Republican, who was also "much intoxicated," demanded to know what evidence Doddridge had for such a claim. The former replied that Jefferson had recommended the colonization of free blacks in his famous *Notes*, but when asked to implement such a policy five times by the Virginia legislature, he had "coldly evaded their application." In saying this, Doddridge was breaking an oath not to "divulge the secret proceedings of the Senate, of which he had been a member." Mercer, however, was under no such oath. Intrigued with the idea of removing free blacks, who he believed were "every day polluting and corrupting public morals" in his state, Mercer used the resolutions to found the American Colonization Society the following December, an organization that he ran until 1833. While some of its members prayed that the colony of Liberia would accomplish what the Assembly of 1802 had hoped—motivate slaveholders to emancipate their slaves and colonize them outside the United States—Mercer was always careful to say that his society had "nothing, whatever, to do with domestic slavery." Having been taken over by the Colonization Society, Venable's resolutions lost their abolitionist flavor.[47]

If the singular drama of two widespread conspiracies in as many years had not shaken white Virginians from their complacency, nothing ever would. Having failed in its small efforts to gradually bring the peculiar institution to an end, the Virginia Assembly next prepared to scurry in the opposite direction and reimpose the restraints that had lapsed since the Revolution. "[W]e have the wolf by the ear," Jefferson lamented toward the end of his long life, "and we can neither hold him, nor safely let him go." That was tragically incorrect. As the editor of the *Richmond Virginian* later conceded, the legislature of 1802 had "aim[ed] at a general and unconditional emancipation." They had tried to free the beast. Now they would do all they could to hold it.[48]

11

The Power in That Name

The steps the Assembly had taken were small enough. The chambers, halls, and cloakrooms had not heard eloquent denunciations of human bondage. The legislature had not openly debated a specific plan for gradual emancipation. But clearly the legislature, terrified by two massive conspiracies launched by charismatic rebel leaders, had hoped that its program of colonization would precipitate numerous private manumissions and provide a homeland for already-free blacks who had grown weary of endless insults and constant demands for deference. But the plan had come to nothing. Now the lawmakers would do all they could to hold the wolf by the ears and make their peculiar system safe and permanent.

For all their pretensions as bookish and philosophical men, members of the Virginia planter class could be hardheaded and pragmatic enough when they had to be. The legislators of 1802 realized they had only two choices. "The question now is a plain one," observed one Virginian, rather bluntly. "Shall we abolish slavery, or shall we continue it? There is no middle course to steer." If slavery was to endure, the relative freedom that slaves had enjoyed during the decades after the Revolution would have to end. "If we continue it," the anonymous writer insisted, "we must restrict it. We must re-enact all those rigorous laws which experience has proved necessary to keep it within bounds. In a word, if we will keep a ferocious monster in our country, we must keep him in chains."[1]

More than a few white Americans, north and south, prayed that the conspiracies would shake the Virginians out of their complacency. But these were individuals unaware of what had transpired behind closed doors in the capitol building. Samuel White of Delaware, speaking on the floor of Congress, called upon the national government to strike at the "horrid evil of slavery." Only the "interposition [of] an unusual thunderstorm," he warned, "prevented the Slaves, only two years since, from destroying Richmond." The *New England Palladium*, gloating over Jefferson's brush with the "spirit of resistance" he routinely advocated for northern states, even waxed poetic:

Remember ere too late,
The tale of St. Domingo's fate.
Tho Gabriel dies, a host remain
Oppress'd with slavery's galling chain.
And soon or late the hour will come
Mark'd with Virginia's dreadful doom.[2]

For those privy to the secrets of the Virginia Assembly and the diplomatic correspondence with William Wilberforce, it was all too clear that reform had failed. For a planter class that could not envision abandoning colonization and undertaking more dramatic action, repression alone remained. "It is a pity," Charles Pettigrew grumbled in response to the Easter plot, but "slavery & Tyranny must go together." And so in the years following 1802, the General Assembly adopted Pettigrew's advice and methodically set out to restore tyranny and make plots like those led by Gabriel and Sancho all but impossible.[3]

The first laws were constructed with the conspiracies of 1800 and 1802 specifically in mind. The most obvious danger was the woefully unprepared state of the city's defenses; none doubted that Gabriel's army could have marched largely unmolested into the heart of the city had the clouds not opened. In late 1802, Monroe established the Public Guard of Richmond, a nighttime police force designed to protect the public buildings and militia arsenals. The guard also bore the responsibility of rounding up all bondpersons after the town bell clanged at 9:00 P.M. Officers herded tardy slaves into pens near the market square, where, unless their owners promptly rescued them, they were stripped and beaten with "as many stripes" as the guard officer "might see proper to inflict." At the dawn of the nineteenth century, few American cities employed police forces. They were especially rare in the impoverished South. But thanks to Gabriel, Richmond had one of the most efficient—if also one of the most brutal—forces in the country.[4]

The need to bolster urban defenses was only one of the lessons of 1800. A second was the need to eliminate the ability of Richmond bondmen to communicate with slaves in other river or port towns. Jacob, the black skipper, was dead—either by his own hand or by that of his captors—but hundreds of other black Virginians plied the Chesapeake's complex network of rivers and bays. In that same year of 1802, the Assembly cracked down on black sailors by forbidding any "negro or mulatto," even if free, to obtain a pilot's license. Slaves found at the helm of a vessel would receive thirty-nine lashes. Those already possessing a license were allowed to continue their profession. But black pilots were now a closed caste, and more than a few discovered that nervous town merchants suddenly preferred to deal with white skippers. As if that were not enough, subsequent legislation held that any "waterman of colour" found "strolling from his boat above the banks of the river" was to be seized and whipped. To put an end to the underground economy, black boatmen found with goods not formally listed on their manifests would incur heavy fines.[5]

Two years later, the Assembly acted again. This time the gentry dealt a blow to the slaves' extralegal right to gather in the evenings or on Sundays after their labor was finished. Since these traditional revels in the summer of 1800 had all too often provided cover for the recruitment of rebels, the legislature wanted them stopped. The "common practice [for] slaves to assemble in considerable numbers at meeting houses and places of religious worship, in the night," read the statute, "may be productive of considerable evil." Justices of the peace were empowered to invade these "unlawful assemblages" and "inflict corporal punishment on the offender[s]." The act was specifically designed to control the slave-heavy eastern counties; the provisions of this law did not extend to any county west of the Blue Ridge.[6]

The Assembly also saw to it that the state would produce no more literate slaves who possessed the ability to scrawl simple letters and peruse newspapers—and thus understand the world beyond their masters' gateposts. In 1805, overseers of the poor who bound out "black or mulatto orphan[s]" were to caution these new guardians against teaching their young charges "reading, writing, or arithmetic." The few slaves who could read, however, probably learned their lessons at the knee of a parent, a local freeman, or even, as appears to be the case with Gabriel, from a plantation mistress. The state could not guard against the last, aside from publicly frowning on the practice, but it could deal with free black tutors. In 1811 an angry Richmond mob destroyed a school for freemen and slaves run by several free blacks. Eight years later, the legislature even passed a law denying readmission to the state to free blacks who traveled north in search of an education. In one of history's ironies, several days later the same set of men proudly chartered the University of Virginia.[7]

As the gentry went down the list of conditions that had allowed the two slave plots to develop, they noticed that the ability of masters to hire out their surplus slaves had not been addressed. Now it was. In early 1808 the practice was formally outlawed. (Since 1792 it had been illegal for slaves to hire their own time.) Because so many white artisans had fled to northern cities, merchants and master craftsmen long on orders and short on laborers often had little choice but to ignore the law. But the practice of hiring out was never again as widespread as it had been in the 1790s. Essentially, it was driven underground. The crowds of slaves for hire disappeared from the steps of the Henrico Courthouse, and both whites and blacks who continued the practice had to be discreet; white offenders faced stiff fines, blacks were subject to savage beatings.[8]

Circumscribing the economic opportunities of skilled slaves was not enough for some nervous whites. "Slaves ought to be solely employed in agricultural or other occupations of plain labour," editorialized the *Richmond Virginian*. Skilled bondmen had "the means, without much exertion [of] forming plots and conspiracies." The editor realized that the elimination of an entire class of slaves might damage the economy of the state and infringe on the economic needs of the master class, but there was little choice. "Peace, quiet industry on one hand—robbery, scouring, hanging, alarms and insurrections on the other." The proposal came to nothing. Skilled slaves were too crucial to the state's economic well-being. But the editorial was an accurate barometer of how far most whites would go in controlling their laboring class.[9]

Pacification—or tyranny, to borrow Pettigrew's apt phrase— was well established in the cradle of liberty by 1806. All of the statutes and regulations that an embarrassed gentry had allowed to lapse since the year of Gabriel's birth had been restored, link by link. But in 1806 the Assembly abandoned the piecemeal approach and went after a bigger danger: the large number of free blacks in the commonwealth. Even in the absence of a Jesse or Reuben Byrd, the planters regarded men like them as subversive. Mobile and moderately prosperous, free blacks provided a dangerous model of liberty to their enslaved cousins and nephews and husbands. Even when free blacks turned their backs on revolutionary talk, the very presence of the caste presented problems to men who wished to thwart the potential for slave insurrection. As a result, "any slave hereafter emancipated" had twelve months to leave the state. All newly freed bondpersons who remained after that time would "forfeit" their "right" to freedom and would "be apprehended and sold" back into bondage. Proceeds from these sales would fall to "the [white] poor of such county."[10]

The law of 1806 did not go so far as to overturn the manumission act of 1782, which allowed masters unencumbered by debt to free their slaves without the permission of the governor. But it did the act considerable injury. Leaving the state upon gaining freedom often meant leaving behind relations still in bondage. It meant leaving the land of their fathers for a strange and often unfriendly place; few northern states willingly accepted impoverished black emigrants. The law had the effect, therefore, of turning free blacks into a closed class. Those who were already free scrambled, as indeed they had ever since the chaos of 1800, to register with their respective towns as "free Negroes & Mulattoes." And those who yearned to become free now viewed any change in their status as a mixed blessing. Slaves who bought their freedom or heard it pronounced in an aged master's will had either to petition the legislature for an exemption or to stay and risk reenslavement—or to begin the long journey north toward the uncharitable arms of Maryland or Pennsylvania.[11]

Virginia society took its tone from the Assembly. And so it was predictable that the eastern elite fell into line with the intent of this extensive legislation, which, unlike the colonization resolutions, was not debated behind shuttered windows. The ruling class was particularly interested in fracturing the interracial urban working class. Whenever the small planter clique found itself in danger of losing its hegemony, it invariably appealed to racism in hopes of disrupting any potentially threatening labor movement. Norfolk mayor John Cowper, for one, railed against back-alley tavern keepers who not only sold rum to blacks but even invited them to imbibe in their own homes. Such practices, Cowper cautioned, seduced slaves away "from the service of [their] owners, and [taught] them bad habits."[12]

Of even greater concern than the dockside gambols were slave artisans who entered into serious relationships with white servant women. From the planters' perspective, miscegenation was something better left to them, as their illicit relationships with slave women produced only light-skinned slaves, not free mulattoes who threatened the social order. In 1803, "Many old Citizens" of Norfolk petitioned the legislature to prohibit white women from taking "Black Husband[s]." (Interracial marriages had long been illegal; the Norfolk residents used the term "husbands" in reference to stable, long-term relationships.) The penalty for love, these charitable citizens urged, should be no less than thirty-nine lashes for each partner, well laid on. These unions, the petitioners warned, were more "injurious than gambling" dens.[13]

Nor were black churches and black preachers allowed to retain their autonomy. Sunday patrols now demanded that slaves leaving their master's residence for services carry a written pass, yet fewer and fewer masters demonstrated any inclination to provide them. Those few bondpersons who could obtain a "ticket" often arrived to find a staid service that they hardly recognized; white Baptists and even Methodists increasingly turned away from the lively revivals toward more decorous services. Faced with growing white hostility and a dwindling number of slave congregants, many mixed churches simply collapsed. Typical was the case of the Davenport Baptist Church of Petersburg. Founded in 1788 by Israel Decoudry, a free black of Caribbean birth, the church folded in 1802 after the Easter plot turned city fathers against such sources of black empowerment. Later that same year Jacob Bishop, who had tried to create a Norfolk church openly based on African traditions, closed his doors in the face of white animosity and fled to Baltimore.[14]

In this atmosphere of fear and repression, elite liberalism could not long survive. When the eighth convention of American abolition societies met in Philadelphia in the summer of 1803, not a single delegate represented Virginia. The Virginia contingent had never been large in previous years, but a few wealthy denizens had always ridden north to demonstrate their support for an end to human bondage. Now even those aristocrats who dared to express such sentiments in the privacy of their own parlors over a pipe and a bowl of Madeira found themselves ostracized by old acquaintances. As far as the men who knew the secrets of the resolutions were concerned, the matter had been debated. That was an end to it. There was no room for further discussion.[15]

Individual planters, of course, might continue to harbor private reservations about their system. But as the decade wore on, public expressions of guilt over owning humans, so common in the quarter century since the Revolution, disappeared with astonishing speed. Many slaveholders had never expressed any doubts about the correctness of their way of life. But many more had wrestled with their consciences as they placed the injustice of slavery on the scale beside their inability to maintain their agrarian empires without unpaid laborers. For these men, the sound of legal repression emanating from the capitol was like manna from heaven. In a sense they now were emancipated from their own guilt. With the tacit backing of the legislature, the gentry could shove aside their misgivings and start advancing alternate notions of morality and right. Their new pronouncements on their duty to their childlike black wards were yet laced with occasional hints of guilt, but the Virginia ruling class had begun the long march down the road toward the notion that slavery was a positive good in itself.[16]

Worse was to follow. The sentiments then being expressed in the Virginia statehouse were also being heard in the nation's capital, for the repression being implemented in the Old Dominion spilled over its borders; it was carried into Washington in the psychological luggage of Thomas Jefferson. The chief executive, however, was not interested in petty piecemeal legislation designed to inhibit the growth of conspiracies. Rather, the president wished to eliminate the foremost model of black autonomy in the New World. In 1787, Jefferson had pronounced "a little rebellion now and then [to be] a good thing." Since then he had witnessed the role that a successful slave revolution in Saint Domingue had played in inspiring an unsuccessful slave revolution in his home state. As James Monroe insisted, the "occurrences in St. Domingo for some years past . . . doubtless did excite some sensation among our Slaves." Now the president would do anything necessary to isolate or defeat that model of freedom.[17]

Isolating Saint Domingue would not be easily accomplished. The Caribbean sugar island played a crucial role in the American economy. Even before the slave uprising of 1791, Saint Domingue ranked second only to Great Britain on America's list of trading partners; despite its French ownership, the colony imported more goods from the United States than any other nation. That thriving commerce continued to blossom during the Adams years, as the Federalist administration quietly labored to seduce General-in-Chief Louverture away from his former Parisian masters. By the time Jefferson took his oath of office in March 1801, as many as thirty-two vessels could be counted on any given day at the docks of Le Cap François alone.[18]

All of this bustling activity meant contact with American ports, many of them in southern states. Every barrel and crate imported to American shores, in the president's eyes, was contaminated with the disease of black liberty. "[B]lack crews, & supercargoes, & missionaries" from the island, he insisted, proved a very real danger to Virginia. If these "cannibals" could be "introduced among us under any veil whatever, we have to fear it." Within days of taking office, Jefferson recalled Edward Stevens, Adams's envoy to the island. The able Stevens had performed his duties too well and had become a valued, though unofficial, adviser to Toussaint. As his replacement, the Sage of Monticello chose Tobias Lear, a pedestrian jack-of-all-trades who had once served George Washington by slyly returning several slaves to Mount Vernon just before they came under the provisions of the Pennsylvania emancipation act of 1783.[19]

As it happened, Jefferson's determination to quarantine the island neatly dovetailed—or so he thought—with a second objective of his administration: the acquisition of Louisiana. Upon taking office, the president began to hear whispers of the secret treaty of San Ildefonso of 1800, which transferred New Orleans and the trans-Mississippi West from Spanish to French control. At the same time, it became clear that Napoleon was interested in reasserting French control over Saint Domingue. Toussaint had guessed right. Despite the abolition of slavery by the Convention in 1794 and the titles heaped upon him by the Directory, his freedom and that of the Dominguan people might last only so long as did the war in Europe. Now with peace between France and Britain on the horizon, Toussaint could expect war with the *premier consul*. To Jefferson, it appeared that the best way to obtain Louisiana would be to conciliate Bonaparte by assisting him in bringing down Toussaint, which, after all, would serve his purposes as well. As a result, in July 1801, Jefferson calmly informed Louis Andre Pichon, the French chargé d'affaires in Washington, that "nothing would be more simple than to furnish your army and your fleet with everything and to starve out Toussaint."[20]

News of Jefferson's support for a move against Toussaint flew across the water. Charles Maurice de Talleyrand, continuing in the foreign office, counseled Bonaparte that American support was all he needed to reenslave Saint Domingue. "France ought to expect from the amity of the United States," he observed, "that they interdict very private adventure [that] may be destined to the ports of St. Domingo, occupied by the rebels." In early 1802 an expeditionary force of twenty-five thousand men sailed west. Led by Charles Victor Leclerc, Napoleon's brother-in-law and one of his ablest generals, the army was able to seize Toussaint through treachery. Toussaint died the following year in a French dungeon, but his soldiers, led by his lieutenants Jean Jacques Dessalines and Henri Christophe, successfully fought on. Thousands of Frenchmen died at the hands of the Dominguan army; thousands more, including Leclerc himself, succumbed to yellow fever. In November 1804 the battered remnants of the French army fled the island, never to return. Eleven months earlier, on January 1, 1804, Dessalines had proclaimed himself ruler of the independent black republic, which the victorious Dominguans renamed Haiti, meaning a "higher place."[21]

In point of fact, Toussaint's valorous army saved Louisiana for the United States. There was a crucial connection in Bonaparte's diplomacy that Jefferson utterly failed to perceive. The *premier consul* desired the Mississippi valley as a breadbasket to feed the reenslaved Dominguans, all of whom would be employed in producing sugar, not grains. Far from obtaining Louisiana by conciliating Bonaparte, Jefferson's tragic willingness to help "starve out Toussaint" nearly cost the new president his western prize. Had Leclerc succeeded in his mission, Bonaparte would have refused to sell the region. Only when his dream of a reenslaved island lay in ashes did the French dictator discover he no longer needed Louisiana. Jefferson's greatest achievement came not because of adroit diplomacy or skillful negotiation but because of the courage of half a million black rebels who refused to be reenslaved.[22]

If Jefferson ever grasped the role that men he derided as "canibals" played in his greatest achievement, it was an irony he did not savor. Indeed, in the mind of the president, an independent Haiti led by Dessalines was even more dangerous than a black colony governed by Toussaint. The latter had merely overthrown a small number of white and mulatto planters; the former had crushed one of the most formidable generals in

Europe. If anything, Haiti now stood as an even greater monument to black resiliency. In late 1804 and again in his message to Congress in late 1805, Jefferson, himself a former revolutionary well versed in the ways of usurping power from the British Crown, called for an end to American trade with "the usurped government of that unfortunate island."[23]

The first to rise to the bait was Senator George Logan of Pennsylvania. Even those Republicans who welcomed an end to intercourse with Haiti thought it odd that Logan should be the one to call for it. As staunchly antislavery as he was timid in his personal demeanor, Logan had recently angered his southern colleagues by presenting Quaker petitions praying for an end to the international trade in humans. But Logan was also a pacifist. Despite the failure of the Leclerc expedition, Bonaparte haughtily continued to insist that Haiti still belonged to France. American trade with the island thus presented a potential trouble spot that threatened to engulf the United States in the woes of Europe, which had again exploded into war in May of 1803. Logan thought it wise policy to inform France that trade between American shores and Haiti was outlawed, so that "if the merchants would carry it on they must do it at their peril." With this idea in mind, Logan rose unsteadily to his feet on December 20, 1805, and "asked leave to bring in a bill to suspend the commercial intercourse between the United States and the French island of St. Domingo [sic]."[24]

On the other side of the capitol building, the Logan bill found a ready advocate in Virginia congressman John W. Eppes, the son-in-law of the president. The fiery young man had once sworn he would "pledge the Treasury of the United States, that the Negro government should be destroyed," and now he saw his chance to make good on that promise. Speaking from the floor, Eppes denied that Haiti had proved its independence; the fact that France was of the opposite opinion was enough for him. "We are called on by a nation friendly to us to put a stop to this infamous traffic," he shouted. What was more, trade with the black republic daily threatened to "bring immediate and horrible destruction on the fairest portion of America."[25]

Since the measure carried the endorsement of the administration, there was little doubt as to the outcome. With scant debate, the Senate passed the Logan bill on February 20, 1806, by a vote of 21 to 8. Andrew Moore of Virginia sided with the majority; William Branch Giles, Virginia's other senator, was then absent from Washington. Among the minority could be found the two Federalist senators from Massachusetts, John Quincy Adams, the son of the former president, and Timothy Pickering, who, when secretary of state, had quietly urged Toussaint to declare independence in the late 1790s.[26]

Five days later, the bill came before the House a final time. Here too the advocates of continuing commerce with the victorious rebels were hopelessly outnumbered. While many Federalists, especially those north of the Chesapeake, were hostile to any measure that stood in the way of American shipping, their party had taken a brutal beating in the election of 1804, and few southern congressmen wished to go on record as being friendly to armed slaves. The clerk recorded a lopsided tally of 93 to 26. Of the seventeen-member Virginia delegation, fourteen men, including Eppes, Thomas Newton, and Peterson Goodwyn (the last two were veterans at putting down slave conspiracies), voted with the majority. The remaining three—John Randolph, John Clopton, and Joseph Lewis, the popular Federalist from Loudoun County—found it expedient to be away from the floor when their names were called.[27]

On Friday, February 28, a much-relieved Jefferson affixed his signature to the bill. The ban on trade lasted only one year, but in the early spring of 1807 Congress renewed the law for a second year. Before that period ended, the Embargo Act of 1807, passed in retaliation for the British seizure of four sailors (two of whom were black) from the American frigate *Chesapeake*, ended all American trade with Haiti, as well as with the rest of the globe. Trade with Haiti was not legal again until President James Madison signed Macon's Bill No. 2 into law on May 1, 1810. By that time, however, Haiti's economy had deteriorated too much to ever again play a significant role in American shipping. Southerners, having assisted the French in shattering the Haitian economy, crowed that the island's disastrous financial condition provided a valuable lesson against black self-government. Not until June 5, 1862, under the relentless prodding of Abraham Lincoln and Massachusetts senator Charles Sumner, did Congress resume normal diplomatic relations with the republic of Haiti.[28]

White Virginians, at least the genteel sort, were relieved that a wall of silence had been built around Haiti. But the Logan bill could do little to restore nerves forever jangled by Gabriel's followers. In the end, the true legacy of the conspiracies was not the new and tighter shackles forged by the Virginia Assembly, nor even Thomas Jefferson's fatal policies toward Haiti. Instead, the legacy that counted the most was the impact that the near revolts had on the people who lived through them, both the men who put them down and the insurgents who helped to plan them and somehow squirmed free of the hangman's noose.

For the gentry, the sight of hundreds of terror-stricken militiamen, every one of them pale as death, guarding the streets of Richmond, was one never to be forgotten. Even the Tucker cousins, staunch progressives when measured against their white brethren, had told themselves that their smiling slaves were harmless children. Now they knew otherwise. Strong, smart, ambitious, and self-reliant, Gabriel left as permanent a scar on the southern psyche as if he had put it there with his scythe sword. One can pardon Benjamin Howard for taking his pistol with him when he went "a courting" in the fall of 1800. But the fear Howard felt as he rode down lonely forest paths would not fade for decades, if it ever did. "I speak from facts when I say that the night bell never tolls for fire in Richmond," John Randolph remarked in later years, "that the mother does not hug the infant more closely to her bosom."[29]

The fear of sudden death at the hands of vengeful slaves, in a somewhat different fashion, haunted not only the planter class for years after, but also those bondmen who had assisted in bringing the rebels to the bar of white justice. One of these was Ben Woolfolk. No minor conspirator, the young recruiter had turned against his fellows in exchange for pardon. By the time the trials ground to a halt in December 1800, Woolfolk had implicated or testified against no fewer than sixteen rebels. On January 15, 1801, Woolfolk strolled out of jail after spending four months behind bars. For his "services" in the Henrico and Caroline courtrooms, a grateful state paid Woolfolk $22.36 and presented him with a suit of new clothes. The state was not grateful enough, however, to reward Woolfolk with his freedom; that prize was reserved for Tom and Pharoah, the two "loyal" slaves who had never joined the plot. It is probably well that the historian, gazing down from the safety of the present day, not judge young Woolfolk too harshly for doing what he thought he had to do. But Paul Graham's other slaves, not to mention Gabriel's friends in the city and country, looked upon the young mulatto in less charitable terms. Bondmen who violated the code of ethics of the quarters found themselves outcasts and objects of insult and injury. After leaving jail, Woolfolk disappeared from the eyes of history. But it may not be presuming too much to suspect that Woolfolk, only eighteen years old, did not enjoy a long and happy life.[30]

Indeed, the fate of the other chief witness for the state, Ben, the unhappy property of Thomas Prosser, provides a clue to the future of those who cooperated too closely with the courts of oyer and terminer. Like Woolfolk, Ben was released from custody on January 6, 1801. For implicating twenty slaves and testifying against nearly that many (including Solomon and Watt, the first and last slaves to be tried), the governor rewarded Ben with a new suit of clothes, "including Shoes, Stockings, &c." But also like Woolfolk, Ben did not walk out of jail a free man. He kept his life, but he returned to the decidedly hostile quarters at Brookfield.[31]

Ben obviously expected more than a suit of clothes for his efforts. To be sentenced to a life of labor at Brookfield, where he had to endure the glares and kicks of resentful slaves, not to mention the savagery of a master who knew he was not to be trusted, was all too much. The record on what happened next is unclear, but evidently Ben again began to plan for his freedom, this time with two other Prosser slaves, Ned and Isaac. Once more he was found out, and once more, on May 10, 1806, Ben found himself before the Henrico court of oyer and terminer, charged with "conspiracy and insurrection." As Ben eyed the justices he saw familiar faces: Daniel Hylton, Pleasant Younghusband, and George Williamson. But this time Ben had the wit to stay silent, as did his friends. His lawyer, William B. Chamberlayne, entered the requisite plea of not guilty. With no turncoat to speak against any of the three, the court had little choice but to thrice return findings of not guilty. Like Woolfolk, Ben thence dropped from sight of the historical record. But it would be most unusual if Prosser did not conclude that the time had arrived to sell this troublesome slave to the lower South.[32]

Neither Pharoah nor Tom, it is safe to say, exactly enriched his reputation in the slave community by his actions in August 1800. But unlike Woolfolk and Ben, the Sheppard slaves were no longer slaves. As "loyal" chattel who had never entered into the plot, the two men emerged from the testy bartering over their prices as free men. Neither one, therefore, had to endure baleful stares from former friends; few slaves would be foolish enough to cross free blacks who had powerful white patrons. Pharoah, therefore, decided to remain in the county. As an act of fealty, Pharoah adopted the surname of Sheppard. In turn, Mosby Sheppard eventually purchased his former slave's son, Pharoah Junior, from an Albemarle County man and presented him to the older Pharoah. But Pharoah was unable to free his son and so remained Pharoah Junior's owner of record. Had he freed his boy, the child would have had to leave the state to comply with the law of 1806.[33]

Pharoah and his legally idiosyncratic family remained in the area. As a freeman, Pharoah performed odd jobs and wielded a scythe for neighboring farms. Every spring he returned to his old home to help harvest the wheat; Mosby Sheppard dutifully recorded the small amounts of "Cash Paid [to] Pharoah Sheppard" for his labors. Pharoah followed this pattern until just after the War of 1812, when he finally disappeared from the Sheppard ledgers.[34]

If many of Pharoah's former friends turned away as they saw him approach, he at least had the companionship of Tom, whose life took much the same path. Five years Pharoah's senior, Tom was a rather more ambitious man. He too worked around the county, but his rise was more dramatic. By 1809 "Tom Sheppard (Free Negro)"—he also adopted the Sheppard name—had put aside enough cash to rent "Mitchells," a small farm, from Mosby Sheppard. But he too returned to the old house every spring to help bring in the wheat, although he often did so in the capacity of "driver." As a black man with a whip and a license from a white employer to use it, Tom would have been more despised in the slave community than Pharoah. He also would have been more feared. Tom Sheppard continued to rent land and drive slaves for his former owner until 1825, when, at the age of fifty-eight, he too dropped from the family account books.[35]

When placed on a scale beside the prosperity of Tom Sheppard, the accomplishments of those black Virginians who knew of one or the other of the conspiracies and yet said nothing add up to little enough. But their satisfied consciences must have outweighed any pecuniary gain they had let pass by, and the doors of rude cabins or smoky basement taverns never banged shut against them. In the same category could be found Jesse and Reuben Byrd, who in after years returned to their modest carpentry business in Petersburg.[36] Robert Cowley, the ancient doorkeeper who surely knew of the plot but cautiously decided to keep his options open until the final second, lived another two decades beyond the summer of 1800. When he died on February 8, 1820, many old dwellers of Richmond believed that Cowley had lived to be "one hundred and twenty-five years [old]."[37]

Of the 1802 rebels, Lewis, after his escape while being transferred from Richmond to Goochland, was never heard from again. More tragic was the fate of Rochester Jumper, the free black who had first told Lewis of the Easter plot. Seized near his home in Petersburg, Jumper was awaiting trial at the time of Lewis's escape. Because his case never came before a court—the Dinwiddie justices were awaiting Lewis's testimony—Jumper never obtained a court-appointed lawyer. Even the least capable lawyer would have been able to point out that Lewis's testimony was inadmissible, coming as it was from a slave at the trial of a free man. The Petersburg jailor evidently had no idea what to do with Jumper and so shipped him north under guard to the Richmond penitentiary. There Jumper remained in solitary confinement for forty months, until someone finally caught the error and released him in February 1806.[38]

This somber event, however, did little to convince Virginia authorities that their legal system, as it pertained to African Americans, was a fraud. Certainly it did little to deter James Rind, who had defended so many of the accused in 1800, from continuing his busy practice as court-appointed counsel. Rind was no doubt convinced that his lethargic services were essential in providing the accused with their just due. In early 1801, he was back before the Henrico court, dispensing advice to Stephen, a slave of Lucy Redford's, who was accused of killing Miles Selden's Aaron. Typically, Stephen was found guilty, notwithstanding Rind's expert defense, and sentenced to die. (Typically also, Rind did not forget to collect his ten dollar fee from Redford.) Rind's one attempt at a political career fared little better. In 1802 he stood for election to the Richmond City seat once held by Charles Copland, who had defended Gabriel in 1799. Rind lost to Dr. John Adams, the Federalist candidate; as one who had but recently "deserted" the Republican party for the Federalist fold, Rind enjoyed few friends on either side of the aisle.[39]

Of all the principal actors, none rose so high, and then fell so far, as Thomas Henry Prosser. Only a man completely lacking in energy and imagination—that is, most men—would have thought that to serve as master to a slave who had nearly succeeded in turning the world upside down presaged a dismal future in Virginia society. Yet Prosser was but momentarily distracted in his quest for financial gain; he was hardly defeated. He used most of the money paid him for his executed and transported slaves to purchase replacements. By the end of 1801 he owned forty-five slaves over the age of twelve, just three fewer than before the conspiracy exploded.[40]

Aggressive and impatient in love as he was in business—if the two could ever be said to be separated in Virginia society—young Prosser continued in his quest to win the daughter of Daniel Hylton. Either his southern charm or his head for business (perhaps the former appealed to the daughter, the latter to her merchant father) carried the day. On Thursday, June 25, 1801, the twenty-five-year-old merchant and planter wed Lucy Bolling Hylton in St. John's Church. Over time, the couple produced four children. Two of them, at least, were boys, Albert and Daniel.[41]

For more than a few years, Thomas Prosser did well for himself. His urban mercantile company prospered, and the dispirited slave community at Brookfield caused him no further trouble—with the exception of the minor affair with Ben in 1806. Prosser also continued to garner the laurels necessary for the rise of any young man in the Tidewater. In 1803 he became a justice of the peace in the Henrico court of common law and chancery. During the War of 1812 he served as captain for a troop of cavalry for part of the summer of 1814, a short period of service that allowed him to adopt the customary—and essential—title of "colonel" for the remainder of his life. Financially, he was more than secure; just before the war his father-in-law passed away, and Prosser inherited much of the Hylton estate.[42]

For all that, like many restless young Virginians, Prosser looked to the west in search of greater fortune and fame. Within a few years of the war, "Col. T. H. Prosser" moved to Wilkinson County, Mississippi. The southwestern frontier, however, proved unhealthy to his growing family. In 1821 two of his children died. The tragedy weakened Lucy even more than the steamy climate did, and in the following year she "followed [them] to the tomb." Four years after, in 1826, Prosser's oldest child, Albert Prosser, who had trained as a doctor, died suddenly "in the 24th year of his age."[43]

At length Prosser remarried, but his second wife, Elizabeth, bore him no children. In 1839, at the age of sixty-three, Prosser envisioned "the approach of [his] latter End." He prepared a simple will and divided his estate "between [his] beloved wife Elizabeth and [his] only surviving Son, Daniel H. Prosser." Francis Gildart, the judge of probate, recorded the will during the December term of 1839. Then Thomas Henry Prosser too dropped from the sight of history.[44]

The remaining principals had all disappeared from the historical record long before that date. Richardson Taylor, the Methodist skipper who ferried Gabriel to Norfolk, vanished into the hidden inlets and back bays of the maritime world. Arrested in Norfolk on the charge of "intentionally aiding and assisting in [Gabriel's] escape," Taylor was "bound over" to appear before Richmond mayor James McClurg "to answer for his conduct." Unwisely, however, Norfolk authorities released the captain on his own "recognizance." One night in early October the *Mary* quietly slipped away from the dock. Taylor never arrived in Richmond. Nor was he seen again in Norfolk.[45]

The shadowy Frenchmen remained equally elusive, and from James Monroe's perspective, that was all to the good. Monroe was many things, but never a fool; he scarcely would have sanctioned the trial of two white French soldiers during an election in which his party daily was being charged with an unholy alliance with Bonaparte. For those who inquired, Monroe had a ready answer. The conspiracy was "quite a domestic one," and no "white men were engaged in it." Most likely, Charles Quersey fled the state and joined Alexander Beddenhurst at the French Boarding-House on the corner of Coats' Alley.[46]

The greatest mystery remains the fate of Gabriel's wife, Nanny. Perhaps she was left alone. Certainly she was never arrested or, as far as the extant evidence indicates, even questioned. The court records demonstrated that she was aware of the plot, but no testimony ever placed her outside of Brookfield. Given the patriarchal attitudes of the court, the justices may have assumed that Nanny was but a timid follower of a domineering husband and thus posed no danger in his absence. Nanny may have presumed as much. Although she was with Gabriel on the morning of Sunday, August 31, she made no attempt to flee with him.[47]

Although all of the participants of the singular events of 1800 and 1802 dropped from sight one by one, the events themselves, and the legend of Gabriel, were never forgotten, especially by the folk in the slave quarters. Sixty years later, black soldiers in uniforms of Union blue, most of them slaves only months before, marched toward Atlanta and Petersburg and Richmond to do battle with their former masters. As they advanced down the dusty roads they sang their own version of "Battle Hymn of the Republic" as they honored their own divine messenger.

> We are done with hoeing cotton,
> We are done with hoeing corn,
> We are colored Yankee soldiers,
> As sure as you are born.
> When Massa hears us shouting,
> He will think 'tis Gabriel's horn,
> As we go marching on.[48]

Much later still, in a different century, Melvin Gabriel Wilmot, a resident of the urban North, provided a clue to the fate of the nine slaves transported to New Orleans in early 1801. The son of a Louisiana man, Wilmot told an inquiring sociologist that his father "named me Gabr'l for one of them slavery time prophets, and you better believe there is some power in that name."[49]

APPENDIX 1

Gabriel's Religion

Of all the myths and legends surrounding the events of the summer of 1800, surely the most durable is the idea that Gabriel was a messianic figure, an early national Nat Turner who wore his hair long in imitation of his hero, Samson. Perhaps Gabriel's biblical name has given longevity to the idea. Perhaps the myth is fueled by the historical knowledge that radical Christianity has always carried an implicit message of earthly equality and the understanding that the Virginia countryside of 1800 was deep in the midst of religious fervor. Perhaps also, the legend has been sustained by the knowledge that Gabriel recruited after Sunday "preachings"—although the fact that he also searched for followers after funerals and barbecues has not given rise to the tale that the black revolutionary was an undertaker or a caterer.

Compelling logic there may be for such a view, but the simple fact is that it is wholly untrue. Evidence does exist that Gabriel and his brother Martin were familiar with both the Bible and the evangelical brand of Christianity practiced by the Baptists and the Methodists. Gabriel's ability to obtain benefit of clergy in 1799 indicated the capacity to recite a passage from the Bible. But the single reference to religion in the vast trial testimony comes from Martin, not Gabriel. It implies only that like most Virginians, white and black, Martin had a working knowledge of the Bible, and that like most slaves, he was particularly fond of the Old Testament. There is not a *single* extant primary document that supports the contention that Gabriel was a deeply religious slave or that Martin was a slave preacher. What exists instead is Thomas Henry Prosser's 1800 description of his twenty-four-year-old property: a tall young man with "short black knotty hair."[1]

The Samson myth is of uncertain origin. Three scholars writing in the mid- to late nineteenth century—Robert R. Howison, Joshua Coffin, and Thomas W. Higginson—made no mention of either Gabriel's religion or a Samson complex.[2] But in the last decades of the century Marion Harland published a novel titled *Judith: A Chronicle of Old Virginia*. Even by the standards of the late 1800s, *Judith* was an astonishingly racist epic. Perhaps designed to counteract the somewhat more sympathetic view of Gabriel put forth by Coffin and Higginson, Harland made her slave rebel a bit of a religious charlatan: "His hair was long and thick, and had never been cut. He wore it generally in a cue [*sic*], like a gentleman's, but this night he let it hang loose on his shoulders to remind his men of Samson's hair, 'wherin his great strength lay.'"[3]

The first modern scholar to support the myth in print was Joseph C. Carroll in his pioneering (if careless) *Slave Insurrections in the United States* (1938). Carroll's Gabriel was "a careful student of the Old Testament, where he believed that he found his own prototype in the picturesque and legendary figure of Samson." No citation was given for this assertion; perhaps by this time Harland's fictional embellishment had become a part of the popular historical consciousness.[4]

Since Carroll's work, which is still in print, the Samson story has appeared in virtually every reference to the conspiracy. It has been repeated by Philip S. Foner, William J. Kimball (twice), Lerone Bennett, Jr., Barbara Clark Smith, George P. Rawick, and Nicholas Halasz. Each writer has added his or her own twist to the legend; Halasz certainly has contributed the most color: "[Gabriel] thought himself a man of mission, put to a hard test by an exacting divinity. He spoke little and his words sounded like paraphrases of the Scriptures."[5] In point of fact, Gabriel's words—peppered as they were with references to merchants and property—sounded like no such thing. Yet the more the story was repeated, the more there existed works for still other unsuspecting scholars to build upon.

A handful of more cautious historians, however, have carried on the substance of the story while dropping its more dramatic elements. In *Roll, Jordan, Roll: The World the Slaves Made*, Eugene D. Genovese mentions only that Gabriel "relied on Christian preaching but stressed secular themes," a careful pronouncement that does not go far beyond the primary sources. The same author's important *From Rebellion to Revolution: Afro-American Slave Revolts in the Making of the Modern World* drops even this minor reference to Gabriel's faith. Equally reserved are Winthrop D. Jordan and Albert J. Raboteau. The former relishes the "compelling irony [that] some of the slaves seem to have been influenced by Christian training," while the latter merely notes that Gabriel recruited at prayer meetings. (Raboteau does, however, repeat the fiction that Martin was a plantation preacher.)[6] No historian, of course, can ever check every primary source. One naturally tends to trust in the accuracy of previously published works, which makes the healthy skepticism of Genovese and Jordan all the more admirable.

Less admirable, but more curious, is the rise of a second religious corollary to the Samson myth, what may be called the Moses myth. The Samson of legend was an Israelite warrior, but unlike Moses he did not lead his people out of bondage. Still, the Gabriel described by Harvey Wish in a 1937 article was inspired by "the emancipation of the ancient Israelites from Egypt." Joanne Grant made much the same point in 1968 in her *Black Protest: History, Documents, and Analysis*. The most highly developed version of this twist appears in John W. Blassingame's *The Slave Community: Plantation Life in the Antebellum South*. This Gabriel inspired "the faint-hearted with apocalyptic visions from the Scriptures of God delivering the Israelites from the hands of their oppressors." In an example of how ingrained the religious myth has become, Blassingame cites only Higginson, who made no mention of Gabriel's religion.[7]

In recent years several scholars have returned to the original sources, and so the image of the messianic Gabriel does not grace the pages of two excellent monographs: Gerald (Michael) W. Mullin's *Flight and Rebellion: Slave Resistance in Eighteenth-Century Virginia* (1972) and Philip J. Schwarz's *Twice Condemned: Slaves and the Criminal Law of Virginia, 1705–1865* (1988).[8] Neither, however, explicitly denounced the myth, and so it has not vanished yet. Mechal Sobel takes Mullin to task in *Trabelin' On: The Slave Journey to an Afro-Baptist Faith*, 2d ed. (1988) for de-emphasizing the role of religion in Gabriel's plot. Program notes to a 1987 Smithsonian Institution symposium, "Race and Revolution: African-Americans, 1770–1830," describe Gabriel as a "deeply religious slave." The revised edition of Sidney and Emma Kaplan, *The Black Presence in the Era of the American Revolution* (1989), refers to the rebel leader as a preacher. Elliott J. Gorn, *Constructing the American Past: A Source Book of a People's History* (1991), commits the same error. In all three cases the only source cited is Mullin.[9]

APPENDIX 2

The Frenchmen

Historians who are determined to uphold the myth of Gabriel as a religious zealot are equally determined to characterize as myth one story here described as fact: the involvement of two white Europeans known to the slaves as the Frenchmen. In a critical way, the legend of Gabriel's religion and the story he told of white men who would aid in the uprising are interlocking. If Gabriel is viewed as an unsophisticated preacher whose power emanated from his shaggy locks, it is easy to believe that his claims of aid from two white radicals, one of them knowledgeable in soldiering, was nothing but an irrational dream. But if Gabriel is understood to be a literate artisan whose breadth of vision was truly international and whose pragmatic decisions were based upon information drawn from the urban press, the claim is not so easily dismissed. Scholars who accept the Samson myth as fact, however, naturally tend to brush aside the factual story of the two Europeans as myth, discounting with it a great deal of supporting evidence.

To deny the story is also to patronize the conspirators, for one must conclude that these were foolish men who believed outlandish tales. But the list of prominent scholars who have done so is surprisingly long. William Joel Ernst, in his 1968 master's thesis, "Gabriel's Revolt: Black Freedom, White Fear," explicitly denounces the story, as do Harry Ammon, Barbara Clark Smith, Richard R. Beeman, and, inexplicably, Gerald (Michael) W. Mullin. Herbert Aptheker argues that the "alleged implication of two Frenchmen in the Gabriel Plot [was used] to embarrass the Republicans in the political campaign of 1800." The fact, however, that the Federalists tried to use the information hardly makes it false in itself.[1]

Only a very few writers have been willing to take the conspirators at their word. James H. Johnston, in a 1931 essay, accepted the slaves' testimony at face value and supported their claims of white involvement. Philip J. Schwarz agrees that the story might be true: "Gabriel and his followers perhaps relied on at least one Frenchman for military advice."

Arna Bontemps's 1936 novel, *Black Thunder: Gabriel's Revolt Virginia 1800*, which was loosely based on trial testimony, depicts Frenchmen "M. Creuzot" and "Alexander Biddenhurst" as being on the periphery of the conspiracy.[2]

The evidence relating to the two men is circumstantial yet compelling. Almost all of the insurgents, even those outside of Richmond, knew of the two men, although only the rebel leadership knew who they were. To discount the story as nonsense is therefore to discount the nearly unanimous testimony of the slaves. Jack Ditcher, for example, told Ben "that two White Frenchmen" were deeply involved in "the Insurrection." Wisely, he refused to divulge their names. On the night the conspiracy collapsed, a Petersburg slave informed his owner, Benjamin Harrison, that "two white men" were "concerned" in the aborted rising.[3]

It is even possible to piece together a picture of the two men. Gabriel told more than a few of his followers that "a man from Caroline" County who had fought on the American side during the Revolution was to meet him at Brook Bridge on the night of the assault and help to organize the men. Several slaves informed William Young's Gilbert that the man in question was Charles Quersey, who had lived in Caroline with Francis Corbin two years earlier. Quersey himself previously told Gilbert, who at the time was hired out in Caroline, that "he would help them & shew them how to fight," and several conspirators now observed that Quersey and another white man were "very active" in "this late Business" in Norfolk.[4]

Unfortunately, the mysterious Quersey, never having become a property owner, remains a shadowy figure in the public records. But Francis Corbin, with whom the slaves insisted he had lived, is not. County records indicate that at the time Quersey was said to have been living with Corbin, the Virginian did indeed rent a room to an unidentified adult white male.[5]

Charles Quersey's name, however, was given in oral testimony, and neither white nor black Virginians were particularly adept at pronouncing or spelling French names. (Perhaps the correct spelling was "Quercy," taken from the French town of the same name.) The imprecision in spelling thus provides a number of potential suspects. A Charles Quary lived in Hanover County at the turn of the century. But Quary appears in the Hanover tax records every year from 1788 to 1802. He could not, therefore, have been living in Caroline with Francis Corbin when Gilbert said he was.[6]

A Guillaume Querenet was an engineer with the French army at the siege of Yorktown, but his first name varies too greatly from "Charles" for him to be a likely candidate.[7] Equally unlikely—even impossible—is Alexander Quesnay. The grandson of the celebrated physiocrat Francois

Quesnay, Alexander arrived in Philadelphia in 1780. He tried his hand at teaching but enrolled few pupils. He moved his failing academy first to New York and then, in early 1786, to Richmond.[8] But success eluded him in Virginia as well, and in December 1786 he sailed for home. Quesnay died in 1820 without ever returning to America.[9] No other name found in the public record comes close. Surely the simple answer is the best: the man's name was Charles Quersey, and he was one of the many French soldiers who landed in the Chesapeake with Rochambeau's army and remained in the region but lived on the margins of society.

The second Frenchman, Alexander Beddenhurst, remains equally shadowy, yet here as well can be seen the outline of a man far too substantial to be the figment of so many slaves' imaginations. As noted in the text, Beddenhurst was probably not French at all but had arrived in Virginia with the German-speaking Fourth Regiment under the Duke of Deux-Ponts.[10] According to an anonymous correspondent for the Fredericksburg *Virginia Herald*, John Scott, a Petersburg rebel, even had a Philadelphia address for Beddenhurst: "the corner house of Coats' Alley." This tiny street appears as a line, with no name given, on a contemporary street map. Therefore Scott could not have designated the street by randomly picking a name from a Philadelphia map; he must have gotten the address elsewhere.[11]

The simple address captured with Scott neglected to mention that the corner house, according to the 1795 Philadelphia City Directory, was "The French Boarding-House," owned and operated by John Boulanger. Nor did it mention that the alley boasted a large population of French nationals.[12]

In weighing this evidence, one might do well to recall Sherlock Holmes's famous maxim: "When you have eliminated the impossible, whatever remains, however improbable, must be the truth." There are three possible scenarios. First, to impress potential recruits, Scott fabricated the name of a Frenchman and a Philadelphia street address. Even if we assume that Scott would bother to consult a Philadelphia street map—or that he could obtain one—he would not have been able to find a reference to the tiny Coats' Alley.

A second possibility is that the correspondent for the *Virginia Herald*, who was clearly a Federalist, fabricated the story of the address found in Scott's pocket—a document that is absent from the trial material in the Virginia State Library—to embarrass the Republicans on the eve of the presidential election. But the anonymous informant, like Scott, never mentioned that the corner house was named "The French Boarding-House." If the correspondent made the story up as a campaign tactic, he achieved a coincidence of truly Dickensian proportion.

That leaves only a third possibility: that Alexander Beddenhurst did exist and that this friend of Charles Quersey's gave Scott directions to his home base should the conspiracy collapse. (Scott, after all, was boarding a stage for Norfolk when he was captured.) What then to make of James Monroe's desperate public assertion that if "white men were involved in it, it is a fact of which we have no proof"?[13] What to make of the absence of the Scott letter from the public documents relinquished by Governor Monroe upon leaving office? What to make of the absence of the lists kept by the leaders or the correspondence captured with Gabriel and the black captain? People in three cities—Richmond mayor James McClurg, William Prentis of Petersburg, and the anonymous newspaper source—insisted that such documents had been seized and sent directly to the governor, where they vanished from sight. The clear implication is that Monroe, holding evidence that would do considerable damage to his party, knew the truth but kept it—and the incriminating documents—from all but a trusted few. It is an impossible charge to prove. But it is the only plausible conclusion. And in a day of Oval Office tape recorders and shredded documents, it is, perhaps, no longer hard to believe.

APPENDIX 3

Virginia Slaves Executed in 1800 and 1802

When Gabriel's War of Independence began, the leading conspirators were all young, strong men in their prime; when it ended, gravediggers in far too many counties had taken up their shovels far too many times. Given the general confusion surrounding Gabriel—the myths about his religion, his surname, his place of birth—it is not surprising that historians have been equally confused about the number of his followers who paid with their lives for their desire to breathe free.

In determining the number hanged in the fall of 1800, most scholars have followed the lead of Herbert Aptheker, who has done more than any historian to rescue Gabriel and his spiritual heirs from the most insidious myth of all: the fiction of slave docility. Professor Aptheker made a careful study of the pay vouchers but failed to uncover the 1806 master list of slaves transported outside of Virginia. As a result, he assumed that one could discover the number of slaves hanged by counting the number of white masters who received payment from the state. His calculation of thirty-five is thus too high, as owners of slaves transported—like Charles Carter, whom Aptheker counts three times—also received payment for their lost property.[1]

The number thirty-five, however, has been generally accepted. John Hope Franklin, in his classic text *From Slavery to Freedom: A History of Negro Americans*, Virginius Dabney, in both his history of Virginia and his valuable monograph on Richmond, and W. Carrington Tate, in a Henrico County publication, all accept the figure as accurate. Louis H. Manarin and Clifford Dowdey, in their study of Henrico County, choose the slightly higher tally of thirty-six.[2]

Only one writer adopts a figure higher than Manarin's. Nicholas Halasz, who exaggerates virtually every aspect of the conspiracy, somehow arrived at a figure of forty-five.[3] Rather closer to the mark are U. B. Phillips, whose research (as apart from his basic assumptions about African Americans) was never in question, and Gerald (Michael) W. Mullin. Phillips lists twenty-five as executed. Mullin places the number around twenty.[4]

On the absurdly low side can be found Julia C. Pollard. In *Richmond's Story* (1954), Pollard insists that only "Gabriel and two of his leaders were . . . put to death; others were acquitted or pardoned." The author cites only Franklin, who, following Aptheker, in fact places the number far too high. More likely, Pollard fashioned her account from Marion Harland's racist novel, *Judith*: "Gabriel, and I think, three others of the ring-leaders, were taken in different hiding-places and brought to Richmond jail. They had a fair trial and were condemned to death."[5]

Within reason, there is good cause for much of this confusion. Because the trial records in several crucial Virginia counties, including Norfolk and Dinwiddie, are incomplete, it will probably never be known precisely how many blacks were *tried* for complicity in the plot. Moreover, the harried Henrico clerk copied the records of four trials—those of Burton's Isaac, Jones's John, Mosby's Will, and Price's James—into the county court order book twice, once in September and once in October.[6] James Monroe lost track of the death toll early on; his letters describing the number tried or hanged on any given day were rarely correct. James Callender, who had a better view of the proceedings from his temporary home in the Richmond jail, proved a more accurate observer, although one of his letters, written on September 18, was misdated September 13, and so leads to further confusion.

Regardless of where the insurgents were tried, however, if they were *executed* a record was retained in Richmond, so it is possible to ascertain with some certainty the number hanged. By cross-matching the death certificates and payments to owners in the file Auditor's Item 153, box 2, Condemned Slaves 1800, with the material in Condemned Slaves 1800–1801, Executed, Gabriel's Insurrection; Condemned Slaves 1801, Transported; List of Slaves Reprieved for Transportation and Sold, March 8, 1806, Executive Papers; and Pardons, September–December, 1800, Executive Papers (all in the Virginia State Library), the number who died in 1800 comes to twenty-seven. This figure includes William Wilson's Jacob, the black skipper, who allegedly hanged himself while in custody. (Most of the slaves tried in 1800, and all of those hanged, are listed in the useful appendix "Slaves Hanged or Transported for Conspiracy or Insurrection, 1785–1831," in Philip J. Schwarz's *Twice Condemned*.)[7]

There appears to be little controversy about the number of slaves who died in the Easter plot of 1802. Professor Aptheker does not devote much attention to the second conspiracy, but he does argue that, in Virginia alone, as many as thirty-seven slaves were executed in 1802. He bases this figure on owners compensated, and again, many were compensated for slaves who were transported. Moreover, the assumption that all slaves who were hanged or transported were part of various conspiracies is not supported by the trial records. Many were guilty of isolated capital crimes, not insurrection. In all, ten Virginia slaves swung for their involvement in Sancho's plot. Fifteen more North Carolina slaves were executed by the state.[8]

NOTES

CHAPTER ONE

1. On slave midwifery, see Savitt, *Medicine and Slavery*, 182, and Charles Joyner, "The World of the Plantation Slaves," in Campbell and Rice, eds., *Before Freedom Came*, 59.

For Gabriel's date of birth, see Chapter 2. Throughout the notes I have identified the slaves by including the last name of the owner before the slave's name, except in the rare instances of a slave who had a surname. (While some historians refer to Gabriel as Gabriel Prosser, no contemporary document does so, and hence I have avoided that form here.) This usage is as necessary as it is clumsy, as many of the conspirators share the same first—and only—name. There were numerous bondmen involved named John, several Bens and Solomons, and even two Gabriels, in addition to a Jack Gabriel.

2. Rhys Isaac, "Preachers and Patriots: Popular Culture and the Revolution in Virginia," in Young, ed., *The American Revolution*, 129; D. P. Jordan, *Political Leadership in Jefferson's Virginia*, 7.

3. Main, *The Antifederalists*, 2–3; Isaac, "Preachers and Patriots," 131.

4. Pole, "Representation and Authority in Virginia," 29.

5. Genovese, *World the Slaveholders Made*, 16, 97.

6. Genovese suggests in *Roll, Jordan, Roll* that the closing of the international slave trade was the final factor in the creation of paternalism; the borrowing of feudal legal elements was the first step. Thus Genovese describes the maturation of paternalism as an antebellum phenomenon. But as discussed below, by the time of the Revolution there was an unusually large native-born slave class in Virginia, and large-scale importations of Africans into the colony had been tapering off for decades. Philip Morgan correctly, in my view, thus suggests that the shift from patriarchalism to paternalism was well under way in Virginia by the close of the century ("Three Planters and Their Slaves: Perspectives on Slavery in Virginia, South Carolina, and Jamaica, 1750–1790," in Jordan and Skemp, eds., *Race and Family in the Colonial South*, 39–40). But Duncan J. MacLeod goes perhaps too far in writing of the pre-Revolutionary Virginia planter: "If slavery was ever characterized by paternalism, this was the time and place" ("Toward Caste," in Berlin and Hoffman, eds., *Slavery and Freedom*, 227). Frey, in *Water from the Rock*, attributes the reformulation of paternalism to the influence of evangelical Christianity.

7. Isaac, *Transformation of Virginia*, 308–09.

8. Peter Wood, "'The Dream Deferred': Black Freedom Struggles on the Eve of White Independence," in Okihiro, ed., *In Resistance*, 173–74.

9. Broadside, [November 7], 1775, John Murray (Earl of Dunmore) Papers; Quarles, "Lord Dunmore as Liberator," 497; Berlin, *Slaves without Masters*, 16.

10. Frey, "The British and the Blacks," 229; Quarles, *Negro in the American Revolution*, 115.

11. Frey, "Between Slavery and Freedom," 380–82.

12. Frey, "The British and the Blacks," 229–33; Frey, "Between Slavery and Freedom," 396.

13. McColley, *Slavery and Jeffersonian Virginia*, 88; Kulikoff, *Tobacco and Slaves*, 419.

14. Wood, "'The Dream Deferred,'" 177–78.

15. Morgan, *American Slavery, American Freedom*, 374.

16. Essig, "A Very Wintry Season," 174–75.

17. Albert J. Raboteau, "The Slave Church in the Era of the American Revolution," in Berlin and Hoffman, eds., *Slavery and Freedom*, 203; O'Brien, "Factory, Church, and Community," 521; Christian, *Richmond*, 56.

18. Isaac, "Evangelical Revolt," 354–55; Sobel, *Trabelin' On*, 98–109. On the problems of maintaining the purity of African religion in the new land, see Boles, *Black Southerners*, 37.

19. Genovese, *Roll, Jordan, Roll*, 170–71; Jackson, "Religious Development of the Negro in Virginia," 172–73.

20. Daniel, "Virginia Baptists and the Negro," 66.

21. Scott and Wyatt, *Petersburg's Story*, 104–05; Frey, *Water from the Rock*, 286; Sobel, *Trabelin' On*, 208; "An Act Further Declaring What Shall Be Deemed Unlawful Meetings of Slaves," January 24, 1804, in Shepherd, ed., *Statutes at Large*, 3:108; Daniel, "Virginia Baptists and the Negro," 62–63.

22. Sobel, *Trabelin' On*, 117; Mullin, *Flight and Rebellion*, 130.

23. Genovese, *Roll, Jordan, Roll*, 275, 283; Raboteau, "Slave Church," 202; Essig, "A Very Wintry Season," 175–76, 183.

24. Isaac, *Transformation of Virginia*, 309. Genovese doubts that guilt over slaveholding was widespread in the later antebellum period, but concedes that it might have "express[ed] itself as a social question" in an earlier period (*World the Slaveholders Made*, 146).

25. W. D. Jordan, *White over Black*, 350–51; McColley, *Slavery and Jeffersonian Virginia*, 54; Deyle, "The Irony of Liberty," 14–15.

26. Fields, "Slavery, Race, and Ideology," 114; Alden, *The South in the Revolution*, 334–35.

27. Richard S. Dunn, "Black Society in the Chesapeake," in Berlin and Hoffman, eds., *Slavery and Freedom*, 51.

28. Schwarz, *Twice Condemned*, 193; Flexner, *Washington*, 388–92.

29. Stampp, *Peculiar Institution*, 411. Fogel and Engerman argue that slave prices were not soft after the Revolution, although they make no distinction between the depleted lands of the Chesapeake and the fresher soil of the lower South (*Time on the Cross*, 86–88). The far more careful analysis of Robert McColley, however, supports their view by noting the generally low price level of basic com-

modities in the early national period and observing that a good field hand cost as much as a town lot in Norfolk. See his *Slavery and Jeffersonian Virginia*, 25.

30. Stampp, *Peculiar Institution*, 96; David Meade to Judge [Joseph] Prentis, July 23, 1801, Prentis Family Papers.

31. Miller, *Wolf by the Ears*, 22. John Adams wrote of Jefferson's *Notes*: "The passages upon slavery are worth diamonds. They will have more effect than volumes written by mere philosophers." See P. Smith, *John Adams*, 2:626.

32. MacLeod, "Toward Caste," 231.

33. Berlin, *Slaves without Masters*, 28; Hoffman, *Spirit of Dissension*, 147; *Minutes of the Proceedings of the Fourth Convention of Delegates from the Abolition Societies*, 39.

34. W. D. Jordan, *White over Black*, 346; *Memorials Presented to the Congress of the United States of America by the Different Societies Promoting the Abolition of Slavery*.

35. St. George Tucker, *Dissertation on Slavery*, 91–94.

36. Ibid., 82–83, 93–103.

37. [George Tucker], *Letter to a Member*, 6; Thomas Jefferson to St. George Tucker, August 28, 1797, in P. L. Ford, ed., *Writings of Jefferson*, 7:168. Some scholars assume that St. George Tucker was the author of the anonymous *Letter to a Member* as well as of *Dissertation*. Two letters from George Tucker to his cousin St. George Tucker, March 7, [1801; misdated 1800], and [January] 18, [1801; misdated 1800], both in Tucker-Coleman Papers, prove that George Tucker was the author of the former. Both missives mention "my *Letter to a Member*."

38. *Journal of the House of Delegates of Virginia*, 52.

39. *Virginia Argus* (Richmond), July 17, 1802; "An Act to Amend the Act Concerning Slaves, Free Negroes, and Mulattoes," January 25, 1798, in Shepherd, ed., *Statutes at Large*, 2:77. This is not to imply that before 1796 no white Virginian defended slavery, only that after 1796 the steady, if timid, moves toward reform stopped. For some examples of early proslavery ideology, see Schmidt and Wilhelm, eds., "Early Proslavery Petitions in Virginia," 145.

40. Berlin, *Slaves without Masters*, 36–41; James Monroe to the General Assembly, January 16, 1802, Executive Papers.

41. David Meade to Judge [Joseph] Prentis, September 4, 1799, Prentis Family Papers.

42. Klein, "Slaves and Shipping in Eighteenth-Century Virginia," 409–10; Minchinton, King, and Waite, eds., *Virginia Slave Trade Statistics*, 177–89.

43. Dunn, "Black Society," 68–69; Mary Beth Norton, Herbert G. Gutman, and Ira Berlin, "The Afro-American Family in the Age of Revolution," in Berlin and Hoffman, eds., *Slavery and Freedom*, 177.

44. Kulikoff, "A 'Prolifick' People," 413–14; Kulikoff, *Tobacco and Slaves*, 359–60; Sobel, *World They Made Together*, 124. White convincingly argues that when planters claimed to keep families together they meant only the mother and children, not the father (*Ar'n't I a Woman?*, 145).

45. Unidentified newspaper clipping, William Palmer Scrapbook; Steward, *Twenty-two Years a Slave*, 12; J. Davis, *Travels of Four Years and a Half*, 400, 418–20.

46. In recent years the debate over the nature of slavery in postwar Virginia has taken on a sharper focus. Although differences of interpretation separate almost all scholars of the period from each other, two sides, generally speaking, have emerged. The first broad interpretation holds that the Revolution brought a cultural and social transformation to Virginia that, in the words of Rhys Isaac, made slavery a "problem." In addition to Isaac, those who hold this view include Jan Lewis (*The Pursuit of Happiness*), and Mullin, who argues that "the last quarter of the eighteenth century may well have been one of the most relaxed and tolerant periods in race relations in Virginia" (*Flight and Rebellion*, 127). MacLeod suggests that the Revolutionary generation missed a crucial opportunity to abolish slavery, although this notion is based on the idea that slavery before 1776 "was a racial institution, but not avowedly so," a thesis rejected by most scholars (*Slavery, Race, and the American Revolution*, 8–13).

On the other side of the debate stand Allan Kulikoff and Robert McColley. Both emphasize stability over change, and the latter's careful analysis has demonstrated that slavery was hardly on the economic ropes before the rise of the cotton kingdom.

The argument made here is an attempt to bridge the historiographical gap. As noted in the text, I agree with Isaac and Lewis to the extent that at least some leading members of the gentry found it impossible to rationalize human bondage with their own demands for liberty and equality. There is no question that slavery was economically healthy and that slave prices were not low, or that the institution had spread into the Piedmont, but this change of mind by leading politicians did threaten to weaken the system permanently. When forced by St. George Tucker in 1796 to take corporate action, the gentry took its stand and moved to retighten controls. The year 1796 was, I argue, a watershed year that has not been appreciated by historians. After that date the small moves toward reform stopped, although troubled planters found it difficult to reimpose controls. Hence Mullin too is right. Slavery was "relaxed." But the state was not reforming the system out of existence.

CHAPTER TWO

1. For contemporary views of turn-of-the-century Richmond, see Weld, *Travels through North America*, 1:187–88; Carter, ed., *Papers of Latrobe*, 1:966; Mordecai, *Richmond*, 45–46; Sutcliff, *Travels through North America*, 50–51.

2. Weld, *Travels through North America*, 1:188–89; Pollard, *Richmond's Story*, 76; Dabney, *Richmond*, 78–82.

3. Rhodes, *Landmarks of Richmond*, 10; Mordecai, *Richmond*, 58.

4. The public whipping post was used also as punishment by the state. See trial of Price's John, September 30, 1800, Henrico County Court Order Book. On the white, free black, and bond population of Richmond and Henrico County in 1800, see *Return of the Whole Number of Persons within the Several Districts of the United States*, 69–70.

5. An unidentified newspaper clipping in the William Palmer Scrapbook describes the appearance of the Prosser house, which is no longer standing. Brookfield was in what is now the Chamberlayne Farms suburb of Richmond. Brook Creek is now Brook Run, and the stone bridge that crossed the creek probably stood where Interstate 95 now crosses the stream. The 1806 insurance map of Brookfield does not include the slave cabins, which were not worth insuring. See Brookfield, Mutual Assurance Society Policies, Map, vol. 40, no. 1119, August 3, 1806.

6. Henrico County Court Order Book, no. 9, p. 256; Meade, *Old Churches, Ministers, and Families of Virginia*, 1:141; Patrick Henry Account Book, 1762–70, folio 39. I am grateful to Philip J. Schwarz for the last citation.

7. On Thomas Henry Prosser's date of birth, see Charles Copland Petition, December 5, 1798, Af 119, Richmond City Legislative Petitions. Goode incorrectly lists Thomas Henry Prosser as Elizabeth's father (*Virginia Cousins*, 59). He was her brother.

8. Thomas Prosser, Henrico County Personal Property Tax, 1783. This postwar tax was the only one in Virginia history to name all of the slaves assessed instead of simply providing the number of taxable persons (slaves above age twelve). Gabriel and Solomon appear near the bottom of the list. Martin, who was older, is listed far above. It is likely that the names appear in order roughly according to age.

9. The fact that all three brothers were on the same plantation at a time when Gabriel was but seven years old implies that Gabriel was born at Brookfield (ibid.). Moreover, in 1800 Thomas Henry Prosser described Gabriel by saying, without doubt: "Gabriel is twenty-four years of age" (*Virginia Argus* [Richmond], September 23, 1800). Such exactitude indicates firsthand knowledge of Gabriel's birth year. For the fact that Martin was far older than his two other brothers, see the testimony of Prosser's Ben at trial of Prosser's Martin, September 12, 1800, Executive Papers, Negro Insurrection). On slave naming and the use of biblical names, see Genovese, *Roll, Jordan, Roll*, 447, and Gary B. Nash, "Forging Freedom: The Emancipation Experience in the Northern Seaport Cities, 1775–1820," in Berlin and Hoffman, eds., *Slavery and Freedom*, 22.

On the question of Gabriel's religion, see Appendix 1.

10. The description of early national Chesapeake slave cabins is drawn from Weld, *Travels through North America*, 1:148; Steward, *Twenty-two Years a Slave*, 11; Henson, *Father Henson's Story*, 18; Vlach, *By the Work of Their Hands*, 60, 221.

11. Blassingame, *Slave Community*, 184; Stampp, *Peculiar Institution*, 378; Henson, *Father Henson's Story*, 17.

12. White, *Ar'n't I a Woman?*, 53; *Norfolk Herald*, September 16, 1800; Miller, *Wolf by the Ears*, 256–57; Genovese, *Roll, Jordan, Roll*, 563; Stampp, "Rebels and Sambos," 367. Higginson incorrectly states that Gabriel was illiterate (*Travellers and Outlaws*, 190). Marion Harland's late-nineteenth-century novel *Judith: A Chronicle of Old Virginia* is astonishingly racist but still grounded in tradition. She wrote: "Gabriel was an unusually intelligent negro. His master had petted him from his childhood and his mistress taught him how to read" (excerpt in Goode, *Virginia Cousins*, 59).

13. Kulikoff, *Tobacco and Slaves*, 373; Stampp, *Peculiar Institution*, 378.

14. Pinchbeck, *Virginia Negro Artisan*, 32, 47; Stampp, *Peculiar Institution*, 58–59; Boles, *Black Southerners*, 112.

15. Norton, *Liberty's Daughters*, 30; Norton, Gutman, and Berlin, "Afro-American Family," in Berlin and Hoffman, eds., *Slavery and Freedom*, 181–82; Boles, *Black Southerners*, 145.

16. Stampp, *Peculiar Institution*, 334–35; Steffen, *Mechanics of Baltimore*, 38; Henson, *Father Henson's Story*, 18–19.

17. *Virginia Argus* (Richmond), September 23, 1800; *Norfolk Herald*, September 16, 1800; James Callender to Thomas Jefferson, September 13, 1800, Jefferson Papers. The description of the clothes that Gabriel likely wore is drawn from advertisements for runaway Virginia slave artisans. See Windley, ed., *Runaway Slave Advertisements*, 1:38–39, 196, 110, 178, 217, 227.

18. Testimony of Burton's Daniel at trial of Burton's Isaac, September 11, 1800, Executive Papers, Negro Insurrection; Norton, Gutman, and Berlin, "Afro-American Family," in Berlin and Hoffman, eds., *Slavery and Freedom*, 178–79; White, *Ar'n't I a Woman?*, 97; Charles Joyner, "World of the Plantation Slaves," in Campbell and Rice, eds., *Before Freedom Came*, 61; interview with Georgina Gibbs, January 15, 1937, in Rawick, ed., *American Slave*, 16:15.

19. Thomas Prosser, Henrico County Personal Property Tax, 1783. On living "abroad," see White, *Ar'n't I a Woman?*, 154; Blassingame, *Slave Community*, 164; Norton, Gutman, and Berlin, "Afro-American Family," in Berlin and Hoffman, eds., *Slavery and Freedom*, 178.

20. *Virginia Gazette and General Advertiser* (Richmond), October 9, 1798. The Richmond City Legislative Petitions, Af-121, lists the date of death as October 13. Presumably the former, being closer in time to the fact, is correct.

21. Sentence of Smith's George, September 19, 1800, Executive Papers, Negro Insurrection; William Mosby to James Monroe, November 10, 1800, *Journal of the Senate of Virginia*, 26; Council Journal, July 3, 1802, p. 265; *Virginia Gazette and General Advertiser* (Richmond), February 7, 1800; Mordecai, *Richmond*, 92.

22. For a description and a map of Prosser's townhouse, see Mutual Assurance Society Policies, vol. 54, no. 845, July 7, 1817; Thomas Prosser, Henrico County Personal Property Tax, 1800. In that year Prosser had forty-eight taxable slaves; slaves under the age of twelve were neither taxed nor counted, hence it is impossible to tell exactly how many bondpersons he owned in 1800. For the location of the house, see Virginia Lee Cox, "How Richmond Founder Began Naming Streets," *Richmond Times-Dispatch*, January 20, 1924. I am grateful to Sarah Huggins for finding this article.

23. Will of Daniel L. Hylton, February 4, 1811, Henrico County Will Book, no. 4, pp. 104, 204. Advertisement placed by Daniel Hylton in *Virginia Gazette* (1782) in Windley, ed., *Runaway Slave Advertisements*, 1:335–36. Benjamin Henry Latrobe painted *View from Windsor*. See Carter, ed., *Papers of Latrobe*, 2:526.

24. James Callender to Thomas Jefferson, September 13, 1800, Jefferson Papers.

25. Stampp, *Peculiar Institution*, 38; Pinchbeck, *Virginia Negro Artisan*, 31; Genovese, *Roll, Jordan, Roll*, 392–93. Six works that describe Gabriel as free

are Nash and Jeffrey, *The American People*, 291; Nash, *Race and Revolution*, 79; Miller, *Wolf by the Ears*, 126; Federal Writers' Project, *Virginia*, 78; Brodie, *Thomas Jefferson*, 342; Gorn, *Constructing the American Past*, 1:199.

26. Wade, *Slavery in the Cities*, 42; Hughes, "Slaves for Hire," 261; Entry of October 18, 1798, David Erskine Copybook; Bascom Diary, December 25, 1801, in Roeber, ed., "New England Woman's Perspective," 289.

27. Wade, *Slavery in the Cities*, 39. Hughes argues that McColley estimates too high when he suggests that skilled slaves hired "from fifty to one hundred dollars per year" (*Slavery and Jeffersonian Virginia*, 78). The highest annual rent that Hughes discovered between 1787 and 1803 was the $54.95 that Miles King paid for Tom, an adult male ("Slaves for Hire," 261, 275, n. 36). Still, that was a considerable sum of money.

28. Hughes, "Slaves for Hire," 265; Account Book, vol. 3, n.p., Robinson Papers; *Richmond Recorder* April 9 and 13, 1803; Certification of William Young, September 26, 1800, Condemned Slaves 1800, Auditor's Item 153, box 2. Sawney belonged to William Lewis of Henrico.

29. William Bowler [Jr.] to James Monroe, September 27, 1800, Executive Papers, Negro Insurrection; Caroline County Board, February 12, 1799, Condemned Slaves 1801, Transported, Auditor's Item 153, box 2; *Norfolk Herald*, September 27, 1800. In 1797 William Bowler, Sr., owned four slaves; see Caroline County Personal Property and Land Book, 1797.

30. Stampp, *Peculiar Institution*, 72; Genovese, *Roll, Jordan, Roll*, 392; Boles, *Black Southerners*, 129; Clement Eaton, "Slave-Hiring," 672; Starobin, *Industrial Slavery*, 135; Testimony of Ben Woolfolk at trial of Smith's George, September 19, 1800, Executive Papers, Negro Insurrection; Testimony of Ben Woolfolk at trial of Sam Byrd, Jr., September 27, 1800, ibid.

31. Eaton, "Slave-Hiring," 677–78; Manarin and Dowdey, *History of Henrico County*, 166; Bogger, "Slave and Free Black Community," 189; "An Act . . . Concerning Slaves, Free Negroes, and Mulattoes," December 17, 1792, in Shepherd, ed., *Statutes at Large*, 1:126.

32. Main, *Social Structure*, 63; Boles, *Black Southerners*, 129; David R. Goldfield, "Black Life in Old South Cities," in Campbell and Rice, eds., *Before Freedom Came*, 131.

33. Genovese, *World the Slaveholders Made*, 16, 121, 125.

34. Rediker, *Between the Devil and the Deep Blue Sea*, 167, 200; Thompson, "Patrician Society, Plebian Culture," 385.

35. Schweninger, "Underside of Slavery," 8.

36. Pinchbeck, *Virginia Negro Artisan*, 47; Sobel, *World They Made Together*, 49–50; Nash, *Urban Crucible*, 16.

37. Thompson, "Time, Work-Discipline, and Industrial Capitalism," 60; Berlin, *Slaves without Masters*, 28.

38. Wilentz, *Chants Democratic*, 28; Nash, *Urban Crucible*, 4, 18.

39. Bogger, "Slave and Free Black Community," 167; Testimony of Prosser's Ben at trial of Gabriel, October 6, 1800, Executive Papers, Negro Insurrection.

40. Genovese, *Roll, Jordan, Roll*, 563; Boles, *Black Southerners*, 126.

41. Berlin, *Slaves without Masters*, 241–42; Pinchbeck, *Virginia Negro Artisan*, 38, 60–61; Testimony of Williamson's Daniel at trial of Jones's John, September 11, 1800, Executive Papers, Negro Insurrection.

42. Berlin, *Slaves without Masters*, 223; "An Act . . . to Restrain the Practice of Negroes Going at Large," December 10, 1793, in Shepherd, ed., *Statutes at Large*, 1:238.

43. E. Foner, *Tom Paine*, 48–51; Berlin, *Slaves without Masters*, 260–61.

44. Boles, *Black Southerners*, 128; Rediker, "American Revolution," 16; Wade, *Slavery in the Cities*, 85; *Norfolk Herald*, October 2, 1800; Berlin, *Slaves without Masters*, 261–62.

45. Thompson, "Patrician Society, Plebian Culture," 397; Sheldon, "Black-White Relations in Richmond," 31.

46. Eaton, *Growth of Southern Civilization*, 270; MacLeod, "Toward Caste," in Berlin and Hoffman, eds., *Slavery and Freedom*, 229; Schwarz, *Twice Condemned*, 120.

47. Testimony of Prosser's Ben at trial of Gabriel, October 6, 1800, Executive Papers, Negro Insurrection.

48. Confession of Prosser's Solomon, September 15, 1800, Executive Letterbook. Genovese argues persuasively that post-Revolutionary slave revolts "must be understood primarily as part of the most radical wing of the struggle for a democracy that had not yet lost its bourgeois moorings" (*From Rebellion to Revolution*, 2). Ernst states that Gabriel's goals were "muddled" ("Gabriel's Revolt," 30–31). He fails, however, to distinguish among the levels of conspirators. The testimony of Solomon and Prosser's Ben, both close to Gabriel, is given equal weight to that of Ben Woolfolk, an illiterate agricultural worker who was not in a position to understand Gabriel's economic demands. Moreover, because he does not ground Gabriel—and his goals—in place, class, and time, Ernst finds the rebel's emphasis on property "particularly curious."

49. Trial of Prosser's Gabriel, October 7, 1799, Henrico County Court Order Book; Trial of Wilkinson's Jupiter, September 23, 1799, ibid. Absalom Johnson was taxed on sixteen slaves over the age of twelve in 1800. See Henrico County Personal Property Tax, 1800. On the attitude of slaves toward the appropriation of the property of their owners, see Lichtenstein, "'That Disposition to Theft.'" Thompson discusses the stealing of deer as an attack upon one of the "symbols of authority" (*Whigs and Hunters*, 64).

50. Isaac, *Transformation of Virginia*, 92; *Minutes of the Proceedings of the Fourth Convention of Delegates from the Abolition Societies*, 58; "An Act . . . Concerning Slaves, Free Negroes, and Mulattoes," December 17, 1792, in Shepherd, ed., *Statutes at Large*, 1:126. On the 1692 creation of the courts of oyer and terminer, see Schwarz, *Twice Condemned*, 17.

51. Trial of Wilkinson's Jupiter, September 23, 1799, Henrico County Court Order Book; "An Act against Hog Stealing," December 8, 1792, in Shepherd, ed., *Statutes at Large*, 1:111.

52. Trial of Prosser's Solomon, September 23, 1799, Henrico County Court Order Book.

53. Trial of Prosser's Gabriel, October 7, 1799, ibid.; "An Act . . . Concerning

Slaves, Free Negroes, and Mulattoes," December 17, 1792, in Shepherd, ed., *Statutes at Large*, 1:127; Preyer, "Crime, the Criminal Law, and Reform," 54, n. 6. During the year before his defense of Gabriel, Charles Copland earned an impressive $6,022.44 from his legal practice. See Charles Copland Diary, April 1799. Sawyer errs in writing that the practice was abolished in Virginia in 1796 as it was "repugnant" to most Virginians (" 'Benefit of Clergy,' " 66). Benefit of clergy was abolished only for whites; physical punishments on black bodies were more acceptable.

54. Complaint of Absalom Johnson, November 4, 1799, Henrico County Court Order Book; Prosser Bond, November 5, 1799, ibid. Schwarz suggests that Prosser left Gabriel in jail for the month of October as a form of control ("Gabriel's Challenge," 285). But the court record does not indicate that Gabriel was to remain in jail after his branding, and Prosser was quick to raise the bond to secure Gabriel's release after Johnson's second complaint. Schwarz, however, is especially good on the problems that Johnson faced as a newcomer to the region.

55. Ballagh claims that Gabriel did not have "an especial personal grievance to inspire him" (*Slavery in Virginia*, 92). Aside from his bondage and that of his wife being a "personal grievance," certainly the public branding of this proud slave by a white jailor counted as a special form of humiliation, as it was meant to be.

CHAPTER THREE

1. William Vans Murray to John Quincy Adams, December 9, 1800, in W. C. Ford, ed., "Letters of Vans Murray," 663.

2. Flexner, *Washington*, 369.

3. Brown, *Presidency of John Adams*, 48–51; Cunningham, *In Pursuit of Reason*, 213.

4. *Aurora* (Philadelphia), May 28, 1798; *Gazette of the United States* (Philadelphia), June 21, 1798.

5. Entry of December 9, 1798, David Erskine Copybook; *Annals of Congress*, 5th Cong., 2d Sess., 575, 586, 589, 599, 609, 2028, 2093, 2171.

6. [Virginia] Resolution, December 21, 1798, in Shepherd, ed., *Statutes at Large*, 2:192–93.

7. Lowery, *James Barbour*, 34–35; Ketcham, *James Madison*, 403–4.

8. Cunningham, *In Pursuit of Reason*, 222.

9. *Norfolk Herald*, May 31, 1800; Durey, *"With the Hammer of Truth,"* 133. The best discussion of Callender's trial is still J. M. Smith, *Freedom's Fetters*, chap. 15.

10. Entry of December 11, 1798, David Erskine Copybook; *Virginia Herald* (Fredericksburg), May 9, 1800; *Virginia Gazette and General Advertiser* (Richmond), January 25, 1799.

11. Koch writes that the rumors of Republicans stockpiling guns were just that (*Jefferson and Madison*, 194), and Davidson demonstrated that the Assembly voted money for the armory before the passage of the acts ("Virginia and the Alien and Sedition Laws"). But Malone observed: "Very likely there was belligerent talk by hotheads" (*Jefferson and His Time*, 3:416 and n. 17). Given the sedition act

trials, it would be odd if individual Republicans were *not* discussing disunion. The point here is not that the nation was on the verge of civil war but that Gabriel believed it to be. William Vans Murray and other Federalists believed it to be so, and they were hardly naive men. See Murray's letter to John Quincy Adams, December 9, 1800 (W. C. Ford, ed., "Letters of Vans Murray," 663).

12. Genovese suggests that Gabriel's conspiracy "matured in the wake of divisions or apparent divisions in the ruling classes" (*Roll, Jordan, Roll*, 593). This thesis would seem more applicable to the Vesey conspiracy of 1822, by which time the relative racial flexibility of 1800 had ended. Vesey, unlike Gabriel, wished to use the split among whites to flee the country; he could not envision joining either side or remaining in the American South.

13. Broussard, *Southern Federalists*, 5; James Monroe to Thomas Jefferson, April 23, 1800, Jefferson Papers; Charles Copland Diary, April 1800.

14. Stewart, *Opposition Press*, 346; Lowery, *James Barbour*, 24; *Virginia Gazette and General Advertiser* (Richmond), July 18, 1800.

15. Link, *Democratic-Republican Societies*, 13–16; Wilentz, *Chants Democratic*, 70. On such "conjunctions" see Thompson, *Making of the English Working Class*, 168.

16. Wilentz, *Chants Democratic*, 70–71. The view presented here dissents from that of Mathews, who suggests that the agrarian/pastoral Jefferson was in some ways more progressive—with his "distinctly nonmarket ethos"—than the petit bourgeois artisans (*Radical Politics of Thomas Jefferson*, 19–33). Aside from the fact that for Jefferson rhetoric and reality were rarely one and the same, Mathews fails to note that the artisans drew distinctions between property acquired by one's own labor and property—like Jefferson's—accumulated from the labor of others.

17. *Porcupine's Gazette* (Philadelphia), April 3, 1798; Lowery, *James Barbour*, 21.

18. Benjamin Henry Latrobe to Giambattista Scandella, April 17, 1798, in Carter, ed., *Papers of Latrobe*, 2:368–70. Hobsbawm and Rude make the same point in only a slightly different context (*Captain Swing*, 88–89). An example was the Hudson Valley slaveowner who sold a bondwoman because she "require[d] an attentive eye—being a Republican *of the Present day* [1803]." See Kurth, "Wayward Wenches and Wives," 206.

19. Isaac, *Transformation of Virginia*, 103; Weld, *Travels through North America*, 1:191.

20. Mayer, *Son of Thunder*, 241–45; Box 668, Account Book A, 1798–1827, Mosby Sheppard Papers.

21. Rediker, "American Revolution," 13; Testimony of Prosser's Sam at trial of Jack Ditcher, October 29, 1800, Executive Papers, Negro Insurrection.

22. This interpretation of the southern class system follows Morgan (*American Slavery, American Freedom*, 328, 380–81). On Gabriel's identification of the "merchants" as his enemies, see testimony of Prosser's Ben at trial of Gabriel, October 6, 1800, Executive Papers, Negro Insurrection.

23. David Meade to Judge [Joseph] Prentis, September 7, 1798, Prentis Family Papers.

24. McColley, *Slavery and Jeffersonian Virginia*, 4; D. B. Davis, *Revolutions*, 38; John Randolph to Creed Taylor, September 13, 1798, Taylor Papers.

25. Childs, *French Refugee Life*, 147–48; D. B. Davis, "American Equality and Foreign Revolutions," 731.

26. P. Smith, *John Adams*, 2:912–13; Ammon, *James Monroe*, 173.

27. Palmer, *Age of Democratic Revolution*, 514; Childs, *French Refugee Life*, 146; Gary B. Nash, "Forging Freedom: The Emancipation Experience in the Northern Seaport Cities, 1775–1820," in Berlin and Hoffman, eds., *Slavery and Freedom*, 8.

28. Genovese, *World the Slaveholders Made*, 6; *Boston Gazette*, October 9, 1800.

29. Joseph Selden to Wilson Cary Nicholas, January 1, 1801, Randolph Papers; Lerche, "Jefferson and the Election of 1800," 480.

30. Kennett, *French Forces in America*, 162.

31. Ibid., 156–57; McColley, *Slavery and Jeffersonian Virginia*, 83; Quarles, *Negro in the American Revolution*, 160–62.

32. Scott and Wyatt, *Petersburg's Story*, 54. P. Smith writes: "As many as thirty-thousand Frenchmen were estimated to be in America, many of them active agents in the Revolution" (*John Adams*, 2:977). Although the number of French nationals is generally correct, especially when the Dominguan refugees are included, few historians have accepted the conspiratorial notion that "many" were active agents of the Directory. Still, some radicals surely acted on their own to further what they believed to be the principles of 1776 and 1789.

33. Confession of Prosser's Solomon, September 15, 1800, Executive Communications, Letterbook. Confession of Young's Gilbert, September 23, 1800, Executive Papers, Negro Insurrection. For a discussion of the evidence on the Frenchmen, see Appendix 3.

34. Confession of Young's Gilbert, September 23, 1800, Executive Papers, Negro Insurrection; *Genealogies of Virginia Families*, 2:346–49; George Washington to Francis Corbin, July 24, 1798, in Fitzpatrick, ed., *Writings of Washington*, 36:362; Francis Corbin, Caroline County Personal Property and Land Book, 1799.

35. Confession of Young's Gilbert, September 23, 1800, Executive Papers, Negro Insurrection; Unsigned letter to editor, September 13, 1800, in *Virginia Herald* (Fredericksburg), September 23, 1800; Philadelphia Map, 1802, Genealogical Research Aids Room, National Archives, Washington, D.C.; Philadelphia City Directory, 1795, pp. 27, 35, 74; Nash, "Forging Freedom," 40. Whitridge briefly discusses the German-speaking Fourth Regiment (*Rochambeau*, 78–79).

36. Testimony of Prosser's Ben at trial of Prosser's Solomon, September 11, 1800, Executive Papers, Negro Insurrection; Confession of Prosser's Solomon, September 15, 1800, Executive Communications, Letterbook; *Spectator* (New York), October 1, 1800.

37. "An Act to Amend . . . the Act Concerning Slaves, Free Negroes, and Mulattoes, January 25, 1798," in Shepherd, ed., *Statutes at Large*, 2:77.

38. Curtin, *Rise and Fall of the Plantation Complex*, 166; James's *Black Jacobins* remains the classic work on the island revolt, but see also Ott's *Haitian Revolution*. Although many scholars spell the black leader's surname with an

apostrophe, he spelled it Louverture. As a slave, he was typically called Toussaint Breda, after the plantation of his birth.

39. Hunt, *Haiti's Influence*, 33; *Virginia Herald* (Fredericksburg), May 16, 1800. It was not until the preliminaries of peace were signed on October 1, 1801, that Bonaparte gave the word for the Leclerc expedition to sail for Saint Domingue; see James, *Black Jacobins*, 274.

40. *Norfolk Herald*, January 25, 1800; Robert G. Harper to his constituents, March 20, 1799, in Donnan, ed., *Papers of Bayard*, 2:90; Ott, *Haitian Revolution*, 54.

41. Hickey, "America's Response," 365; Joseph W. Cox, *Champion of Southern Federalism*, 144.

42. Hunt, *Haiti's Influence*, 101; E. Foner, *Nothing But Freedom*, 41–42; MacLeod, *Slavery, Race, and the American Revolution*, 153–54.

43. Bogger, "Slave and Free Black Community," 112–13; Weld, *Travels through North America*, 1:175–76.

44. Geggus, *Slavery, War, and Revolution*, 305; Berlin, *Slaves without Masters*, 40; [Norfolk mayor] John Cowper to James Monroe, March 11, 1802, Executive Papers; James Monroe to John Cowper, March 17, 1802, Executive Letterbook; James Monroe to Brigadier General Mathews, March 17, 1802, Executive Letterbook.

45. Unidentified newspaper clipping, William Palmer Scrapbook, 101; Scott, "Afro-American Slave Revolts," 10, 12.

46. C. Wilson, *Criminal History of Mankind*, 477.

47. As Hobsbawm and Rude have suggested, "Human beings do not react to the goad of hunger and oppression by some automatic and standard response of revolt. What they do, or fail to do, depends on their situation among other human beings, on their environment, culture, tradition, and experience" (*Captain Swing*, 56).

48. On the gap between the artisans and laboring poor in northern cities, see E. Foner, *Tom Paine*, 52–53; Hobsbawm's discussion of urban crowd action in only a slightly different setting is found in his *Primitive Rebels* (111).

49. Testimony of Prosser's Ben at trial of Prosser's Gabriel, October 6, 1800, Executive Papers, Negro Insurrection; Unsigned letter to editor, September 13, 1800, in *Virginia Herald* (Fredericksburg), September 23, 1800; Confession of Ben Woolfolk, September 17, 1800, Executive Papers, Negro Insurrection. The decision to spare poor white women was based on class, not sexual, considerations and should not be seen as supporting the traditional racist fantasy of black men lusting after white women. Historians who have interpreted this comment in such a way include Howison (*History of Virginia*, 2:390), Little (*History of Richmond*, 101), and Morgan (*James Monroe*, 228).

50. James Monroe to Thomas Jefferson, April 22, 1800, in Aptheker, *American Negro Slave Revolts*, 220, n. 38.

CHAPTER FOUR

1. Confession of Prosser's Solomon, September 15, 1800, Executive Letterbook; Testimony of Prosser's Ben at trial of Prosser's Solomon, September 11, 1800, Executive Papers, Negro Insurrection; William Mosby to James Monroe, November 10, 1800, in *Journal of the Senate of Virginia*, 26.

2. See Rediker, *Between the Devil and the Deep Blue Sea*, 227–29, for a profile of a conspiracy in a similar context.

3. Unsigned letter to editor, September 20, 1800, in *Norfolk Herald*, October 18, 1800; Confession of Prosser's Solomon, September 15, 1800, Executive Letterbook; Testimony of Prosser's Ben at trial of Prosser's Gabriel, October 6, 1800, Executive Papers, Negro Insurrection; John Randolph to Joseph Nicholson, September 26, 1800, Nicholson Papers; Thompson, "Moral Economy of the English Crowd," 112. Mullin criticizes Gabriel's plan as being too complex and starting too far outside of the city (*Flight and Rebellion*, 151). The Brook Bridge, however, was only four miles outside of Richmond, far enough away for slaves to gather in large numbers without being detected but close enough to the city that they could easily march upon it before daybreak. James Callender, who was in the city jail, insisted the scheme "could hardly have failed of success"; see his letter to Thomas Jefferson, September [18; misdated 13], 1800, Jefferson Papers. John Randolph also had no doubts about its chances of success; see his letter to Joseph Nicholson, cited above.

4. On this point, see D. B. Davis, *Revolutions*, 29.

5. Testimony of Ben Woolfolk at trial of Prosser's Gabriel, October 6, 1800, Executive Letterbook; Testimony of Prosser's Ben at trial of Prosser's Gabriel, October 6, 1800, Executive Papers, Negro Insurrection. See Thornton on the use of banners by West African armies ("African Dimensions of the Stono Rebellion," 1111).

6. Confession of Ben Woolfolk, September 17, 1800, Executive Papers, Negro Insurrection. Mullin correctly takes Gabriel to task for slighting the religious dimension (*Flight and Rebellion*, 159–60).

7. Testimony of Ben Woolfolk at trial of George Smith, September 19, 1800, Executive Papers, Negro Insurrection; Raboteau, *Slave Religion*, 13–14; Stuckey, *Slave Culture*, 34. Harding wisely suggests that Gabriel should have taken the traditions of Africa more seriously (*There Is a River*, 56).

8. Testimony of Prosser's Ben at trial of Prosser's Martin, September 12, 1800, Executive Papers, Negro Insurrection.

9. Unsigned letter to editor, September 20, 1800, in *Norfolk Herald*, October 18, 1800; Testimony of Prosser's Ben at trial of Burton's Isham, September 15, 1800, Executive Papers, Negro Insurrection.

10. Stuckey, *Slave Culture*, 69; White, *Ar'n't I a Woman?*, 75–76.

11. Pinchbeck, *Virginia Negro Artisan*, 30; Schwarz, *Twice Condemned*, 223, n. 51; Isaac, *Transformation of Virginia*, 52–53.

12. Manarin and Dowdey, *History of Henrico County*, 167; Testimony of Prosser's Ben at trial of Prosser's Solomon, September 11, 1800, Executive Papers, Negro Insurrection; Joseph Jones to James Madison, September 9, 1800, Execu-

tive Papers, Negro Insurrection. That some of the plans were laid after religious services on Sunday does not mean the conspiracy had evangelical overtones. It was simply a safe place to congregate. The 1358 Jacquerie rising, for example, was planned in meetings held after vespers. See Barbara W. Tuchman, *A Distant Mirror: The Calamitous Fourteenth Century* (New York, 1978), 176.

13. *Richmond Recorder*, April 9, 1803; Testimony of Prosser's Ben at trial of Gregory's Charles, September 12, 1800, Executive Papers, Negro Insurrection.

14. Testimony of Ben Woolfolk at trial of George Smith, September 19, 1800, Executive Papers, Negro Insurrection; Confession of Ben Woolfolk, September 17, 1800, ibid.; Unsigned letter to editor, September 20, 1800, in *Norfolk Herald*, October 18, 1800.

15. Unsigned letter to editor, September 20, 1800, in *Norfolk Herald*, October 18, 1800; Testimony of Ben Woolfolk at trial of Sam Byrd, Jr., September 27, 1800, Executive Papers, Negro Insurrection; *Kentucky Gazette* (Lexington), November 3, 1800.

16. Testimony of Patrick at trial of Gregory's Charles, September 12, 1800, Executive Papers, Negro Insurrection; Testimony of Ben Woolfolk at trial of Woodfin's Jacob, September 30, 1800, ibid.; Testimony of Ben Woolfolk at trial of Williamson's Lewis, October 1, 1800, [misfiled in] Executive Papers, 1802, Pardon Papers.

17. Testimony of Prosser's Ben at trial of Young's Gilbert, September 22, 1800, Executive Papers, Negro Insurrection; Testimony of Prosser's Ben at trial of Gregory's Billey, September 12, 1800, ibid. On the use of the term "business" as Atlantic basin slang for revolutionary activity, see Richard H. Condon, "Col. Edward Despard," in Baylen and Grossman, eds., *Biographical Dictionary of Modern British Radicals*, 1:119.

18. *Richmond Recorder*, April 13, 1803; Testimony of Prosser's Ben at trial of Mosby's Will, September 11, 1800, Executive Papers, Negro Insurrection; John Randolph to Joseph Nicholson, September 26, 1800, Nicholson Papers; James T. Callender to Thomas Jefferson, September [18; misdated 13], 1800, Jefferson Papers; Unsigned letter to editor, September 20, 1800, in *Norfolk Herald*, October 18, 1800.

19. Testimony of Prosser's Ben at trial of Prosser's Solomon, September 11, 1800, Executive Papers, Negro Insurrection; Testimony of Ben Woolfolk at trial of Sam Byrd, Jr., September 27, 1800, ibid.

20. Wade suggests that urban areas hindered slave revolts on the grounds that urban bondmen, because of their better conditions, would have less incentive to rise up (*Slavery in the Cities*, 226). Lofton dissents from that view by noting that "revolutionary movements have usually been led and widely supported, not by the most deprived class but by those who already enjoyed certain privileges and who wanted to remove remaining vestiges of tyranny precisely because they could visualize and appreciate the advantages of freedom" (*Denmark Vesey's Revolt*, xi). Genovese agrees with Lofton and suggests that "urban centers, like great plantation districts, offered especially favorable conditions as well as special dangers" (*From Rebellion to Revolution*, 14).

21. Undated notation in James Monroe's hand, Executive Papers, Negro Insurrection; Trial of Thomas Jordan Martin, October 6, 1800, Henrico County Court Order Book.

22. Testimony of Ben Woolfolk at trial of Nicholas's King, October 3, 1800, Executive Papers, Negro Insurrection; Larkin Stanard to James Monroe, October 30, 1800, ibid.; Testimony of Philip Nicholas at trial of Nicholas's King, September 25, 1800, Executive Papers.

23. Confession of Young's Gilbert, September 23, 1800, Executive Papers, Negro Insurrection; Undated notation in James Monroe's hand, ibid.

24. Confession of Young's Gilbert, September 23, 1800, ibid.

25. Testimony of Prosser's Ben at trial of Wilkinson's Jupiter, September 15, 1800, ibid.; Unidentified newspaper clipping, William Palmer Scrapbook; Mordecai, *Richmond*, 312–13.

26. "An Act to Fix the Salaries of Certain Officers," February 2, 1802, in Shepherd, ed., *Statutes at Large*, 2:334; Obituary of Robert Cowley, in *Daily Compiler* (Richmond), February 10, 1820; Confession of William Young's Gilbert, September 23, 1800, Executive Papers, Negro Insurrection.

27. Confession of Prosser's Solomon, September 15, 1800, Executive Letterbook; Testimony of Owen's Ned at trial of Owen's Michael, September 11, 1800, Executive Papers, Negro Insurrection; *Richmond Recorder*, April 13, 1803.

28. Testimony of Prosser's Ben at trial of Wilkinson's Jupiter, September 15, 1800, Executive Papers, Negro Insurrection; Testimony of Ben Woolfolk at trial of George Smith, September 19, 1800, ibid. This is not to imply that Gabriel looked down on the less-assimilated plantation slaves, only that their cultural domain was so different that he and they had little in common—aside from their obvious interest in freedom. Certainly they had little understanding of his emphasis on property and a fair share of the wealth of society. On relations between skilled bondmen and field hands, see Genovese, *Roll, Jordan, Roll*, 393. Denmark Vesey's conspiracy was largely urban, although Gullah Jack Pritchard, who had no counterpart in the 1800 plan, recruited among the plantation slaves outside of Charleston; see Lofton, *Denmark Vesey's Revolt*, 135–38.

29. Testimony of Prosser's Ben at trial of Prosser's Gabriel, October 6, 1800, Executive Papers, Negro Insurrection; Testimony of Ben Woolfolk at trial of Sam Byrd, Jr., September 27, 1800, ibid.; Scott and Wyatt, *Petersburg's Story*, 90.

30. Weld, *Travels through North America*, 1:185; Chastellux, *Travels in North America*, 2:426; *Return of the Whole Number of Persons within the Several Districts of the United States*, 70; Scott and Wyatt, *Petersburg's Story*, 65, 351.

31. William Prentis to James Monroe, September 24, 1800, Executive Papers, Negro Insurrection; Confession of Young's Gilbert, September 23, 1800, ibid.; Petersburg City Personal Property Tax, 1795–1803.

32. Unidentified newspaper clipping, William Palmer Scrapbook; William Prentis to James Monroe, September 6, 1800, Executive Papers, Negro Insurrection.

33. Carter, ed., *Papers of Latrobe*, 1:127; Sentence of Claiborne's Peter, October 20, 1800, Condemned Slaves 1800, Auditor's Item 153, box 2. For a brief Claiborne family history, see Hatfield, *William Claiborne*, 3.

34. [Richmond mayor] James McClurg to James Monroe, n.d., Executive Papers, Negro Insurrection; Unsigned letter to editor, September 13, 1800, in *Virginia Herald* (Fredericksburg), September 23, 1800.

35. Carter, ed., *Papers of Latrobe*, 1:75; *Return of the Whole Number of Persons within the Several Districts of the United States*, 70; Weld, *Travels through North America*, 1:173–74; Bogger, "Slave and Free Black Community," 201; Wertenbaker, *Norfolk*, 125–26.

36. Pay warrant to Joel Thomas, March 3, 1801, Gabriel's Insurrection, Military Papers; Thomas Booth to Alexander McCrea, October 5, 1800, Executive Papers; William Prentis to James Monroe, n.d., Executive Papers, Negro Insurrection. Most contemporary newspaper sources incorrectly described Jacob as a free man.

37. Thomas Booth to Alexander McCrea, October 5, 1800, Executive Papers; A.W. to B.H., September 20, 1800, Executive Papers (the only extant letter from a conspirator of 1800); *Norfolk Herald*, October 2, 1800.

38. Testimony of Ben Woolfolk at trial of George Smith, September 19, 1800, Executive Papers, Negro Insurrection; Testimony of Prosser's Ben at trial of Young's Sawney, September 13, 1800, ibid.; Testimony of Prosser's Ben at trial of Ben Woolfolk, September 18, 1800, Executive Papers.

39. Testimony of Ben Woolfolk at trial of Thilman's Thornton, October 30, 1800, Executive Papers.

40. On the Christmas plot of 1769, see Schwarz, *Twice Condemned*, 180 and n. 27.

41. Testimony of Ben Woolfolk at trial of Thilman's Dick, October 6, 1800, Executive Papers, Negro Insurrection; Confession of Sam Graham, n.d., Executive Papers; Testimony of Ben Woolfolk at trial of Jack Gabriel, October 29, 1800, ibid.

42. Carter, ed., *Papers of Latrobe*, 2:326; Confession of Young's Gilbert, September 23, 1800, Executive Papers, Negro Insurrection.

43. Testimony of Ben Woolfolk at trial of Sam Byrd, Jr., September 27, 1800, Executive Papers, Negro Insurrection; Sentence of Smith's Ben, October 1, 1800, Louisa County Court Order Book.

44. Confession of Young's Gilbert, September 23, 1800, Executive Papers, Negro Insurrection.

45. *Richmond Recorder*, April 13, 1803; Confession of Ben Woolfolk, September 17, 1800, Executive Papers, Negro Insurrection; Testimony of Prosser's Ben at trial of Prosser's Watt, December 1, 1800, Executive Papers.

46. Testimony of Prosser's Ben at trial of Burton's Isham, September 15, 1800, Executive Papers, Negro Insurrection; Testimony of Williamson's Daniel at trial of Jones' John, September 11, 1800, ibid. William Burton testified that the barbecue was on July 20; see his testimony at trial of his slave Isham, September 15, 1800, ibid.

47. Testimony of Jones's John at trial of Prosser's Frank, September 12, 1800, Executive Papers, Negro Insurrection; John Foster to James Monroe, September 9, 1800, ibid.; Testimony of Williamson's Daniel at trial of Jones's John, September 11, 1800, ibid.

48. William Young to Samuel Pleasants, September 24, 1800, *Virginia Argus*

(Richmond), October 3, 1800; Testimony of Price's John at trial of Young's Gilbert, September 22, 1800, Executive Papers, Negro Insurrection.

49. Testimony of Prosser's Ben at trial of Prosser's Solomon, September 11, 1800, Executive Papers, Negro Insurrection; Confession of Ben Woolfolk, September 17, 1800, ibid.

50. Confession of Prosser's Solomon, September 15, 1800, Executive Letterbook; Confession of Ben Woolfolk, September 17, 1800, Executive Papers, Negro Insurrection; Unsigned letter to editor, September 13, 1800, in *Virginia Herald* (Fredericksburg), September 23, 1800; Unsigned letter to editor, September 20, 1800, in *Norfolk Herald*, October 18, 1800.

51. Testimony of Prosser's Ben at trial of Prosser's Gabriel, October 6, 1800, Executive Papers, Negro Insurrection; Testimony of Mosby's Will at trial of Prosser's Solomon, September 11, 1800, ibid.; Unsigned letter to editor, September 13, 1800, in *Virginia Herald* (Fredericksburg), September 23, 1800. At the trial of Sam Byrd, Jr. (September 27, 1800, Executive Papers, Negro Insurrection), Ben Woolfolk testified that Byrd told him that the "french would join them against the White people." Woolfolk did not understand; Byrd meant only that two Frenchmen had joined, not that he expected any help from the country of France. Aptheker nonetheless writes that Gabriel "knew of the strained relations between the United States and France . . . and this led [him] to hope for assistance from France once their own rebellion was under way" (*American Negro Slave Revolts*, 101). As far as the extant evidence indicates, he did not.

52. Unsigned letter to editor, September 20, 1800, in *Norfolk Herald*, October 18, 1800; Confession of Ben Woolfolk, September 17, 1800, Executive Papers, Negro Insurrection. The quotations attributed to Martin are the only references to religion in all of the trial testimony. They do not support the myth that Martin was a slave preacher. They indicate only that Martin, like most Virginians, had a working knowledge of the Bible and that he, like most black Virginians, had a fondness for the Old Testament.

53. Testimony of Ben Woolfolk at trial of Sam Byrd, Jr., September 27, 1800, Executive Papers, Negro Insurrection; Unsigned letter to editor, September 20, 1800, in *Norfolk Herald*, October 18, 1800.

54. Testimony of Price's John at trial of Williamson's Laddis, September 16, 1800, Executive Papers, Negro Insurrection; Testimony of Price's John at trial of Sam Graham, September 29, 1800, ibid.

55. Testimony of Price's John at trial of Jack Ditcher, October 29, 1800, ibid.

56. Ibid.

57. Testimony of Winston's Charles at trial of Jones's John, September 11, 1800, ibid; Confession of Ben Woolfolk, September 17, 1800, ibid.

58. Testimony of Ben Woolfolk at trial of Thilman's Thornton, October 30, 1800, Executive Papers; Testimony of Ben Woolfolk at trial of John Fells, October 30, 1800, ibid.; Testimony of Ben Woolfolk at trial of Jack Gabriel, October 29, 1800, ibid.; Confession of Sam Graham, n.d., ibid.

59. Testimony of Ben Woolfolk at trial of Leftwich's Randolph, October 6, 1800, Executive Letterbook. There is, however, no evidence to support the assertion

made by Halasz that all blacks "were to be forced to join the rebels or die like whites" (*Rattling Chains*, 92).

60. Confession of Young's Gilbert, September 23, 1800, Executive Papers, Negro Insurrection; *Virginia Herald* (Fredericksburg), September 19, 1800, October 3, 1800.

61. J. Grammer to Augustine Davis, August 9, 1800, in Flourney, ed., *Calendar of Virginia State Papers*, 9:128; [Richmond mayor] James McClurg to James Monroe, August 10, 1800, ibid.

62. Testimony of Prosser's Ben at trial of Wilkinson's Daniel, September 15, 1800, Executive Papers, Negro Insurrection; Testimony of Prosser's Ben at trial of Prosser's Watt, December 1, 1800, Executive Papers; Testimony of Prosser's Ben at trial of Ben Woolfolk, September 18, 1800, ibid.; Confession of Ben Woolfolk, September 17, 1800, Executive Papers, Negro Insurrection; Confession of Sam Graham, n.d., Executive Papers. Thornton was one of at least fifteen slaves owned by Paul Thilman; slaves under the age of twelve were not taxed or listed in tax records. See Paul Thilman, Hanover County Personal Property Tax, 1799.

63. Testimony of Prosser's Ben at trial of Prosser's Solomon, September 11, 1800, Executive Papers, Negro Insurrection; John Randolph to Joseph Nicholson, September 26, 1800, Nicholson Papers; *Kentucky Gazette* (Lexington), November 3, 1800; *Virginia Argus* (Richmond), October 10, 1800.

CHAPTER FIVE

1. *Norfolk Herald*, June 19, 1800.

2. James Callender to Thomas Jefferson, September [18; misdated 13], 1800, Jefferson Papers; Unsigned letter to editor, September 20, 1800, in *Norfolk Herald*, October 18, 1800; James Monroe to General Assembly, December 5, 1800, Letterbook, Executive Communications.

3. Testimony of Prosser's Ben at trial of Owen's Michael, September 11, 1800, Executive Papers, Negro Insurrection; Testimony of Prosser's Ben at trial of Prosser's Frank, September 12, 1800, ibid.; Testimony of Prosser's Ben at trial of Prosser's Gabriel, October 6, 1800, ibid. The events of the night of August 30 have led to a great deal of undocumented speculation on the part of scholars. Both Ballagh (*Slavery in Virginia*, 92) and Aptheker (*American Negro Slave Revolts*, 221) have suggested that one thousand slaves met at Brookfield. The trial records are not specific on this point, but they do indicate that because of the heavy rain, very few arrived at the Prosser plantation. In any case, Gabriel never estimated the number of his followers to be nearly that high. George Morgan wrote that Prosser, "warned by a servant, escaped from his dwelling, by leaping through a window" (*Life of James Monroe*, 228). Not surprisingly, no source was provided. The most inventive of all is Giddings, who argues that "one thousand slaves met outside of Richmond and marched on the city [but] were routed by the militia" (*When and Where I Enter*, 40).

4. Testimony of Sheppard's Pharoah at trial of Owen's Michael, September 11, 1800, Executive Papers, Negro Insurrection; Testimony of Sheppard's Pharoah at

trial of Prosser's Solomon, September 11, 1800, ibid.; Gibbons, "Meadow Farm," 67–69. The current house was built by Mosby Sheppard in 1810; see *Meadow Farm Museum: Crump Park* (Henrico County Brochure).

5. William Sheppard, Henrico County Personal Property Tax, 1782; Mosby Sheppard, Henrico County Personal Property Tax, 1799; Unidentified newspaper clipping, William Palmer Scrapbook; Box 456, Financial Records and Deeds, 1799–1824, Mosby Sheppard Papers; Samuel Coleman to James Monroe, February 28, 1801, in Flournoy, ed., *Calendar of Virginia State Papers*, 9:201.

6. Samuel Coleman to James Monroe, February 28, 1801, in Flournoy, ed., *Calendar of Virginia State Papers*, 9:201–02; James Monroe to Philip Shephard [*sic*], March 5, 1801, in Hamilton, ed., *Writings of Monroe*, 3:266; Box 456, Financial Records and Deeds, 1799–1824, Mosby Sheppard Papers.

7. Genovese, *Roll, Jordan, Roll*, 8–9; Box 668, Account Book, Household, 1794–1812, Mosby Sheppard Papers; Mosby Sheppard, Henrico County Personal Property Tax, 1799; Christian, *Richmond*, 53.

8. Box 668, Account Book, Household, 1794–1812, Mosby Sheppard Papers. Sheppard bought Pharoah "1 Hatt, 1 Boys Hatt, and 1 White Hatt [Bonnet]."

9. Box 668, Account Book, Household, 1794–1812, Mosby Sheppard Papers; Box 457, Financial Records, Philip Sheppard Papers. On the fate of traitors in the African afterlife, see Stuckey, *Slave Culture*, 6.

10. Samuel Coleman to James Monroe, February 28, 1801, in Flournoy, ed., *Calendar of Virginia State Papers*, 9:201; Unidentified newspaper clipping, William Palmer Scrapbook.

11. Mosby Sheppard to James Monroe, August 30, 1800, in *Journal of the Senate of Virginia*, 26.

12. William Mosby to James Monroe, November 10, 1800, in ibid.

13. James Monroe to the General Assembly, December 5, 1800, Letterbook, Executive Communications; William Mosby to James Monroe, November 10, 1800, in *Journal of the Senate of Virginia*, 26; Joseph Jones to James Monroe, September 9, 1800, Executive Papers, Negro Insurrection.

14. Ammon, *James Monroe*, 185–86; *Norfolk Herald*, September 27, 1800; James Monroe to Thomas Jefferson, September 15, 1800, Jefferson Papers.

15. Testimony of Prosser's Ben at trial of Jack Ditcher, October 29, 1800, Executive Papers, Negro Insurrection; *Richmond Recorder*, April 9, 1803.

16. Testimony of William Gentry at trial of Burton's Isaac, September 11, 1800, Executive Papers, Negro Insurrection; *Richmond Recorder*, April 6, 1803; Unsigned letter to editor, September 20, 1800, in *Norfolk Herald*, October 18, 1800; George Tucker to St. George Tucker, September 1, 1800, Tucker-Coleman Papers.

17. Testimony of Prosser's Ben at trial of Prosser's Watt, December 1, 1800, Executive Papers; Testimony of Ben Woolfolk at trial of Young's Gilbert, September 22, 1800, Executive Papers, Negro Insurrection.

18. *Virginia Argus* (Richmond), October 10, 1800; Paul Thilman to James Monroe, n.d., Executive Papers; Christopher Hudson to James Monroe, September 24, 1800, Executive Papers, Negro Insurrection.

19. Testimony of Mary Martin at trial of Nicholas's King, September 25, 1800, Executive Papers.

20. Testimony of Ben Woolfolk at trial of Williamson's Lewis, October 1, 1800, Executive Papers, 1802, Pardon Papers, (misfiled); Thomas Booth to Alexander McCrea, October 5, 1800, Executive Papers; A.W. to B.H., September 20, 1800, ibid. The A.W. letter is the extant letter written by a conspirator. Although the writer A.W. probably did not know where Gabriel was hiding, A.W. obviously was literate and could read in the newspapers that Gabriel had not been arrested. Since all of the other leaders save Ditcher had been captured, Gabriel doubtless was the "brother X," referred to in the letter, who was still at large.

21. John Foster to James Monroe, September 9, 1800, Executive Papers, Negro Insurrection.

22. Payroll, May 12, 1801, Gabriel's Insurrection, Military Papers; Accounts, n.d. ibid. On the structure of the militia see Tillson, *Gentry and the Common Folk*, 47. (Some of the accounts are in dollars, others in pounds, a few in both. I have converted all of the figures into dollars using the exchange rate of £1 to $3.33, which was the rate then used by the State of Virginia.)

23. Payroll, March 2, 1801, Gabriel's Insurrection, Military Papers; Payroll, November 24, 1800, ibid.; Accounts, January 31, 1801, ibid.; Accounts, February 24, 1801, ibid.

24. Mayo Carrington to James Monroe, September 17, 1800, Executive Papers, Negro Insurrection; Aptheker, *American Negro Slave Revolts*, 223, n. 49; General Accounts, January 6, 1801, Gabriel's Insurrection, Military Papers; Militia Rolls, December 10, 1800, ibid.; General Accounts, October 6, 1800, ibid.; John Randolph to Joseph Nicholson, September 26, 1800, Nicholson Papers.

25. Accounts, November 24, 1800, Chesterfield Militia, Gabriel's Insurrection, Military Papers; Payroll, n.d., Chesterfield Militia, ibid.; Payroll, November 24, 1800, (William Fendley) Chesterfield Militia, ibid.; Militia Rolls, November 24, 1800, Chesterfield Militia, ibid.; Payroll, November 24, 1800, (William Branch) Chesterfield Militia, ibid.; Pay Warrant, November 24, 1800, (William Ball) Chesterfield Militia, ibid.; Pay Warrant, November 24, 1800, (Henry Featherston) Chesterfield Militia, ibid.; Pay Warrant, November 24, 1800, (William Goode) Chesterfield Militia, ibid.; Pay Warrant, November 24, 1800 (Richard Baugh) Chesterfield Militia, ibid.; Pay Warrant, November 24, 1800, (Henry Winfree) Chesterfield Militia, ibid.; Pay Warrant, November 24, 1800, (Reuben Brumal) Chesterfield Militia, ibid.; Pay Warrant, November 24, 1800, (William Friend) Chesterfield Militia, ibid.; Pay Warrant, November 24, 1800, (Mathew Cheatham) Chesterfield Militia, ibid.; Pay Warrant, November 24, 1800, (Edward Friend) Chesterfield Militia, ibid.; Pay Warrant, November 24, 1800, (Robert Hills) Chesterfield Militia, ibid.; Pay Warrant, November 24, 1800, (Daniel Wooldrigger) Chesterfield Militia, ibid.; Pay Warrant, November 24, 1800, (John Goode) Chesterfield Militia, ibid.; Pay Warrant, November 24, 1800, (Francis Lockett) Chesterfield Militia, ibid.

26. William Wilkinson to James Monroe, October 1, 1800, Executive Papers, Negro Insurrection; *Virginia Argus* (Richmond), October 10, 1800; *Norfolk Herald*, October 2, 1800; Warrant, March 3, 1801, Gabriel's Insurrection, Military Papers.

27. Caroline Guards, March 17, 1801, Gabriel's Insurrection, Military Papers; Payroll, January 1, 1801, ibid.; Payroll, December 11, 1800, ibid.

28. Edmund Pendleton, Jr., to James Monroe, October 22, 1800, Executive Papers, Pardons Papers; Pay Warrant, December 27, 1800, Gabriel's Insurrection, Military Papers; William Radford to John Preston, September 14, 1800, Preston Family Papers.

29. George Tucker to St. George Tucker, September 1, 1800, Tucker-Coleman Papers; *Virginia Gazette and General Advertiser* (Richmond), September 12, 1800, in *Virginia Herald* (Fredericksburg), September 16, 1800.

30. Quoted in Fitzgerald, *A Different Story*, 65; *Kentucky Gazette* (Lexington), November 3, 1800.

31. James Callender to Thomas Jefferson, September [18; misdated 13], 1800, Jefferson Papers; John Randolph to Joseph Nicholson, September 26, 1800, Nicholson Papers.

32. Thomas Newton to James Monroe, December 29, 1800, Executive Papers; [Williamsburg mayor] John Bracken to James Monroe, September 20, 1800, Executive Papers, Negro Insurrection.

33. George Braikensridge to Francis Jerdone, November 12, 1800, Jerdone Papers.

34. *Kentucky Gazette* (Lexington), October 6, 1800. See W. D. Jordan on white fears of black sexuality during times of slave uprisings (*White over Black*, 151–54). The assumption that oppressed peoples desired the wives of the ruling class was not limited to Gabriel's Virginia. The French aristocracy assumed that the rape of their wives, not injustice, was the motivation behind the Jacquerie uprising of 1358; see Barbara W. Tuchman, *A Distant Mirror: The Calamitous Fourteenth Century* (New York, 1978), 176.

35. "An Act . . . Concerning Slaves, Free Negroes, and Mulattoes," December 17, 1792, in Shepherd, ed., *Statutes at Large*, 1:125. The punishment was not common, yet it persisted into the nineteenth century. In 1802 John Gibbs's Jack was found guilty of the attempted rape of Eliza Rowlett and sentenced to be "castrated on Thursday next." The "operation," which was to be performed by Dr. Thomas A. Taylor, was never done. See Chesterfield County Court Order Book, July 12, 1802, pp. 301, 306. The assumption that Gabriel's men desired white women, not surprisingly, found its way into Marion Harland's late-nineteenth-century novel *Judith: A Chronicle of Old Virginia*. Harland's Gabriel planned to spare "only some young women . . . half a dozen who were to marry the principle men." Nanny would be disposed of in favor of "Mrs. Randolph, a beautiful widow [who would be] his queen" (excerpt in Goode, *Virginia Cousins*, 59).

36. On this point, see Litwack, *Been in the Storm So Long*, 266.

37. James Monroe to Thomas Jefferson, September 9, 1800, Jefferson Papers.

38. John Randolph to Joseph Nicholson, September 26, 1800, Nicholson Papers; Militia Rolls, December 27, 1800, Gabriel's Insurrection, Military Papers; Militia Rolls, December 10, 1800, ibid.

39. Accounts, n.d., Gabriel's Insurrection, Military Papers; Accounts, November 20, 1800, ibid.; Accounts, n.d., ibid.

40. Thomas Newton to James Monroe, September 24, 1800, Executive Papers, Negro Insurrection; *Boston Gazette*, October 9, 1800; *Norfolk Herald*, September 25, 1800; *Spectator* (New York), October 4, 1800. Most of the newspaper accounts claim that Gabriel was carrying a bayonet fixed on a stick when he boarded the *Mary*. The scythe swords, however, were tied to wooden handles and would have resembled a crude bayonet.

CHAPTER SIX

1. James Monroe to Thomas Jefferson, September 9, 1800, Jefferson Papers; *Virginia Herald* (Fredericksburg), September 16, 1800.

2. Unsigned letter to editor, September 20, 1800, in *Norfolk Herald*, October 18, 1800; Mordecai, *Richmond*, 125.

3. Gaines, "Courthouses of Henrico and Chesterfield," 33; Unsigned letter to editor, September 20, 1800, in *Norfolk Herald*, October 18, 1800; Flanigan, "Criminal Procedure in Slave Trials," 544; McColley, *Slavery and Jeffersonian Virginia*, 64; Schwarz, *Twice Condemned*, 51, n. 27.

4. *Minutes of the Proceedings of the Fourth Convention of Delegates from the Abolition Societies*, 58; "An Act . . . Concerning Slaves, Free Negroes, and Mulattoes," December 17, 1792, in Shepherd, ed., *Statutes at Large*, 1:126–27. Stampp writes that when a slave was condemned, the compensation paid the owner was "something less than the full value assessed by a jury" (*Peculiar Institution*, 198–99). That was not the case in Virginia.

5. St. George Tucker, *Dissertation on Slavery*, 62; "An Act . . . Concerning Slaves, Free Negroes, and Mulattoes," December 17, 1792, in Shepherd, ed., *Statutes at Large*, 1:125.

6. Douglas Hay, "Property, Authority, and the Criminal Law," in Hay, ed., *Albion's Fatal Tree*, 29; Roeber, "Authority, Law, and Custom," 39.

7. Wren, "A 'Two-Fold Character,'" 420–21; Isaac, *Transformation of Virginia*, 94. Sutcliff, *Travels in North America*, 50. Some scholars believe that Sutcliff was describing the trial of slaves executed in an 1804 conspiracy, a plot for which there is no other evidence. Evidently the term "lately" used here by Sutcliff means "in recent years." Moreover, internal evidence suggests that the trial he was discussing was held in 1800. Sutcliff alluded to slaves tried in Richmond but hanged in "a field" north of the city. Several conspirators, including George Smith and Prosser's Tom, were tried in Richmond but hanged north of town near Prosser's tavern. During the Easter 1802 conspiracy no slaves were hanged either in or north of Richmond.

8. Stampp, *Peculiar Institution*, 226–27; Flanigan, "Criminal Procedure in Slave Trials," 556. The refusal to allow slaves to testify against free persons was based upon Roman slave law and was not in its origins racist, as it became in Virginia. See Watson, *Slave Law in the Americas*, chap. 2.

9. Gervas Storrs and Joseph Selden to James Monroe, September 8, 1800, Executive Papers, Negro Insurrection; *Kentucky Gazette* (Lexington), November 3, 1800; Flanigan, "Criminal Procedure in Slave Trials," 543–44.

10. *Virginia Herald* (Fredericksburg), September 16, 1800; *Norfolk Herald*, September 27, 1800.

11. Trial of Prosser's Solomon, September 11, 1800, Henrico County Court Order Book; *Richmond Recorder*, June 9, 1802.

12. Testimony of Prosser's Ben at trial of Prosser's Solomon, September 11, 1800, Executive Papers, Negro Insurrection; Sentence of Prosser's Solomon, September 11, 1800, ibid.; Copy of sentence in Condemned Slaves 1800, Auditor's Item 153, box 2.

13. Testimony of Williamson's Daniel at trial of Jones's John, September 11, 1800, Executive Papers, Negro Insurrection; Sentence of Jones's John, September 11, 1800, ibid.; Copy of sentence in Condemned Slaves 1800, Auditor's Item 153, box 2.

14. Testimony of Prosser's Ben, Holman's Toby, and Burton's Dan at trial of Mosby's Will and Burton's Isaac, September 11, 1800, Executive Papers, Negro Insurrection; Sentence of Mosby's Will, September 11, 1800, ibid.; Copy of sentence in Condemned Slaves 1800, Auditor's Item 153, box 2; Sentence of Burton's Isaac, September 11, 1800, Executive Papers, Negro Insurrection; Copy of sentence in Condemned Slaves 1800, Auditor's Item 153, box 2. The trial records for Jones's John, Burton's Isaac, and Mosby's Will are inexplicably repeated in the Henrico County Court Order Book under the date of October 11, thereby making it appear that more slaves were tried than actually were.

15. Trial of Owen's Michael, September 11, 1800, Henrico County Court Order Book; Testimony of Prosser's Ben at trial of Owen's Michael, September 11, 1800, Executive Papers, Negro Insurrection; Sentence of Owen's Michael, September 11, 1800, ibid.; Copy of sentence in Condemned Slaves, Auditor's Item 153, box 2.

16. Trial of Parson's Ned, September 11, 1800, Henrico County Court Order Book; Testimony of Mosby's Wiltshire at trial of Parson's Ned, September 11, 1800, Executive Papers, Negro Insurrection; Sentence of Parson's Ned, September 11, 1800, ibid.; Copy of sentence in Condemned Slaves, Auditor's Item 153, box 2.

17. Trial of Gregory's Billey, September 11, 1800, Henrico County Court Order Book.

18. Petition of Prosser's Solomon, September 12, 1800, Executive Papers, Negro Insurrection; Confession of Prosser's Solomon, September 15, 1800 (dated after the fact), Executive Letterbook. Schwarz errs in suggesting that Prosser's Solomon "would escape the gallows by incriminating other slaves" ("Gabriel's Challenge," 284). The useful appendix in his *Twice Condemned* correctly lists Solomon as "hanged" (324).

19. Unidentified newspaper clipping, William Palmer Scrapbook; William Rose to James Monroe, September 12, 1800, Executive Papers, Negro Insurrection.

20. Peter Linebaugh, "The Tyburn Riot against the Surgeons," in Hay, ed., *Albion's Fatal Tree*, 67; Ayers, *Vengeance and Justice*, 136; Jones, *Born a Child of Freedom, Yet a Slave*, 91; Unidentified newspaper clipping, William Palmer Scrapbook; Miller, *Wolf by the Ears*, 20.

21. James Monroe to General Assembly, December 5, 1800, Executive Communications; John Mayo to Samuel Pleasants, September 24, 1800, in *Virginia Argus*

(Richmond), October 3, 1800; Unidentified newspaper clipping, William Palmer Scrapbook; Certification of death for Mosby's Will, signed by Mosby Sheppard, n.d., Condemned Slaves 1800, Auditor's Item 153, box 2; Pay Warrant for Will to John Mosby, n.d., ibid.; Certification of death for Owen's Michael, signed by Mosby Sheppard, September 19, 1800, ibid.; Pay Warrant for Michael to Judith Owen, n.d., ibid.; *Virginia Argus* (Richmond), October 3, 1800; Certification of death for Parson's Ned, September 14, 1800, Condemned Slaves 1800, Auditor's Item 153, box 2; Pay Warrant for Ned to Ann Parsons, n.d., ibid.; Certification of death for Burton's Isaac, n.d., ibid. There is no extant description of the death of the 1800 conspirators. Benjamin Henry Latrobe witnessed a 1796 hanging of a Richmond slave, William Harris. Harris was bound and blindfolded outside of the jail and then driven to the gallows in "the Cart." See Carter, ed., *Papers of Latrobe*, 1:191.

22. For the funeral practices of West Africans and black Americans, see Stuckey, *Slave Culture*, 108–09; Creel, "*A Peculiar People*," 54–55; Frey, *Water from the Rock*, 301; Sobel, *World They Made Together*, 174; Vlach, *By the Work of Their Hands*, 44–45.

23. Trial of Gregory's Billey, September 12, 1800, Henrico County Court Order Book; Sentence of Gregory's Billey, September 12, 1800, Executive Papers, Negro Insurrection; Copy of sentence in Condemned Slaves 1800, Auditor's Item 153, box 2.

24. Trial of Prosser's Martin, September 12, 1800, Henrico County Court Order Book; Testimony of Prosser's Ben and Jones's Martin at trial of Prosser's Martin, September 12, 1800, Executive Papers, Negro Insurrection; Sentence of Prosser's Martin, September 12, 1800, ibid.; Copy of sentence in Condemned Slaves 1800, Auditor's Item 153, box 2.

25. Trial of Gregory's Charles, September 12, 1800, Henrico County Court Order Book; Testimony of Prosser's Ben at trial of Gregory's Charles, September 12, 1800, Executive Papers, Negro Insurrection; Sentence of Gregory's Charles, September 12, 1800, ibid.; Copy of sentence in Condemned Slaves 1800, Auditor's Item 153, box 2.

26. Trial of Prosser's Frank, September 12, 1800, Henrico County Court Order Book; Testimony of Prosser's Ben and Jones' John at trial of Prosser's Frank, September 12, 1800, Executive Papers, Negro Insurrection; Sentence of Prosser's Frank, September 12, 1800, ibid.; Copy of sentence in Condemned Slaves 1800, Auditor's Item 153, box 2.

27. *Aurora* (Philadelphia), September 19, 1800; *Virginia Herald* (Fredericksburg), September 19, 1800; Certification of death for Prosser's Solomon, signed by Mosby Sheppard, n.d., Condemned Slaves 1800, Auditor's Item 153, box 2; Certification of death for Jones's John, signed by Mosby Sheppard, n.d., ibid.

28. Trial of Gregory's Martin, September 12, 1800, Henrico County Court Order Book; Testimony of Gregory's Billy and Price's Moses at trial of Gregory's Martin, September 12, 1800, Executive Papers, Negro Insurrection.

29. Trial of Burton's George, September 12, 1800, Henrico County Court Order Book; Trial of Burton's George, September 13, 1800, ibid.; Trial of Wilkinson's Frank, September 13, 1800, ibid.

30. Trial of Lewis's Sawney, September 13, 1800, Henrico County Court Order

Book; Sentence of Lewis's Sawney, September 13, 1800, Executive Papers, Negro Insurrection; Copy of sentence in Condemned Slaves 1800, Auditor's Item 153, box 2. William Young certified on September 26, 1800, that Sawney belonged to William Lewis of Henrico but was hired out to him; see ibid.

31. Sentence of Price's James, September 13, 1800, Executive Papers, Negro Insurrection. The records of this trial are repeated in the Henrico County Court Order Book for September 30, 1800, a mistake perhaps attributable to the crush of paperwork facing the court clerk.

32. Trial of Brooke's Daniel, September 13, 1800, Henrico County Court Order Book.

33. *Journal of the Senate of Virginia*, 29; Certification of death for Gregory's Charles, signed by Mosby Sheppard, September 18, 1800, Condemned Slaves 1800, Auditor's Item 153, box 2; Certification of death for Gregory's Billey, September 18, 1800, ibid.; Pay Warrant for Billey and Charles to Roger Gregory, ibid.; Certification of death for Prosser's Frank, signed by Mosby Sheppard, n.d., ibid.; Certification of death for Prosser's Martin, signed by Mosby Sheppard, n.d., ibid.

34. Council Journal, September 15, 1800; James Monroe to Thomas Jefferson, September 15, 1800, Jefferson Papers.

35. Trial of Brooke's Daniel, September 15, 1800, Henrico County Court Order Book.

36. Trial of Prosser's Peter, September 15, 1800, Henrico County Court Order Book; Sentence of Prosser's Peter, September 15, 1800, Executive Papers, Negro Insurrection; Trial of Wilkinson's Jupiter, September 15, 1800, Henrico County Court Order Book; Sentence of Wilkinson's Jupiter, September 15, 1800, Executive Papers, Negro Insurrection; Copy of sentence in Condemned Slaves 1800, Auditor's Item 153, box 2.

37. Trial of Wilkinson's Sam, September 15, 1800, Henrico County Court Order Book; Testimony of Prosser's Ben at trial of Wilkinson's Sam, September 15, 1800, Executive Papers, Negro Insurrection; Sentence of Wilkinson's Sam, September 15, 1800, ibid.; Copy of sentence in Condemned Slaves 1800, Auditor's Item 153, box 2.

38. Trial of Burton's Isham, September 15, 1800, Henrico County Court Order Book; Testimony of Prosser's Ben at trial of Burton's Isham, September 15, 1800, Executive Papers, Negro Insurrection; Sentence of Burton's Isham, September 15, 1800, ibid.; Copy of sentence in Condemned Slaves 1800, Auditor's Item 153, box 2.

39. Trial of Wilkinson's Daniel, September 15, 1800, Henrico County Court Order Book; Testimony of Prosser's Ben at trial of Wilkinson's Daniel, September 15, 1800, Executive Papers, Negro Insurrection. On Wilkinson's age and his inability to control his slaves, see Schwarz, "Gabriel's Challenge," 290.

40. Trial of Young's Ned, September 16, 1800, Henrico County Court Order Book; Sentence of Young's Ned, September 16, 1800, Executive Papers, Negro Insurrection; Trial of Allen's Isaac, September 16, 1800, Henrico County Court Order Book; Sentence of Allen's Isaac, September 16, 1800, Executive Papers, Negro Insurrection; Copy of sentence in Condemned Slaves 1800, Auditor's Item 153, box 2; Trial of Williamson's Laddis, September 16, 1800, Henrico County

Court Order Book; Sentence of Williamson's Laddis, September 16, 1800, Executive Papers, Negro Insurrection; Copy of sentence in Condemned Slaves 1800, Auditor's Item 153, box 2.

41. Trial of Austen's Ned, September 16, 1800, Henrico County Court Order Book; Trial of Austen's Joe, September 16, 1800, ibid.; Trial of Austen's Harry, September 16, 1800, ibid.; Trial of Billy Chicken, September 16, 1800, ibid.

42. Unsigned letter to editor, September 20, 1800, in *Norfolk Herald*, October 18, 1800; Hay, "Property, Authority, and the Criminal Law," in Hay, ed., *Albion's Fatal Tree*, 42.

43. Confession of Ben Woolfolk, September 17, 1800, Executive Papers, Negro Insurrection; Trial of Ben Woolfolk, September [18; misdated 16], 1800, Henrico County Court Order Book; Testimony of Price's James and Prosser's Ben at trial of Ben Woolfolk, September 18, 1800, Executive Papers; Sentence of Ben Woolfolk, September 18, 1800, Executive Papers, Negro Insurrection; Council Journal, September 18, 1800; Pollard, *Richmond's Story*, 74.

44. James Callender to Thomas Jefferson, September [18; misdated 13], 1800, Jefferson Papers; *Spectator* (New York), October 1, 1800; Certification of death for Burton's Isham, signed by Mosby Sheppard, n.d., Condemned Slaves 1800, Auditor's Item 153, box 2; Certification of death for Wilkinson's Jupiter, signed by Mosby Sheppard, September 24, 1800, ibid.; Certification of death for Lewis's Sawney, signed by Mosby Sheppard, September 26, ibid.; Certification of death for Prosser's Peter, signed by Mosby Sheppard, n.d., ibid.; Certification of death for Wilkinson's Sam, signed by Mosby Sheppard, September 24, 1800, ibid.; Pay Warrant for Isaac and Isham to William Burton, n.d., ibid.; Pay Warrant for Frank, Peter, Solomon, and Martin to Thomas Henry Prosser, n.d., ibid.

45. On the distinction between executions on the gallows and hangings from a cart, see McLynn, *Crime and Punishment*, 269.

46. Trial of George Smith, September 19, 1800, Henrico County Court Order Book; Sentence of George Smith, September 19, 1800, Executive Papers, Negro Insurrection; Copy of sentence in Condemned Slaves 1800, Auditor's Item 153, box 2; Certification of death for Allen's Isaac, signed by Mosby Sheppard, September 26, 1800, ibid. No death certificate exists for Laddis in the Virginia State Library. He was, however, neither pardoned nor transported.

47. Thomas Jefferson to James Monroe, September 20, 1800, Jefferson Papers; James Monroe to Thomas Jefferson, September 22, 1800, ibid.

48. Unsigned letter to editor, September 20, 1800, in *Norfolk Herald*, October 18, 1800; John Randolph to Joseph Nicholson, September 26, 1800, Nicholson Papers.

49. Trial of Young's Gilbert, September 15, 16, 17, 22, 1800, Henrico County Court Order Book; Sentence of Young's Gilbert, September 22, 1800, Executive Papers, Negro Insurrection; Copy of sentence in Condemned Slaves 1800, Auditor's Item 153, box 2; Trial of Prosser's Tom, September 22, 1800, Henrico County Court Order Book; Sentence of Prosser's Tom, September 22, 1800, Executive Papers, Negro Insurrection; Copy of sentence in Condemned Slaves 1800, Auditor's Item 153, box 2; Trial of Young's William, September 22, 1800, Henrico

County Court Order Book; Sentence of Young's William, September 22, 1800, Condemned Slaves 1800, Auditor's Item 153, box 2.

50. Trial of Sam Byrd, Jr., September 27, 1800, Henrico County Court Order Book; Sentence of Sam Byrd, Jr., September 27, 1800, Executive Papers, Negro Insurrection; Copy of sentence in Condemned Slaves 1800, Auditor's Item 153, box 2; Trial of Goode's Michael, September 27, 1800, Henrico County Court Order Book; Sentence of Goode's Michael, September 27, 1800, Condemned Slaves 1800, Auditor's Item 153, box 2.

51. Trial of Sam Graham, September 22, 27, 29, 1800, Henrico County Court Order Book; Sentence of Sam Graham, September 29, 1800, Condemned Slaves 1800, Auditor's Item 153, box 2; Trial of Burton's Abraham, September 29, 1800, Henrico County Court Order Book; Sentence of Burton's Abraham, September 29, 1800, Executive Papers, Negro Insurrection; Gervas Storrs and Joseph Selden to James Monroe, September 30, 1800, ibid.; Trial of Jim Allen, September 29, 1800, Henrico County Court Order Book; Trial of Price's Moses, September 29, 1800, ibid.

52. Trial of Woodfin's Jacob, September 30, 1800, Henrico County Court Order Book; Sentence of Woodfin's Jacob, September 30, 1800, Executive Papers, Negro Insurrection; Trial of Smith's Dick, September 30, 1800, Henrico County Court Order Book; Sentence of Smith's Dick, September 30, 1800, Executive Papers, Negro Insurrection; Trial of Lewis's Solomon, September 29, 30, 1800, Henrico County Court Order Book; Benjamin Goode to James Monroe, October 6, 1800, Executive Papers, Pardons; Pardon of Lewis's Solomon, Executive Papers, Pardons.

53. *Norfolk Herald*, September 25, 1800; John Moss to James Monroe, September 28, 1800, Executive Papers, Negro Insurrection.

CHAPTER SEVEN

1. Gaines, "Courthouses of Henrico and Chesterfield," 33–34; Trial of Nicholas's King, September 25, 1800, Richmond City Court Order Book; Sentence of Nicholas's King, September 30, 1800, Condemned Slaves 1800, Auditor's Item 153, box 2, Transported; Larkin Stanard to James Monroe, October 30, 1800, Executive Papers, Negro Insurrection.

2. Trial of Anderson's Brutus (alias Julius), September 25, 1800, Richmond City Court Order Book; Schwarz, *Twice Condemned*, 326.

3. Trial of Smith's Ben, October 1, 1800, Louisa County Court Order Book.

4. "Negroes Living in Hanover and Caroline," n.d., Executive Papers; Edmund Pendleton, Jr., to James Monroe, October 22, 1800, Pardons, Executive Papers. Mays argues that five of the slaves Pendleton prosecuted were hanged (*Edmund Pendleton*, 2:329). He used only the court order books, however, and did not examine the transportation lists or pardon papers. All five of those condemned to die in Caroline were either pardoned or transported out of the country.

5. John Hoomes to James Monroe, October 27, 1800, Executive Papers, Negro Insurrection; Council Journal, October 24, 1800.

6. Trial of Carter's Ben, October 22, 1800, Caroline County Court Order Book.

7. Carter Berkeley to Charles Carter, October 19, 1802, Berkeley Papers.

8. Trial of Carter's John, October 22, 1800, Caroline County Court Order Book; Trial of Thilman's George, October 22, 1800, ibid.; Trial of Thilman's Scipio, October 22, 1800, ibid.; John Hoomes to James Monroe, October 27, 1800, Executive Papers, Negro Insurrection.

9. Edmund Pendleton, Jr., to James Monroe, October 22, 1800, Pardons, Executive Papers; Trial of Jack Gabriel, October 29, 1800, Caroline County Court Order Book; Trial of Garland's Humphrey, October 29, 1800, ibid.; Trial of Penn's Billy, October 29, 1800, ibid.

10. Trial of Thilman's Thornton, October 30, 1800, Caroline County Court Order Book; Trial of John Fells, October 30, 1800, ibid.

11. Paul Thilman to James Monroe, n.d., Executive Papers. The county court order books for Hanover no longer exist, so it is impossible to know which two slaves had been condemned to death. (Many county records were lost or burned during the Civil War.) Thilman's Holmy was on the list of Hanover slaves provided by Woolfolk, whom Monroe ordered arrested.

12. *Norfolk Herald*, October 2, 1800; *Virginia Argus* (Richmond), October 10, 1800.

13. Carter, ed., *Papers of Latrobe*, 1:75 and n. 3; *Virginia Argus* (Richmond), October 10, 1800. The Norfolk County Court records are also lost. Still, it is clear that only two men were tried, and if either was convicted a copy of the record would exist in the Condemned Slaves file in Richmond, which is intact.

14. Benjamin Duvall to James Monroe, December 25, 1800, in Flournoy, ed., *Calendar of Virginia State Papers*, 9:173.

15. James McClurg to James Monroe, n.d., Executive Papers, Negro Insurrection; Joseph Jones to James Monroe, September 9, 1800, ibid.

16. William Prentis to James Monroe, September 6, 1800, Executive Papers, Negro Insurrection; William Prentis to James Monroe, September 24, 1800, ibid.

17. William Prentis to James Monroe, September 24, 1800, Executive Papers, Negro Insurrection. For the view that ruling class lawmakers were the "prisoners" of their own "games of power," see Thompson, *Whigs and Hunters*, 263.

18. Scott and Wyatt, *Petersburg's Story*, 51; Sentence of Claiborne's Peter, October 20, 1800, Condemned Slaves 1800, Auditor's Item 153, box 2. The Dinwiddie County Court Order Book is also not extant, but as six African Americans were arrested and four released, only one other man could have been tried, and if so, he was not found guilty.

19. James Monroe to William Prentis, October 11, 1800, Executive Letterbook; Unidentified newspaper clipping, William Palmer Scrapbook.

20. Trial of Williamson's Lewis, October 1, 1800, Henrico County Court Order Book; Sentence of Williamson's Lewis, October 1, 1800, Executive Papers, Negro Insurrection; Copy of sentence in Condemned Slaves 1801, Transported, Auditor's Item 153, box 2.

21. Trial of Nathaniel Lipscombe's Billy, October 1, 1800, Henrico County Court Order Book; Sentence of Nathaniel Lipscombe's Billy, October 1, 1800, Executive Papers, Negro Insurrection; Trial of Ambrose Lipscombe's Billy, September 30,

October 1, 1800, Henrico County Court Order Book; Sentence of Ambrose Lipscombe's Billy, October 1, 1800, Executive Papers, Negro Insurrection; Trial of Williamson's Peter, October 1, 1800, Henrico County Court Order Book; Sentence of Williamson's Peter, October 1, 1800, Executive Papers, Negro Insurrection.

22. John Randolph to Joseph Nicholson, September 26, 1800, Nicholson Papers; Sutcliff, *Travels in North America*, 50.

23. Testimony of Prosser's Ben at trial of Prosser's Solomon, September 11, 1800, Executive Papers, Negro Insurrection; Testimony of Prosser's Ben at trial of Mosby's Will, September 11, 1800, ibid.; Confession of Prosser's Solomon, September 15, 1800, Executive Letterbook; Confession of Ben Woolfolk, September 17, 1800, Executive Papers, Negro Insurrection; Testimony of Ben Woolfolk at trial of Sam Byrd, Jr., September 27, 1800, ibid. On the belief that French arms could aid in overcoming conservative political domination, so common in the Atlantic world of the 1790s, see Thompson, *Making of the English Working Class*, 173.

24. Unsigned letter to editor, September 13, 1800, in *Virginia Herald* (Fredericksburg), September 23, 1800; *Spectator* (New York), October 1, 1800.

25. Lerche, "Jefferson and the Election of 1800," 480; Hayden, *Virginia Genealogies*, 738; *Virginia Argus* (Richmond), September 12, 1800; Unsigned letter to editor, September 13, 1800, in *Virginia Herald* (Fredericksburg), September 23, 1800.

26. Testimony of Prosser's Ben at trial of Prosser's Solomon, September 11, 1800, Executive Papers, Negro Insurrection; Testimony of Ben Woolfolk at trial of Sam Byrd, Jr., September 27, 1800, ibid.; John Foster to James Monroe, September 9, 1800, ibid.; *Virginia Herald* (Fredericksburg), September 19, 1800.

27. William Prentis to James Monroe, September 6, 1800, Executive Papers, Negro Insurrection; William Prentis to James Monroe, n.d., ibid.

28. William Prentis to James Monroe, September 24, 1800, Executive Papers, Negro Insurrection; Confession of Young's Gilbert, September 23, 1800, ibid.; John Mayo to Samuel Pleasants, September 24, 1800, in *Virginia Argus* (Richmond), October 3, 1800.

29. Thomas Newton to James Monroe, September 24, 1800, Executive Papers, Negro Insurrection; *Spectator* (New York), October 4, 1800.

30. "An Act to Amend . . . the Act Concerning Slaves, Free Negroes, and Mulattoes," January 25, 1798, in Shepherd, ed., *Statutes at Large*, 2:78; Thomas Newton to James Monroe, September 24, 1800, Executive Papers, Negro Insurrection.

31. Linebaugh, *London Hanged*, 135–36; Undated notation by James Monroe, Executive Papers, Negro Insurrection.

32. Thomas Newton to James Monroe, September 24, 1800, Executive Papers, Negro Insurrection.

33. Richard E. Lee to James Monroe, September 25, 1800, ibid.; Thomas Newton to James Monroe, September 27, 1800, ibid.; John Moss to James Monroe, September 28, 1800, ibid.

34. *Virginia Herald* (Fredericksburg), October 3, 1800; *Norfolk Herald*, September 25, 1800; John Moss to James Monroe, September 28, 1800, Executive Papers, Negro Insurrection; *Spectator* (New York), October 8, 1800. The Federal Writers' Project erroneously claims that Gabriel "was captured in a vessel about

to sail *for* Norfolk" (*Virginia*, 78). Kimball is unfairly harsh toward Taylor, who he believes did not try to apprehend Gabriel, as he was "concerned that his hands would not assist him" ("The Gabriel Insurrection of 1800," 153). If anything, Taylor should have been concerned that his hands could not keep silent.

35. Thomas Newton to James Monroe, September 24, 1800, Executive Papers, Negro Insurrection; *Spectator* (New York), October 11, 1800.

36. Council Journal, October 16, 1800. Thomas J. Davis found similar examples of class and race-based rewards in colonial New York; see his *Rumor of Revolt*, 39.

37. *Virginia Herald* (Fredericksburg), October 3, 1800; Thomas Newton to James Monroe, September 24, 1800, Executive Papers, Negro Insurrection.

38. Thomas Newton to James Monroe, September 24, 1800, Executive Papers, Negro Insurrection; Richard E. Lee to James Monroe, September 25, 1800, ibid.; Unidentified newspaper clipping, William Palmer Scrapbook; *Norfolk Herald*, September 25, 1800.

39. James Monroe to Council, September 28, 1800, Executive Papers, Negro Insurrection; [Councilman] A. Blair to Keeper of Penitentiary, September 28, 1800, in Flournoy, ed., *Calendar of Virginia State Papers*, 9:156.

40. *Virginia Argus* (Richmond), September 30, 1800; *Virginia Herald* (Fredericksburg), October 3, 1800.

41. *Virginia Argus* (Richmond), September 30, 1800; James Monroe to Council, September 28, 1800, Executive Papers, Negro Insurrection; Ammon, *James Monroe*, 187–188; James Callender to Thomas Jefferson, September 29, 1800, Jefferson Papers; *Virginia Herald* (Fredericksburg), October 3, 1800; *Norfolk Herald*, October 2, 1800.

42. Trial of Leftwich's Randolph, October 6, 1800, Henrico County Court Order Book; Sentence of Leftwich's Randolph, October 6, 1800, Executive Papers, Negro Insurrection; Trial of Thilman's Dick, October 6, 1800, Henrico County Court Order Book; Sentence of Thilman's Dick, October 6, 1800, Executive Papers, Negro Insurrection; Trial of Thilman's Bristol, October 6, 1800, Henrico County Court Order Book; Trial of Thomas Jordan Martin, [October; misdated September] 6, 7, 1800, Henrico County Court Order Book.

43. *Norfolk Herald*, October 11, 1800; Trial of Prosser's Gabriel, October 6, 1800, Henrico County Court Order Book; Testimony of Prosser's Ben at trial of Prosser's Gabriel, October 6, 1800, Executive Papers, Negro Insurrection.

44. Testimony of Ben Woolfolk at trial of Prosser's Gabriel, October 6, 1800, Executive Papers, Negro Insurrection.

45. Sentence of Prosser's Gabriel, October 6, 1800, ibid.; Copy of sentence in Condemned Slaves 1800, Auditor's Item 153, box 2; *Norfolk Herald*, October 11, 1800.

46. *Virginia Herald* (Fredericksburg), October 14, 1800; Gervas Storrs to James Monroe, October 10, 1800, Executive Papers, Negro Insurrection; Council Journal, October 16, 1800; *Norfolk Herald*, October 19, 1800. Dabney incorrectly observes that Ditcher "was taken early, but Gabriel eluded his pursuers for several weeks" (*Richmond*, 185–86).

47. Thomas Booth to Alexander McCrea, October 2, 1800, Executive Papers; Pay Warrant to Joel Thomas, March 3, 1801, Gabriel's Insurrection, Military

Papers; William Prentis to James Monroe, n.d., Executive Papers, Negro Insurrection.

48. *Norfolk Herald*, October 18, 1800; Certification of death for Goode's Michael, signed by Samuel Mosby, December 8, 1800, Condemned Slaves 1800, Auditor's Item 153, box 2; Certification of death for Young's William, signed by Benjamin Sheppard, October 11, 1800, ibid.; Certification of death for Sam Graham, signed by Benjamin Sheppard, n.d., ibid. Both James Callender, who was usually correct on this point, and James Monroe, who lost track of how many slaves were executed, were mistaken as to the number of slaves hanged on October 10. Callender said the number was ten; Monroe put it at "10 or 12"; see James Callender to Thomas Jefferson, October 11, 1800, Jefferson Papers, and James Monroe to James Madison, October 8, 1800, Madison Papers.

49. Certification of death for Prosser's Tom, signed by Samuel Mosby, October 15, 1800, Condemned Slaves 1800, Auditor's Item 153, box 2; Certification of death for Young's Gilbert, signed by Samuel Mosby, October 11, 1800, ibid.; Certification of death for George Smith, signed by Samuel Mosby, October 20, ibid.; Pay Warrant for Gilbert and William to William Young, n.d., ibid. Sam Byrd, Jr., for unknown reasons, was never certified dead. James Monroe, however, stated that he was hanged on October 10, and no pardon was issued in his name; see James Monroe to William Prentis, October 11, 1800, Executive Letterbook.

50. *Virginia Herald* (Fredericksburg), October 14, 1800; Certification of death for Prosser's Gabriel, signed by Mosby Sheppard, October 20, 1800, Condemned Slaves 1800, Auditor's Item 153, box 2; Pay Warrant for Gabriel and Tom to Thomas Henry Prosser, October 20, 1800, ibid. Howison insists that Gabriel lost his nerve on the gallows, a position for which there is no documentation (*History of Virginia*, 2:392). One unsigned letter to the editor, September 20, 1800, in *Norfolk Herald*, October 18, 1800, written before Gabriel's death, noted that the rebels "have uniformly met death with fortitude." There is no reason to think that Gabriel died any differently.

There is also a great deal of confusion about when Gabriel died and who died with him. Virginius Dabney suggests that Gabriel and Ditcher died together (*Virginia*, 186). The unreliable Carroll argued that Gabriel was executed on October 7 (*Slave Insurrections*, 54). Unfortunately, many historians have followed his lead on this question. See, for example, Malone, *Jefferson and His Time*, 3:480, n. 64; Kimball, "Gabriel Insurrection," 155 (who also has Gabriel dying with Ditcher); and W. D. Jordan, *White over Black*, 393.

51. Oates, *Fires of Jubilee*, 12. Denmark Vesey also bought his freedom that year with his winnings from the 1799 East Bay Street Lottery; see Lofton, *Denmark Vesey's Revolt*, 75.

52. Pay Warrant, Penitentiary Guards, March 7, 1801, Gabriel's Insurrection, Military Papers. Oates suggests that in 1831, as in 1800, "the most effective brake on summary justice was financial considerations" (*Fires of Jubilee*, 117).

53. James Monroe to James Madison, October 8, 1800, Madison Papers; Thomas Jefferson to James Monroe, September 20, 1800, Jefferson Papers.

54. James Monroe to Joseph Cabell, February 8, 1828, Monroe Papers; *Boston Gazette*, October 13, 1800.

55. "A List of Slaves Reprieved for Transportation and Sold," March 8, 1806, Executive Papers; Miles Selden to James Monroe, November 22, 1800, Executive Papers; Henrico Justices to James Monroe, October 6, 1800, Executive Papers, Negro Insurrection; Pay Warrant, April 27, 1801, Condemned Slaves 1801, Transported, Auditor's Item 153, box 2; Pay Warrant, February 19, 1801, ibid.

56. Trial of Price's Absolam, November 3, 4, 1800, Henrico County Court Order Book; Trial of Wood's Emanuel, November 3, 4, ibid.; Trial of Prosser's Watt, December 1, 1800, ibid.; Sentence of Prosser's Watt, December 1, 1800, Executive Papers; "A List of Slaves Reprieved for Transportation and Sold," March 8, 1806, Executive Papers; Pay Warrant, January 31, 1801, Condemned Slaves 1801, Transported, Auditor's Item 153, box 2.

57. Trial of Jack Ditcher, October 29, 1800, Henrico County Court Order Book; Sentence of Jack Ditcher, October 29, 1800, Executive Papers, Negro Insurrection; "A List of Slaves Reprieved for Transportation and Sold," March 8, 1806, Executive Papers.

58. Pay Warrant, January 23, 1801, Condemned Slaves 1800, Auditor's Item 153, box 2; *Journal of the House of Delegates of Virginia* [1801], 42.

59. *Virginia Herald* (Fredericksburg), September 19, 1800; A Private Citizen to James Monroe, December 10, 1800, in *Norfolk Herald*, December 18, 1800.

60. *Boston Gazette*, October 9 and 23, 1800; Robert Troup to Rufus King, October 1, 1800, in King, ed., *Life and Correspondence of Rufus King*, 3:316; *Porcupine's Gazette* (Philadelphia), September 25, 1800.

61. James T. Callender to Samuel Pleasants, October 1, 1800, in *Virginia Argus* (Richmond), October 3, 1800; Mordecai, *Richmond*, 163; James Monroe to John Drayton, October 21, 1800, in Hamilton, ed., *Writings of Monroe*, 3:217.

62. Unsigned letter to editor, September 13, 1800, in *Virginia Herald* (Fredericksburg), September 23, 1800; *Russell's Gazette, Commercial and Political* (Boston), September 29, 1800; John Randolph to Joseph Nicholson, September 26, 1800, Nicholson Papers. Beeman incorrectly suggests that "neither party attempted to make political capital of" the alleged French involvement (*Old Dominion and the New Nation*, 228 and n. 22).

63. *Aurora* (Philadelphia), September 24 and 26, 1800. On the trial of Duane, see Smith, *Freedom's Fetters*, chap. 13.

64. Testimony of Price's John at trial of Young's Gilbert, September 22, 1800, Executive Papers, Negro Insurrection; Joseph Selden to Wilson C. Nicholas, January 1, 1801, Randolph Papers.

CHAPTER EIGHT

1. Compared to other slave conspiracies, that of 1802 has received surprisingly little attention. Aptheker regards the unrest as isolated acts of physical resistance, not as a larger two-state conspiracy (*American Negro Slave Revolts*, 230). Wyatt-Brown doubts the existence of a slave conspiracy anywhere in Virginia in 1802, but concentrates on Norfolk and Hanover, not Halifax (*Southern Honor*, chap. 15). Parramore suggests that no conspiracy existed except in the feverish minds of

"[e]xcited whites" ("Aborted Takeoff," 121). (See, however, my "A Rejoinder" to Parramore, especially on his use of sources.)

John Scott Strickland examines white fears of slave plots and thus implicitly denies the actuality of any conspiracy ("The Great Revival and Insurrectionary Fears in North Carolina," in Burton and McMath, eds., *Class, Conflict, and Consensus*, 57–95). Crow dissents from that view but does not present the North Carolina plot as the wing of a larger network ("Slave Rebelliousness and Social Conflict in North Carolina," 96–101, and *Black Experience in Revolutionary North Carolina*, 89–91). Taylor covers the plot in one paragraph ("Slave Conspiracies in North Carolina," 31).

2. Pinchbeck, *Virginia Negro Artisan*, 31; Farr, *Black Odyssey*, 170–71; Bogger, "Slave and Free Black Community," 163.

3. Quarles, *Negro in the American Revolution*, 87; Quarles, "Lord Dunmore as Liberator," 503–04; Frey, "Between Slavery and Freedom," 383.

4. Nash, *Urban Crucible*, 16; "An Act Authorizing the Potowmac Company to Open the Shenandoah River," January 13, 1802, in Shepherd, ed., *Statutes at Large*, 2:359.

5. Crittenden, "Inland Navigation in North Carolina," 149; Carter, ed., *Papers of Latrobe*, 1:92.

6. Berlin, *Slaves without Masters*, 218–19.

7. Ibid., 159.

8. Hughes, "Slaves for Hire," 269.

9. Wade, *Slavery in the Cities*, 48–51, 66; Rediker, *Between the Devil and the Deep Blue Sea*, 200.

10. Bolster, "'To Feel Like a Man,'" 1187, 1189; Gary Nash, "Forging Freedom: The Emancipation Experience in the Northern Seaport Cities," in Berlin and Hoffman, eds., *Slavery and Freedom*, 10; Rediker, "Motley Crew of Rebels," 31.

11. Kay and Carey, "Slave Runaways," 18–19; Farr, *Black Odyssey*, 180–81; Windley, ed., *Runaway Slave Advertisements*, 1:294; *Norfolk Herald*, October 2, 1800.

12. Duncan J. MacLeod, "Toward Caste," in Berlin and Hoffman, eds., *Slavery and Freedom*, 227; Pinchbeck, *Virginia Negro Artisan*, 32. For an excellent discussion on how craftsmen provided a link to the wider world for unskilled laborers in another agrarian society, see Hobsbawm and Rude, *Captain Swing*, 18.

13. This analysis follows the lead of Genovese, *From Rebellion to Revolution*, xx–xxii.

14. John B. Scott to James Monroe, April 21, 1802, Executive Papers; Unidentified newspaper clipping, William Palmer Scrapbook.

15. J.L.C. to unknown, n.d., Slave Collection, 1748–1856. This letter was from a Virginia conspirator. Parramore argues that the J.L.C. letter was written by a slave trader to bring down prices ("Aborted Takeoff," 116). But would a trader know, or wish to suggest, that "the poor [white] sort that has no blacks," if presented with a massive uprising, would "be not only willing to Acknowledge, liberty & Equality, but purchase their lives at any price"? That would be a dangerous admission that southern racial barriers were not as monolithic as the ruling class liked to imply. What Parramore suggests, therefore, is that a Machiavellian trader,

in trying to soften prices, wrote a letter that so terrified gullible authorities in two states that they beat and tortured large numbers of slaves in an attempt to get them to support the story in the letter (and in the case of Halifax and Norfolk, to identify Easter as the moment of the rising). Curiously, in his *Southampton County*, Parramore regards the letter as authentic (66).

16. Testimony of Smith's Robin at trial of Smith's Abram, May 1, 1802, Executive Papers, 1802, Pardon Papers; Isaac, *Transformation of Virginia*, 103; Testimony of Smith's Abram at trial of Booker's Sancho, April 23, 1802, Executive Papers, 1802, Pardon Papers.

17. Testimony of Smith's Abram at trial of Booker's Sancho, April 23, 1802, Executive Papers, 1802, Pardon Papers.

18. Testimony of Smith's Abram at trial of Robertson's Frank, April 23, 1802, Executive Papers, 1802, Pardon Papers.

19. Testimony of Prosser's Ben at trial of Prosser's Gabriel, October 6, 1800, Executive Papers, Negro Insurrection; J.L.C. to unknown, n.d., Slave Collection, 1748–1856; John Scott to James Monroe, April 23, 1802, Executive Papers; Rediker, "American Revolution," 18; Bolster, "'To Feel Like a Man,'" 1177–79; John Scott to James Monroe, April 23, 1802, Executive Papers.

20. Testimony of Smith's Robin at trial of Smith's Abram, May 1, 1802, Executive Papers, 1802, Pardon Papers; John B. Scott to James Monroe, April 21, 1802, Executive Papers; Testimony of Sandifer's Bob at trial of Booker's Sancho, April 23, 1802, Executive Papers, 1802, Pardon Papers.

21. Testimony of Ned at trial of Hillard's Absalom, April 26, 1802, Halifax County Court Order Book; J.L.C. to unknown, n.d., Slave Collection, 1748–1856.

22. Sentence of Booker's Sancho, April 23, 1802, Condemned Slaves 1802, Executed, Auditor's Item 153, box 2; Scott and Wyatt, *Petersburg's Story*, 90.

23. Testimony of Green's Ned at trial of Royall's Bob, January 7, 1802, Executive Papers.

24. Testimony of Jones's Hampton at trial of Jones's Joe, January 7, 1802, Executive Papers; Richard Jones to William Prentis, January 2, 1802, ibid.

25. William R. Davie to Benjamin Williams, February 17, 1802, Historical Society of Pennsylvania Papers. Davie was writing from Halifax Town, North Carolina, but his letter was based upon news from "Virginia," where his correspondents informed him that the plot extended from Petersburg "at least to Roanoke," a hamlet actually west of Halifax County, Virginia.

26. Carter, ed., *Papers of Latrobe*, 1:137; Grief Green to James Monroe, n.d., Executive Papers, 1802, Slave Insurrection; Grief Green to Peterson Goodwyn, May 1, 1802, Executive Papers; Confession of Brown's Lewis, May 5, 1802, ibid.

27. Frank Goode to Roling Pointer, January 18, 1802, Executive Papers; Horatio Turpin to James Monroe, January 22, 1802, ibid.

28. Grief Green to James Monroe, n.d., Executive Papers, 1802, Slave Insurrection; Weld, *Travels through North America*, 1:190; Carter, ed., *Papers of Latrobe*, 1:94–95.

29. Thomas Newton to James Monroe, May 14, 1802, Executive Papers, 1802, Slave Insurrection.

30. Bogger, "Slave and Free Black Community," 201; Testimony of Walke's Will

at trial of Ingram's Ned, June 20, 1802, Norfolk County Court Order Book; *Virginia Herald* (Fredericksburg), May 18, 1802.

31. "Families of Lower Norfolk and Princess Anne Counties," 148–51; Unidentified newspaper clipping, William Palmer Scrapbook.

32. Broussard, *Southern Federalists*, 5; Bogger, "Slave and Free Black Community," 165; Thomas Mathews to James Monroe, March 10, 1802, Executive Papers.

33. Testimony of Jackson's Adam at trial of Wilkes's Isaac, February 11, 1802, Executive Papers; Testimony of Jackson's George at trial of Wilkes's Isaac, February 11, 1802, ibid.; Testimony of Wilkes's Jeffrey at trial of Wilkes's Isaac, February 11, 1802, ibid.

34. Testimony of Jackson's Raysom at trial of Wilkes's Isaac, February 11, 1802, Executive Papers; Unidentified newspaper clipping, William Palmer Scrapbook.

35. Jeffrey, *State Parties and National Politics*, 17; McColley, *Slavery and Jeffersonian Virginia*, 11; Scott and Wyatt, *Petersburg's Story*, 73; "Document: Journal of a French Traveller," 737; *Raleigh Register*, July 27, 1802. As Jeffrey J. Crow has written: "The interconnecting waterways of eastern North Carolina evidently made the transmission of information not only feasible but unstoppable" ("Slave Rebelliousness," 97).

36. Deposition of Bearmas's George, June 1802, Slave Collection, 1748–1856; Deposition of Dick Blacksmith, June, 1802, ibid.; Thomas Blount to John Gray Blount, June 28, 1802, in Masterson, ed., *John Gray Blount Papers*, 3:517.

37. *Spectator* (New York), August 4, 1802; Testimony of Boston at trial of Salem, June 1802, Slave Collection, 1748–1856; Deposition of Turner's Isaac, June 1802, ibid. Guns and bayonets were found in the homes of slaves in Currituck and other counties, but these alleged conspiracies do not appear to be connected to the main conspiracy. On the arms found, see the *Spectator* (New York), August 4, 1802, and *Virginia Herald* (Fredericksburg), May 18, 1802.

38. Testimony of Bostom at trial of Salem, June 1802, Slave Collection, 1748–1856; Deposition of Turner's Emanuel, June 1802, ibid.

39. Unsigned letter to editor, June 14, 1802, in *Alexandria Times*, June 28, 1802; Deposition of Turner's Emanuel, June 1802, Slave Collection, 1748–1856; Deposition of Hunter's Simon, June 1802, ibid.; *Virginia Herald* (Fredericksburg), June 29, 1802; *Raleigh Register*, July 27, 1802. The choice of June 10, the date of the quarterly meetings of the Kehukee Baptist associations, like the choice of Easter, appears to have had no religious significance other than being a moment of weakness for Carolina whites.

40. *Raleigh Register*, July 27, 1802; Deposition of Dick Blacksmith, June 1802, Slave Collection, 1748–1856.

41. Deposition of Hunter's Simon, June 1802, Slave Collection, 1748–1856; Richard Dobbs Spaight to John Steele, July 12, 1802, Walter Clark Manuscripts.

CHAPTER NINE

1. William Prentis to James Monroe, January 5, 1802, Executive Papers.

2. Testimony of Willis Pillar at trial of Jones's Joe, January 7, 1802, ibid; Richard Jones to William Prentis, January 2, 1802, ibid.

3. William Martin to James Monroe, January 2, 1802, ibid.; William Prentis to James Monroe, January 4, 1802, ibid.; James Monroe to General Assembly, January 16, 1802, Letterbook, Executive Papers.

4. Horatio Turpin to James Monroe, January 22, 1802, Executive Papers.

5. Frank Goode to Roling Pointer, January 18, 1802, Executive Papers; Council Journal, January 23, 1802; James Monroe to Littleberry Mosby, January 23, 1802, Letterbook, Executive Papers; James Monroe to John Harris, January 23, 1802, ibid.

6. James Monroe to Richard Adams, May 11, 1802, Letterbook, Executive Papers; Joseph Bingham to James Monroe, January 5, 1802, Executive Papers; James Monroe to Richard Adams, May 8, 1802, Letterbook, Executive Papers; William Prentis to James Monroe, January 5, 1802, Executive Papers.

7. James Monroe to Richard Adams, July 26, 1802, Letterbook, Executive Papers; James Monroe to Alexander Quarrier, July 26, 1802, ibid.; James Monroe to Alexander Quarrier, May 5, 1802, ibid.

8. Sentence of Jones's Joe, January 7, 1802, Condemned Slaves 1802, Executed, Auditor's Item 153, box 2; Sentence of Royall's Bob, January 7, 1802, ibid.; James Monroe to General Assembly, January 16, 1802, Letterbook, Executive Papers, 1802; Certification of death for Royall's Bob, signed by William Cabanis, January 16, 1802, Condemned Slaves 1802, Executed, Auditor's Item 153, box 2; Certification of death for Jones's Joe, signed by William Cabanis, January 16, 1802, ibid.

9. Richard Jones to William Prentis, January 2, 1802, Executive Papers, 1802.

10. Testimony of Jackson's George, Jackson's Adam, and Wilkes's Jeffrey at trial of Wilkes's Isaac, February 3, 1802, Executive Papers; Sentence of Wilkes's Isaac, February 3, 1802, Condemned Slaves 1802, Executed, Auditor's Item 153, box 2; Sentence of Hagood's Phill, February 3, 1802, ibid.; Certification of death for Isaac, signed by James Rice and John Tucker, September 13, [1802; misdated 1800], ibid.; Certification of death for Phill, September 13, [1802; misdated 1800], ibid.; Pay warrant for Isaac to estate of Joseph Wilkes, n.d., 1802, ibid.; Council Journal, February 11, 1802.

11. *Virginia Herald* (Fredericksburg), May 18, 1802; *Alexandria Advertiser*, May 18, 1802; John Cowper to James Monroe, April 17, 1802, Executive Papers.

12. *Spectator* (New York), May 22, 1802; *Alexandria Advertiser*, May 18, 1802; *Virginia Herald* (Fredericksburg), May 18, 1802; Testimony of Walke's Will at trial of Ingram's Ned, June 20, 1802, Norfolk County Court Order Book; Testimony of Caleb Boush at trial of Ingram's Ned, June 20, 1802, Executive Papers.

13. "Families of Lower Norfolk and Princess Anne Counties," 149, 151; Testimony of Walke's Will at trial of Ingram's Ned, June 20, 1802, Norfolk County Court Order Book; Testimony of John Floyd at trial of Ingram's Ned, June 20, 1802, ibid.; Testimony of Walke's Will at trial of Walke's Ned, April 26, 1802, Executive Papers, 1802, Pardon Papers. Wyatt-Brown argues that Jarvis and Floyd used "threats of torture" on Will (*Southern Honor*, 430). Certainly in such a situation the possibility of white violence was always implicit, but, as noted in the text, Floyd testified that no overt threats were made.

14. John Cowper to James Monroe, April 17, 1802, Executive Papers; *Raleigh*

Register and North Carolina Gazette, May 18, 1802; *Alexandria Advertiser*, May 18, 1802; Roeber, ed., "New England Woman's Perspective," 307.

15. Thomas Newton to James Monroe, May 14, 1802, Executive Papers, 1802; [General] Thomas Mathews to James Monroe, March 10, 1802, ibid.; James Monroe to John Nivison, May 12, 1802, Executive Letterbook.

16. *Virginia Herald* (Fredericksburg), May 18, 1802; Sentence of Walke's Ned, April 26, 1802, Condemned Slaves 1802, Transported, Auditor's Item 153, box 2; Sentence of Cornick's Jeremiah, April 26, 1802, Executive Papers, 1802, Pardon Papers; Thomas Newton to James Monroe, May 7, 1802, ibid.; Testimony of Walke's Will at trial of Walke's Ned, April 26, 1802, ibid.

17. George McIntosh to James Monroe, May 5, 1802, Executive Papers, 1802, Pardon Papers; John Cowper to James Monroe, May 18, 1802, ibid.; Thomas Newton to James Monroe, May 7, 1802, ibid.

18. Council Journal, May 8, 1802, p. 227; James Monroe to John Cowper, May 12, 1802, Executive Letterbook; James Monroe to Thomas Newton, May 12, 1802, ibid.; *Spectator* (New York), May 22, 1802; "Circular—To the County Courts," April 16, 1802, Executive Letterbook.

19. Thomas Newton to James Monroe, May 14, 1802, Executive Papers, 1802; John Cowper to James Monroe, May 18, 1802, Executive Papers, 1802, Pardon Papers; *Norfolk Herald*, May 18, 1802; *Spectator* (New York), May 26, 1802.

20. James Monroe to Thomas Newton, May 12, 1802, Executive Letterbook; James Monroe to John Cowper, May 25, 1802, ibid.; James Monroe to Jailor of the Borough of Norfolk, July 12, 1802, ibid.; Council Journal, May 24, 1802, p. 240, June 5, 1802, p. 251; Certification of Daniel Hylton, October 5, 1802, Condemned Slaves 1802, Transported, Auditor's Item 153, box 2.

21. George McIntosh to Henry A. Wise, December 22, 1856, Executive Papers. Wyatt-Brown writes: "There is no indication that [McIntosh] had any pecuniary interest in Jerry's fate" (*Southern Honor*, 428). Perhaps not, but he did in Ned's. The slaves of William and Mary Walke were divided among their five children, one of whom was married to McIntosh. The estate was not yet settled.

22. *Virginia Herald* (Fredericksburg), May 11, 1802; *Norfolk Herald*, May 29, 1802; *Petersburg Intelligencer*, June 4, 1802; *Spectator* (New York), June 9, 1802; Roeber, ed., "New England Woman's Perspective," 316; Certification of death for Cornick's Jeremiah, signed by James Boyce, May 28, 1802, Condemned Slaves 1802, Executed, Auditor's Item 153, box 2.

23. *Virginia Herald* (Fredericksburg), May 18, 1802; Sentence of Ingram's Ned, June 20, 1802, Norfolk County Court Order Book.

24. John Scott to James Monroe, April 30, 1802, Executive Papers, 1802; James Monroe to John Scott, May 1, 1802, Executive Letterbook; Richard Dobbs Spaight to John Gray Blount, July 1, 1802, in Masterson, ed., *John Gray Blount Papers*, 3:518.

25. W. W. Freehling, *Road to Disunion*, 78–79; James Dejarnett to Jailor of Halifax County, April 14, 1802, Executive Papers, 1802, Pardon Papers.

26. Testimony of Smith's Abram and Sandifer's Bob at trial of Booker's Sancho, April 23, 1802, Halifax County Court Order Book; Sentence of Booker's Sancho,

April 23, 1802, Condemned Slaves 1802, Executed, Auditor's Item 153, box 2.

27. Sentence of Daniel Price's Phebe, April 23, 1802, Halifax County Court Order Book.

28. Sentence of Hilliard's Absalom, April 26, 1802, Halifax County Court Order Book; Sentence of Robertson's Frank, April 23, 1802, ibid.; Sentence of Bass's Martin, April 26, 1802, ibid.

29. Testimony of Sandifer's Bob at trial of Smith's Abram, May 1, 1802, Executive Papers, 1802, Pardon Papers; Sentence of Smith's Abram, May 1, 1802, Halifax County Court Order Book.

30. John Scott to James Monroe, April 30, 1802, Executive Papers; Council Journal, May 8, 1802, p. 225; *Norfolk Herald*, June 10, 1802; *Virginia Herald* (Fredericksburg), June 15, 1802; *Raleigh Register and North Carolina Gazette*, June 22, 1802; Certification of death for Booker's Sancho, signed by John Wimbish, May 15, 1802, Condemned Slaves 1802, Executed, Auditor's Item 153, box 2; Certification of death for Hilliard's Absalom, signed by John Wimbish, June 4, 1802, ibid.; Certification of death for Bass's Martin, signed by John Wimbish, July 6, 1802, ibid.; Certification of death for Robertson's Frank, signed by John Wimbish, July 6, 1802, ibid.; Certification of death for Smith's Abram, signed by John Wimbish, July 6, 1802, ibid. In my "'Fly across the River,'" I erroneously stated that Abram died alone on May 16 (105). The five slaves swung together.

31. Grief Green to Peterson Goodwyn, May 1, 1802, Executive Papers, 1802; Confession of Brown's Lewis, May 5, 1802, ibid.; Arthur Farrar to James Monroe (dictated), June 12, 1802, ibid. Wyatt-Brown argues convincingly that the story Lewis attributed to Arthur about the alleged attack on Richmond "bore suspicious resemblance to the public accounts of the Gabriel plot" (*Southern Honor*, 426). Lewis, however, was doubtless involved in the Nottoway-Dinwiddie wing of the plot. As a ferryman on the upper James, it is unlikely, even impossible, that he would not have at least *heard* of the plan. And the story he told about Jumper mentioned the date of Easter.

32. James Monroe to Grief Green, May 1, 1802, Executive Letterbook; James Monroe to Grief Green, May 4, 1802, ibid.

33. Unidentified newspaper clipping, William Palmer Scrapbook; James Monroe to Martin Mims, May 8, 1802, Executive Letterbook.

34. Testimony of Brown's Lewis at trial of Arthur Farrar, May 17, 1802, Executive Papers, 1802; Unidentified newspaper clipping, William Palmer Scrapbook.

35. Sentence of Arthur Farrar, May 17, 1802, Executive Papers, 1802; Copy of sentence in Condemned Slaves 1802, Transported, Auditor's Item 153, box 2.

36. Arthur Farrar to James Monroe (dictated), June 12, 1802, Executive Papers, 1802; James Monroe to William Rose, July 13, 1802, ibid.; Council Journal, July 10, 1802, p. 272. The highly unreliable Carroll incorrectly argues that Farrar was executed (*Slave Insurrections*, 61–62).

37. Testimony of James at trial of Thilman's Glasgow, May 5, 1802, Executive Papers; Testimony of Eve Glasgow, Sr., Ben, and Walker at trial of Thilman's Glasgow, May 5, 1802, ibid.; Paul Woolfolk to Thomas Tinsley, May 31, 1802, ibid.; Council Journal, May 22, 1802, p. 237; James Monroe to Sheriff of Hanover, May 24, 1802, Executive Letterbook; Pay Warrant for Glasgow and Tom to estate

of Paul Thilman, August 27, 1802, Condemned Slaves, 1802, Executed [*sic*], Auditor's Item 153, box 2; Martin Mims to James Monroe, May 25, 1802, Executive Papers, 1802.

38. James Monroe to Grief Green, June 5, 1802, Executive Letterbook; James Monroe to Peterson Goodwyn, June 19, 1802, ibid.; James Monroe to Peterson Goodwyn, October 2, 1802, ibid.; Peterson Goodwyn to James Monroe, June 12, 1802, Executive Papers, 1802.

39. William R. Davie to Benjamin Williams, February 17, 1802, Historical Society of Pennsylvania Papers; Unidentified newspaper clipping, William Palmer Scrapbook; *Virginia Herald* (Fredericksburg), May 18, 1802; Unsigned letter from Murfreesborough, June 9, 1802, in *Alexandria Times*, June 28, 1802; Deposition of Fitt's Dennis, June 15, 1802, Slave Collection, 1748–1856.

40. *Raleigh Register and North Carolina Gazette*, July 6, 1802; Deposition of Fitt's Fed, June 1802, Slave Collection, 1748–1856.

41. *Raleigh Register and North Carolina Gazette*, July 6, 1802; *Virginia Herald* (Fredericksburg), June 29, 1802.

42. *Raleigh Register and North Carolina Gazette*, July 6, 1802.

43. Ibid., July 27, 1802; John Folk to William Williams, June 6, 1802, Slave Collection, 1748–1856.

44. Clark, "Aspects of the North Carolina Slave Code," 151; *Spectator* (New York), July 7, 1802; *Raleigh Register and North Carolina Gazette*, July 27, 1802; Unsigned letter from Murfreesborough, June 14, 1802, in *Alexandria Times*, June 28, 1802.

45. *Raleigh Register and North Carolina Gazette*, July 13, 1802; *Virginia Herald* (Fredericksburg), June 29, 1802; Unsigned letter from Murfreesborough, June 14, 1802, in *Alexandria Times*, June 28, 1802; *North-Carolina Minerva* (Raleigh), June 15, 1802; Crow, "Slave Rebelliousness and Social Conflict in North Carolina," 100. Other slaves were hanged in the neighboring counties of Camden, Currituck, and Perquimans, but there is no evidence connecting this maroon activity to the Roanoke wing of the conspiracy. Aptheker does not devote much attention to the 1802 plot, but he does argue that in Virginia alone as many as thirty-seven slaves were executed for their involvement (*American Negro Slave Revolts*, 230, n. 77). He bases this number on owners compensated, although the state also compensated owners for slaves transported outside the state. Moreover, his assumption that all executed or transported were a part of the conspiracy is not supported by the trial records. Many were guilty of isolated capital crimes, not insurrection.

46. *Norfolk Herald*, June 15, 1802; *Virginia Herald* (Fredericksburg), June 15, 1802; *Virginia Argus* (Richmond), June 23, 1802; *Raleigh Register and North Carolina Gazette*, July 6, August 10, 1802.

CHAPTER TEN

1. Weld, *Travels through North America*, 1:189.

2. James Monroe to General Assembly, December 5, 1800, Executive Letterbook.

3. *Journal of the House of Delegates of Virginia*, 47–48.

4. Ibid., 61, 71.

5. Thomas Brooke to Levin Powell, December 22, 1800, Powell Papers; *Journal of the House of Delegates of Virginia*, 61.

6. "An Act to Purchase Pharoah and Tom," January 14, 1801, in Shepherd, ed., *Statutes at Large*, 1:126; *Journal of the House of Delegates of Virginia*, 61, 67.

7. Samuel Coleman to James Monroe, February 28, 1801, in Flournoy, ed., *Calendar of Virginia State Papers*, 9:201; James Monroe to Philip Shephard [*sic*], March 5, 1801, in Hamilton, ed., *Writings of Monroe*, 3:266; Pay Warrants for Tom and Pharoah to Elizabeth and Philip Sheppard, both March 15, 1801, Condemned Slaves 1801, Slaves Emancipated, Auditor's Item 153, box 2.

8. "An Act to Empower the Governor to Transport Slaves Condemned," January 15, 1801, in Shepherd, ed., *Statutes at Large of Virginia*, 2:279–80.

9. *Journal of the Senate of Virginia*, 60; *Journal of the House of Delegates of Virginia*, 61.

10. Payroll, January 26, 1801, Gabriel's Insurrection, Military Papers; Payroll, January 29, 1801, ibid.; Accounts, June 15, 1801, ibid.; Payroll, December 31, 1800, ibid.

11. "An Act to Amend the Penal Laws," December 15, 1796, in Shepherd, ed., *Statutes at Large*, 2:10; Clark, ed., *Footloose in Jacksonian America*, 27; Council Journal, February 6, 1802, p. 184.

12. List of Slaves Reprieved for Transportation & Sold by the Commonwealth, March 8, 1806, Executive Papers; Schwarz, "Transportation of Slaves from Virginia," 223.

13. *Journal of the House of Delegates of Virginia*, 47–48.

14. Thomas Jefferson to James Monroe, September 20, 1800, Jefferson Papers.

15. George Tucker to St. George Tucker, November 2, 1800, Tucker-Coleman Papers; George Tucker to St. George Tucker, [January] 18, [1801; misdated 1800], ibid.; George Tucker to St. George Tucker, March 7, [1801; misdated 1800], ibid.

16. [George Tucker], *Letter to a Member*, 16.

17. George Tucker to St. George Tucker, November 2, 1800, Tucker-Coleman Papers; *Journal of the Senate of Virginia*, 51; St. George Tucker, *Dissertation on Slavery*, 91–94.

18. Thomas Jefferson to James Monroe, November 24, 1801, Monroe Papers; James Monroe to Thomas Jefferson, December 8, 1801, Jefferson Papers; James Monroe to Thomas Jefferson, December 21, 1801, ibid.; James Monroe to the General Assembly, December 21, 1801, Executive Letterbook.

19. James Monroe to General Assembly, January 16, 1802, Executive Letterbook.

20. *Journal of the House of Delegates of Virginia*, 71; James Monroe to Thomas Jefferson, February 13, 1802, Jefferson Papers. The resolution can be found in Slaughter, *Virginian History of African Colonization*, 5.

21. Second part of resolution, in Slaughter, *Virginian History of African Colonization*, 5. Slaughter presumably got the copies of the resolutions from fellow colonizationist Charles Fenton Mercer, who in early 1816 saw them in the "secret

journals." See my "'Its Origin Is Not a Little Curious,'" 466. I have not found any House or Senate journals that include the resolutions. The emphasis in the quotation is mine.

22. Mercer, *Address to the American Colonization Society*, 18. The standard work on colonization, Staudenraus, *African Colonization Movement*, fails to note the evolution of the resolutions from 1801 to 1802 to include free blacks who might wish to emigrate to Africa. He argues that the "penal colony [was only to be] for rebellious slaves and free Negro criminals" (4). The Assembly's hope that a colony might lead to private emancipations is also missed by Alison G. Freehling (*Drift toward Dissolution*, 112) and W. D. Jordan (*White over Black*, 560–63, which is still, however, the best discussion of pre-1816 colonization attempts). James Monroe also confused the chronology of events later in life when he compressed the two conspiracies into one and indicated that the idea of colonizing free blacks followed Gabriel's conspiracy. "I have no recollection of the correspondence referred to, or how it originated, whether it was, at the instance of the legislature, by the advice of council; by a letter of Mr. Jefferson, on hearing of the occurrence [*sic*], or by one from me to him"; see James Monroe to Joseph C. Cabell, February 8, 1828, Monroe Papers, Virginia Historical Society.

23. James Monroe to Thomas Jefferson, February 13, 1802, Jefferson Papers; James Monroe to Thomas Jefferson, June 15, 1802, ibid.

24. On Jefferson's views on race and colonization, see Mathews, *The Radical Politics of Thomas Jefferson*, 68–75; William Cohen, "Thomas Jefferson and the Problem of Slavery," 523–24; and W. W. Freehling, *Road to Disunion*, 121. Jefferson's 1779 "Bill Concerning Slaves" can be found in Thomas Jefferson, *Notes on the State of Virginia*, in Peterson, ed., *Jefferson*, 263–64.

25. W. D. Jordan argues that for the reasons listed in the text "Virginia was the one [state] where the question of emancipation seemed furthest open" (*White over Black*, 551–52). That view is challenged generally by Richard S. Dunn ("Black Society in the Chesapeake, 1776–1810," in Berlin and Hoffman, eds., *Slavery and Freedom*, 81) and specifically by D. B. Davis (*Problem of Slavery*, 255–56 and n. 1). The view taken here is that the economic and social factors outlined by Jordan would not by themselves have been enough to bring about widespread emancipations, but that those factors combined with the terror inspired by two statewide conspiracies very likely could have led to an elite-led plan of abolition had Jefferson and Monroe proved more willing. The fact is, the Assembly in early 1802 *did* lay the groundwork for large-scale emancipations and removal.

26. Furneaux, *William Wilberforce*, 124–25; Winks, *Blacks in Canada*, 63; Thomas Jefferson to James Monroe, June 2, 1802, Jefferson Papers.

27. Thomas Jefferson to Rufus King, July 13, 1802, Jefferson Papers; Christopher Gore to Thomas Jefferson, October 10, 1802, Executive Papers, 1802.

28. Christopher Gore to Thomas Jefferson, October 10, 1802, Executive Papers, 1802; Rufus King to Thomas Jefferson, December 18, 1802, Jefferson Papers.

29. Thomas Jefferson to James Monroe, November 24, 1802, Executive Papers, 1802; James Monroe to General Assembly, December 9, 1802, Executive Letterbook.

30. Council Journal, April 10, 1802, p. 214.

31. George Goosley to James Monroe, June 5, 1802, Executive Papers, 1802; George Goosley to James Monroe, June 8, 1802, ibid.

32. Notation by James Monroe, on George Goosley to James Monroe, June 5, 1802, Executive Papers, 1802; James Monroe to George Goosley, June 14, 1802, Executive Letterbook; George Goosley to James Monroe, June 24, 1802, Executive Papers, 1802.

33. William Fulcher to James Monroe, July 3, 1802, Executive Papers, 1802; Council Journal, July 10, 1802, p. 271; James Monroe to Martin Mims, July 13, 1802, Executive Letterbook; James Monroe to Martin Mims, July 12, 1802, ibid.

34. Thomas Newton to James Monroe, September 8, 1802, Executive Papers, 1802; Fontaine Maury to James Monroe, August 21, 1802, ibid.; James Monroe to Thomas Newton, September 6, 1802, Executive Letterbook.

35. Memorandum of Negroes Sentenced for Transportation and Sent to the Penitentiary for Safe Keeping, December 2, 1806, Executive Papers; Schwarz, "Transportation of Slaves from Virginia," 224.

36. James Monroe to Thomas Jefferson, June 11, 1802, Jefferson Papers.

37. Ibid.

38. Rufus King to William Wilberforce, January 8, 1803, Jefferson Papers; Rufus King to Henry Thornton, April 30, 1803, ibid.; Wilson, *The Loyal Blacks*, 183–84.

39. Wilson, *The Loyal Blacks*, 383–401; Henry Thornton to Rufus King, May 10, 1803, Jefferson Papers; Rufus King to Thomas Jefferson, May 12, 1803, ibid.

40. *Journal of the House of Delegates of Virginia*, 107.

41. Ibid., 3; Resolution in Slaughter, *Virginian History of African Colonization*, 6.

42. Thomas Jefferson to [Governor] John Page, December 27, 1804, Jefferson Papers.

43. *Journal of the Senate of Virginia*, 66. There is no mention in the *Journal of the House of Delegates of Virginia* of the vote taken on January 22, 1805.

44. Thomas Jefferson to William A. Burwell, January 28, 1805, in Betts, ed., *Thomas Jefferson's Farm Book*, 20.

45. Alison G. Freehling's *Drift toward Dissolution* is the most detailed account of the Virginia slavery debates of 1831–32, although see also Dabney's *Virginia* for a corrective of Freehling's too optimistic view that "antislavery Virginians of abolitionist and moderate persuasion might well regard the 1831–1832 legislative debate not as a repudiation of revolutionary hopes, but as a vigorous 'fresh start' to the age old dream of emancipation-colonization" (167). Dabney counters with the argument "that the unwillingness of the session of 1831–1832 to act affirmatively for gradual emancipation was tragic in its consequences" (228). By 1831, however, it was too late.

46. Tadman demonstrates that for "slave children living in the Upper South in 1820, the cumulative chance of being 'sold South' by 1860 might have been something like 30 percent" (*Speculators and Slaves*, 45).

47. Charles Fenton Mercer to John Hartwell Cocke, April 19, 1818, Cocke Papers. See my "'Its Origin Is Not a Little Curious,'" on how Mercer discovered the secret resolutions and used them as the basis for the American Colonization

Society. The role that colonization played in Mercer's larger economic program can be seen in my *Charles Fenton Mercer and the Trial of National Conservatism*, chap. 7.

48. Thomas Jefferson to John Holmes, April 22, 1820, in Peterson, ed., *Jefferson*, 1434; *Richmond Virginian*, 1808, in Escott and Goldfield, eds., *Major Problems in the History of the American South*, 1:214.

CHAPTER ELEVEN

1. Unsigned letter to editor, September 13, 1800, in *Virginia Herald* (Fredericksburg), September 23, 1800.

2. Brown, ed., *William Plumer's Memorandum*, 115–16; Thomas Jefferson advocated the "spirit of resistance" in his famous letter to William Smith, November 13, 1787, in Boyd, ed., *Papers of Jefferson*, 12:356–57; *New England Palladium*, quoted in Kerber, *Federalists in Dissent*, 46.

3. Charles Pettigrew to Ebenezer Pettigrew, May 19, 1802, in Lemmon, ed., *Pettigrew Papers*, 1:285–86. Manarin and Dowdey argue that "after the initial shock, both whites and blacks appear to have welcomed a return to the status quo" (*History of Henrico County*, 174). When it came to passing restrictive legislation, the Assembly clearly did not wish to maintain the status quo, since the relative freedom of movement enjoyed by bondpersons had allowed Gabriel to plan the conspiracy. Nor is it likely that the slaves welcomed a return to the status quo, since so many of them conspired to overturn it and free themselves.

4. Unidentified newspaper clipping, William Palmer Scrapbook; Sheldon, "Black-White Relations in Richmond," 34–35.

5. "An Act to Amend and Reduce into One the Seven Acts concerning Pilots," January 23, 1802, in Shepherd, ed., *Statutes at Large*, 2:313; Bogger, "Slave and Free Black Community," 168; Farr, *Black Odyssey*, 181; Schweninger, "Underside of Slavery," 3.

6. "An Act Further Declaring What Shall be Deemed Unlawful Meetings of Slaves," January 24, 1804, in Shepherd, ed., *Statutes at Large*, 3:108.

7. "An Act Further to Amend the Act . . . Concerning Slaves, Free Negroes, and Mulattoes," January 31, 1805, in Shepherd, ed., *Statutes at Large*, 3:124; David Goldfield, "Black Life in Old South Cities," in Campbell and Rice, eds., *Before Freedom Came*, 146; Miller, *Wolf by the Ears*, 257.

8. *Journal of the House of Delegates of Virginia*, 85.

9. *Richmond Virginian*, 1808, in Escott and Goldfield, eds., *Major Problems in the History of the American South*, 1:214–15.

10. "An Act to Amend the Several Laws Concerning Slaves," January 25, 1806, in Shepherd, ed., *Statutes at Large*, 3:252; *Virginia Gazette and General Advertiser* (Richmond), February 5, 1806.

11. Adam Craig to Philip N. Nicholas, September 13, 1800, Executive Papers, Negro Insurrection; Richard S. Dunn, "Black Society," in Berlin and Hoffman, eds., *Slavery and Freedom*, 80; Pinchbeck, *Virginia Negro Artisan*, 66. Nash incorrectly states that after the conspiracies "Virginia repealed the [1782] manu-

mission law and reverted to the old prohibition against the private liberation of slaves" (*Race and Revolution*, 115). Masters still had the right to emancipate their slaves without the government's permission. But the freed slaves now had to leave the state.

12. *Norfolk Herald*, January 28, 1802.

13. Ibid., April 15, 1803.

14. Sobel, *Trabelin' On*, 169, 172–73, 190, 192.

15. *Minutes of the Proceedings of the Eighth Convention of Delegates from the Abolition Societies*, 4.

16. Genovese, *World the Slaveholders Made*, 146.

17. Thomas Jefferson to James Madison, January 30, 1787, in Boyd, ed., *Papers of Jefferson*, 11:92–93; James Monroe to General Mathews, March 17, 1802, Executive Letterbook. I have relied heavily on two excellent essays on Jefferson's diplomacy toward Haiti: Hickey, "America's Response," 361–79, and Michael Zuckerman, "The Color of Counterrevolution: Thomas Jefferson and the Rebellion in San Domingo," in Mannucci, ed., *Languages of Revolution*, 83–107. Both authors, however, attribute Jefferson's hostility to Toussaint solely to racism; neither mentions the impact that Gabriel had on the president's actions.

18. Ott, *Haitian Revolution*, 132; Zuckerman, "Color of Counterrevolution," 85.

19. Hickey, "America's Response," 368; Zuckerman, "Color of Counterrevolution," 95.

20. Tucker and Hendrickson, *Empire of Liberty*, 126.

21. Charles M. de Talleyrand to John Armstrong, n.d., in *Virginia Gazette and General Advertiser* (Richmond), January 25, 1806; DeConde, *This Affair of Louisiana*, 100; Palmer, *Age of Democratic Revolution*, 514; Hunt, *Haiti's Influence*, 23–24.

22. Adams, *History of the United States of America during the Administration of Thomas Jefferson*, 316; Robert L. Pacquette, "Revolutionary Saint Domingue in the Making of Territorial Louisiana," in Gaspar and Geggus, *French Revolution and the Greater Caribbean*. Malone concedes that Jefferson's hostility to Toussaint might have been due to Gabriel, but has, I believe, the weaker part of the argument in suggesting that the president could not have understood the connection between Napoleon's attempt to reenslave Saint Domingue and his need for the Louisiana breadbasket (*Jefferson and His Time*, 4:251–53).

23. Zuckerman, "Color of Counterrevolution," 101.

24. *Annals of Congress*, 9th Cong., 1st Sess., 26; Adams, ed., *Memoirs of Adams*, 1:383; Brown, ed., *William Plumer's Memorandum*, 250–51.

25. *Annals of Congress*, 9th Cong., 1st Sess., 499, 515; Brown, ed., *William Plumer's Memorandum*, 243.

26. *Annals of Congress*, 9th Cong., 1st Sess., 138; Adams, ed., *Memoirs of Adams*, 1:414; *Norfolk Gazette*, September 28, 1806; *Virginia Gazette and General Advertiser* (Richmond), March 1, 1806.

27. *Annals of Congress*, 9th Cong., 1st Sess., 515–16. Hickey argues that "Federalists from both sides of the Mason-Dixon line" voted against the Logan bill ("America's Response," 376). That may be generally true, but it was not the case

in Virginia. No Virginian of any political persuasion cast a nay vote. Joseph Lewis, the Federalist congressman from Loudoun County, was absent during the voting.

28. Hickey, "America's Response," 378; Donald, *Charles Sumner and the Rights of Man*, 57.

29. Benjamin Howard to William Preston, October 25, 1800, Preston Family Papers; John Randolph, quoted in McGraw and Kimball, *In Bondage and Freedom*, 66.

30. Testimony of Ben Woolfolk, various dates, Executive Papers, Negro Insurrection; Accounts, January 15, 1801, Gabriel's Insurrection, Military Papers; Pay Warrant to Ben Woolfolk, January 22, 1801, ibid.; Blassingame, *Slave Community*, 316.

31. Testimony of Prosser's Ben, various dates, Executive Papers; Accounts, January 6, 1801, Gabriel's Insurrection, Military Papers; Pay Warrant to Prosser's Ben, January 15, 1801, ibid.

32. Trial of Prosser's Ben, May 10, 1806, Henrico County Court Order Book; Trial of Prosser's Ned, May 10, 1806, ibid.; Trial of Prosser's Isaac, May 10, 1806, ibid.

33. Schwarz, "Emancipators, Protectors, and Anomalies," 320–21.

34. Box 668, Account Book, Household, 1794–1812, Mosby Sheppard Papers; Box 456, Financial Records, 1799–1824, ibid.; Box 668, Account Book, Household, 1816–, ibid.

35. Box 668, Account Book, Household, 1794–1812, Mosby Sheppard Papers; Box 668, Account Book, Agricultural, Ledger A, 1798–1817, ibid.; Box 668, Account Book, Agricultural, Ledger C, 1824–1830, ibid.

36. Petersburg City Personal Property Tax, 1801–03.

37. *Daily Compiler* (Richmond), February 10, 1820. I am grateful to Randall Miller for providing me with this information.

38. Schwarz, *Twice Condemned*, 278, n. 48.

39. Trial of Redford's Stephen, February 2, 1801, Henrico County Court Order Book; *Alexandria Advertiser*, May 5, 1802.

40. Thomas Henry Prosser, Henrico County Personal Property Tax, 1801.

41. *Virginia Argus* (Richmond), June 30, 1801.

42. Henrico County Court Order Book, May 5, 1803; Manarin and Dowdey, *History of Henrico County*, 190; *Richmond Enquirer*, January 22, 1811.

43. *Richmond Enquirer*, October 25, 1822, and December 23, 1826.

44. Thomas Henry Prosser, Last Will and Testament, October 22, 1839, Record of Wills, 1 (1824–45), 213–14, Wilkinson County Courthouse. My thanks to Philip J. Schwarz for making a copy of this document available to me.

45. *Spectator* (New York), October 11, 1800.

46. James Monroe to John Drayton, October 21, 1800, in Hamilton, ed., *Writings of Monroe*, 3:217.

47. Aptheker does not go far beyond the documentation when he writes that Nanny was "active" in the conspiracy (*American Negro Slave Revolts*, 220), a position echoed by Rosalyn Terborg-Penn ("Black Women in Resistance: A Cross-Cultural Perspective," in Okihiro, ed., *In Resistance*, 194). The single reference to

Nanny in the court records hardly, however, supports the thesis that the plot was "led by Nancy [*sic*] Prosser [*sic*] and her husband, Gabriel." See Giddings, *When and Where I Enter*, 40.

48. Genovese, *Roll, Jordan, Roll*, 157.

49. Gwaltney, *Drylongso*, 127.

APPENDIX ONE

1. Description of Gabriel by Thomas Henry Prosser, in *Virginia Argus* (Richmond), September 23, 1800.

2. Howison, *History of Virginia*, 2:390; Higginson, *Travellers and Outlaws*, 190; Coffin, *Some Principal Slave Insurrections*, 24–28.

3. Marion Harland, *Judith: A Chronicle of Old Virginia*, excerpt in Goode, *Virginia Cousins*, 60.

4. Carroll, *Slave Insurrections*, 49.

5. P. S. Foner, *History of Black Americans*, 453; Kimball, "Gabriel Insurrection," 153, and the same author's sketch in Logan and Winston, eds., *Dictionary of American Negro Biography*, 506; Bennett, *Before the Mayflower*, 111; Smith, *After the Revolution*, 129, although the catalog is less explicit on the point than the Smithsonian exhibit itself; Rawick, *From Sundown to Sunup*, 112; Halasz, *Rattling Chains*, 87.

6. Genovese, *Roll, Jordan, Roll*, 593, and his *From Rebellion to Revolution*, 44–46; W. D. Jordan, *White over Black*, 393; Raboteau, *Slave Religion*, 147.

7. Wish, "American Slave Insurrections before 1861," 311; Grant, *Black Protest*, 38; Blassingame, *Slave Community*, 221.

8. Mullin, *Flight and Rebellion*; Schwarz, *Twice Condemned*.

9. Sobel, *Trabelin' On*, 159; Ruffin, Program notes to "Race and Revolution," 17; Sidney Kaplan and Emma Kaplan, *The Black Presence in the Era of the American Revolution*, 111; Gorn, *Constructing the American Past*, 1:198.

APPENDIX TWO

1. Ernst, "Gabriel's Revolt," 37; Ammon, *James Monroe*, 187; Smith, *After the Revolution*, 159; Beeman, *Old Dominion and the New Nation*, 228; Mullin, *Flight and Rebellion*, 152; Aptheker, *American Negro Slave Revolts*, 44, n. 78.

2. Johnston, "Participation of White Men in Virginia Negro Insurrections," 160–61; Schwarz, *Twice Condemned*, 269; Bontemps, *Black Thunder*.

3. Testimony of Prosser's Ben at trial of Prosser's Solomon, September 11, 1800, Executive Papers, Negro Insurrection; Joseph Jones to James Monroe, September 9, 1800, ibid.

4. Confession of Prosser's Solomon, September 15, 1800, Letterbook, Executive Communications; Confession of Young's Gilbert, September 23, 1800, Executive Papers, Negro Insurrection.

5. *Genealogies of Virginia Families*, 2:346–49; Caroline County Personal Property and Land Book, 1797.

6. Hanover County, Personal Property Tax, 1784–1785, 1788–1802.

7. Rice and Brown, eds., *American Campaigns of Rochambeau's Army*, 2:163.

8. Roberts, "Francois Quesnay's Heir"; James Currie to Thomas Jefferson, May 2, 1787, in Boyd, ed., *Papers of Jefferson*, 11:328; Mordecai, *Richmond*, 135.

9. Rev. James Madison to Thomas Jefferson, December 28, 1786, in Boyd, ed., *Papers of Jefferson*, 10:642; Quesnay de Beaurepaire to Thomas Jefferson, March 2, 1789, ibid., 14:606–07; Passports Issued by Jefferson, May 22, 1788, ibid., 15:486.

10. Whitridge, *Rochambeau*, 78–79.

11. Unsigned letter to editor, September 13, 1800, in *Virginia Herald* (Fredericksburg), September 23, 1800.

12. Philadelphia City Directory, 1795, Philadelphia City Archives, City Hall Annex, 27, 35, 74. I am grateful to Billy G. Smith and Tom Gentry for their aid on this point.

13. James Monroe to John Dayton, October 21, 1800, in Hamilton, ed., *Writings of Monroe*, 11:217.

APPENDIX THREE

1. Aptheker, *American Negro Slave Revolts*, 222–23 and n. 49.

2. Franklin, *From Slavery to Freedom*, 153; Dabney, *Virginia*, 186, and the same author's *Richmond*, 57; Tate, "Gabriel's Insurrection," 20; Manarin and Dowdey, *History of Henrico County*, 172.

3. Halasz, *Rattling Chains*, 96.

4. Phillips, *American Negro Slavery*, 475; Mullin, *Flight and Rebellion*, 153.

5. Pollard, *Richmond's Story*, 75–76; Marion Harlan, *Judith: A Chronicle of Old Virginia*, excerpt in Goode, *Virginia Cousins*, 60.

6. Trials of Burton's Isaac, Jones's John, Mosby's Will, and Price's James repeated in error for October 11, 1800, Henrico County Court Order Book, pp. 372–73.

7. Schwarz, *Twice Condemned*, app., 323–35.

8. Aptheker, *American Negro Slave Revolts*, 230, n. 77; Crow, "Slave Rebelliousness and Social Conflict in North Carolina," 100.

BIBLIOGRAPHY

MANUSCRIPTS

Charlottesville, Virginia
Alderman Library, University of Virginia
  John Hartwell Cocke Papers
  David Erskine Copybook
  John Murray (Earl of Dunmore) Papers
  Prentis Family Papers
  Creed Taylor Papers
Henrico County, Virginia
Henrico County Human Services Department
  Mosby Sheppard Papers
  Philip Sheppard Papers
Madison, Wisconsin
State Historical Society of Wisconsin
  John Robinson Papers
Philadelphia, Pennsylvania
Philadelphia City Archives, City Hall Annex
  Philadelphia City Directory, 1795
Raleigh, North Carolina
North Carolina Archives and Records Section
  Walter Clark Manuscripts, 1783–1826
  Historical Society of Pennsylvania Papers, 1760–1888
  Pasquotank County Court Minutes, 1799–1806
  Slave Collection, 1748–1856
Richmond, Virginia
Virginia Historical Society
  Francis Baylor Papers
  Carter Berkeley Papers
  James Monroe Papers
  William Palmer Scrapbook
  James Scott Papers
Virginia State Library
  Amelia County Personal Property Tax
  Brunswick County Court Order Book
  Caroline County Court Order Book

Caroline County Personal Property and Land Book
Chesterfield County Court Order Book
Condemned Slaves 1800–1805
Charles Copland Diary
Council Journals
Executive Communications
Executive Letterbook
Executive Papers
Executive Papers, Negro Insurrection
Executive Papers, 1802, Pardon Papers
Gabriel's Insurrection, Military Papers
Halifax County Court Order Book
Hanover County Personal Property Tax
Henrico County Court Order Book
Henrico County Personal Property Tax
Henrico County Will Book
Louisa County Court Order Book
Mutual Assurance Society Policies
Norfolk County Court Order Book
Patrick Henry Account Book, 1762–1770, Folio 39
Petersburg City Personal Property Tax
Richmond City Court Order Book
Richmond City Legislative Petitions
Southampton County Court Order Book
Washington, D.C.
Library of Congress
   Thomas Jefferson Papers
   James Madison Papers
   James Monroe Papers
   Joseph Nicholson Papers
   Levin Powell Papers
   Preston Family Papers
   William B. Randolph Papers
Williamsburg, Virginia
Swem Library, William and Mary College
   Francis Jerdone Papers
   Tucker-Coleman Papers
Woodville, Mississippi
Wilkinson County Courthouse
   Record of Wills, 1

NEWSPAPERS

Alexandria Advertiser
Alexandria Times

Aurora (Philadelphia)
Boston Gazette
Columbian Centinel (Boston)
Daily Compiler (Richmond)
Gazette of the United States (Philadelphia)
Kentucky Gazette (Lexington)
Norfolk Herald
North-Carolina Minerva (Raleigh)
Petersburg Intelligencer
Porcupine's Gazette (Philadelphia)
Raleigh Register, and North Carolina Gazette
Richmond Enquirer
Richmond Recorder
Russell's Gazette, Commercial and Political (Boston)
Spectator (New York)
Virginia Argus (Richmond)
Virginia Gazette and General Advertiser (Richmond)
Virginia Herald (Fredericksburg)

PUBLIC DOCUMENTS

Annals of Congress. Washington: Gales and Seaton, 1834–56.

Gopsill's Philadelphia City and Business Directory for 1868–1869. Philadelphia: James Gopsill, 1868.

Journal of the House of Delegates of the Commonwealth of Virginia. Richmond: Thomas Nicolson, 1797–1804.

Journal of the Senate of the Commonwealth of Virginia. Richmond: Thomas Nicolson, 1797–1804.

Minchinton, Walter, Celia King, and Peter Waite, eds. *Virginia Slave Trade Statistics, 1698–1775.* Richmond: Virginia State Library, 1984.

Return of the Whole Number of Persons within the Several Districts of the United States. Washington: Apollo Press, 1802.

Shepherd, Samuel, ed. *The Statutes at Large of Virginia, 1792 to 1806.* 3 vols. New York: AMS Press, 1970 reprint of the 1835 edition.

PUBLISHED PRIMARY SOURCES

Adams, Charles Francis, ed. *Memoirs of John Quincy Adams, Comprising Parts of His Diary from 1795 to 1848.* 12 vols. Philadelphia, Pa.: J. B. Lippincott and Company, 1874–77.

Betts, Edwin M., ed. *Thomas Jefferson's Farm Book.* Princeton, N.J.: Princeton University Press, 1953.

Boyd, Julian P., ed. *The Papers of Thomas Jefferson.* 24 vols. to date. Princeton, N.J.: Princeton University Press, 1950–90.

Brown, Everett S., ed. *William Plumer's Memorandum of Proceedings in the United States Senate, 1803–1807.* New York: Macmillan, 1923.

Carter, Edward C., ed. *The Papers of Benjamin Henry Latrobe: Virginia Journals.* Ser. 1, *Journals.* 2 vols. New Haven, Conn.: Yale University Press, 1977.

Chastellux, Marquis de. *Travels in North America in the Years 1780, 1781, and 1782.* 2 vols. Edited by Howard C. Rice, Jr. Chapel Hill: University of North Carolina Press, 1963.

Clark, Thomas D., ed. *Footloose in Jacksonian America: Robert W. Scott and His Agrarian World.* Lexington: Kentucky Historical Society, 1989.

Coffin, Joshua. *An Account of Some of the Principle Slave Insurrections.* New York: American Anti-Slavery Society, 1860.

Davis, John. *Travels of Four Years and a Half in the United States of America, During 1798, 1799, 1800, 1801, and 1802.* Edited by A. J. Morrison. New York: Holt, 1909.

"Document: Journal of a French Traveller in the Colonies, 1765." *American Historical Review* 26 (July 1921): 726–47.

Donnan, Elizabeth, ed. *Papers of James A. Bayard, 1796–1815.* Washington, D.C.: Annual Report of the American Historical Association of 1913, 1915.

Fitzpatrick, John C., ed. *The Writings of George Washington.* 39 vols. Washington, D.C.: U.S. Government Printing Office, 1931–44.

Flournoy, H. W., ed. *Calendar of Virginia State Papers and Other Manuscripts.* 11 vols. Richmond, Va.: James E. Goode, 1875–93.

Ford, Paul L., ed. *The Writings of Thomas Jefferson.* 9 vols. New York: Putnam's Sons, 1892–98.

Ford, Worthington C., ed. "Letters of William Vans Murray to John Quincy Adams." *Annual Report of the American Historical Association.* Washington, D.C., 1914.

Hamilton, Stanislaus M., ed. *The Writings of James Monroe.* 11 vols. New York: Putnam's Sons, 1898–1903.

Hayden, Horace E. *Virginia Genealogies.* 1891. Reprint. Baltimore, Md.: Genealogical Publishing, 1966.

Henson, Josiah. *Father Henson's Story.* Saddle River, Pa.: Literature House, 1970.

King, Charles R., ed. *The Life and Correspondence of Rufus King.* 5 vols. New York: Putnam's Sons, 1896.

Lemmon, Sarah M., ed. *The Pettigrew Papers.* Raleigh: North Carolina Department of Archives and History, 1971.

Masterson, William H., ed. *The John Gray Blount Papers.* 4 vols. Raleigh: North Carolina Department of Archives and History, 1952–82.

Meade, William. *Old Churches, Ministers, and Families of Virginia.* 1857. Reprint. Baltimore, Md.: Genealogical Publishing, 1966.

Memorials Presented to the Congress of the United States of America by the Different Societies Promoting the Abolition of Slavery. Philadelphia, Pa.: Francis Bailey, 1792.

Mercer, Charles Fenton. *An Address to the American Colonization Society at their 36th Annual Meeting.* Geneva, Switzerland: Monroe, English Bookseller, 1854.

Minutes of the Proceedings of the Eighth Convention of Delegates from the Abolition Societies. Philadelphia, Pa.: Z. Poulson, 1803.

Minutes of the Proceedings of the Fourth Convention of Delegates from the Abolition Societies. Philadelphia, Pa.: Z. Poulson, 1797.

Mordecai, Samuel. *Richmond in By-Gone Days.* Richmond, Va.: George West, 1856.

Peterson, Merrill D., ed. *Thomas Jefferson: Writings.* New York: Library of America, 1984.

Rawick, George P., ed. *The American Slave: A Composite Autobiography.* Vol. 16 (Virginia). Westport, Conn.: Greenwood Press, 1972.

Rice, Howard C. Jr., and Anne S. Brown, eds. *The American Campaigns of Rochambeau's Army.* 2 vols. Princeton, N.J.: Princeton University Press, 1972.

Roeber, A. G., ed. "A New England Woman's Perspective on Norfolk, Virginia, 1801–1802: Excerpts from the Diary of Ruth Henshaw Bascom." *Proceedings of the American Antiquarian Society* 88 (1978): 277–325.

Rutland, Robert A., ed. *The Papers of George Mason, 1725–1792.* 3 vols. Chapel Hill: University of North Carolina Press, 1970.

Slaughter, Philip. *The Virginian History of African Colonization.* Richmond, Va.: MacFarlane and Fergusson, 1855.

Steward, Austin. *Twenty-two Years a Slave and Forty Years a Freeman.* Introduction by Jane H. Pease and William H. Pease. Reading, Pa.: Addison-Wesley, 1969.

Sutcliff, Robert. *Travels through Some Parts of North America, in the Years 1804, 1805, and 1806.* Philadelphia, Pa.: B. and T. Kite, 1812.

[Tucker, George.] *Letter to a Member of the General Assembly of Virginia, on the Subject of the Late Conspiracy of the Slaves with a Proposal for Their Colonization.* 2d ed. Richmond, Va.: H. Pace, 1801.

Tucker, St. George. *A Dissertation on Slavery with a Proposal for the Gradual Abolition of It in the State of Virginia.* Philadelphia, Pa.: Mathew Carey, 1796.

Weld, Isaac. *Travels through the States of North America.* 2 vols. 1807. Reprint. New York: Johnson Reprints, 1968.

Windley, Lathan A., ed. *Runaway Slave Advertisements: A Documentary History from the 1730s to 1790.* Vol. 1 (Virginia). Westport, Conn.: Greenwood Press, 1983.

SECONDARY SOURCES

Adams, Henry. *History of the United States of America during the Administration of Thomas Jefferson.* New York: Library of America, 1986.

Alden, John R. *The South in the Revolution, 1763–1789.* Baton Rouge: Louisiana State University Press, 1957.

Ammon, Harry. *James Monroe: The Quest for National Identity.* New York: McGraw-Hill, 1971.

Aptheker, Herbert. *American Negro Slave Revolts.* 5th ed. New York: International Publishers, 1983.

Ayers, Edward L. *Vengeance and Justice: Crime and Punishment in the Nineteenth-Century American South.* New York: Oxford University Press, 1984.

Ballagh, James C. *A History of Slavery in Virginia.* Baltimore, Md.: Johns Hopkins University Press, 1902.

Baylen, Joseph, and Norbert J. Grossman, eds. *Biographical Dictionary of Modern British Radicals.* Vol. 1. Sussex, England: Harvester Press, 1979.

Beeman, Richard R. *The Old Dominion and the New Nation, 1788–1801.* Lexington: University Press of Kentucky, 1972.

Bennett, Lerone, Jr. *Before the Mayflower: A History of the Negro in America, 1619–1962.* Chicago: Johnson Publishing, 1962.

———. *The Shaping of Black America.* Chicago: Johnson Publishing, 1975.

Berlin, Ira. *Slaves without Masters: The Free Negro in the Antebellum South.* New York: Oxford University Press, 1974.

Berlin, Ira, and Ronald Hoffman, eds. *Slavery and Freedom in the Age of the American Revolution.* Urbana: University of Illinois Press, 1986.

Blassingame, John W. *The Slave Community: Plantation Life in the Antebellum South.* Rev. ed. New York: Oxford University Press, 1979.

Bogger, Tommy L. "The Slave and Free Black Community in Norfolk, 1775–1865." Ph.D. diss., University of Virginia, 1976.

Boles, John B. *Black Southerners, 1619–1869.* Lexington: University Press of Kentucky, 1984.

Bolster, W. Jeffrey. "'To Feel Like a Man': Black Seamen in the Northern States, 1800–1860." *Journal of American History* 76 (March 1990): 1173–99.

Bontemps, Arna. *Black Thunder: Gabriel's Revolt Virginia 1800.* 1936. Reprint. Boston: Beacon Press, 1968.

Brodie, Fawn M. *Thomas Jefferson: An Intimate History.* New York: Norton, 1974.

Broussard, James H. *The Southern Federalists, 1800–1816.* Baton Rouge: Louisiana State University Press, 1978.

Brown, Ralph A. *The Presidency of John Adams.* Lawrence: University Press of Kansas, 1975.

Burton, Orville V., and Robert C. McMath, Jr., eds. *Class, Conflict, and Consensus: Antebellum Southern Community Studies.* Westport, Conn.: Greenwood Press, 1982.

Campbell, Edward D. C., and Kym S. Rice, eds. *Before Freedom Came: African-American Life in the Antebellum South.* Charlottesville: University Press of Virginia, 1991.

Carroll, Joseph C. *Slave Insurrections in the United States, 1800–1865.* 1938. Reprint. New York: Negro Universities Press, 1973.

Childs, Frances S. *French Refugee Life in the United States, 1790–1800.* Baltimore, Md.: Johns Hopkins University Press, 1940.

Christian, W. Asbury. *Richmond: Her Past and Present.* Richmond, Va.: L. H. Jenkins, 1912.

Clark, Ernest J., Jr. "Aspects of the North Carolina Slave Code, 1715–1860." *North Carolina Historical Review* 39 (Spring 1962): 148–64.

Cohen, William. "Thomas Jefferson and the Problem of Slavery." *Journal of American History* 56 (December 1969): 503–26.

Cox, Joseph W. *Champion of Southern Federalism: Robert Goodloe Harper of South Carolina*. Port Washington, N.Y.: Kennikat Press, 1972.

Cox, Virginia Lee. "How Richmond Founder Began Naming Streets." *Richmond Times-Dispatch*, January 20, 1924.

Creel, Margaret Washington. *"A Peculiar People": Slave Religion and Community-Culture among the Gullah*. New York: New York University Press, 1988.

Crittenden, Charles C. "Inland Navigation in North Carolina, 1763–1789." *North Carolina Historical Review* 8 (April 1931): 145–54.

Crow, Jeffrey J. *The Black Experience in Revolutionary North Carolina*. Raleigh: North Carolina Department of Cultural Resources, 1977.

——— . "Equal Justice: Afro-American Perceptions of the Revolution in North Carolina, 1750–1800." Paper presented at the annual meeting of the Organization of American Historians, Reno, Nevada, March 1988.

——— . "Slave Rebelliousness and Social Conflict in North Carolina, 1775–1802." *William and Mary Quarterly* 37 (January 1980): 79–102.

Cunningham, Noble E., Jr. *In Pursuit of Reason: The Life of Thomas Jefferson*. Baton Rouge: Louisiana State University Press, 1987.

Curtin, Philip D. *The Rise and Fall of the Plantation Complex: Essays in Atlantic History*. New York: Cambridge University Press, 1990.

Dabney, Virginius. *Richmond: The Story of a City*. New York: Doubleday, 1976.

——— . *Virginia: The New Dominion*. New York: Doubleday, 1971.

Daniel, W. Harrison. "Virginia Baptists and the Negro in the Early Republic." *Virginia Magazine of History and Biography* 80 (1972): 60–69.

Davidson, P. G. "Virginia and the Alien and Sedition Laws." *American Historical Review* 36 (January 1931): 336–42.

Davis, David Brion. "American Equality and Foreign Revolutions." *Journal of American History* 76 (December 1989): 729–52.

——— . *The Problem of Slavery in the Age of Revolution, 1770–1823*. Ithaca, N.Y.: Cornell University Press, 1975.

——— . *Revolutions: Reflections on American Equality and Foreign Liberations*. Cambridge, Mass.: Harvard University Press, 1990.

Davis, John P., ed. *The American Negro Reference Book*. Englewood Cliffs, N.J.: Prentice-Hall, 1966.

Davis, Thomas J. *A Rumor of Revolt: The "Great Negro Plot" in Colonial New York*. New York: Free Press, 1985.

DeConde, Alexander. *This Affair of Louisiana*. New York: Scribner's, 1976.

Deyle, Steven. "The Irony of Liberty: American Independence and the Rise of the Domestic Slave Trade." Paper presented at the annual meeting of the Society for Historians of the Early Republic, Charlottesville, Virginia, July 1989.

Donald, David. *Charles Sumner and the Rights of Man*. New York: Knopf, 1970.

Durey, Michael. *"With the Hammer of Truth": James Thomson Callender and America's Early National Heroes*. Charlottesville: University Press of Virginia, 1990.

Eaton, Clement. *The Growth of Southern Civilization, 1790–1860*. New York: Harper and Row, 1961.

——. "Slave-Hiring in the Upper South: A Step toward Freedom." *Mississippi Valley Historical Review* 46 (March 1960): 663–678.

Egerton, Douglas R. *Charles Fenton Mercer and the Trial of National Conservatism*. Jackson: University Press of Mississippi, 1989.

——. "'Fly across the River': The Easter Slave Conspiracy of 1802." *North Carolina Historical Review* 68 (April 1991): 87–110.

——. "Gabriel's Conspiracy and the Election of 1800." *Journal of Southern History* 56 (May 1990): 191–214.

——. "'Its Origin Is Not a Little Curious': A New Look at the American Colonization Society." *Journal of the Early Republic* 5 (Winter 1985): 463–80.

——. "A Rejoinder." *North Carolina Historical Review* 68 (April 1991): 122–24.

Ernst, William Joel. "Gabriel's Revolt: Black Freedom, White Fear." Master's thesis, University of Virginia, 1968.

Escott, Paul D., and David R. Goldfield, eds. *Major Problems in the History of the American South*. 2 vols. New York: D. C. Heath, 1990.

Essig, James D. "A Very Wintry Season: Virginia Baptists and Slavery, 1785–1797." *Virginia Magazine of History and Biography* 88 (April 1980): 170–85.

"Families of Lower Norfolk and Princess Anne Counties: Walke Family." *Virginia Magazine of History and Biography* 5 (July 1897): 139–53.

Farr, James B. *Black Odyssey: The Seafaring Traditions of Afro-Americans*. New York: Peter Lang, 1989.

Federal Writers' Project. *Virginia, A Guide to the Old Dominion*. New York: Oxford University Press, 1940.

Fields, Barbara J. "Slavery, Race, and Ideology in the United States of America." *New Left Review* 181 (May/June 1990): 95–118.

Fitzgerald, Ruth C. *A Different Story: A Black History of Fredericksburg, Stafford, and Spotsylvania, Virginia*. Fredericksburg: Unicorn Press, 1979.

Fladeland, Betty. *Men and Brothers: Anglo-American Anti-Slavery Cooperation*. Urbana: University of Illinois Press, 1972.

Flanigan, Daniel J. "Criminal Procedure in Slave Trials in the Antebellum South." *Journal of Southern History* 40 (November 1974): 537–64.

Flexner, James T. *Washington: The Indispensable Man*. Boston: Little, Brown, 1969.

Fogel, Robert W., and Engerman, Stanley L. *Time on the Cross: the Economics of American Negro Slavery*. Boston: Little, Brown, 1974.

Foner, Eric. *Nothing But Freedom: Emancipation and Its Legacy*. Baton Rouge: Louisiana State University Press, 1983.

——. *Tom Paine and Revolutionary America*. New York: Oxford University Press, 1976.

Foner, Philip S. *History of Black Americans: From Africa to the Emergence of the Cotton Kingdom*. Westport, Conn.: Greenwood Press, 1975.

Franklin, John Hope. *From Slavery to Freedom: A History of Negro Americans*. 5th ed. New York: Knopf, 1980.

Freehling, Alison G. *Drift toward Dissolution: The Virginia Slavery Debate of 1831–1832.* Baton Rouge: Louisiana State University Press, 1982.

Freehling, William W. "The Founding Fathers and Slavery." *American Historical Review* 77 (February 1972): 81–93.

———. *The Road to Disunion: Secessionists at Bay, 1776–1854.* New York: Oxford University Press, 1990.

Frey, Sylvia. "Between Slavery and Freedom: Virginia Blacks in the American Revolution." *Journal of Southern History* 49 (August 1983): 375–98.

———. "The British and the Blacks: A New Perspective." *The Historian* 38 (February 1976): 225–38.

———. *Water from the Rock: Black Resistance in a Revolutionary Age.* Princeton, N.J.: Princeton University Press, 1991.

Furneaux, Robin. *William Wilberforce.* London: Hamish Hamilton, 1974.

Fyfe, Christopher. *A History of Sierra Leone.* New York: Oxford University Press, 1962.

Gaines, William H., Jr. "Courthouses of Henrico and Chesterfield." *Virginia Cavalcade* 17 (Winter 1968): 30–37.

Gaspar, David Berry, and David P. Geggus, eds. *The French Revolution and the Greater Caribbean.* Urbana: University of Illinois Press, forthcoming.

Geggus, David P. *Slavery, War, and Revolution: The British Occupation of Saint-Domingue, 1793–1798.* New York: Oxford University Press, 1982.

Genealogies of Virginia Families: From the Virginia Magazine of History and Biography. 5 vols. Baltimore, Md.: Genealogical Publishing, 1981.

Genovese, Eugene D. *From Rebellion to Revolution: Afro-American Slave Revolts in the Making of the Modern World.* Baton Rouge: Louisiana State University Press, 1979.

———. *Roll, Jordan, Roll: The World the Slaves Made.* New York: Pantheon, 1974.

———. *The World the Slaveholders Made: Two Essays in Interpretation.* New York: Pantheon, 1969.

Gibbons, Jean N. "Meadow Farm." *Henrico County Historical Society Magazine* 1 (December 1976): 67–69.

Giddings, Paula. *When and Where I Enter: The Impact of Black Women on Race and Sex in America.* New York: William Morrow, 1984.

Goode, G. Brown. *Virginia Cousins: A Study of the Ancestry and Posterity of John Goode of Whitby.* 1888. Reprint. Bridgewater, Va.: C. J. Carrier Company, 1963.

Goolrick, John T. *Historic Fredericksburg: The Story of an Old Town.* Richmond, Va.: Whittet and Shepperson, 1922.

Gorn, Elliott J. *Constructing the American Past: A Source Book of a People's History.* New York: HarperCollins, 1991.

Grant, Joanne. *Black Protest: History, Documents, and Analysis.* New York: Fawcett Press, 1968.

Gwaltney, John Langston. *Drylongso: A Self-Portrait of Black America.* New York: Random House, 1980.

Halasz, Nicholas. *The Rattling Chains: Slave Unrest and Revolt in the Antebellum South.* New York: McKay, 1966.

Harding, Vincent. *There Is a River: The Black Struggle for Freedom in America.* New York: Harcourt Brace Jovanovich, 1981.

Hatfield, Joseph T. *William Claiborne: Jeffersonian Centurion in the American Southwest.* Lafayette: University of Southwestern Louisiana Press, 1976.

Hay, Douglas, ed. *Albion's Fatal Tree: Crime and Society in Eighteenth-Century England.* New York: Pantheon, 1975.

Hickey, Donald R. "America's Response to the Slave Revolt in Haiti, 1791–1806." *Journal of the Early Republic* 2 (Winter 1982): 361–79.

Higginson, Thomas W. *Travellers and Outlaws: Episodes in American History.* Boston: Lee and Shepard, 1889.

Hobsbawm, Eric. *Primitive Rebels: Studies in Archaic Forms of Social Movement in the Nineteenth and Twentieth Centuries.* New York: Norton, 1959.

Hobsbawm, Eric, and George Rude. *Captain Swing: A Social History of the Great English Agricultural Uprising of 1830.* New York: Norton, 1968.

Hoffman, Ronald. *A Spirit of Dissension: Economics, Politics, and the Revolution in Maryland.* Baltimore, Md.: Johns Hopkins University Press, 1973.

Howison, Robert R. *A History of Virginia.* 2 vols. Philadelphia, Pa.: Carey and Hart, 1846.

Hughes, Sarah S. "Slaves for Hire: The Allocation of Black Labor in Elizabeth City County, Virginia, 1782–1810." *William and Mary Quarterly* 35 (April 1978): 260–86.

Hunt, Alfred N. *Haiti's Influence on Antebellum America: Slumbering Volcano in the Caribbean.* Baton Rouge: Louisiana State University Press, 1988.

Isaac, Rhys. "Evangelical Revolt: The Nature of the Baptists' Challenge to the Traditional Order in Virginia, 1765–1775." *William and Mary Quarterly* 31 (July 1974): 345–68.

———. *The Transformation of Virginia, 1740–1790.* Chapel Hill: University of North Carolina Press, 1982.

Jackson, Luther P. "Religious Development of the Negro in Virginia from 1760 to 1860." *Journal of Negro History* 16 (January 1931): 168–239.

James, C. L. R. *The Black Jacobins: Toussaint L'Ouverture and the San Domingo Revolution.* 2d ed. New York: Vintage, 1963.

Jeffrey, Thomas E. *State Parties and National Politics: North Carolina, 1815–1861.* Athens: University of Georgia Press, 1989.

Johnston, James H. "The Participation of White Men in Virginia Negro Insurrections." *Journal of Negro History* 16 (April 1931): 158–67.

———. "Race Relations in Virginia and Miscegenation in the South, 1776–1860." Ph.D. diss., University of Chicago, 1937.

Jones, Norrece T. *Born a Child of Freedom, Yet a Slave: Mechanisms of Control and Strategies of Resistance in Antebellum South Carolina.* Hanover, N.H.: University Press of New England, 1990.

Jordan, Daniel P. *Political Leadership in Jefferson's Virginia.* Charlottesville: University Press of Virginia, 1983.

Jordan, Winthrop D. *White over Black: American Attitudes toward the Negro, 1550–1812.* Chapel Hill: University of North Carolina Press, 1968.

Jordan, Winthrop D., and Sheila Skemp, eds. *Race and Family in the Colonial South*. Jackson: University Press of Mississippi, 1987.

Kaplan, Sidney, and Emma Kaplan. *The Black Presence in the Era of the American Revolution*. Rev. ed. Amherst: University of Massachusetts Press, 1989.

Kay, Marvin L. Michael, and Lorin Lee Carey. "Slave Runaways in Colonial North Carolina, 1748–1775." *North Carolina Historical Review* 63 (January 1986): 1–39.

Kennett, Lee. *The French Forces in America, 1780–1783*. Westport, Conn.: Greenwood Press, 1977.

Kerber, Linda K. *Federalists in Dissent: Imagery and Ideology in Jeffersonian America*. Ithaca, N.Y.: Cornell University Press, 1970.

Ketcham, Ralph. *James Madison: A Biography*. New York: Macmillan, 1971.

Kilson, Marion D. "Towards Freedom: An Analysis of Slave Revolts in the United States." *Phylon* 25 (Summer 1964): 175–87.

Kimball, William J. "The Gabriel Insurrection of 1800." *Negro History Bulletin* 34 (November 1971): 153–56.

Klein, Herbert S. "Slaves and Shipping in Eighteenth-Century Virginia." *Journal of Interdisciplinary History* 5 (Winter 1975): 382–412.

Koch, Adrianne. *Jefferson and Madison: The Great Collaboration*. New York: Knopf, 1950.

Kulikoff, Allan. "A 'Prolifick' People: Black Population Growth in the Chesapeake Colonies, 1700–1790." *Southern Studies* 16 (Winter 1977): 391–428.

———. *Tobacco and Slaves: The Development of Southern Cultures in the Chesapeake, 1680–1800*. Chapel Hill: University of North Carolina Press, 1986.

Kurth, Jan. "Wayward Wenches and Wives: Runaway Women in the Hudson Valley, New York, 1785–1830." *National Women's Studies Association Journal* 1 (Winter 1988–89): 199–220.

Lerche, Charles O., Jr. "Jefferson and the Election of 1800: A Case Study in the Political Smear." *William and Mary Quarterly* 5 (October 1948): 467–91.

Lewis, Jan. *The Pursuit of Happiness: Family and Values in Jefferson's Virginia*. New York: Cambridge University Press, 1983.

Lichtenstein, Alex. " 'That Disposition to Theft, with Which They Have Been Branded': Moral Economy, Slave Management, and the Law." *Journal of Social History* 21 (Spring 1988): 413–40.

Linebaugh, Peter. *The London Hanged: Crime and Civil Society in the Eighteenth Century*. New York: Cambridge University Press, 1992.

Link, Eugene P. *Democratic-Republican Societies, 1790–1800*. New York: Columbia University Press, 1942.

Little, John P. *History of Richmond*. Richmond, Va.: Dietz Printing, 1933.

Litwack, Leon. *Been in the Storm So Long: The Aftermath of Slavery*. New York: Vintage, 1980.

Lofton, John. *Denmark Vesey's Revolt: The Slave Plot That Lit a Fuse to Fort Sumter*. Kent, Ohio.: Kent State University Press, 1983.

Logan, Raford W., and Michael R. Winston, eds. *Dictionary of American Negro Biography*. New York: Norton, 1982.

Lowery, Charles D. *James Barbour: A Jeffersonian Republican.* University: University of Alabama Press, 1984.

McColley, Robert. *Slavery and Jeffersonian Virginia.* 2d ed. Urbana: University of Illinois Press, 1973.

MacLeod, Duncan J. *Slavery, Race, and the American Revolution.* London: Cambridge University Press, 1974.

McLynn, Frank. *Crime and Punishment in Eighteenth-Century England.* New York: Oxford University Press, 1991.

Main, Jackson Turner. *The Antifederalists: Critics of the Constitution, 1781–1788.* Chapel Hill: University of North Carolina Press, 1961.

————. *The Social Structure of Revolutionary America.* Princeton, N.J.: Princeton University Press, 1965.

Malone, Dumas. *Jefferson and His Time.* 6 vols. Boston: Little, Brown, 1948–81.

Manarin, Louis H., and Clifford Dowdey. *The History of Henrico County.* Charlottesville: University Press of Virginia, 1984.

Mannucci, Loretta V., ed. *Languages of Revolution.* Milan, Italy: Milan Group in Early United States History, 1989.

Mason, Clifford. "Gabriel: The Story of a Slave Rebellion." In *Black Drama Anthology,* edited by Woodie King and Ron Milner. New York: New American Library, 1971.

Mathews, Richard K. *The Radical Politics of Thomas Jefferson: A Revisionist View.* Lawrence: University Press of Kansas, 1984.

Mayer, Henry. *A Son of Thunder: Patrick Henry and the American Republic.* New York: Franklin Watts, 1986.

Mays, David J. *Edmund Pendleton, 1721–1803: A Biography.* Cambridge, Mass.: Harvard University Press, 1952.

Meadow Farm Museum: Crump Park. Brochure. Henrico County, Virginia.

Meier, August, and Elliott Rudwick, eds. *The Making of Black America: Essays in Negro Life and History.* 2 vols. New York: Antheneum, 1969.

Miller, John C. *The Wolf by the Ears: Thomas Jefferson and Slavery.* New York: Free Press, 1977.

Morgan, Edmund S. *American Slavery, American Freedom: The Ordeal of Colonial Virginia.* New York: Norton, 1975.

Morgan, George. *The Life of James Monroe.* 1921. Reprint. New York: Arno Press, 1969.

Mullin, Gerald (Michael) W. *Flight and Rebellion: Slave Resistance in Eighteenth-Century Virginia.* New York: Oxford University Press, 1972.

Mutersbaugh, Bert M. "The Background of Gabriel's Insurrection." *Journal of Negro History* 68 (Spring 1983): 209–11.

Nash, Gary B. *Race and Revolution.* Madison, Wis.: Madison House, 1990.

————. *The Urban Crucible: Social Change, Political Consciousness, and the Origins of the American Revolution.* Cambridge: Harvard University Press, 1979.

Nash, Gary B., and Julie Roy Jeffrey. *The American People: Creating a History and a Society.* New York: HarperCollins, 1986.

Norton, Mary Beth. *Liberty's Daughters: The Revolutionary Experience of American Women, 1750–1800*. Boston: Little, Brown, 1980.

Oates, Stephen B. *The Fires of Jubilee: Nat Turner's Fierce Rebellion*. New York: Harper and Row, 1975.

O'Brien, John T. "Factory, Church, and Community: Blacks in Antebellum Richmond." *Journal of Southern History* 44 (November 1978): 509–36.

Okihiro, Gary Y., ed. *In Resistance: Studies in African, Caribbean, and Afro-American History*. Amherst: University of Massachusetts Press, 1986.

Ott, Thomas O. *The Haitian Revolution, 1789–1804*. Knoxville: University of Tennessee Press, 1973.

Palmer, Robert R. *The Age of Democratic Revolution: The Struggle*. Princeton, N.J.: Princeton University Press, 1964.

Parramore, Thomas C. "Aborted Takeoff: A Critique of 'Fly across the River.'" *North Carolina Historical Review* 68 (April 1991): 111–21.

———. *Southampton County, Virginia*. Charlottesville: University Press of Virginia, 1978.

Phillips, U. B. *American Negro Slavery: A Survey of the Supply, Employment, and Control of Negro Labor as Determined by the Plantation Regime*. 1918. Reprint. Baton Rouge: Louisiana State University Press, 1966.

Pinchbeck, Raymond B. *The Virginia Negro Artisan and Tradesman*. Richmond, Va.: William Byrd Press, 1926.

Pole, J. R. "Representation and Authority in Virginia from the Revolution to Reform." *Journal of Southern History* 24 (February 1958): 16–50.

Pollard, Julia C. *Richmond's Story*. Richmond, Va.: Public School Press, 1954.

Preyer, Kathryn. "Crime, the Criminal Law, and Reform in Post-Revolutionary Virginia." *Law and History Review* 1 (1983): 53–85.

Putney, Martha S. *Black Sailors: Afro-American Merchant Seamen and Whalemen prior to the Civil War*. Westport, Conn.: Greenwood Press, 1987.

Quarles, Benjamin. "Lord Dunmore as Liberator." *William and Mary Quarterly* 15 (October 1958): 494–508.

———. *The Negro in the American Revolution*. Chapel Hill: University of North Carolina Press, 1961.

Raboteau, Albert J. *Slave Religion: The "Invisible Institution" in the Antebellum South*. New York: Oxford University Press, 1979.

Rawick, George P. *From Sundown to Sunup: The Making of the Black Community*. Westport, Conn.: Greenwood Press, 1972.

Rediker, Marcus. "The American Revolution and the Cycles of Rebellion in the Eighteenth-Century Atlantic." Paper presented at the United States Capital Historical Society, Washington, D.C., March 1989.

———. *Between the Devil and the Deep Blue Sea: Merchant Seamen, Pirates, and the Anglo-American Maritime World, 1700–1750*. New York: Cambridge University Press, 1987.

———. "A Motley Crew of Rebels: Sailors, Slaves, and the Coming of the American Revolution." Unpublished manuscript.

Rhodes, Marylou. *Landmarks of Richmond*. Richmond, Va.: Garrett and Massie, 1938.

Roberts, John G. "Francois Quesnay's Heir." *Virginia Magazine of History and Biography* 50 (April 1942): 143–50.

Roeber, A. G. "Authority, Law, and Custom: The Rituals of Court Day in Tidewater Virginia, 1720–1750." *William and Mary Quarterly* 37 (January 1980): 29–52.

Ruffin, Faith Davis. Program notes to "Race and Revolution: African-Americans, 1770–1830," Smithsonian Institution Symposium, Washington, D.C., February 1987.

Savitt, Todd L. *Medicine and Slavery: The Diseases and Health Care of Blacks in Antebellum Virginia.* Urbana: University of Illinois Press, 1978.

Sawyer, Jeffrey K. " 'Benefit of Clergy' in Maryland and Virginia." *American Journal of Legal History* 34 (1990): 49–68.

Schmidt, Frederika Teute, and Barbara Ripel Wilhelm, eds. "Early Proslavery Petitions in Virginia." *William and Mary Quarterly* 30 (1973): 145.

Schnore, Leo, ed. *The New Urban History.* Princeton, N.J.: Princeton University Press, 1975.

Schwarz, Philip J. "Emancipators, Protectors, and Anomalies: Free Black Slaveholders in Virginia." *Virginia Magazine of History and Biography* 95 (July 1987): 317–38.

———. "Gabriel's Challenge: Slaves and Crime in Late Eighteenth-Century Virginia." *Virginia Magazine of History and Biography* 90 (July 1982): 283–309.

———. "The Transportation of Slaves from Virginia, 1801–1865." *Slavery and Abolition* 7 (December 1986): 215–40.

———. *Twice Condemned: Slaves and the Criminal Law of Virginia, 1705–1865.* Baton Rouge: Louisiana State University Press, 1988.

Schweninger, Loren. "The Underside of Slavery: The Internal Economy, Self-Hire, and Quasi-Freedom in Virginia, 1785–1865." *Slavery and Abolition* 12 (September 1991): 1–22.

Scott, James G., and Edward A. Wyatt. *Petersburg's Story: A History.* Petersburg, Va.: Titmus Optical Company, 1960.

Scott, Julius. "Afro-American Slave Revolts in the 1790s." Paper presented at the annual meeting of the Organization of American Historians, Reno, Nevada, March 1988.

Sheldon, Marianne Buroff. "Black-White Relations in Richmond, Virginia, 1782–1820." *Journal of Southern History* 45 (February 1979): 27–44.

"Slave Owners in Princess Anne County, Virginia." *William and Mary Quarterly.* 1st ser., 2 (January 1894): 52–62.

Smith, Barbara Clark. *After the Revolution: The Smithsonian History of Everyday Life in the Eighteenth Century.* New York: Pantheon, 1985.

Smith, James M. *Freedom's Fetters: The Alien and Sedition Laws and American Civil Liberties.* Ithaca, N.Y.: Cornell University Press, 1956.

Smith, Page. *John Adams.* 2 vols. New York: Doubleday, 1962.

Sobel, Mechal. *Trabelin' On: The Slave Journey to an Afro-Baptist Faith,* 2d ed. Princeton, N.J.: Princeton University Press, 1988.

———. *The World They Made Together: Black and White Values in Eighteenth-Century Virginia.* Princeton, N.J.: Princeton University Press, 1987.

Stampp, Kenneth M. *The Peculiar Institution: Slavery in the Antebellum South.* New York: Random House, 1956.

————. "Rebels and Sambos: The Search for the Negro's Personality in Slavery." *Journal of Southern History* 37 (August 1971): 367–92.

Starobin, Robert S. *Industrial Slavery in the Old South.* New York: Oxford University Press, 1970.

Staudenraus, P. J. *The African Colonization Movement, 1816–1865.* New York: Columbia University Press, 1961.

Steffen, Charles G. *The Mechanics of Baltimore: Workers and Politics in the Age of Revolution, 1763–1812.* Urbana: University of Illinois Press, 1984.

Stewart, Donald H. *The Opposition Press of the Federalist Period.* Albany: State University of New York Press, 1969.

Stuckey, Sterling. *Slave Culture: Nationalist Theory and the Foundations of Black America.* New York: Oxford University Press, 1987.

Tadman, Michael. *Speculators and Slaves: Masters, Traders, and Slaves in the Old South.* Madison: University of Wisconsin Press, 1989.

Tate, W. Carrington. "Gabriel's Insurrection." *Henrico County Historical Society Magazine* 3 (Fall 1979): 13–20.

Taylor, R. H. "Slave Conspiracies in North Carolina." *North Carolina Historical Review* 5 (January 1928): 20–34.

Thompson, E. P. *The Making of the English Working Class.* New York: Pantheon, 1963.

————. "The Moral Economy of the English Crowd in the Eighteenth Century." *Past and Present* 50 (February 1971): 76–136.

————. "Patrician Society, Plebian Culture." *Journal of Social History* 7 (Summer 1974): 382–405.

————. "Time, Work-Discipline, and Industrial Capitalism." *Past and Present* 38 (December 1967): 56–97.

————. *Whigs and Hunters: The Origins of the Black Act.* New York: Random House, 1975.

Thornton, John K. "African Dimensions of the Stono Rebellion." *American Historical Review* 96 (October 1991): 1101–13.

Tillson, Albert H. *Gentry and the Common Folk: Political Culture on a Virginia Frontier, 1740–1789.* Lexington: University Press of Kentucky, 1991.

Tucker, Robert W., and David Hendrickson. *Empire of Liberty: The Statecraft of Thomas Jefferson.* New York: Oxford University Press, 1990.

Tyler-McGraw, Marie, and Gregg D. Kimball. *In Bondage and Freedom: Antebellum Black Life in Richmond, Virginia.* Chapel Hill: University of North Carolina Press, 1988.

Vlach, John Michael. *By the Work of Their Hands: Studies in Afro-American Folklife.* Charlottesville: University Press of Virginia, 1991.

Wade, Richard C. *Slavery in the Cities: The South, 1820–1860.* New York: Oxford University Press, 1964.

Watson, Alan. *Slave Law in the Americas.* Athens: University of Georgia Press, 1989.

Wertenbaker, Thomas. *Norfolk: Historic Southern Port*. 2d ed. Durham, N.C.: Duke University Press, 1962.

White, Deborah Gray. *Ar'n't I a Woman? Female Slaves in the Plantation South*. New York: Norton, 1985.

Whitridge, Arnold. *Rochambeau*. New York: Macmillan, 1965.

Wilentz, Sean. *Chants Democratic: New York City and the Rise of the American Working Class, 1788–1850*. New York: Oxford University Press, 1984.

Wilson, Colin. *A Criminal History of Mankind*. New York: Putnam's Sons, 1984.

Wilson, Ellen G. *The Loyal Blacks*. New York: Putnam's Sons, 1976.

Winks, Robin W. *The Blacks in Canada: A History*. New Haven, Conn.: Yale University Press, 1971.

Wish, Harvey. "American Negro Slave Insurrections before 1861." *Journal of Negro History* 22 (July 1937): 299–320.

Wren, J. Thomas. "A 'Two-Fold Character': The Slave as Person and Property in Virginia Court Cases, 1800–1860." *Southern Studies* 24 (Winter 1985): 417–31.

Wyatt-Brown, Bertram. *Southern Honor: Ethics and Behavior in the Old South*. New York: Oxford University Press, 1982.

Young, Alfred F., ed. *The American Revolution: Explorations in the History of American Radicalism*. Urbana: University of Illinois Press, 1976.

INDEX

Abolitionists, 13, 15, 42, 159

Abraham (Burton's), 94; sentenced to hang, 94; pardoned, 94

Abram (Smith's), 125; turns state's evidence, 139; sentenced to hang, 140; executed, 141

Absalom (Hilliard's), 125; sentenced to hang, 140; executed, 141

Absalom (Price's), 113; acquitted, 113

Adams, John, 34–35, 46, 169

Adams, John Quincy, 34, 171

Africa, 22, 52, 53, 71, 85–86, 111, 123, 154, 159, 168

African American Christianity, 8, 85, 168; as ideology of freedom, 9, 17; and magic, 52; and resistance, 52, 65, 165; and afterlife, 70, 111; and rebirth, 111; legislation directed against, 165, 167

African retentions, 21; religious traditions, 8, 168; housing patterns, 16; crafts, 21; marriage customs, 22; secret societies, 53; funeral practices, 85–86

Alien and Sedition Acts, 35

Allen, James, 90

Allen, Jim, 94; acquitted, 94

American Colonization Society, 162

American Revolution, 5–7, 42, 148; as black liberation struggle, 5–6, 14, 43, 119–20; and racism, 10–11; egalitarianism of, 10–11, 17, 30, 38, 133, 155, 192 (n. 46)

Anderson, William, 74, 96

Appomattox River, 120, 125, 127

Aptheker, Herbert, 183, 186–87

Arnold, Benedict, 6

Arson, 57, 64, 131, 134

Artisans. See Craftsmen

Austen, Thomas, 90

Austin, William, 72, 75

Awakenings, 7, 17

Banners, 51, 66, 109

Baptist churches, 7–9, 32, 51, 131, 167; appeal to blacks, 8, 179; and antislavery sentiment, 8–9

Baptist General Committee, 9–10

Barrow, David, 7, 9

Beddenhurst, Alexander, 44, 60, 67, 103, 107, 114, 177; evidence regarding, 184–85

Ben (Carter's), 62, 96; sentenced to hang, 97; transported, 112, 150–51

Ben (Prosser's), 28, 49–50, 54, 63–64, 72–73, 102; joins conspiracy, 52; turns state's evidence, 82–83; testifies, 83, 86–91, 93, 108–9, 113; pardoned, 173–74

Ben (Smith's), 63; acquitted, 96

Benefit of clergy, 32, 81, 179

Benn, John, 9

Berkeley, Carter, 97

Biko, Stephen, 114

Billey (Gregory's), 55, 66, 84; sentenced to hang, 86; testifies, 87; executed, 88–89

Billy (Hornett's), 151

Billy (King's), 104, 120; turns in Gabriel, 105–7

Billy (Ambrose Lipscombe's), 101; sentenced to hang, 101; pardoned, 101
Billy (Nathaniel Lipscombe's), 101; sentenced to hang, 101; pardoned, 101
Billy (Penn's), 98; acquitted, 98
Bishop, Jacob, 9, 168
Black preachers, 52–53, 98, 167
Blacksmith, Dick, 131
Black Thunder (Bontemps), ix, 183
Bland, Edward, 134
Blandum, Jacob, 60, 100
Boatmen. *See* Watermen
Bob (slave), 57
Bob (Royall's), 126, 132; sentenced to hang, 134; executed, 134
Bob (Sandifer's), 125, 140
Bonaparte, Napoleon, 42, 169–70, 177
Bontemps, Arna, ix, 183
Booker, John, 60, 119
Boukman, 45
Boulanger, John, 44, 184
Boush, Caleb, 135
Bowler, William, 113
Bowling Green, Va., 96
Bracken, John, 77
Braikensridge, George, 77
Branding, 32, 48, 145. *See also* Torture
Breckenridge, James, 42
Bristol (Carter's), 62, 97
Bristol (Gilliam's), 122
Bristol (Thilman's), 108; acquitted, 108
Brook Bridge (Henrico Co.), 19, 50, 53, 63, 66, 69, 90
Brooke, John, 88
Brooke, Thomas, 148
Brookfield plantation, 19–20, 22, 24, 40, 48, 50, 53, 64, 69–70, 72, 93, 110, 113
Brown, John, 127, 141, 143
Brown, John G., 151
Brown, Joseph, 144
Brown, King, 130–31, 144; sentenced to hang, 145; executed, 145
Brutus (Anderson's), 74; acquitted, 96
Buckner, Thomas, 61

Burton, Thomas, 94
Burton, William, 53, 83, 87, 90
Burwell, William, 161
Byrd, Jesse, 59, 100, 119, 126, 148, 166, 175
Byrd, Reuben, 59, 100, 119, 126, 148, 166, 175
Byrd, Sam, Jr., 25, 52, 54, 56, 65–66, 110, 126; recruits outside Henrico, 59, 62–63, 68, 91, 96, 100; sentenced to hang, 94; executed, 110
Byrd, Sam, Sr., 63, 101

Callender, James Thomson, 36–37, 69, 77, 92, 104, 114, 187; *The Prospect before Us*, 36
Capitalism, 26, 28, 122; and cash wage, 26, 30, 121
Caroline County Jail, 76
Carroll, Joseph C., 180
Carter, Charles, 62, 67, 73, 96–97, 112, 150
Carter, Landon, 10
Carter, Robert, 24, 62
Castration, 78
Cemeteries. *See* Hanging, execution by
Chamberlayne, William, 174
Charles (Gregory's), 54–55, 66; sentenced to hang, 86–87; executed, 88–89
Charlottesville, Va., 63
Chase, Samuel, 37
Chickahominy River, 79
Chicken, Billy, 74; acquitted, 91
Children (slave), 16, 20–22; literacy, 20; work duties of, 20–21; and white children, 20–21, 50; and parents' occupations, 21
Christophe, Henri, 170
Claiborne, Richard, 100
Claiborne, William, 60, 100, 113
Clarke, Jane, 59
Clarkson, Thomas, 155
Clinton, Henry, 5–7
Clopton, John, 172

Clothing (of slaves), 11, 20, 22, 24
Cocke, Bowler, 83, 86
Coffin, Joshua, 179
Collaborators and informants, 70–71,
    91, 107, 139, 173; motives of, 70, 139;
    and afterlife, 71; rewards for, 71, 82,
    107, 144–49; used by courts, 82, 91,
    139; and pardons, 91; retaliation
    against, 173
Colonization, 12, 112–13, 147, 149–62.
    See also American Colonization
    Society
Cooper, Edmund, 135
Cooper, Jack, 158
Copland, Charles, 32, 38, 147, 176
Corbin, Francis, 44, 183
Cornwallis, Charles, Lord, 6, 120
Courts, oyer and terminer, 31, 78,
    80–81, 151, 173; creation of, 31; in
    Henrico, 82, 94, 101–10, 174; and
    rules of evidence, 82, 100, 139; in
    Richmond, 95–96, 141–42; in Louisa,
    96; in Caroline, 96–98; in Hanover,
    98; in Norfolk, 98–99, 136–39; in
    Dinwiddie, 99–101; in Nottoway,
    134; in Brunswick, 135; in Halifax,
    139–40
Cowley, Robert, 57–58, 65, 101, 175
Cowper, John, 135–38, 167
Craftsmen (black), 21, 23–24, 27, 38;
    privileges of, 21; blacksmiths, 21, 53;
    carpenters, 21, 59, 142; wage rela-
    tions, 26; relationship with white
    artisans, 27, 30; relationship with
    merchants, 27–28, 38; as freemen,
    28; and property, 39, 57; training of,
    53
Craftsmen (white), 26–27, 38, 48, 63,
    165; egalitarian attitudes of, 13, 27,
    40; and slave hires, 26–27; as slave-
    holders, 27; political affiliation of,
    38–39; and property, 39; and Jacobin
    clubs, 41
Craig, Adam, 84, 90, 101
Cropping (of ears), 145. *See also*
    Torture

Dan (Burton's), 83
Daniel (Brooke's), 88; acquitted, 89
Daniel (Wilkinson's), 68; acquitted, 90
Daniel (Williamson's), 83
Davie, William, 143–44
Davis, Augustine, 67
Davy (Ashbourne's), 130–31
Decoudry, Israel, 167
Dejarnett, Daniel, 124
Dejarnett, James, 139
Dessalines, Jean Jacques, 170
Dick (slave), 17
Dick (Smith's), 94; sentenced to hang,
    94; pardoned, 94
Dick (Thilman's), 108; sentenced to
    hang, 108; pardoned, 108
Ditcher, Jack, 40, 44, 56, 67–69, 72,
    102; joins conspiracy, 52; challenges
    Gabriel for leadership, 66; surren-
    ders, 110; sentenced to hang, 113;
    transported, 113, 147, 150–51
Docility, myth of, 186. *See also*
    Aptheker, Herbert
Doddridge, Philip, 162
Drayton, John, 114
Drivers, 175
Duane, William, 114
Dunmore, John Murray, Earl of, 5–7,
    37, 42, 51, 68, 77, 120, 155, 159

Election of 1800, 37–42
Ellis's Tavern (Caroline Co.), 62
Emancipation, 149, 155–56; white atti-
    tudes toward, 11–15, 149, 161–63
Emanuel (Wood's), 113; acquitted, 113
Eppes, John, 171–72

Families (slave), 16, 20, 22; extended
    community, 16; forced separation of,
    16, 60; "abroad" wives, 22; marriage
    rituals, 22; interracial, 29, 76, 78, 99,
    167
Farrar, Arthur, 141; sentenced to hang,
    142; transported, 142, 158
Fed (Fitts's), 144
Federalist party, 35–39, 42, 114

Fells, John, 62, 67; sentenced to hang, 98; transported, 112, 150–51
Floyd, John, 135–36
Foushee, William, 32
France, 11, 34–35, 41
Frank (Prosser's), 72, 78; sentenced to hang, 87; executed, 88–89
Frank (Robertson's), 124; sentenced to hang, 140; executed, 141
Frank (Sumner's), 130–31, 144; sentenced to hang, 145; executed, 145
Frank (Wilkinson's), 88; acquitted, 88
Fredericksburg, Va., 39, 76, 114
Free blacks, 28, 57, 82, 120–21, 148, 154; in Chesapeake, 15, 121; and slaves, 28; in cities, 28, 59; legislation directed against, 29, 57, 148, 166–67; and rules of testimony, 100
Frey, Sylvia, 189 (n. 6)
Fristoe, William, 7, 9
Fulcher, William, 157–58
Funerals. *See* Hanging, execution by

Gabriel, Jack, 62, 67, 96; sentenced to hang, 98; transported, 112, 147, 150–51
Gabriel: The Story of a Slave Rebellion (Mason), ix
Gabriel (free black), 71
Gabriel (Prosser's): birth and childhood, 3, 19–20; education, 20; religious training, 20, 51, 179; apprentice artisan, 21–22; appearance as young man, 21–22, 179; marriage to Nanny, 22; hired out, 24; relationship with merchants, 28–31, 41; attacks Absalom Johnson, 31–33; and election of 1800, 37–40; and Saint Domingue, 45–47; begins to plan rebellion, 49–52; recruits followers, 53–58; produces weapons, 55–56; sends recruiters outside Henrico, 58–63; reveals plan at Brook Bridge, 63–64; recruits at Young's Spring, 64–65; elected "general," 66; distributes swords, 68; plot

collapses, 69–70; flees Brookfield, 73; boards *Mary*, 79, 104–5; arrested, 106–7; tried for conspiracy, 108–9; sentenced to hang, 109; executed, 111, 219 (n. 50)
Garland, Edward, 98
Genovese, Eugene D., 180–81, 189 (n. 6), 196 (n. 48)
Gentry, William, 73, 84
George (Bearmas's), 130
George (Burton's), 87; acquitted, 88
George (Thilman's), 62, 96; acquitted, 97
Gerry, Elbridge, 35
Gilbert (Young's), 44, 55, 57–58, 65–67, 73–74, 90, 104; sentenced to hang, 93; executed, 110
Gildart, Francis, 177
Giles, William Branch, 37, 108, 171
Glasgow (Thilman's), 142; sentenced to die, 142; transported, 143, 158
Goode, Benjamin, 83
Goode, Elizabeth Prosser, 19
Goode, Frank, 127, 132
Goode, Robert, 19
Goode, Thomas, 19, 24–25, 54, 73, 94
Goodwyn, Peterson, 143, 172
Goosley, George, 157
Gore, Christopher, 156
Graham, Paul, 54, 94, 173
Graham, Sam, 66, 74; sentenced to hang, 94; executed, 110
Great Britain, 11, 41
Green, Grief, 126
Gregory, Roger, 54–55, 72, 84
Gregory's Tavern (Henrico Co.), 64
Grog shops, 28, 40, 43, 60, 133
Gunn, Obediah, 106–8

Hagood, Randolph, 135
Haiti. *See* Saint Domingue
Hamilton, Alexander, 35, 114
Hampton Roads, Va., 6
Hanging, execution by, 85, 87–89, 92–93, 110–11, 138; in chains, 85; from gallows, 85, 87, 92; as method

of control, 85, 93, 123; funeral rites and, 85–86; from cart, 92; slaves executed (1800), 186–87; slaves executed (1802), 187–88

Hanover Town, Va., 62–63

Harland, Marion, 179, 187, 193 (n. 12); *Judith*, 180

Harper, Robert Goodloe, 46

Harrison, Edmund, 147–48, 150–51, 158

Harrison, Benjamin, 72, 74, 147

Harrison, John, 75

Harry (Austen's), 90; acquitted, 91

Henley, Hezekiah, 32, 83, 142

Henrico County, Va., 3, 19, 23, 50, 61, 73

Henrico County Courthouse, 3, 24, 31–32, 76, 80, 85, 95, 113, 166

Henrico County Jail, 24, 32, 48, 73, 80, 85

Henry, Patrick, 3–4, 10, 19, 40, 51

Higginson, Thomas W., 179

Hog stealing, 31

Holman, John, 83

Holmes, John, 150

Holmes, Sherlock, 184

Holmy (Thilman's), 98; sentenced to hang, 98; escapes, 98

Hoomes, John, 96, 98

Hornett, Jane, 151

Howard, Benjamin, 173

Howison, Robert, 179

Humphrey (Garland's), 98; acquitted, 98

Humphrey (Wilborne's), 125

Hylton, Daniel Lawrence, 19, 23, 83, 88, 90, 113, 138, 174, 176

Hylton, Mehitable, 23

Hylton, Sarah, 23

Hymns, 85

Isham (Burton's), 53; sentenced to hang, 90; executed, 92

Isham (free black), 104–5

Isaac, Rhys, 192 (n. 46)

Isaac (Allen's), 90; sentenced to hang, 90; executed, 92

Isaac (Burton's), 73; sentenced to hang, 83–84; executed, 85

Isaac (Prosser's), 174

Isaac (Wilkes's), 129–30; sentenced to hang, 135; executed, 135

Jack (Riddell's), 88

Jacob (Wilson's), 61, 67, 74, 76, 99, 110, 120, 128, 164; death of, 113–14

Jacob (Woodin's), 55; sentenced to hang, 94; pardoned, 94

James (Price's). *See* John (Price's)

James River, 6, 7, 18, 120

Jay's Treaty, 42

Jefferson, Thomas, 3, 12, 35–36, 38, 40, 49, 77, 85, 89; *Notes on Virginia*, 12, 162; and colonization, 12–13, 112, 151–62; and black rebelliousness, 14, 161; argues against further hangings, 92–93; and Saint Domingue, 168–72

Jeffrey (Wilkes's), 135

Jerdone, Francis, 77

Jeremiah (Cornick's), 135; sentenced to hang, 136; executed, 138

Joe (Austen's), 90; acquitted, 91

Joe (Jones's), 126, 132; sentenced to hang, 134; executed, 134

John (Buckner's), 61

John (Carter's), 62, 96; acquitted, 97

John (Jones's), 29, 64; sentenced to hang, 83; testifies, 86–87; executed, 87

John (Price's), 74, 76, 82, 91, 93; sentenced to hang, 88; pardoned, 112

Johnson, Absalom, 31–33, 50, 64, 71

Jones, Batt, 126, 134

Jones, James, 134

Jones, Joseph, 100

Jones, Mary, 29, 64, 83

Jones, Richard, 132, 134

Jumper, Rochester, 127, 141, 143, 175

Jupiter (Wilkinson's), 31–32, 52, 58; sentenced to hang, 89; executed, 92

Judges, 32, 79, 81; and pardons, 91

King, Miles, 24, 106, 120
King, Rufus, 114, 155–56, 159–60
King (Nicholas's), 56–57, 73–74; sentenced to hang, 95; pardoned, 95; transported, 112, 150–51

Laddis (Williamson's), 66; sentenced to hang, 90; executed, 92
Latrobe, Benjamin Henry, 99
Lear, Tobias, 169
Leclerc, Charles Victor, 170
Leftwich, Nancy, 67, 108
Leland, John, 9
Lewis, Joseph, 94, 172
Lewis, William, 61, 88
Lewis (Brown's), 127; recruits in Richmond, 128; arrested, 141–42; escapes, 143, 175
Lewis (Williamson's), 55, 74; sentenced to hang, 101; pardoned, 101; transported, 112, 150–51
Liberia, 162
Lincoln, Abraham, 172
Literacy: of slaves, 20, 39, 56, 64, 70, 130, 165; of free blacks, 165; laws prohibiting, 165
Littlepage's Bridge (Caroline Co.), 67
Living conditions (of slaves), 20–21
Locke, John, 10
Logan, George, 171–72
Louverture, Toussaint, 45–48, 169–71; spelling of name, 199–200 (n. 38)
Lucas (white laborer), 56

McClurg, James, 67, 95, 104, 106, 177
McColley, Robert, 190 (n. 29), 192 (n. 46)
McCrea, Alexander, 60, 102
McGraw, Samuel, 142
McIntosh, George, 136–38
Madison, James, 35–36, 172; *Report of 1800,* 36
Marriages. *See* Families (slave)
Marsh, Samuel, 139
Marshall, John, 35, 39–40
Martin, Jacob, 127, 133

Martin, Macky, 108
Martin, Mary, 95
Martin, Thomas Jordan, 56–57; acquitted, 108
Martin, William, 132, 140
Martin (Bass's), 140; sentenced to hang, 140; executed, 141
Martin (Gregory's), 87; acquitted, 87
Martin (Prosser's), 19–21, 50, 52, 54, 65, 78, 179; sentenced to hang, 86; executed, 88–89
Mason, Clifford, ix, x
Mason, George, 11, 13
Mathews, Thomas, 136
Mayo, John, 18, 75, 104
Mayo, William, 86
Mayo's Bridge, 18, 51, 75
Meade, David, 12, 15, 41
Meadow Farm (Henrico Co.), 70–71
Mercer, Charles Fenton, 162
Merchants, 27–28, 38–39, 50, 109; and wage conflict, 28; of Richmond, 30, 38; and politics, 38–39
Methodist churches, 7–9, 49, 51, 109, 167, 177; and antislavery sentiment, 8–9, 105; appeal to blacks, 8–9, 179
Michael (Goode's), 24–25, 54, 73; sentenced to hang, 94; executed, 110
Michael (Owen's), 58, 69, 104; sentenced to hang, 84; executed, 85
Midwifery (slave), 3
Militias, 72, 74–77, 96, 99, 132–34, 136, 148, 172
Mims, Martin, 79, 111, 150, 157–58
Minor, Dabney, 162
Minor, John, 76
Moncure, V. M., 23
Monroe, James, 15, 34, 41, 47, 49–50, 65, 67, 79, 89, 91, 93, 97, 168; elected governor, 42; notified of plot, 72–74; calls out militia (1800), 74–76; and evidence of French involvement, 103–4, 114–15, 177, 185; isolates Gabriel, 107; recommends transportation, 112–13, 142–43, 147, 149–50; notified of Easter plot, 132–33;

calls out militia (1802), 133–34, 136; and colonization, 153–60

Moore, Andrew, 171

Morris, William, 151

Morse, John, 106

Mosby, John, 83

Mosby, Joseph, 24, 73

Mosby, Samuel, 110

Mosby, William, 71–72

Moses, 87

Moses (free black), 9

Moses (Price's), 94; acquitted, 94

Moss, John, 106

Mullin, Gerald W., 181–82, 187, 192 (n. 46), 201 (n. 3)

Murray, William Vans, 34, 37

Naming practices, 20, 189 (n. 1); adoption of surnames, 174–75

Nanny (Gabriel's wife), 22, 30, 50, 68–69, 111, 177

Ned (Austen's), 90; acquitted, 91

Ned (Green's), 126

Ned (Ingram's), 135; acquitted, 139

Ned (Owen's), 84

Ned (Parson's), 84; sentenced to hang, 84; executed, 85

Ned (Prosser's), 174

Ned (Young's), 90; sentenced to hang, 90; pardoned, 112

Ned (Walke's), 135, 137; sentenced to hang, 136; transported, 138, 146, 158

Newton, Thomas, 77, 99, 106–7, 136–37, 172

Nicholas, Philip, 56–57, 95, 97

Nicholson, Joseph, 93

Norfolk, Va., 9, 24, 26, 29, 38, 40, 44, 60–61, 67–68, 70, 77, 98–99, 114, 128–29, 135, 177

Owen, Judith, 58, 84

Page, Elizabeth, 96

Page, John, 160

Paine, John, 47

Parson, Anne, 84

Passes, 27, 66, 68, 167; forging of, 27, 73, 127

Patriarchalism, 4, 16, 23, 26, 78, 121; and paternalism, 4, 189 (n. 6)

Patrick (slave), 55

Patrols, 8, 53, 67, 72–73, 76, 99, 127, 132–34, 136, 144, 148

Pendleton, Edmund, 96, 98, 155

Penitentiary (Richmond, Va.), 65, 75, 79, 83, 92, 108, 150, 156–57, 175

Penn, William, 98

Peter (Claiborne's), 60, 100; sentenced to hang, 101; executed, 113

Peter (Prosser's), 66; sentenced to hang, 89; executed, 92

Peter (Williamson's), 101; sentenced to hang, 101; pardoned, 101

Petersburg, Va., 9, 24, 38, 44, 59, 67, 74, 99–100, 114, 126, 129, 132–33

Pettigrew, Charles, 164, 166

Pharoah (Sheppard's), 40, 73, 124; reveals conspiracy, 70–71; testifies, 83–84; freed, 149, 173–75

Pharoah, Jr., 174

Phebe (Price's), 140; acquitted, 140

Philadelphia, Pa., 43–44, 67, 114, 168

Phill (Hagood's), 129; sentenced to hang, 135; executed, 135

Pichon, Louis Andre, 170

Pickering, Timothy, 46, 171

Pidgeon, John, 60, 100

Pinckney, Charles Cotesworth, 34–35

Planters, 13, 16, 19, 38, 60, 78, 92, 133, 154, 161, 163

Pointer, Roling, 127, 133

Powell, Levin, 148

Prentice, William, 100, 104, 110, 132–34

Price, Daniel, 140

Price, Elisha, 74

Price, William, 113

Prosser, Albert, 176–77

Prosser, Ann, 19–20

Prosser, Daniel, 176–77

Prosser, Lucy Bolling Hylton, 23, 177; death of, 177

Prosser, Thomas, 3, 19, 22; slaves owned, 19; death of, 22
Prosser, Thomas Henry, ix, 20–21, 32–33, 40, 50, 64, 71, 83, 92–93, 109, 174; birth of, 19; assumes control of plantation, 22–23; marries Lucy Bolling Hylton, 176; remarries, 177
Public Guard (Richmond, Va.), 164

Quakers, 11, 49, 51, 109, 171
Quersey, Charles, 43–45, 48, 50, 67, 69, 104, 107, 110, 114, 177; evidence regarding, 183–84

Ralph (Page's), 96; acquitted, 96
Randolph, John, 41, 77, 79, 93, 102, 114, 172–73
Randolph (Leftwich's), 67; sentenced to hang, 108; pardoned, 108
Ransom (Jackson's), 129
Rape, 38, 78; of slave women, 78; feared by slaves, 38, 78
Rappahannock River, 6
Redford, Lucy, 175
Republican party, 35–37, 45, 49, 102; and France, 103–4, 114–15
Richmond, Va., 9, 18–19, 22–24, 28–29, 38, 48, 56, 64, 72, 77, 95, 133–34, 164, 172
Riddell, Lucy, 88
Rind, James, 83, 86–92, 96, 175–76
Roanoke River, 120, 125, 129–30
Robb, Robert, 97
Robertson, Archer, 124
Rochambeau, Count de, 43–44
Rockett's Warehouse (Richmond, Va.), 56, 64
Rose, William, 80, 85
Royall, John, 126
Runaway slaves, 15, 33, 42, 120, 122

Sailors. See Watermen
Saint Domingue, ix, 45–48, 160–61, 168–72
St. John's Church (Richmond, Va.), 19, 88, 176

Salem (slave), 130
Sam (Foord's), 145; executed, 145
Sam (Prosser's), 40, 113
Sam (Wilkinson's), 89; sentenced to hang, 90; executed, 92
Samson myth, ix, 20, 51–52, 179–81
Sancho (Booker's), 60, 153; plans Easter conspiracy, 119, 123–25; loses control of plot, 126–27, 130–32; sentenced to hang, 139–40; executed, 141
Sawney (Lewis's), 25, 61, 74; sentenced to hang, 88; executed, 92
Schwarz, Philip J., 181–82, 187
Scipio (Thilman's), 62, 96; sentenced to hang, 97–98; pardoned, 98
Scott, John, 60–61, 68; captured, 102–3
Scott, Matt, 57
Second Continental Congress (1775), 5
Seigneurialism, 26
Selden, Joseph, 82, 84, 88, 91, 103, 113–14
Selden, Miles, 83, 89, 101, 103, 109–10, 175
Self-purchase, 12, 30, 161
Sharp, Granville, 13, 155
Shelton, Hugh, 74
Sheppard, Benjamin, 110
Sheppard, Elizabeth, 70–71, 149
Sheppard, Mosby, 40, 70–72, 75, 87, 89, 111, 149, 174–75
Sheppard, Philip, 70–71, 149
Sheppard, William, 70
Sierra Leone, 155–56, 158–60
Simmons, John, 13
Simon (Thilman's), 68
Slave hiring, 23–24, 70, 121, 165; and contracts, 24; division of wages, 25, 88, 121; self-hire, 25–26, 52, 121, 165
Slaves, 49, 155; African-born, 15, 59; as agricultural workers, 16, 50, 59, 63, 70, 124, 166; urban, 19, 24, 38, 42, 48
Slave trade, 150–51, 157–58, 161; domestic, 12, 16, 161; transatlantic, 15
Smith, Charles, 62

Smith, George, 25, 52–54, 57, 59, 61, 63, 65–66, 69, 74, 91, 110; sentenced to hang, 92; executed, 110
Smith, George William, 31
Smith, Jacob, 25
Smith, Jesse, 94
Smith, Peter, 110
Smith, William, 139
Sobel, Mechal, 181
Solomon (Lewis's), 94; sentenced to hang, 94; pardoned, 94
Solomon (Prosser's), 19–21, 24, 31–32, 50, 56, 64, 68, 72, 90, 173; joins conspiracy, 52; captured, 78; sentenced to hang, 83; confesses, 84; executed, 87
Spaight, Richard, 131
Stanard, Larkin, 95
Stealing, 31
Stevens, Edward, 169
Storrs, Gervas, 32, 82, 84, 88, 91, 110, 147
Styron, William, x
Suffolk, Va., 68–69, 76–77
Sumner, Charles, 172
Sumner, David, 131, 144
Swan Tavern (Richmond, Va.), 37

Talleyrand, Charles Maurice de, 35, 41, 170
Tayloe, John, 122
Taylor, George, 38
Taylor, Richardson, 79, 104–6, 120, 122, 177
Thilman, Paul, 62, 68, 96, 98, 108, 142
Thornton (Thilman's), 62, 66, 68, 96; sentenced to hang, 98; transported, 150–51
Thornton, Edward, 155
Thornton, Henry, 159–60
Tobacco, 11, 18, 56
Toby (Holman's), 83
Tom (Prosser's), 93; sentenced to hang, 93; executed, 110
Tom (Sheppard's), 40, 71, 73, 124; freed, 149, 175

Tom (slave), 24
Tom (Thilman's), 142; sentenced to hang, 142; transported, 143, 158
Torture, 32, 141
Transportation. See Colonization
Troup, Robert, 114
Tucker, George, 14, 76, 154, 161, 172; Letter to a Member, 152, 191 (n. 37)
Tucker, St. George, 13–15, 17, 152, 161, 172; A Dissertation on Slavery, 13
Turner, Benjamin, 111
Turner, Nat, ix, x, 51, 111, 124, 161, 179

Underground economy (of slaves), 27, 56, 123, 165

Venable, Abraham, 153–54, 159, 161–62
Virginia Court of Chancery, 12
Virginia Declaration of Rights (1776), 11, 13
Virginia Slavery Debates (1831–32), 161

Wade, Richard, 202 (n. 20)
Walke, Mary, 128
Walke, William, 128
Walker, Quok, 12
Washington, George, 11, 34, 102, 112, 169
Washington, Sarah, 86
Watermen, 29, 39, 60, 119–23, 128–29; egalitarian attitudes of white, 60, 105, 122, 128–29; as freemen, 120; hierarchy among, 120; wage relations, 120–21; as slaves, 120–23; economic relations with merchants, 121, 165; legislation directed against, 164–65
Watson's Tavern (Richmond, Va.), 23; as place of execution, 92–94, 110
Watt (Prosser's), 63, 73, 173; recruits in Goochland, 68; sentenced to hang, 113; transported, 113, 147, 150–51
Weisner, Samuel, 75
Weld, Isaac, 147

Wesley, John, 8, 105; *Thoughts Upon Slavery*, 8
Whipping, 19, 31, 88, 141, 145, 165–67
White, Samuel, 163
Whitlock's Mill (Suffolk Va.), 68–69, 73, 76, 99
Wilberforce, William, 159, 164
Wilkes, Henrietta, 134
Wilkes, Joseph, 129, 135
Wilkinson, Nathaniel, 31, 89–90
Will (Mosby's), 55; sentenced to hang, 83–84; executed, 85
Will (Walke's), 128, 135–36
William (Young's), 66; sentenced to hang, 93; executed, 110
Williams, Benjamin, 143
Williamsburg, Va., 5, 7, 18, 77
Williamson, Allan, 101
Williamson, Dabney, 72, 74, 101
Williamson, George, 32, 83, 142, 174
Williamson, John, 83, 90
Wilmot, Melvin Gabriel, 178
Wilson, Robert, 106
Wilson, William, 61, 113, 120
Women (slave), 78, 81, 85, 124, 155; beating of, 22; childbirth, 22; family

role, 53; revolts and, 53–54, 57, 140, 177
Wood, Drewry, 113
Wood, Leigh, 79
Woodfin, Thomas, 94
Woolfolk, Ben, 54–55, 69, 73–74, 88, 96, 143; recruits in Caroline, 61–62, 66–67; sentenced to hang, 91; turns state's evidence, 91; pardoned, 91, 173; testifies in Henrico, 92–95, 101, 108–9; testifies in Caroline, 97–98
Woolfolk, Paul, 54, 73, 143
Work, 27; collective, 27; and culture, 29–30, 60
Wythe, George, 12–13, 155

XYZ Affair, 35

Yancey, Charles, 96
Yancey, David, 96
Yancey, Robert, 96
Yorktown, Va., 5, 43, 85
Young, William, 25, 53, 54–55, 64, 88, 90, 93, 112
Younghusband, Pleasant, 32, 83, 174